AF771673

Beyond Borders, Beyond Banking

Heather A. Clark

Beyond Borders, Beyond Banking

The ACLEDA Bank Story, 2005–2019

Springer

Heather A. Clark
Albuquerque, NM, USA

ISBN 978-981-15-1686-3 ISBN 978-981-15-1687-0 (eBook)
https://doi.org/10.1007/978-981-15-1687-0

© Springer Nature Singapore Pte Ltd. 2020
This work is subject to copyright. All rights are reserved by the Publisher, whether the whole or part of the material is concerned, specifically the rights of translation, reprinting, reuse of illustrations, recitation, broadcasting, reproduction on microfilms or in any other physical way, and transmission or information storage and retrieval, electronic adaptation, computer software, or by similar or dissimilar methodology now known or hereafter developed.
The use of general descriptive names, registered names, trademarks, service marks, etc. in this publication does not imply, even in the absence of a specific statement, that such names are exempt from the relevant protective laws and regulations and therefore free for general use.
The publisher, the authors, and the editors are safe to assume that the advice and information in this book are believed to be true and accurate at the date of publication. Neither the publisher nor the authors or the editors give a warranty, expressed or implied, with respect to the material contained herein or for any errors or omissions that may have been made. The publisher remains neutral with regard to jurisdictional claims in published maps and institutional affiliations.

This Springer imprint is published by the registered company Springer Nature Singapore Pte Ltd.
The registered company address is: 152 Beach Road, #21-01/04 Gateway East, Singapore 189721, Singapore

"Socially responsible business models in the financial services sector are instrumental to the achievement of the Sustainable Development Goals, by ensuring financial agency and inclusion for populations typically left behind by less inclusive financial service pathways.... The ACLEDA story is notable in the ACLEDA Group's steadfast determination to unlock barriers to both financial and human capital, at scale, in Cambodia, the Lao PDR, and Myanmar. In its quest to serve millions of low-income customers with financial services, ACLEDA showed its peers why value-driven, customer-centered policies, products, and practices are critical for the growth of an inclusive banking sector. ACLEDA's commitment to building human capital goes beyond banking to higher education, instilling these values in the next generation of bankers."

Judith Karl, Executive Secretary, United Nations Capital Development Fund (UNCDF)

"As an innovative microfinance institution founded almost at the same time as those in China, ACLEDA's development experience and successful story have great reference value to the microfinance industry and financial inclusion in China. The ACLEDA Institute of Business has and will continue to play the role of an exchange platform between China and Cambodia in the field of financial inclusion."

Bai Chengyu, Secretary General, China Association of Microfinance (CAM)

"Heather Clark shows how ACLEDA Bank's ethical leaders, working with committed policy-makers in Cambodia and beyond, contributed to the 'rational exuberance' that has brought growth with equity to the Southeast Asia region. Her highly readable account reveals the keys to development at its best: sound values, dedication to the people, purposeful experimentation, honest dialogue, and perseverance. This is a book to inform and inspire a new generation of finance and development professionals."

Dr. Elisabeth Rhyne, Founder, Center for Financial Inclusion at Accion

"The book explores topics of good governance and why these are important from a Governing Board perspective. An effective Board should promote diversity and a culture of ethical behavior, integrity, and transparency…and Independent Directors bring an outsiders perspective, and specialists' skills…they act as a neutral referee in any disputes."

John Brinsden, Chairman of the Board ACLEDA Bank, Plc. (2014–2015)

"…The leadership of ACLEDA Bank has always recognized the importance of education. With the ACLEDA Institute of Business, ACLEDA Bank has taken an important step in creating an environment in which Cambodia's future leaders are given every opportunity to grow and develop themselves, their fellow students, the businesses and institutions they work for, or those that they will create themselves."

Dr. Gerhardus J.A. Hummels, Social Entrepreneurship Chair in Ethics, Organisations, and Society, Utrecht University, and Professor, School of Economics, Maastricht University

"With innovative methods of learning and leveraging on strategic industry partnerships, the ACLEDA Institute of Business seeks to broaden the talent pool, deepen the expertise, and develop a future workforce that will contribute to the growth of the country and the region in the years ahead."

Dr. Eric Teo Khee Hwee, Professor, Nanyang Business School, Singapore

"I really enjoyed reading about how ACLEDA's use of digital payments in collaboration with Cambodia's regulatory and tax authorities helped to weed out corruption in the financial sector—a triumph for all proponents, as am I, of a market systems approach to financial sector development."

Mayada El-Zoghbi, Managing Director, Center for Financial Inclusion, Accion

"An insightful book by Heather Clark argues that ACLEDA Bank's original core values—no tolerance for corruption, honesty and personal integrity, customer service, staff ownership, and governance—have been and continue to be key drivers of the bank's growth. Long before it became fashionable, ACLEDA 'put customers at the center'… ensuring services matched customer needs and enabling customer's more productive, useful, and profitable financial management practices. By listening to customers, ACLEDA's leadership acknowledges that their customers are the 'builders' of the bank… and that they grow together with the evolution of the bank."

Dr. Monique Cohen, Founder, Microfinance Opportunities

"ACLEDA Bank Plc. and ACLEDA Securities Plc. leadership and staff welcome the People's IPO in keeping with our beliefs and aims to reach all segments of the population with appropriate financial services and to share ACLEDA Bank Plc.'s financial growth with all people who want to participate as well as to make our contribution to the development of Cambodia's securities sector."

Mrs. Mar Amara, Board Chairwoman of ACLEDA Securities Plc., and
Mr. Prom Visoth, President and CEO of ACLEDA Securities, Plc.

"We are very excited and honored to be part of the milestone IPO project for ACLEDA as well as the Cambodian Capital market. The People's IPO is going to open a new chapter for ACLEDA Bank as the Cambodian people's bank. ACLEDA has been the most trusted and loved bank by the Cambodian people, and now the Cambodian people will also own it. The IPO will bring a fundamental change to the Cambodian capital market by tripling market size and reviving trading activity."

KT Han, Managing Director, and the Team at Yuanta Securities (Cambodia)

"The Norwegian Investment Fund for Developing Countries (NORFUND) invests to promote more access to finance. We value the positive impact that ACLEDA Bank Lao is making in the Lao PDR, providing competitive and first-class service to small and medium-sized enterprises in the country. We are proud to be part of ACLEDA Bank Lao's journey and success."

Fay Chetnakarnkul, Regional Director (Asia), NORFUND

"Since its establishment, ACLEDA MFI Myanmar Co., Ltd. has been devoted to supporting local poor people with financial services. As an international bank, ICBC Yangon Branch takes poverty alleviation as a very important social responsibility and supports ACLEDA MFI Myanmar Co., Ltd., which is one of the top microfinance companies in Myanmar."

Ms. Huo Li Juan, Head of Financial Institutions Department, Industrial and Commercial Bank of China Limited (ICBC) Yangon Branch

"TMB is a bank that endeavors to challenge the status quo—not only in order to help the lives of our customers but to improve society in general. We are proud of our ongoing support for ACLEDA Bank Lao, as we can see how their efforts to sustainably improve the livelihoods of small business owners, particularly women in rural areas, continue to make a real difference to the people, as well as for the local economy."

Alexander Nondh Langfeldt, Head of Corporate Banking, TMB Bank Public Company Limited

"The Myanmar government promotes financial inclusion, providing access to affordable financial services as a means to reduce poverty. Historically, ACLEDA Bank's strong microfinance presence in Cambodia enabled ACLEDA MFI Myanmar Co., Ltd (AMM) to rapidly place among the top 10 MFIs out of over 177 MFIs in the country. We are happy to successfully cooperate with AMM and hope to do more in the future."

Yang Chiang Ying, Assistant Vice President, E.SUN Commercial Bank, Ltd. (Yangon Branch)

"ACLEDA's focus on small and microenterprise as a driving force in the Cambodian economy grew into a bank for the future. The central principles of transparency, team work, an emphasis on customer service, and policies and procedures in place so that everyone can perform well and comply, provide quality services to our customers. Our effort to build ACLEDA Institute of Business (AIB) focuses on a new generation…the quality and trust carries from the ACLEDA Bank to AIB."

Ly Thai, Executive Vice President and Group Chief Administrative Officer, Board Chair of the ACLEDA Institute of Business

"The bank's success is owed to the employee's trust, honesty, and their equity participation, a strong belief in the bank's long-term vision and mission, a resilient corporate culture of transparency, and zero tolerance for corruption."

Rath Yumeng, EVP and Group Chief Treasury Officer, Shareholder Representative of ACLEDA Staff Association, ASA Plc.

"ACLEDA Bank Plc. moves from success to success, seemingly without effort. But as Heather Clark reveals, success is based on hard work, careful planning, and tireless dedication to providing inclusive financial services. The vision of ACLEDA Bank is now shared with the people of Laos and Myanmar as the bank expands regionally, serving people without access to appropriate financial services. But in the midst of international expansion, ACLEDA Bank has not forgotten its mission in Cambodia by establishing a business school, designing a People's IPO, and continuing a commitment to excellence in providing traditional and digital financial services. This is a success story that needs to be replicated throughout the world."

Bretton G. Sciaroni, Board Member, ACLEDA Financial Trust Shareholder, and Senior Partner, Sciaroni and Associates Law Office

"ACLEDA is an innovative, client-centric, and visionary global leader and pioneer in inclusive financial services. ACLEDA Bank Plc. and its leadership have been a source of great inspiration and learning for the whole field over many years. Hats off!"

Elizabeth Littlefield, Former President and CEO Overseas Private Investment Corporation (OPIC) and Senior Counselor at Albright Stonebridge Group

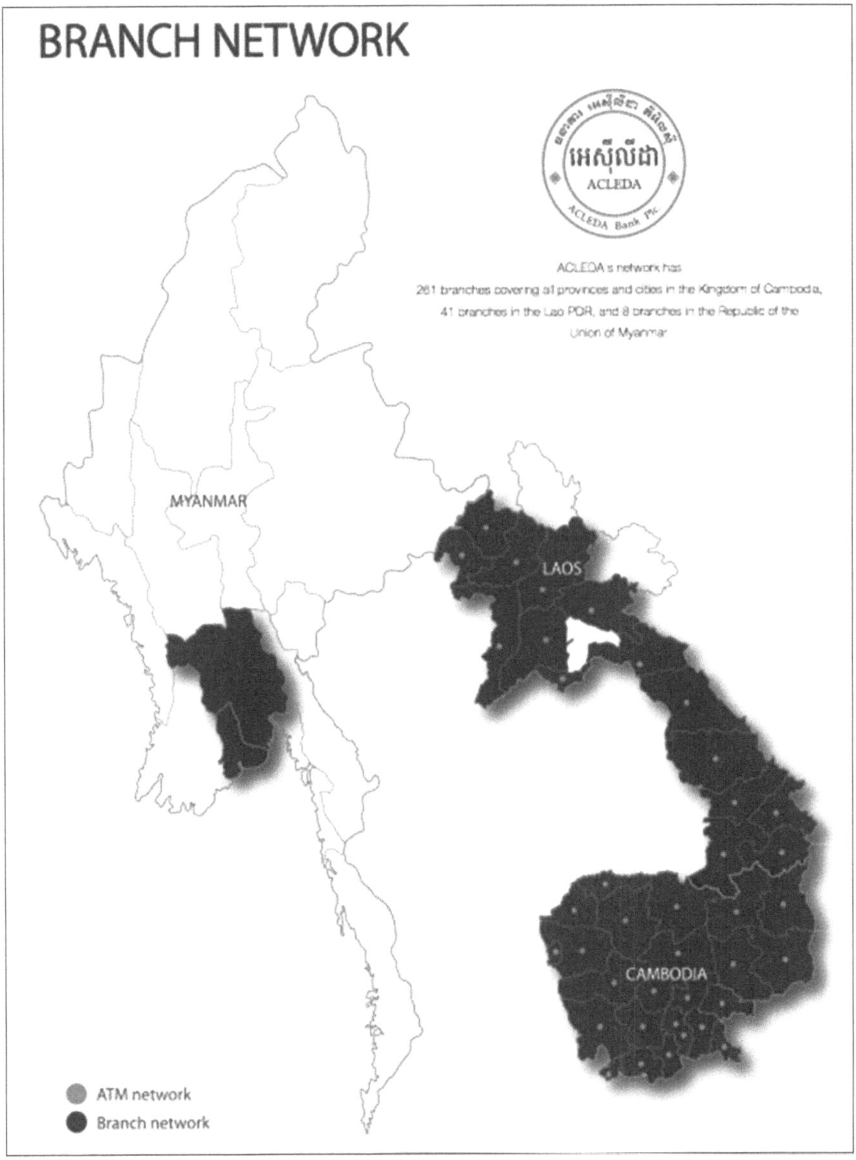

Map of Cambodia, Lao PDR and Myanmar with ACLEDA Bank Plc., ACLEDA Bank Lao, Ltd. and ACLEDA MFI Myanmar Operations
"We go further to get your transactions closer!"
Source: ACLEDA Bank Plc. Annual Report 2018

"I believe that, if managed well, the Fourth Industrial Revolution can bring a new cultural renaissance, which will make us feel part of something much larger than ourselves: a true global civilization. I believe the changes that will sweep through society can provide a more inclusive, sustainable and harmonious society."

"New technologies will dramatically change the nature of work across all industries and occupations."

Klaus Schwab, The Fourth Industrial Revolution
The World Economic Forum

Foreword

Financial sector development presents difficult challenges along with phenomenal opportunities. Markets within the financial sector often seem fragile, even when they are dynamic and the fundamentals are strong. Sometimes financial markets are neglected, and sometimes they are supported by over-exuberance. They can be destroyed overnight with untimely and unexpected events or can be nurtured with care and prudent policy.

Often, I am asked about the challenge of rebuilding a banking sector that suffered complete destruction. During my tenure as Minister of Economy and Finance, we placed great emphasis on building the financial sector and re-creating a vibrant and inclusive banking system. I invite you to read the prequel to this book, *When There Was No Money*. It tells a wonderful story about the initial stages of Cambodia's efforts to develop a banking system that worked for the people.

At that time, we believed financial inclusion was the backbone of our future financial sector—a financial sector that would have a strong foundation in the banking system and focus investment in microenterprises and small and medium enterprises. We have not been disappointed, and we redoubled efforts in that direction.

From a time when there was no money, this book traces the recent growth of the Cambodian financial sector and tells the story of the increasing strength and prominence of Cambodia's leading bank, ACLEDA Bank Plc.

Outside of Cambodia, ACLEDA Bank Plc. is supporting new endeavors together with innovators in neighboring countries. As regional initiatives in financial inclusion begin, grow, and prosper, new pathways for mutual learning, investment, and benefit emerge. The first ACLEDA Bank venture in Lao PDR shows a difficult beginning, a worsening trend, and then a solid "turnaround." This amazing turnaround story is rarely accomplished once an operation gets into trouble with non-performing loans. We see how the operation recovered and re-established its reputation for transparency and highly ethical practices.

The second venture in Myanmar brings ACLEDA Bank Cambodia back to its roots as a microfinance institution. It shows us the "dream" of how microfinance works well in a difficult regulatory environment and reaches women micro-entrepreneurs with credit and deposit services to build their businesses and support their families. The story is not without its lessons that tested preconceived ideas about how to support innovation in a new environment.

The third journey returns to Cambodia to create and develop a new kind of education for eager students of finance and business. The ACLEDA Institute of Business opened its doors to the first bachelor's degree candidates in early 2017. These students will carry on the traditions of innovation, transparency, and ethical banking that ACLEDA Bank Plc. is renowned for throughout the world.

I believe that this is truly an exciting time for financial inclusion and regional cooperation. Notably, it offers the promise for the new generation to hone their talents and build their values to advance the field far into the future. I see this in the rich analysis and splendid storytelling about a decade of ACLEDA Bank's growth. The analysis may seem advanced for the causal reader, but the engaging stories appeal to even the new student of finance.

The focus of this book is on the people, how they think and what they do to overcome challenges and solve problems, making new endeavors work well. And, as Ms. Clark narrates, the skills that have enabled the growth of the ACLEDA Bank group of companies are not only technical. Rather, success is based on a firm code of ethics and a timeless belief in the future and the potential of subsequent generations. This type of experience is quite rare in a sector where short-term gain is tempting and there are substantial incentives to ignore poor and low-income people.

This book takes us on an honest journey through the significant successes and difficulties in expansion and the attempts to repeat—but not copy—the ACLEDA Bank Cambodia experience in other countries. The perspectives of customers, thinkers and innovators, organizational architects, and policy makers who influenced the development of the ACLEDA Banks and the ACLEDA Microfinance Institution show us the experience over time and across borders.

The book examines recent trends in Cambodia, a highly competitive financial services market that continues to become more crowded with new players who have differing objectives and capacities for change and commitment. Each chapter tells a different story about how a small group of people grew to make a great difference in the way financial services reach the Cambodian people and how that same group of ethical financial entrepreneurs sought to repeat that experience with their neighboring counterparts in Lao PDR and Myanmar.

We see how these innovators pushed the envelope, creating new institutions and operational models that appealed to customers, investors, policy makers, and regulatory authorities alike in Lao PDR and Myanmar. Later, these wider groups in different countries redouble their efforts to ensure they support the people to sustain and build their businesses now and in the future.

Policy makers, bank and MFI staff, management, leadership, and investors renew their commitments to building inclusive finance within the region. New partners emerged in Cambodia, and new products are developed that facilitate transactions, expand service hours, lower costs, and advance financial services in a new age.

Shared commitment to a worthy goal is strengthened by a practice that combines the best of innovation with tested experience. Bringing the Fourth Industrial Revolution to Cambodia's financial sector, ACLEDA Bank Plc. was the first bank to start online electronic banking, furthering Fintech and promoting financial inclusion throughout the country, the region, and internationally.

As the World Economic Forum so sagely noted in its 2016 Global Agenda, "We do not yet know just how it (the Fourth Industrial Revolution) will unfold, but one thing is clear: the response to it must be integrated and comprehensive, involving all stakeholders of the global polity, from the public and private sectors to academia and civil society" (Schwab 2016).

This is a story about these practices and how they continue to evolve in Cambodia, Lao PDR, and Myanmar. It is a story that is relevant to all of us now and to the future generations who will lead the financial sectors in their countries with a fundamental understanding of what it takes to begin, evolve, and build an inclusive financial sector.

Keat Chhon, MP

Former Deputy Prime Minister and Former
Minister of Economy and Finance,
The Royal Government of Cambodia
Honorary Chairman of the Supreme
National Economic Council
August 2019

Reference

Schwab, K. (2016) The Fourth Industrial Revolution: What It Means, How to Respond. World Economic Forum, Global Agenda January 2016. Geneva. Available www.weforum.org/agenda/2016/01 Accessed 12 December 2017

Acknowledgments

This book was made possible only through the significant contributions of many people. ACLEDA Bank staff, management, board members, and former technical advisors revealed their stories one by one.

I thank Mr. Chhay Soeun and his predecessors, Mr. John Brinsden and Mr. Chea Sok, who held the position of Chairman of the Board of Directors of ACLEDA Bank Plc. With each individual perspective, they reached back into their memories about the early history of ACLEDA Bank Plc. and the company's first forays abroad to develop ACLEDA Bank Lao and ACLEDA MFI Myanmar. They recalled Cambodia's first banking system, how it dissolved overnight, and how it progressed further than most people thought was possible in only a decade.

This story explores the growth of the ACLEDA group of companies during a new decade, from 2005 to 2019, a significantly different transition than the earlier ones from a donor project to a commercial institution. A decade later, I am still inspired by ACLEDA's Group Managing Director, Dr. In Channy, and ACLEDA's Technical Advisors, Roel Hakemulder, Peter Kooi, and John Brinsden. My original wish, over a decade ago, is redoubled with the certainty that such talent, commitment, and flexibility should accompany every fledgling organization as it continues to grow to reach greater potential.

The expertise in governance is a recognized value and a well-developed skill of the people who built the ACLEDA group of companies. They practice it everyday, and each day, they put into practice the art of a learning organization. Often there is an artificial separation between management and governance. Yet, good governance is practiced in the Board Room, as well as the offices and corridors of any company. The practices of good governance and examples of seamless operations—as well as crisis management—are related in Cambodia, Lao PRD, Myanmar, and the ACLEDA Institute of Business.

These examples are narrated by Buntay Sovanny, Buth Bunsayha, Chhan Ponloeu, Chan Serey, Hou Rasmey, In Siphann, Kaysone Linthong, Meng Mariane, Nittaya Thirasack, Htet Htet Khaing, Su Sandy Win, Moeurng Rotha, Min Aung, Han Su Kyaw, Khin Myo Htet, Su Htwe Htwe Zaw, Kim Bunsocheat, Kim Sotheavy, Ly Thay, Terry Mach, Mar Amara, Nay Sok Samnang, Peuo Tit Mithona, Phon

Narin, Prom Visoth, Rath Yumeng, Sen Sokla, So Phonnary, So Sovannareth, Svay Hay, Tauch Ngam Youra, Tourt Sovanne, Thong Chandara, and Somphathay Thongmanyla, whom I sincerely thank.

Each unique perspective, from internal auditor to branch manager and from credit officer to long-time and new customers and to current AIB students—the Class of 2020—helped put an important piece of history into place and show a clear vision for the future.

I also thank Nget Nary, Sen Sokla, So Seyha, Sok Hay, Sok Piseth, Thath Dynoth, Tum Sokchamreoun, and AIB students. Each ACLEDA staff member and AIB student that I had the privilege to interview impressed me with the importance the new generation attributes to belonging to an organization that represents a different way of doing business in Cambodia.

A most impressive and unforgettable briefing was with the first class of students matriculating at the ACLEDA Institute of Business (AIB). Their perspectives showed a keen blend of realism and altruism, as youthful perspectives should be, if one day they will change the world. And I do believe that Yang Sophaktra, Choemroeun Sereyboth, Rov Chara, Say Sovadhka, Bin Chen Bin, Bunth Sopheakneath, Ron Yanaury, and Sam Chanlika will be able to accomplish their aims. I thank them for their perspectives on development and relating their intentions to influence a future that awaits them. They inspire me.

I am particularly grateful to HE Keat Chhon, Former Minister of Economy and Finance and Deputy Prime Minister. His expertise served Cambodia well with an optimistic view of the potential for developing an inclusive formal financial system in the country and extending honest and transparent financial services throughout the country.

My sincere appreciation is extended to HE Chea Serey and HE Neav Chanthana of the National Bank of Cambodia and their most energetic and knowledgeable staff who are engaged in financial education and advancing policy, regulation, and supervision for their perspectives on the developments of Cambodia's financial system.

Robert Cater, Eric Duflos, Ing Varony, Paul Luchtenberg, Gerald Lazar, Daniel Rozas, Hout Ieng Tong, William Naing, and Sim Senacheert provided valuable insights based on their experience in Cambodia, Lao PDR, and Myanmar, as well as a wealth of international experience in the development and expansion of financial systems. I am grateful for their comments, interpretations of current events, and views of the future. Chuluun Ganhuyag, Kimanthi Mutua, Maria Otero, Elizabeth Rhyne, Richard Rosenberg, Stuart Rutherford, John Tucker, J. D. von Pischke, and Graham Wright helped interpret ACLEDA's experience from a broader international perspective and the evolution of these financial systems from a time when there was no money for the great majority.

I thank my editorial board—John Brinsden, In Channy, Peter Kooi, Gerald Lazar, and Brett Scarloni—for their careful reading, substantive comments, and helpful advice on many aspects of this book. Their balanced and critical reviews helped improve the analysis of developments over the last decade, and why they are important to ACLEDA's legacy and future. Michael Hayes provided expert manuscript editing, improving quality and coherence. He dedicated care to exploring many details that enhanced the storytelling of *Beyond Borders, Beyond Banking* and in the process making it a richer account of history.

I am grateful to William Aucher and Ameena Jafar of Springer Nature for their professional and attentive dedication to seeing this next phase of ACLEDA's contributions to the financial sectors in Cambodia, Lao PDR, and Myanmar as an important part of financial sector development in the ASEAN region. I would also like to thank Anushangi Weerakoon, Sanjeev Keerthi Kumari, Albert Paap and Nitesh Shrivastava for showing exquisite care and attention to detail in the preparation of the manuscript.

Finally, I cannot thank my husband, Marshall Bear, enough for his dedication to—and enthusiasm for— the market systems approach to financial inclusion. His expert editorial advice, reader-friendly style, and creative and tasty cuisine sustained me throughout the writing of this book.

I extend my deepest appreciation for the opportunity to have worked with a wonderful team of professionals—in both private and public sectors—who translated their vision for a better world into reality, and they continue to advance. Individually and collectively, their story is an exceptional one, and I am grateful to have been chosen to write it.

January 2020 Heather A. Clark

Contents

Abbreviations

ABC	Association of Banks in Cambodia
ABL	ACLEDA Bank Lao Ltd.
ACLEDA	Association of Cambodian Local Economic Development Agencies
ADB	Asian Development Bank
AFD	Agence Française de Développement
AMM	ACLEDA MFI Myanmar Co., Ltd.
ASA	ACLEDA Staff Association, Inc.
ASEAN	Association of Southeast Asian Nations
BOL	Bank of the Lao PDR
BRI	Bank Rakyat Indonesia
BMZ	German Federal Ministry for Economic Cooperation and Development
CARERE	Cambodian Resettlement and Rehabilitation Programme
CBM	Central Bank of Myanmar
CCRD	Coordinating Committee on Rural Development
CFD	Caisse Française de Développement
CGAP	Consultative Group to Assist the Poor
CMA	Cambodia Microfinance Association
CMEA	Council for Mutual Economic Assistance
CPI	Consumer Price Index
CPP	Cambodian People's Party
CRS	Catholic Relief Services
DEG	Deutsche Investitions- und Entwicklungsgesellschaft
DFI	Development Finance Institution
EAP	East Asia and the Pacific Region
EU	European Union
ESOP	Employee Stock Ownership Plan
ESS	Environmental and Social Sustainability
FDI	Foreign Direct Investment
FRD	Financial Regulatory Department (Myanmar)
FMO	Netherlands Development Finance Company

FUNCINPEC	National United Front for an Independent, Neutral, Peaceful and Cooperative Cambodia
GDP	Gross Domestic Product
GIZ	Deutsche Gesellschaft für Internationale Zusammenarbeit
GRET	Groupe de recherche et d'échanges technologiques
GSMA	Global System for Mobile Communications Association
HEI	Higher Education Institution
ICT	Information and Communications Technology
IFC	International Finance Corporation
ILO	International Labour Organization
IMF	International Monetary Fund
KfW	Kreditanstalt für Wiederaufbau
LEDA	Local Economic Development Agencies
MDI	Microfinance Deposit Taking Institution
MFI	Microfinance Institution
MIS	Management Information System
MKK	Myanmar Kyat
MMFA	Myanmar MicroFinance Association
MoEF	Ministry of Economy and Finance
MoEYS	Ministry of Education, Youth and Sport (Cambodia)
MPDF	Mekong Project Development Facility
NBC	National Bank of Cambodia
NGO	Nongovernmental Organization
NPAT	Net Profit After Tax
NPL	Non-performing Loan
OTC	Over the Counter
P2P	Peer to Peer
PAR	Portfolio at Risk
PRASAC	Programme de Réhabilitation et d'Appui au Secteur Agricole
Prodem	Foundation for the Promotion and Development of Microenterprise
RDB	Rural Development Bank
SEISP	Small Enterprise and Informal Sector Promotion Project
Sida	Swedish International Development Cooperation Agency
SNC	Supreme National Council
SOE	State-Owned Enterprise
UNAMIC	United Nations Advance Mission in Cambodia
UNDP	United Nations Development Programme
UNCDF	United Nations Capital Development Fund
UNFPA	United Nations Population Fund
UNHCR	United Nations High Commissioner for Refugees
UNICEF	United Nations Children's Fund
UNTAC	United Nations Transitional Authority in Cambodia
USAID	United States Agency for International Development
VAT	Value-Added Tax
WTWNM	*When There Was No Money*
YoY	Year on Year

List of Figures

List of Tables

Part I
A Decade of Growth

Prologue

The Future Perspective

"We are at the beginning of a global transformation that is characterized by the convergence of digital, physical, and biological technologies in ways that are changing both the world around us and our very idea of what it means to be human. The changes are historic in terms of their size, speed, and scope.

This transformation—the Fourth Industrial Revolution—is not defined by any particular set of emerging technologies themselves, but rather by the transition to new systems that are being built on the infrastructure of the digital revolution. As these individual technologies become ubiquitous, they will fundamentally alter the way we produce, consume, communicate, move, generate energy, and interact with one another...

The fundamental and global nature of this revolution also poses new threats related to the disruptions it may cause—affecting labor markets and the future of work, income inequality, and geopolitical security as well as social value systems and ethical frameworks" (Schwab 2016).

Reference

Schwab, Klaus (2016) The Global Competitiveness Report 2016–2017. Adapted from Klaus Schwab, *The Fourth Industrial Revolution,* 2016. World Economic Forum, Geneva.

Chapter 1
Introduction: Building the Future—Beyond Borders, Beyond Banking

In 2005 the book *When There Was No Money* was published. It began with "This is a story about the unlikely success of microfinance in a war-torn country. It is a story about building small legends and big dreams. This is not a romantic tale; it is a story about poverty produced by war and neglect."

When There Was No Money explored the history of the market-driven approach to microfinance from 1992 to 2005 as practiced by ACLEDA Bank in Cambodia. At the time, the market approach to providing credit to poor and low-income people and small and microenterprises was still underdeveloped in many countries, perhaps with the exception of Bolivia. Also, at the time, it was thought to be too complicated and risky to develop such a commercial approach in a country that was still experiencing the aftermath of devastating war, genocide, resurgence of violence, and an ongoing military struggle with the Khmer Rouge that did not finally end until 1998.

An unquiet peace ebbed and peaked for most of the 1990s.

As one United Nations official remarked, even in 1998, "Cambodia is not yet ready for microfinance."

The ACLEDA story in *When There Was No Money* traced the trials and triumphs of a group of people as they implemented a quickly designed International Labour Organization (ILO) employment generation project for demobilized soldiers in Cambodia in 1992. At the time, the objective was clear: to get something on the ground as quickly as possible following the October 23, 1991, Paris Peace Accords.

The story examined the two approaches to microfinance that emerged as early as 1992—the social welfare approach to microfinance and the financial market systems approach. The financial systems approach to microfinance advocated independence from donor funding for microfinance institutions (MFIs). It was believed that this second approach could be achieved by connecting microfinance institutions to the greater financial system in the countries where they operated and with investors locally and globally.

© Springer Nature Singapore Pte Ltd. 2020

H. A. Clark, *Beyond Borders, Beyond Banking*,
https://doi.org/10.1007/978-981-15-1687-0_1

The theory behind the financial systems approach was that with the right regulatory framework, and a strong supportive infrastructure, MFIs would become an intrinsic part of the financial system. And MFIs would become a permanent part of an inclusive financial system in the countries where they operated. They would fill important gaps in the financial system by providing access to formal financial services for poor and low-income people.

These new financial institutions would also bring innovation to the financial system, by providing new products and services that were useful and attractive to poor and low-income people, owners of small and microenterprises, and the workforce that began to grow throughout the early 2000s. New financial institutions were also concerned with constructing the supporting functions that would promote their own expansion and risk management systems to ensure safe and sound practices. By emphasizing innovation, these new financial services providers could provide the key to reaching new customer segments that were neglected by the prevailing system.

But first, financial services providers would need to develop new ways of delivering products to broad segments of excluded customers. These pioneers would focus on building financial institutions that could manage risk, reduce costs, develop products, and maintain quality services to underserved and financially excluded people.

ACLEDA pursued both approaches to microfinance, one after the other. And what they found lacking in the first approach that relied on donors became their rationale for adopting the financial systems approach to building a better financial future for their customers.

Yet, the driving force for ACLEDA's actions and plans was always rooted in their beliefs about how they should behave in society and how they should treat others. Their beliefs centered on the way transparent operations and no tolerance for corruption offered poor and low-income people a fair stake in a system that had long denied them one.

When There Was No Money was a story of corporate values and the people who believe in them. It was a story of perseverance and professionalism; it was a story about how ACLEDA attempted to influence the way banking and business worked in Cambodia at the most fundamental level.

By 2003, ACLEDA Bank Ltd. became the first Cambodian microfinance institution (MFI) to have transformed into a commercial bank. And, by 2004, ACLEDA Bank Plc. became Cambodia's largest commercial retail bank network, managing 119 branches and smaller service posts in rural areas that provided basic banking services in 21 out of Cambodia's 24 provinces. ACLEDA Bank Plc. also gained the standing as the first Cambodian bank to be issued an international credit rating.

At that time, in 2003, ACLEDA Bank Plc. served over 122,000 small and micro-entrepreneurs in rural and urban areas with credit, deposits, and domestic and international funds transfer services. The bank employed 2,108 staff throughout the country and later became the largest employer in Cambodia's private financial sector.

ACLEDA Bank's experience gained global attention in the specialized and focused field of financial inclusion. From the early days through 2018, ACLEDA's success prompted over 142 foreign organizations from 30 countries and 244 local organizations to send over 5,800 visitors and course participants to ACLEDA Bank Plc. in Cambodia to learn about the Bank's operations, standards and ethics, and their secrets of success.

Visitors and course participants discovered ACLEDA's early lessons in good governance, product design, customer service, and the consultative working relationship with their regulator, the National Bank of Cambodia. They also gained a practical understanding of why ACLEDA Bank Plc. considered professional development a leading priority—one that built strong pillars for ACLEDA Bank's growth over two decades.

Foreign visitors met with the National Bank of Cambodia, to hear the story of how an enabling regulatory framework supported both ACLEDA and its competition to emerge and grow on a level playing field, despite the occasional political opposition. They also found, just as ACLEDA had, that competition and cooperation with other MFIs were the best ways to serve the market with products that were safe, sound, and profitable for both the customer and the bank.

Later, the ACLEDA Training Center (ATC) was built in 2011 to serve the capacity building needs of the domestic market, as well as to respond to the expanding training needs for the newly recruited staff of ACLEDA Bank Plc. The ATC became a center of excellence in Cambodia and the microfinance world of developing and emerging economies. In early 2016, the ATC transformed into the ACLEDA Institute of Business, when the Ministry of Education, Youth and Sport (MoEYS) granted a license to AIB to operate as an institute of higher education in Cambodia.

Now, 15 years after the publication of ***When There Was No Money***, ACLEDA Bank Plc. looks a lot different than it did in 2004, and so does Cambodia's economy and financial sector. So much has changed at the national level, not the least of which are Cambodia's striking annual economic growth rates reaching 7% per annum on average for the past 10 years.

Other dramatic changes include the presence of a supportive infrastructure for the financial sector, such as an industry-owned credit bureau that follows international standards and stronger industry associations, such as the Cambodia Microfinance Association and the Association of Banks in Cambodia. Practices of formally licensed MFIs and banks encourage financial consumer protection, even though the legal and regulatory framework lags behind.

And nascent government-supported financial education initiatives are engaging a dynamic staff cadre at the National Bank of Cambodia. There are expanding career and professional development choices for new recruits to the banking sector and those who have not yet chosen to follow the banker's path. In addition, Cambodia developed a stock market, the Cambodia Securities Exchange (CSX), in 2010.

Rules and norms—regulations and practices—continue to develop. These include stricter capital and liquidity requirements, price controls on interest rates, and the encouragement of new entrants. Support for mergers and acquisitions within the banking sector is another new development that has dramatically changed the composition and the face of the banking sector since its "flight to quality" in 1999.

New questions emerge in the context of Cambodia's rapid growth and significant change within the financial sector:

First, how in the world did an ILO employment generation project for demobilized soldiers in 1992 become recognized by 2016 as one of top 100 banks in the ASEAN region by the Banker Global Financial Intelligence Service?

How did a post-conflict country, overrun with international donors, teach the advocates of financial inclusion something about a market-driven approach to microfinance and inclusive finance within the formally regulated banking system?

How did Cambodia become the only country able to meet its Millennium Development Goal of halving poverty by 2009?

What new regulations and practices enable or erode safer and sounder growth in a market that is often described as extremely competitive and sometimes overheated by encouraging more debt than consumers can absorb? What have been the effects on the core market—both service providers and customers—of new regulatory controls on interest rates and higher capital requirements?

How has the market been influenced by the expansion in the numbers of credit organizations that have increased dramatically in the last decade?

Is over-indebtedness a concern, and is it increasing or decreasing with the established interest rate ceiling?

Does local ownership matter in the current context of mergers, acquisitions, and encouragement of new foreign entrants to retail banking? What kind of ownership matters most for the long-term benefit of Cambodia and its citizens?

How did a bank adhere to values, and commit to social change and educational advances for the next generation, all the while committing itself to sound business principles and ethical decision-making in an atmosphere often tainted by corruption?

How and why did ACLEDA Bank Plc. in Cambodia establish subsidiaries in the Lao PDR and Republic of the Union of Myanmar? What lessons does expansion beyond borders to other countries in the region offer?

Can a bank build an institution of higher education or a university and infuse it with the same corporate ethos, favoring innovation while managing risk? Why would a commercial bank take on such a responsibility that is beyond its own boundaries?

What is Cambodia's competitive advantage in ASEAN for embracing innovation, technology, and entrepreneurship, as well as new business practices that require higher levels of transparency, elimination of corruption, and more equitable treatment across the board?

And, lastly, how will Cambodia and its local institutions begin to match the highest standards set in the ASEAN region, readying the country for the challenge of regional and global integration? Will the aim to ensure benefits for Cambodia's new generation secure future economic and social gain or at the least ensure that they will not be left behind?

In 2005, I set out to tell a story about how a new kind of bank emerged in a country devastated by war and neglect. More than a decade has passed since "there was no money." It has become apparent that it is time to tell the next chapter of this story. This book addresses issues and questions for a new millennium and a new generation. They extend beyond borders and beyond boundaries.

1.1 Part I: A Decade of Growth

Part 1: A Decade of Growth sets the context of a society and economy that has achieved 7 percent growth rates nearly every year during the last decade.

Chapter 2: The Big Picture: Cambodia Then, Cambodia Now (2004–2019) examines the process and the structure of Cambodia's economic growth over more than a decade. The chapter provides an overview of the sector's contribution to growth, the drivers of growth, and an analysis of growth with equity. Set in the context of the World Economic Forum's Fourth Industrial Revolution, the discussion provides a broad overview of the socioeconomic context with an examination of Cambodia's Competitiveness Index and trends in this index over time.

1.2 Part II: Flight to Quality

Part II begins with a historical perspective of the initial "flight to quality" in the banking sector in 1999, two decades ago.

Chapter 3: Cambodia's Financial Market System (2004–2019): History, Structure, and Performance identifies major players and financial market system functions, as well as some of the major accomplishments of Cambodia's financial market system over the past decade. An analysis of the market system is featured. The chapter highlights progress and growth as well as issues and questions that arise with the growth of competition, implementing a safer and sounder regulatory regime, and the emergence of stronger supporting infrastructure, including the Cambodia Securities Exchange. Selected topics of current importance and great debate for the future are discussed in more detail later in Chap. 4.

Chapter 4: The Dynamics of Growth Over Time complements Chap. 3 with more in-depth analysis. It examines several major trends related to the structure, incentives, and recent policies in the financial sector. Chapter 4 discusses the advent and growth of "mergers and acquisitions" of Cambodia's microfinance deposit-taking institutions (MDIs). The phenomenal growth of new players serving the bottom of the pyramid and operating under the regulatory radar is discussed. The hotly contested debate about over-indebtedness is analyzed, with a focus on how the interest rate cap plays a significant role among other factors that may promote over-indebtedness.

Chapter 4 closes with a discussion of recent regulatory changes and market dynamics, such as interest rate caps, the phenomenal growth in the number of financial services providers (FSPs) at the bottom of the pyramid, and other challenges within the financial sector that require attention by all the market players, including banks and MFIs as well as the regulator.

1.3 Part III: ACLEDA Bank Plc.: Traditions and Transitions

Part III presents a summary history of ACLEDA Bank Plc. focusing on the principles of ACLEDA's operation that were established from the outset and the people who established them.

Chapter 5: ACLEDA Bank Plc.: Principles and Practices revisits the history of ACLEDA Bank's philosophy and how the values built a culture of integrity that laid the foundation of ACLEDA's ethical banking practices. The chapter analyzes the importance of four major traditions that have led to ACLEDA Bank's success: no tolerance for corruption, understand the customer, a role for staff ownership and governance, and capacity leads, capital follows.

Chapter 6: **Pioneers and Protégés** focuses on one of ACLEDA Bank's fundamental traditions—local ownership and governance. The chapter traces the evolution in the thinking of the original ACLEDA staff—the pioneers—and how their views and values have been adopted by a new generation.

Chapter 7: Products and Performance presents an analysis of ACLEDA Bank's performance over the last decade. It discusses financial performance and also market performance. The focus is on ACLEDA's product and customer service innovations that enabled growth. It also highlights the National Bank of Cambodia and ACLEDA Bank's joint experiment with digitizing corruption out of the market.

1.4 Part IV: ACLEDA Bank Plc.: Expanding Beyond Borders, Beyond Banking

Part IV follows ACLEDA management and staff on their journey beyond Cambodia's borders to the Lao PDR and the Republic of the Union of Myanmar and into the higher educational sector in Cambodia. All three ventures represent three very different worlds than the commercial retail-banking sector in Cambodia.

The story begins with ACLEDA Bank Plc.'s welcome to build a bank in the Lao People's Democratic Republic (PDR).

Chapter 8: Building ACLEDA Bank Lao Ltd. examines how ACLEDA Bank Lao developed in a difficult environment similar to Cambodia in some respects but also very different from what the ACLEDA pioneers expected. The chapter highlights regulatory environments and practices that support financial inclusion and those that do not.

Chapter 9: Banking on the Future: ACLEDA MFI Myanmar Co. Ltd. in the Evolving Financial Sector of the Republic of the Union of Myanmar brings ACLEDA Bank Plc. back to its roots in establishing a microfinance institution in Myanmar.

Chapters 8 and 9 examine lessons about building two very different kinds of retail-banking organizations—a commercial bank and a microfinance institution—in two very different environments in the Lao PDR and Myanmar.

These environments are also unlike Cambodia at any time in recent history. The chapters examine performance and relate successes, challenges, and lessons experienced by staff, management, and customers about ACLEDA's expansion beyond borders.

Chapter 10: ACLEDA Institute of Business: A New Generation of Bankers explores the fascinating history of the ACLEDA Institute of Business (AIB), the people who built it and the reasons why. The chapter begins by setting the context within the education sector in Cambodia and the higher education sub-sector within it. It provides a brief overview of the challenges of the primary, secondary, and higher education sectors as the context to explore ACLEDA Bank Plc.'s dedication to improve professional education in the financial sector.

Chapter 10 explores why ACLEDA expanded beyond banking into Cambodia's higher education sector. To some this appears to be an anomaly; to others it appears as just another step to reach the dream of the original ACLEDA Bank staff—a dedicated group of teachers with high ideals and a vision about the future of their country.

The three chapters combine to show how the ACLEDA pioneers in foreign lands and different sectors of the Cambodian economy welcomed new challenges in pursuit of building something of value for the country and its people.

1.5 Epilogue

The Epilogue highlights the ACLEDA Bank legacy and the contributions the ACLEDA Group of Companies has brought to millions of people in Cambodia, the Lao PDR, and the Republic of the Union of Myanmar. This concluding chapter summarizes the experiences building inclusive financial sectors from ACLEDA Bank's history and the three financial sectors as they continue to develop in Cambodia, the Lao PDR, and Myanmar.

The Epilogue also examines prospects for the future—both challenges and opportunities—with the advent of the Cambodian Stock Exchange (CSX) and as ACLEDA Bank Plc. and ACLEDA Bank Lao continue to forge ahead with fintech innovation in Cambodia and the Lao PDR. The reason for the growing customer base of small and medium enterprises and fintech users in rural and urban areas is examined. ACLEDA Microfinance Myanmar (AMM) stays true to its original vision and mission, expanding outreach to new customers and building a cadre of young microfinance bankers for the benefit of the sector.

Chapter 2
The Big Picture: Cambodia Then, Cambodia Now (2004–2019)

By 2016 Cambodians were not just enjoying something very much like genuine peace, they were also working hard to gain something close to real wealth. For the first time since the Paris Peace Accords were signed in 1991, Cambodia won the designation as a lower middle-income country, up one notch from low-income country status on the World Bank's international growth classifications.

This chapter examines Cambodia's recent decade-plus of growth, with a focus on growth with equity. Matching past performance and future prospects, the chapter also takes a look at obstacles and advantages for Cambodia's economy. The final section examines drivers of future growth.

2.1 More than a Decade of Growth

The hard-won but not so surprising new status as a lower middle-income country was the result of Cambodia's economic growth rate over the period from 2004 through 2017. Annual economic growth averaged over 7% during the last 10 years, with a 4-year high of 7.5% in 2018, placing Cambodia among the most rapidly growing economies in the world (Ly et al. 2019; World Bank 2016a, b, c, d).

Increases in gross national income (GNI) per capita reached USD 1,229 by early 2017 and USD 1,380 in 2018. Steady growth offered a glimpse of prosperity to over 15 million Cambodians, even though the percentage increases in growth were established on a very low base. Although many Cambodians are at risk of slipping back into poverty, there are positive signs of greater equity in Cambodia's growth as indicated by decreases in poverty rates and increases in income and consumption growth for the lower segments of the population (World Bank 2014, 2016a, b, c, d, 2019). [1]

[1] The next section of this chapter continues the discussion of growth with equity, which shows that consumption growth of the lowest quintile of the population was significantly higher than that of

© Springer Nature Singapore Pte Ltd. 2020
H. A. Clark, *Beyond Borders, Beyond Banking*,
https://doi.org/10.1007/978-981-15-1687-0_2

Fig. 2.1 Sector contribution to employment 2004 (Reproduced from ILOSTAT database, 2018) Source: International Labour Organization, ILOSTAT database. Data retrieved in November 2017

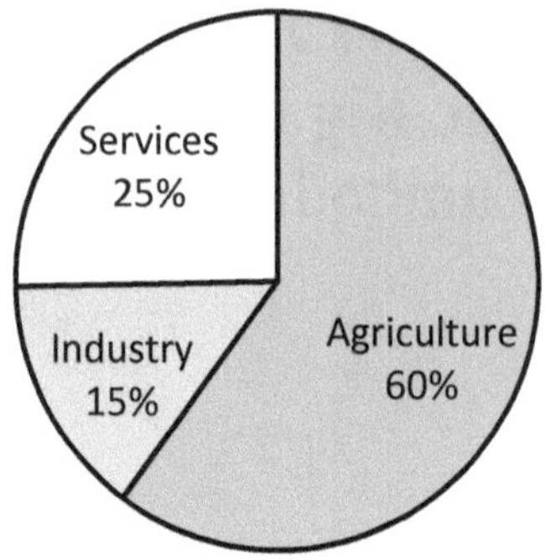

Cambodians appreciated opportunities brought on by the prosperity that came with sustained peace. Their nascent market economy was performing much better than it had at any other time in the past 60 years.

Agriculture Sector Dynamics The agricultural sector, dominated by exports of high-quality Khmer rice, continued to offer employment [2] and income opportunities to women and men in the rural areas, where about 90% of Cambodia's poor people live. However, the agricultural sector's contribution to job growth steadily declined with Cambodia's modest success in diversifying its overall economy over the 14-year period from 2004 to 2017. See Figs. 2.1 and 2.2.

The agricultural sector contributed irregularly to GDP growth from 2004 through 2016. Agriculture's contribution to GDP growth spiked in 2012 and flattened during 2014–2015 caused by a combination of drought, sluggish improvement in yields, and depressed agriculture commodity prices (Ly 2016). See Fig. 2.3.

By 2016, even with a slight recovery, agriculture's share of GDP declined to 26.3 %, down from about one-third a decade ago (World Bank 2017). Even though the agriculture sector recently increased productivity, over the last 2 years, the sector contributed less than 1% to the overall 7% GDP growth in 2016 and 2017 as shown in Fig. 2.3.

The Garment and Apparel Industry The greatest gains in GDP growth have come in the garment and apparel industry and other light industries, such as electronics and auto parts. (See Fig. 2.3.) The recent domestic construction boom also

the highest quintile of the population. This shows that Cambodia achieved growth with equity during the 10-year period up to and including 2015.

[2] Employment is defined as persons of working age who were engaged in any activity to produce goods or provide services for pay or profit, whether at work during the reference period or not at work due to temporary absence from a job, or to working-time arrangement. The services sector consists of wholesale and retail trade and restaurants and hotels; transport, storage, and communications; financing, insurance, real estate, and business services; and community, social, and personal services, in accordance with divisions 6–9 (ISIC 2) or categories G–Q (ISIC 3) or categories G–U (ISIC 4). International Labour Organization, ILOSTAT database. Data retrieved on 20 July 2018.

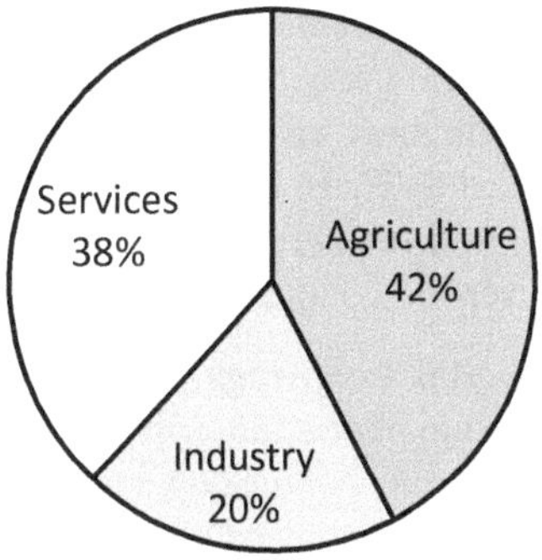

Fig. 2.2 Sector contribution to employment 2017 (Reproduced from ILOSTAT database, 2018) Source: International Labour Organization, ILOSTAT database. Data retrieved in November 2017

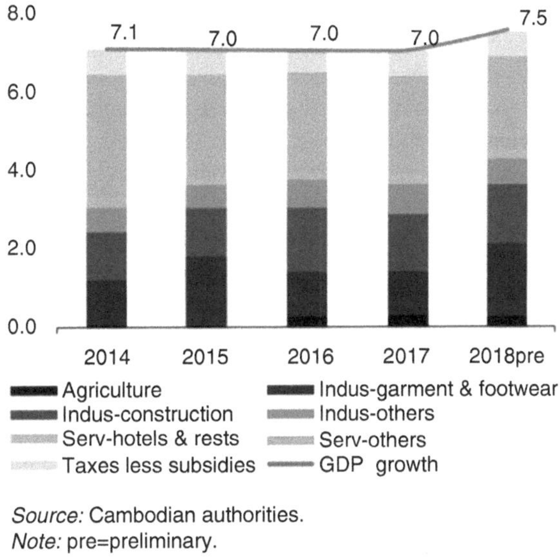

Fig. 2.3 Sector contribution to GDP growth, percent (Reproduced from Ly et al. May 2019)

contributed heavily to GDP growth and employment during this period. Growth in each of these industries is fueled by foreign direct investment (FDI).

Together, the garment and apparel industry, construction industry, and other light industries accounted for approximately one-half of GDP growth in 2017. These sectors of the economy also boosted the steady urban employment rates that had been established earlier by the garment industry alone. (See Figs. 2.1 and 2.2.)

The Service Industry The service industry also rebounded since 2014, including real estate, trade, banking, and tourism, as shown in Fig. 2.3. Tourism is another main contributor to Cambodia's employment, and the sector added steadily to GDP growth over the decade. Foreign tourist arrivals increased 6% on average from 2014 to 2016 and accelerated to 10% increase during 2018. The growth trend enabled Cambodia's tourism industry to attract more than 6 million foreign visitors in 2018, up dramatically from 1.4 million in 2005 (Ministry of Tourism 2017, 2018; World Bank 2015, 2016e, 2017, 2018).

The employees of these urban industries have their roots and extended families in rural areas. Fortunately, a well-developed and fine-tuned professional banking community enabled the daughters and sons of rural families to generate new rural wealth. These newly skilled urban employees took advantage of safe and efficient digital funds transfer services through accounts with MFIs and banks, as well as over-the-counter transactions from a variety of financial services providers.

Digital Leapfrogging By early 2019, Cambodia boasted more than 25 million mobile phone subscriptions for a population of 16 million. About 12.5 million people or most of the population has access to the Internet. Ninety percent of all Internet access is achieved via satellite, instead of cable and landlines. [3]

By using satellite technology, Cambodia was able to "leapfrog" over landlines, and the physical infrastructure required supporting landline technology. As HE Chea Serey, Director General of the National Bank of Cambodia, notes, "Twenty years ago, telecommunication cost in Cambodia was the highest in ASEAN according to an ADB study, but now I can confidently say that access to Internet in Cambodia is the cheapest in ASEAN" (Chea 2018).

The rapid increase in cell phone ownership and Internet access makes urban to rural funds transfers inexpensive, convenient, and safer than alternative means. The volume of digital domestic funds transfers was estimated at USD1 billion in 2013 (Morton 2014).[4] Within 4 years, by 2017, the amount and the number of digital remittances increased by more than 1,200% in both KHR and USD combined, a growth trend expected to continue into the foreseeable future (National Bank of Cambodia 2016).

By the end of 2017, the NBC registered 86.6 million transfers made during the year by mobile banking operations alone (National Bank of Cambodia 2017). Even though mobile banking transactions are greater in number than Internet banking by almost 12 times, Internet banking transactions are made in greater amounts.

This pattern shows how each service is placed in two diverse segments of the market. The general public uses mobile money and makes a greater number of transactions in smaller amounts. Businesses and government operations use Internet banking to support their operations which require a smaller number of transactions, but for larger amounts, for example, to support payroll or office operating expenses.

These statistics and the story behind them also show that mobile banking and Cambodia's "leapfrog digital infrastructure" have contributed positively to increased financial inclusion.

---

[3] For an up-to-date statistical database, see We Are Social and Hootsuite's latest collection, available at https://www.slideshare.net/DataReportal/digital-2019-cambodia-january-2019-v01, and Digital 2019: Global Internet Use Accelerates. The information source is updated regularly and an asset to the financial services industry.

[4] For the year 2013, Wing, Cambodia's premier mobile money operation, saw "…an increase in domestic remittances – transferring money to someone inside the country for a small fee via mobile phone or by visiting one of the company's Wing Cash Xpress outlets – drove transaction volumes to $1.5 billion. At least $1 billion of the total came from remittances" (Morton 2014).

2.2 Growth with Equity

Cambodia's growth has come with increasing equity. According to the World Bank: "The poverty rate dropped from 52.2 % of the population in 2004 to 20.5 % in 2011, surpassing all expectations and exceeding the country's Millennium Development Goals (MDGs) of halving poverty by 2009. Among 69 countries that have comparable data, Cambodia ranked fourth in terms of the fastest poverty reduction in the world from 2004–2008" (World Bank 2014).

The **income Gini coefficient** is a measure economists use to measure income inequality in a country. It measures the distribution of income among individuals or households within a country from a perfectly equal distribution. The Gini index is the Gini coefficient expressed as a percentage and is equal to the Gini coefficient multiplied by 100. A value of 0 represents absolute equality and a value of 100 absolute inequality.

Source: World Bank (2014)

In addition, consumption growth among the bottom 40 % of the population averaged an annual 6.3% increase between 2008 and 2013, twice the consumption growth of the top 60 % of the population (World Bank 2014).

As a result, "Cambodia's Gini Index, a measure of income inequality, fell sharply from 41.14 in 2007 to 30.76 by 2013, the latest year for which data are available" (World Bank 2016a, b, c, d). See Fig. 2.4 [5]

Drivers of Growth with Equity One of the main drivers of Cambodia's economic growth and growth with equity is the promotion of the garment industry and the employment it generates. A recent World Bank report found that a vibrant garment sector can improve the well-being of the bottom 40 % in any society, and evidence from Cambodia confirms this finding.

"Poor households with members working in the sector are more likely to experience consumption gains; suffer less from food insufficiency; and report higher rates of school enrollment for their children. The sector also has a much lower gender wage gap than other industries and is a main reason Cambodia has been able to incorporate women into the productive economy." (World Bank 2016a, b, c, d)

Rural areas have also benefitted from growth. Although agriculture's economic importance as a percentage of GDP growth has been declining, the agricultural sec-

[5] Data are based on primary household survey data obtained from government statistical agencies and World Bank country departments and PovcalNet (http://iresearch.worldbank.org/PovcalNet/index.html).

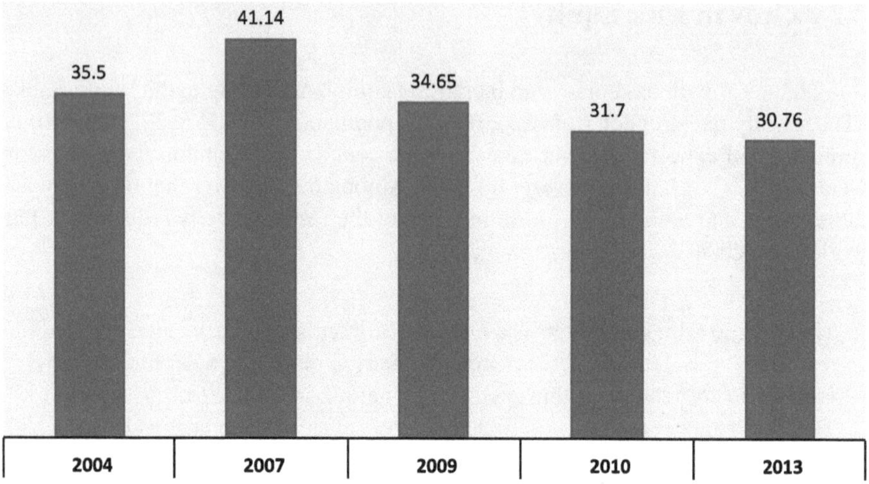

Fig. 2.4 Trends in the Gini index, Cambodia, 2004–2013
Source: World Bank, Development Research Group. Data are based on primary household survey data obtained from government statistical agencies and World Bank country departments. For more information and methodology, please see PovcalNet (http://iresearch.worldbank.org/PovcalNet/index.htm)

tor narrowed income inequality in rural areas over the last decade. Farm incomes from agricultural crops, mainly paddy rice, more than doubled between 2004 and 2009.

The recent increasing importance of nonfarm self-employment and rising wages in Cambodia's rural areas cannot be underestimated when it comes to reducing rural income inequality. Average per capita daily wage labor incomes among rural residents rose 9.5% annually during 2004–2009, and as of 2013, wages and salaries represented 43% of total rural household income. This is a major shift in the fundamental composition of rural household income (World Bank 2014; 2016a, b, c, d).

Financial Services Drive Growth with Equity One of Cambodia's major accomplishments in increasing growth, with modest but growing equity, is developing an expanding inclusive financial sector, particularly with respect to the retail-banking system.

The banking sector includes a strong microfinance presence in both dedicated microfinance institutions (MFIs) and commercial and specialized banks, mostly notably ACLEDA Bank Plc. and Wing (Cambodia) Limited Specialized Bank. These banks and MFIs have digital capacity in addition to physical branches, or agents as in the case of Wing, in rural and urban areas. Cambodia's dynamic banking and microfinance sector focuses on providing basic banking services for the majority of the population including deposit accounts and credit and money transfer services within the country and internationally.

Even though financial inclusion lags in rural areas, basic banking services are in high demand in both rural and urban areas. According to the FinScope Consumer Survey, at least 96% to 98% of the population is aware of, or using (71%), mobile money, small and micro loans from MDIs, MFIs, bank branches, agents, ATMs, and digital financial services (FinScope 2015).

As such, the banking sector, particularly those banks and MFIs that serve poor and low-income people, positively influences the upward trend in "growth with equity." There are more—and more convenient—options for more people in rural and urban areas to keep their money safe, finance investments regardless of size, and move money when they need to.

2.3 Growth and Poverty

As the World Bank notes, while Cambodia achieved the Millennium Development Goal (MDG) of halving poverty in 2009, the vast majority of families who escaped poverty were only able to do so by a small margin. Thus, around 8.1 million people are near poor, living on less than USD 2.30 a day (World Bank 2016a, b, c, d).

The 8.1 million people who are near poor—more than half the population—remain highly vulnerable, even to small shocks, which could quickly bring them back into poverty. A recent World Bank study found that a small shock of 30 cents a day would double the nation's poverty rate (World Bank 2016a, b, c, d).

Over 1.1 million Cambodians work abroad. For every ten Cambodians in the workforce, one of them works abroad. These men and women are major contributors to increasing incomes and Cambodia's economic prosperity. They generated over USD 900 million in remittances in 2017 alone, accounting for 4.5% of Cambodia's GDP for that year (Chheng 2018).

The great push to foster growth with equity requires well-matched policy advances, prudent management, and vigilant implementation, lest those gains be lost or begin to reverse. This is particularly important, as Cambodia's gains in poverty reduction are fragile. And some of these gains are dependent on workers abroad who respond to employment opportunities created by economies in other countries.

The drive to advance growth with equity requires increasing investment in competitiveness and innovation to ensure that the accomplishments of the next decade match those of the last decade.

2.4 Competitiveness and Innovation

Cambodia appears to be on the way to joining more prosperous ASEAN member nations to mutual advantage. With a gross national income (GNI) per capita of USD 1,380 in 2018, and the real GNI projected to increase between 7% and 6.9% each year for the next 3 years, the distance seems ambitious but attainable.

Yet, significant steps forward for any country to maintain growth with equity are always accompanied by significant challenges. Cambodia is no exception. Building regional and global competiveness is both a challenge and a great opportunity with anticipated ASEAN regional integration and new global economic partners.

2.4.1 The Global Competitiveness Index (GCI)

There are many global rating indices that might be used to analyze an economy. The Cambodian economy is in transition from a very low base compared to other ASEAN countries. Economic competitiveness, particularly considering the economy's export orientation, will be a main consideration as Cambodia positions itself to become a substantial player in the ASEAN region and continue its global export capacity.

The World Economic Forum's (WEF) Global Competitiveness Index (GCI) is well suited to analyze Cambodia's main challenges and advantages at this stage of its economic growth. In addition, the WEF introduced a new Global Competitiveness Index in 2018. The new Index has refocused indicators in light of the new challenges and opportunities brought about by the Fourth Industrial Revolution (Schwab 2018), and it is also comparable to earlier GCI [6]. In this way, the newly revised Index brings analytics for an economy's competitive positioning to inform a possibly disruptive future.

As the authors of the GCI note, "A key message from the report is the need for a broad-based approach to raising competitiveness – a strong performance in one area cannot make up for a weak performance in another. This is especially true when it comes to innovation: while it is true that a strong focus on technology can provide leapfrogging opportunities for low and middle income countries, governments must not lose sight of 'old' developmental issues, such as governance, infrastructure and skills. In this light one worrying factor thrown up by this year's Index is the fact that, for 117 of the 140 economies surveyed, quality of institutions remains a drag on overall competitiveness" (Schwab 2018).

Cambodia is included in this category.

The 12 Pillars of Competitiveness Twelve drivers of productivity support the new Global Competiveness Index framework. These 12 pillars are institutions; infrastructure; technological readiness; macroeconomic context; health; education and skills; product market; labor market; financial system; market size; business dynamism; and innovation. There are 98 supportive indicators.

The World Economic Forum defines national competitiveness as the set of institutions, policies, and factors that determine the level of productivity of an economy.

[6] See the Prologue to Part 1 for a brief description of the Fourth Industrial Revolution. Also refer to https://www.weforum.org/center-for-the-fourth-industrial-revolution/.

Table 2.1 shows Cambodia's scores for the 2018 GCI, using the new methodology that emphasizes an economy's productivity (Schwab 2018).[7] Twelve pillars and their 98 supportive indicators, such as "economic and financial development, education, health, and labor readiness, among others, capture concepts that matter for productivity and long-term prosperity."[8] See Table 2.1 The twelve global competitiveness pillars and Cambodia's ranking 2018.

Cambodia's competitiveness in the region and globally improved substantially since 2007, when it ranked 109th out of 134 countries and was one of the four least competitive countries in the Asian region (Schwab and Porter 2008). In the 2007 GCI, Cambodia's financial market development ranked 130th out of 134 countries participating in the index, indicating a common perception that it required substantial improvement.

In the 2016–2017 World Economic Forum's Global Competitiveness Index (GCI), Cambodia ranked 89th out of 138 countries (Schwab 2016). Among Asian nations, Cambodia showed the largest overall improvement between 2007 (when it ranked 109th) and 2016–2017 (when it ranked 89th).

The most recent GCI for 2018 (see Table 2.1) shows that Cambodia's overall ranking fell slightly to 110th out of 140 countries participating in the Index. Scoring of indicators reveals a stable profile across most pillars, although by 2018 Cambodia lost some of the gains it made in 2016.

Overall Performance and Trends Even though Cambodia's overall competitiveness trend has been positive since 2007, the country's challenges are diverse and significant when it comes to global competitiveness. Cambodia ranks no better than 65th place in any of the 12 pillars in the 2018 Competitiveness Index, in which 140 countries participated.

In half of the pillars, Cambodia places beyond the 100th mark (out of 140 economies). Of particular concern is the mediocre performance in three of the four areas that constitute the basic drivers of competitiveness: "institutions" (126th place and decreasing since 2017), "infrastructure" (112th place and decreasing since 2017), and "skills" (a category which includes education and labor force skills) in 121st place.

Between 2012 and 2017–2018, some countries that were ranked in the CGI have moved ahead, while others have fallen behind. Cambodia's competitiveness ranking overall has remained constant or decreased only slightly for the past 6 years. In a global competitive world, "constant" could also mean "standing still." One could reasonably infer that Cambodia's ranking suggests that it may not be investing in the

[7]According to the WEF, "the World Economic Forum's Global Competitiveness Index 4.0 builds on four decades of experience in benchmarking competitiveness. New composite indicators assess the set of factors that determine an economy's level of productivity—widely considered as the most important determinant of long-term growth." Further details on methodology and the full 2018 report, as well as previous reports, can be found at https://www.weforum.org/reports.

[8]The Global Competitiveness Report indicators are described in greater detail in Appendix C of The Global Competitiveness Index 4.0 Methodology and Technical Notes (Schwab 2018).

Table 2.1 Global competitiveness pillars and Cambodia's ranking 2018 (Schwab 2018)

		Score out of a possible 100	Ranking out of a possible 140	Trend since 2017
Overall performance		**50th**	**110th**	↔
Pillars: enabling environment				
1	Institutions: rights protections, courts, government efficiency	42	126	↑
2	Infrastructure: transport, electricity, connectivity, water, and sanitation	52	112	↑
3	ICT adoption	44	92	↑
4	Macroeconomic stability (inflation and debt dynamics)	74	74	↓
Pillars: human capital				
5	Health	63	104	↑
6	Skills	41	121	↑
	Mean years of schooling (4.6 years)	31	125	↔
	Skill sets of graduates	42	111	↓
	Ease of finding skilled employees	40	121	↓
Pillars: markets				
7	Product market	50	114	↓
8	Labor market	60	65	↓
9	Financial system	54	92	↑
	Domestic credit to private sector % GDP	66	52	↑
	Financing of SMEs	46	70	↓
	Venture capital availability	31	73	↓
	Soundness of banks	58	91	↑
	Non-performing loans % loan portfolio value	97	35	↓
10	Market size	46	88	↑
Pillars: innovative ecosystem				
11	Business dynamism	45	128	↑
12	Innovation capability	31	96	↓

components of the economy that will serve it well for steadily advancing its competitiveness or that these investments have not yet matured enough to show results.

Financial Market Development Along with labor market efficiency and the macroeconomic environment, financial market development is ranked as a pillar of competitiveness where Cambodia has made most progress since 2007. By 2017–2018, Cambodia's financial market development ranked 61st among 137 countries, indicating that it achieved substantial improvement. Yet, in late 2018 Cambodia's financial system ranking fell to 92 out of 140 countries, mainly based on lower scores for financing SMEs, availability of venture capital, and an increasing number of non-performing loans.

Higher Education and Skills Training Cambodia ranks 124th out of 137 in higher education and training, Cambodia's poorest performance in any pillar. This ranking places Cambodia's higher education and training below all 22 Asian countries that participated in the 2017–2018 index. Further, Cambodia's trend along this pillar has not improved since 2008. It is estimated that secondary education enrollment hovers around 50%. In an increasingly competitive world, the opportunities to advance, or even to stay the same, are dependent on quality higher education and skills training.

As a final point of this analysis, the WEF 2017–2018 Executive Opinion Survey indicated the top five most problematic factors for doing business in Cambodia were (1) corruption; (2) an inadequately educated workforce; (3) policy instability; (4) an inadequate supply of infrastructure; and (5) crime and theft (Schwab 2017). The top two problematic factors for doing business headed the list of factors during the prior year, although the others moved up substantially.

2.5 The Current and Future Advantage

Cambodia's aspirations for the future rely on positioning itself to become more competitive in the region. This requires Cambodia to invest in the factors that currently limit or prevent those desired competitive advances to materialize.

With a median age of 23.8 years, Cambodia is home to one of the youngest populations in Asia (United Nations 2015). In fact, the youth of the population is now widely considered Cambodia's "demographic advantage" or Cambodia's "demographic dividend," compared to other countries in the region and globally with aging populations. Cambodia has not yet capitalized on this valuable resource. Ensuring access to quality education for all should therefore be a policy priority for improving Cambodia's economic competitiveness.

Building on Opportunity and Experience It is also important to view the future with the benefit of hindsight. As the WEF wrote a decade ago in 2008, "many of the competitive disadvantages noted are common to many countries, but there are variations in the degrees of weakness. For example, in Cambodia, competitive disadvantages manifest in the financial market (130th out of 134 countries) and higher education and training pillars where Cambodia ranked 127th out of 134 countries" (Schwab and Porter 2008).

It is possible to envisage Cambodia being part of a bustling Southeast Asia, playing increasingly diverse and meaningful roles in ASEAN regional integration. There are substantial challenges, particularly with maintaining the gains in "growth with equity" of the past decade. But there is also considerable opportunity to build the human resource capacity of a predominantly youthful society that is not yet—but could be—equipped with education to compete in innovation and technological growth in the region and around the world.

Concerted efforts by both the public and private sectors are required to efficiently and transparently curb practices considered as the most significant barriers to doing business in the country. Cambodia's policy makers know they need to do a lot more just to maintain the hard-earned and celebrated growth with equity rates.

One fundamental change that every Cambodian citizen—no matter rich or poor—would applaud is advancing priority investment in the new generation and the current educational system that holds them back. The new generation will position Cambodia to fulfill its promise, and that promise for generations to come.

Focusing on Barriers Cambodia's financial market development comes to mind when Cambodia's future is viewed with hindsight from the past. Cambodia's financial market surged—from a GCI global rank of 130th out of 134 countries in 2007 to a rank of 61st in 2017–2018. The 2018 GCI report ranks Cambodia's financial market development 92nd out of 140 countries, which shows considerable loss of ground.

Even so, there has been substantial improvement of Cambodia's financial market sophistication and growth with equity within a little over a decade.[9]

The next major undertaking might be to tackle the anti-competitive barrier that Cambodia's weak human capital base presents to promoting Cambodia's innovation and competitiveness regionally and globally. The skill sets of graduates and the ease of finding skilled employees within the higher education and training sector are factors that present a drag on Cambodia's competitiveness in the region and globally.

And, with the opening of the ACLEDA Institute of Business (AIB) in 2016, it is positioned to address a share of the educational and skill set barriers to Cambodia's global competitiveness now and in the future.[10]

References

Chea, Serey (2018) Key Note Speech presented at the Official Launch of the Cambodia FinTech Association at the Singapore FinTech Festival ASEAN Roadshow, Phnom Penh, 15 August 2018. Available https://www.nbc.org.kh/english/news_and_events/speeches.php. Accessed 15 October 2018

Chheng, Channy (2018) The Cambodian Workforce Working Abroad by 2017, compiled by Chheng Channy with statistics from the Ministry of Labor and Vocational Training of Cambodia and the World Bank (2017). Available www.facebook.com. Accessed 30 June 2018. As of 9 January 2019, no longer available

FinScope (2015) Consumer Survey Highlights, Cambodia 2015. Phnom Penh 2015.

FinScope. Available https://finmark.org.za/results-from-finscope-consumer-survey-kingdom-of-cambodia-2015/. Accessed 25 July 2018.

[9] Recent setbacks in Cambodian's financial system and regulatory framework for financial inclusion are discussed in depth in Chaps. 3 and 4.

[10] Chapter 10 is devoted to the ACLEDA Institute of Business and the challenges and opportunities with the higher education sector in Cambodia.

International Labour Organization (2017) ILOSTAT database Available https://www.ilo.org/ilostat. Accessed 25 July 2018.

Ly, Sodeth (2016) *Cambodia - Economic update: improving macroeconomic and financial resilience (English)*. Cambodia Economic update Washington, D.C. World Bank Group. Available http://documents.worldbank.org/curated/en/403961467989523939/Cambodia-Economic-update-improving-macroeconomic-and-financial-resilience Accessed 20 June 2017

Ly, Sodeth; Sanchez Martin, Miguel Eduardo; Phim, Runsinarith; Ky, Linna; Tong, Kimsun; Provo, Anne Marie; Nagpal, Somil; Vashakmadze, Ekaterine T. (2019) *Cambodia Economic Update : Recent Economic Developments and Outlook (English)*. Cambodia Economic Update. Washington, D.C.: World Bank Group. Available http://documents.worldbank.org/curated/en/843251556908260855/Cambodia-Economic-Update-Recent-Economic-Developments-and-Outlook Accessed 30 June 2019

Ministry of Tourism, Statistics and Information Department. (2018) Tourism Statistics Report. Royal Government of Cambodia, Phnom Penh Available https://amchamcambodia.net/wp-content/uploads/2019/04/Year_2018.pdf Accessed 20 June 2019.

Ministry of Tourism, Statistics and Information Department. (2017) Tourism Statistics Report. Royal Government of Cambodia, Phnom Penh Available https://amchamcambodia.net/wp-content/uploads/2019/04/Year_2017.pdf Accessed 15 June 2018.

Morton, Eddie (2014) Local Transfers Push Wing Revenue. The Phnom Penh Post Feb 18, 2014, Phnom Penh. Available https://www.phnompenhpost.com/

National Bank of Cambodia (2016) Annual Report. Royal Government of Cambodia. Phnom Penh. Available https://www.nbc.org.kh

National Bank of Cambodia (2017) Annual Report. Royal Government of Cambodia, Phnom Penh. Available https://www.nbc.org.kh

Schwab, Klaus (ed.) (2018) The Global Competitiveness Report 2018. World Economic Forum, Geneva. Available https://www.weforum.org/reports. Accessed 14 November 2018

Schwab, Klaus (ed.) (2017) The Global Competitiveness Report 2017–2018. World Economic Forum, Geneva. Available https://www.weforum.org/reports. Accessed 14 November 2018

Schwab, Klaus (ed.) (2016) The Global Competitiveness Report 2016–2017. World Economic Forum, Geneva. Available https://www.weforum.org/reports Accessed 14 November 2018

Schwab, Klaus and Michael E Porter (eds.) (2008) The Global Competitiveness Report 2008–2009. World Economic Forum, Geneva Available https://www.weforum.org/reports. Accessed 21 December 2016

World Bank. 2014. "Where Have All the Poor Gone? Cambodia Poverty Assessment 2013." Washington, DC: World Bank.

"World Bank. 2015. Cambodia Economic Update, October 2015: Adapting to Stay Competitive. World Bank, Phnom Penh. © World Bank. https://openknowledge.worldbank.org/handle/10986/22934 License: CC BY 3.0 IGO."

World Bank (2016a) *Cambodia Overview, World Bank*, Last updated: September 2016. Available https://www.worldbank.org/en/country/cambodia/overview Accessed 20 June 2017

World Bank (2016b) Poverty and Shared Prosperity 2016: Taking on Inequity. Key Findings. Washington D. C. Available http://www.worldbank.org/en/publication/poverty-and-shared-prosperity Accessed 20 June 2017

World Bank (2016c) Supporting Inclusive Growth in Cambodia 07/05/2016 Available https://blogs.worldbank.org/eastasiapacific/supporting-inclusive-growth-in-cambodia Accessed 20 June 2017

World Bank (2016d) "Where Have All the Poor Gone? Cambodia Poverty Assessment 2013." Washington, DC: World Bank. Available https://openknowledge.worldbank.org/handle/10986/17546. Accessed 20 June 2017

World Bank (2016e) ASPIRE: The Atlas of Social Protection Indicators of Resilience and Equity, online analytical tool http://datatopics.worldbank.org/aspire/ https://www.slideshare.net/WB_Research/cambodia-poverty-assessment-feb-2014/1. Accessed 20 June 2017

World Bank (2017) Cambodia Economic Update: Cambodia climbing up the manufacturing value chains – October 2017 (English). Washington, D.C. World Bank Group. Available http://documents.worldbank.org/curated/en/628341511277852360/Cambodia-economic-update-Cambodia-climbing-up-the-manufacturing-value-chains-October-2017 World Bank. 2017. Accessed 8 February 2018

World Bank (2018) Cambodia Economic Update, April 2018: Recent Economic Developments and Outlook. World Bank, Phnom Penh. © World Bank. Available https://openknowledge.worldbank.org/handle/10986/29811 License: CC BY 3.0 IGO. Accessed 14 November 2018

World Bank (2019) World Development Indicators database Available http://databank.worldbank.org/data/reports.aspx?source=1277&series=SI.POV.GINI# and https://data.worldbank.org/indicator/NY.GNP.PCAP.CD?locations=KH Last Accessed 3 August 2019.

United Nations (2015) World Population Prospects: The 2017 Revision. Department of Economic and Social Affairs, Population Division. Custom Data acquired via website. https://www.un.org/development/desa/publications/world-population-prospects-the-2017-revision.html Accessed 14 November 2018

Part II
Flight to Quality

"Flight to quality represents the major motive for this action."

HE Keat Chhon and HE Chea Chanto, Statement to the IMF Board of Governors, 2000 Annual Meeting, Prague, Czech Republic, September 2000

Prologue

The Historical Perspective

Over the past decade Cambodia's economic growth rates landed the country right at the top of global charts. The country was also lauded for achieving growth with equity.[1] The financial market system grew to keep pace with the growing demand across all segments of the market—from savers to borrowers, micro-entrepreneurs, and small- and medium-sized enterprises. Users of digital domestic and international transfers and enterprises in need of more sophisticated financial services and systems emerged with the advent of accessible technology and growing businesses and banking institutions.

Customers demanded increasingly more diverse financial products and services. Banks and microfinance institutions, and later digital financial services providers, bolstered efforts to meet customer requirements with better, more flexible, and less costly products and services.

But this vibrant customer-responsive banking sector of the last decade was not always the way Cambodia's banking sector behaved. During the early 1990s, many small local and foreign-owned banks leapt into the Cambodian market (IMF 1998).[2]

[1] See Chap. 2 for a discussion of growth with equity.

[2] From 1991 to 1996, 7 foreign bank branches and 22 private banks began operations. By December 1997, 5 were in operation without renewal of a license (International Monetary Fund 1998).

They offered limited services to the public. They operated mainly in the capital where they exclusively served their country's trade finance and banking requirements.

Other banks were opened for less noble reasons. If the banking sector was lopsided with a concentration of 31 banks in Phnom Penh, it was also focused on the new wave of gray market capitalism and commodities.

Way back then, Cambodia's porous borders, dollarized economy, and newly found capitalist spirit made it an attractive locus and a haven for the trade in less socially acceptable products. Venerable banking institutions, such as the Standard Chartered Bank and Maybank, operated alongside banks with dubious origins and charters that were thought to be present in Cambodia only to engage in money laundering.

After issuing the new Law on Banking and Financial Institutions in late 1999, the National Bank of Cambodia (NBC) ordered all commercial banks to submit re-licensing applications within six months. One by one, and later in groups, 23 commercial banks closed their doors. Many banks liquidated voluntarily; they were unwilling or unable to meet the new minimum capital requirement, which rose from USD 5 million to USD 13 million (National Bank of Cambodia 1999). Others failed the new tests for solvency, prudential ratios, and professional qualifications for shareholders and managers (National Bank of Cambodia 1999).

The Cambodian government was adamant in its approach to reform; it was determined to shrink the sector, ridding it of the large segment of banks undertaking suspicious activities. The new law required background checks on directors. It also obliged banks to prove their sources of capital, verified by outside audits and on-site inspections.

By September 2002 the crowd in the banking sector diminished drastically. Three-quarters of the banks operating in Cambodia in 1996 had their licenses revoked or they left voluntarily because of the new rules and regulations. The twelve remaining private banks played by the rules of the game.

The sweep through the banking system was not as disastrous as some bankers predicted. Some lamented that the new law was "too strict for Cambodia, one of Asia's poorest countries, at this stage of its economic development" (AFTA Online 2004). But, at the time, it was difficult to prove that banks served Cambodia's people, either directly or through enterprise finance that would provide employment. Other bankers supported the new law, saying it would support the growth of a more law abiding and healthy banking industry.

According to HE Keat Chhon, Senior Minister of Economy and Finance, and HE Chea Chanto, Governor of the National Bank of Cambodia, "these measures are necessary to establish a sound banking system, promote savings, and increase the confidence of the public in the banking system" (Keat 2001).

> "Flight to quality represents the major motive for this action." (Keat and Chea 2000).

References

AFTA (2004) ASEAN Free Trade Area Online Banking and Finance Archives, Associated Press Article Accessed June 2004. Cited in *When There Was No Money*, pages 139–140.

International Monetary Fund (1998) Staff Country Report No. 98/54 (Washington, D.C.: IMF, June 1998) See *When There Was No Money*, pages 139–140. IMF Staff Country Report No. 98/54 (Washington, D.C.: IMF, June 1998) See *When There Was No Money*, pages 139–140.

Keat Chhon and Chea Chanto (2000) Statement at the IMF Board of Governors, 2000 Annual Meeting, Prague, Czech Republic, September, 2000. Available http://www.adb.org

Keat Chhon (2001) Governor's Speech at the 34th Annual Meeting of the Board of Governors of the Asian Development Bank May 9, 2001. Available http://www.adb.org

National Bank of Cambodia (1999) The Law on Banking and Financial Institutions Article 18, Phnom Penh: National Bank of Cambodia. Available https://www.nbc.org.kh/english/

Chapter 3
Cambodia's Financial Market System (2004–2019): History, Structure, and Performance

3.1 An Introduction to Cambodia's Financial Market System

Over the past decade, Cambodia's economic growth rates exceeded expectations, contributing to economic well-being for the majority of the population and new status as a lower middle-income country.[1] This chapter begins with a few highlights, issues, and questions that identify some of the major characteristics and accomplishments of Cambodia's financial market system over the past decade. Each of these topics will be discussed in more detail later in this chapter.

3.1.1 Demand and Supply of Financial Services Fuel Economic Growth

Demand for more diversified financial products and services increased. Cambodia's financial market system grew to keep pace with the robust economic growth rates that averaged 7% per year over the past 10 years. The gross domestic product (GDP) in Cambodia expanded 7% in 2017 from the previous year and 7.5% in 2018. The GDP annual growth rate in Cambodia averaged 7.61% from 1994 until 2016, reaching an all-time high of 13.3% in 2005 and a record low of 0.08% in 2009 (National Institute of Statistics of Cambodia 2017, and World Bank Data Bank).

Economic growth spurred demand across all segments of the financial consumer market—the number of savings accounts increased, and the number of borrowers and their loan size increased to support economic investment but also to consolidate debt. More people from both rural and urban areas used domestic and international transfers in more frequent numbers and for higher amounts. The array and number

[1] See Chap. 2 for a discussion of growth with equity.

© Springer Nature Singapore Pte Ltd. 2020

H. A. Clark, *Beyond Borders, Beyond Banking*,
https://doi.org/10.1007/978-981-15-1687-0_3

of financial services providers increased and expanded operations to meet increased demand.

New demand for more digital services also emerged from enterprises and individuals. And financial services providers were there to meet that demand. Some financial services providers specialized in products, such as Wing Specialized Bank's dedication to domestic money transfers. Small, medium, and large enterprises in need of more sophisticated financial services and systems could rely on a growing number of banks and microfinance institutions to provide additional products to finance their businesses and facilitate numerous financial transactions at home and abroad.

With growing demand came increased competition within the microfinance sector. Increased competition improved products, lowered prices, and called for new ways of managing financial sector risk. Financial services providers, the supervisory and regulatory agency, and those organizations that served the financial infrastructure invested to upgrade staff skills and system capacities at all levels.

In these ways the core financial market system stimulated and expanded growth throughout the economy. Importantly, the growth of the financial sector, including the expertise of the National Bank of Cambodia, and the growth of supporting functions to the core market have been recognized as major contributors to "growth with equity" within the national economy as discussed in Chap. 2.

3.1.2 A Responsive Regulatory Framework and Supporting Infrastructure Advance Financial Inclusion

The regulator, the National Bank of Cambodia, redoubled efforts to continue the "flight to quality" at this time within all segments of the market. Sound and safer growth continued to rely on an agile regulatory and supervisory system managed by the National Bank of Cambodia (NBC).

The shape of Cambodia's financial sector—and the vibrant financial services market within it—depended on the willful choices made by policy makers, regulators, and financial services providers to enable poor and low-income people to join the financial system. A highly competitive environment allowed customers in most urban areas and some densely populated and economically diverse rural areas to have a real choice about the financial services provider and the products that they use.

Growth is supported by diverse financial sector infrastructure, from a budding securities market—the Cambodia Securities Exchange (CSX)—to an industry-owned credit bureau, the Credit Bureau of Cambodia. The associations of banks and particularly MFIs are serious about keeping up with industry advances and technology. Industry associations, mainly the Cambodia Microfinance Association (CMA), provide consumer protection information and vigilance as well as training and education for their MFI members. The CMA also facilitates international consumer protection certification for their members. The following section of this chapter provides more details about the financial sector—the core market, rules and norms, and supporting functions.

Efforts to improve the financial capabilities of customers increased. While tepid within most MFIs and banks during much of the early 2000s, microfinance institutions (MFIs) and microfinance deposit-taking institutions (MDIs) began to strengthen customer financial education efforts throughout the broader system. Financial education[2] for customers and higher education initiatives in finance and banking began to support the development of current and future generations of providers and users of financial services.

Perhaps one of the most innovative consumer financial education initiatives in the Cambodian landscape is the NBC's broad-based consumer financial education campaign "Let's Talk Money!". "Let's Talk Money!" started as a public information campaign to promote financial literacy, but it is now poised to expand from its initial targeting of the general public on a temporary basis. It has developed into a concerted effort to incorporate financial education into the primary and high school curricula. The NBC efforts in this regard have the keen collaboration of the Ministry of Education.[3]

As competition increased, customers had more options to select among financial services providers that offered suitable products and respected customer requirements. Experience with several different providers led customers to value fair play and respect from the financial institutions that serve them well.

Overall, Cambodian financial services providers, particularly microfinance institutions (MFIs), microfinance deposit-taking institutions (MDIs), and ACLEDA Bank Plc., know that customers are highly responsive to competitive rates on savings and deposit accounts, speedy service, and customer-friendly features of international remittances and domestic transfers. Many customers make informed decisions based on ease of service, reliability, and competitive pricing of financial products.

Both providers of services and customers know that there are other equally valuable alternatives in the marketplace. Competition has also increased the level of access to financial services, particularly in rural and hard to reach areas, and enabled the financial sector consumer to take advantage of decreases in price and increases in service quality.

Cambodia's overheated credit market is a focus in Chap. 4, which discusses how the microcredit market is tipping rapidly toward excessive access and aggressive competition without adequate prudent safeguards for the borrower or lender.

How did such a vibrant financial services sector develop from 40 years ago when possession of currency was a capital crime against the state? To address this

[2] The Center for Financial Inclusion defines financial literacy as: "The combination of knowledge, skills, attitudes and ultimately behaviors that translate into sound financial decisions and appropriate use of financial services" (CFI).

[3] The "Let's Talk Money!" initiative is discussed in more detail in the section in this chapter on the supporting functions.

question, this chapter discusses the rise and expansion of Cambodia's financial market economy. It considers the development of a robust regulatory framework, the growth of organizations providing supporting functions that make the market work better, and the aspirations and accomplishments of the people that have made such growth possible.

Most stakeholders began to label this stage of financial sector development in Cambodia as one of "rationale exuberance," mainly due to the high annual growth rates of the Cambodian economy, consistently on or about 7% over the past 6 years (National Institute of Statistics of Cambodia, Trading Economics.com, various years). They would acknowledge gaps in sector development, such as financial consumer protection, comprehensive financial education, as well as more appropriate cash flow lending products for SMEs and agriculture. These gaps cry out for innovators to step forward and fill them.

What about the next stage of financial sector development: Will it be one of "irrational exuberance" where unfettered growth, aggressive competition, and the quest for quick profits undermine the very foundations on which the sector has been built?

Or will it be one of "cautious exuberance" (MIMOSA 2015; Rozas 2016)[4] as financial services providers (FSPs) in all segments of the market pay more attention to signs of growing debt saturation and develop the means to manage it for their customers and their organizations?

Chapter 3 continues with an overview of Cambodia's financial market system. First, the core market for financial services is presented and analyzed. Cambodia's financial inclusion rates are discussed, and how they have advanced over the last decade. The probable relationship between financial inclusion rates and poverty reduction rates are presented. A quick look at the expansion of new products and delivery methods developed to serve the growing market is also provided.

Later, the chapter discusses rules and norms that govern the financial system, with a focus on truth in lending, the origins of the policy, and how it worked over time. The chapter closes with a summary of the role of the increasing development of supporting functions in the market system and how these functions strengthen the relationship between the financial services providers and the their customers.

Chapter 3 lays out the structure of the market and the history of how the market developed. The next chapter, The Dynamics of Growth Over Time, complements this one. While Chap. 3 examines the structure of the market, Chap. 4 examines the dynamics of the market, including several major trends related to the structure, incentives, and recent policies in the financial sector.

Chapter 4 discusses the phenomenal growth of new players serving the bottom of the pyramid and operating under the regulatory radar. The hotly contested debate about over-indebtedness is analyzed. The advent and growth of "mergers and acquisitions" of Cambodia's microfinance deposit-taking institutions (MDIs) is discussed. Chapter 4 presents a discussion of some recent surprising regulatory changes

[4] The article suggests "cautious exuberance" will be the predominant sentiment in the market at this time, as there is potential for growth, but reason for caution regarding over-indebtedness.

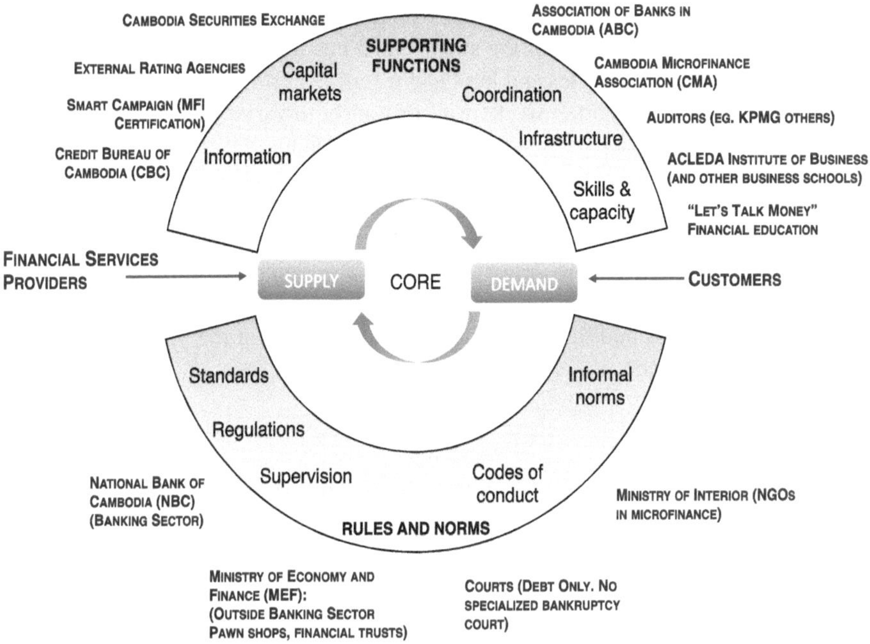

Fig. 3.1 The market system, main market functions, and players (Format Reproduced from Springfield et al. 2015) (Format Source: Reproduced from Springfield Centre et al. 2015) CGAP. 2015. A Market Systems Approach to Financial Inclusion: Guidelines for Funders. Consensus Guidelines. Washington, D.C. CGAP: Creative Commons License Attribution CC BY 3.0

about interest rate ceilings on microcredit, and challenges within the financial sector that require attention by all the market players, including banks and MFIs as well as the regulator.

3.2 Cambodia's Financial Market System

All markets depend on a variety of factors for their start-up and expansion. The financial market is no exception. A multiplayer, multifunction market system framework has three main parts as shown in Fig. 3.1: the market system, main market functions, and players.[5]

[5]The visual depiction of the financial market system was originally created by Springfield Centre (www.springfieldcentre.com). It was later used to illustrate the financial market system in the Consultative Group to Assist the Poor (CGAP) Funder Guidelines. CGAP. 2015. A Market Systems Approach to Financial Inclusion: Guidelines for Funders. Consensus Guidelines. Washington, D.C. CGAP: Creative Commons License Attribution CC BY 3.0. CGAP is a global partnership of 34 leading organizations that seek to advance financial inclusion. CGAP develops innovative solutions through practical research and active engagement with financial service providers, policy makers, and funders to enable approaches at scale. The World Bank hosts CGAP.

At the center of the market system, often called the core market, are the providers of goods and services (the supply) and customers of goods and services (the demand). The formal rules and laws and informal norms influence the behavior of market players. The market works well or poorly to varying degrees depending on the type and intensity of functions in support of its players and the rules of the game.

Figure 3.1 gives a brief overview of the players in the market system in Cambodia.[6] It is a picture of what the market system looks like in 2019. If this picture of the market system were drawn 20 years ago, it would be almost empty. Many of the organizations that provide supporting functions were formed over the last 10 years. The players and the functions that they perform in the system are elaborated in the next section.

3.2.1 A Brief Tour of the Financial Market System: Supporting Functions[7]

As an introduction to the supporting functions in the market today, there are three types of information-providing agencies whose services are used by FSPs with business models to deepen Cambodia's financial sector. They are the Credit Bureau of Cambodia (CBC); external rating agencies, such as Moody's; and specialized microfinance rating agencies, such as MicroRate, MicroFinanza Rating, M-CRIL, and Planet Rating.

The Smart Campaign, initiated in 2008 by a consortium of organizations, such as CGAP and the Center for Financial Inclusion, provides certification in client protection. Nine financial services providers, including all of Cambodia's MDIs and ACLEDA Bank Plc., hold current certifications in client protection. The Smart Campaign serves as an international source of good practice in financial consumer protection and serves as a model to adopt financial consumer protection laws.

Moving clockwise around Fig. 3.1, the recent opening of the Cambodian Stock Exchange (CSX) is noteworthy. It is the first effort to build Cambodia's capital market, which remains underdeveloped, as the CSX opened only in April 2012. However the market is slowly growing and becoming an accepted part of Cambodia's financial market system. There are also several budding securities and brokerage firms, including ACLEDA Securities Plc. that was also established in 2012 to assist customers access the exchange and provide securities brokerage services to individuals and businesses.

[6] The diagram shows only a representative sample of the many organizations that perform functions in the overall financial market system in Cambodia.

[7] The "Brief Tour" of supporting functions and rules and norms is followed in this chapter by a more detailed presentation of the core market, rules and norms, and supporting functions.

Coordination and related advocacy functions are performed by a range of organizations, such as membership associations, including the Cambodia Microfinance Association (CMA) and the Association of Banks in Cambodia (ABC). The CMA and ABC also play important roles in establishing norms through voluntary codes of conduct. In addition, associations play important roles in skills and capacity building.

Finally, business schools and institutes, such as the ACLEDA Institute of Business (AIB), and specialized accounting services and legal firms are among many more market players that perform the skills and capacity building functions for the financial sector. Legal firms, accounting services, and audit services enhance transparency at the firm and organizational level. The "Let's Talk Money!" campaign, championed by the NBC to encourage financial literacy, is an important initiative for the capacity building of future generations of financial customers.

3.2.2 A Brief Tour of the Financial Market System: Rules and Norms

When it comes to formal rules in the financial sector, the National Bank of Cambodia performs the nation's regulatory and supervisory function of the financial sector, issuing laws and regulations and supervising banks, specialized banks, MDIs, MFIs, and rural credit operators to keep the financial system safe and sound.

The Ministry of Economy and Finance oversees the overall economy, including taxation and new forms of financial organizations, such as the newly created Financial Trusts. Financial Trusts are conventionally designed throughout the world to support a variety of financial transactions where one party holds money for another, such as escrow accounts and endowments.[8]

The Ministry of the Interior has the predominant role in overseeing NGO operations. The general court system is responsible for ensuring resolution of disputes. Even as a National Arbitration Centre is set up to resolve general business disputes, it has not yet been recognized or accepted by the court system as a viable alternative, particularly in any case where there is an appeal of a decision. The Centre is not yet specialized in financial transactions, banking, securities, or trust law.

General business transactions are closer to having a dispute arbitration mechanism available that avoids cumbersome and less than transparent deliberations. At this time, there is no specialized court or dispute resolution mechanism specifically set up to resolve disputes within the financial sector, which require a more specific understanding of financial transactions within the system. However, "establishment of a well-functioning dispute handling mechanism" for consumers and providers of financial services appears to be on the NBC's agenda for the future (Chea 2018).

---

[8] The origin, design, and implementation of Financial Trusts in Cambodia are discussed in more detail in Chap. 6.

Following the intent to establish a functioning dispute handling mechanism, in September 2018, the NBC issued a new regulation requiring banks and financial institutions to establish a complaints resolution framework as part of their operations. (See Sect. 3.6.4. on consumer protection, later in this chapter.)

Norms With respect to norms that govern behavior, financial services providers (FSPs) have adopted mechanisms for self-regulation through the design and implementation of codes of conduct. "Self-regulation" is not the preferred mechanism for transparent financial performance and reporting. However, "informal rules" developed as codes of conduct are important contributions to the way financial services providers and customers relate with one another, particularly when competition is strong and customers have choices about which FSPs they use.

When combined with outside financial consumer protection certification, such as that promoted by the Center for Financial Inclusion's Smart Campaign, with the support of the Cambodia Microfinance Association, the codes of conduct and verification of their implementation are credible.

Finally, informal norms and practices in the general population influence the way business gets done in every transaction in every sector of the economy. So while formal rules are written, distributed, and easily available to players in the financial sector, informal norms about the way people treat each other in society and transact business are often more important for influencing how things get done.[9]

3.2.3 *At the Core: Customers and Financial Services Providers*

According to NBC reports from 2006 to the end of 2018, growth in the FSP landscape has been dramatic, as reflected in Figs. 3.2 and 3.3 (National Bank of Cambodia 2006–2019).

The decade began with a reasonably good start with 42 licensed or registered FSPs serving different segments of the market in 2008. They served large industries; rural and urban micro, small, and medium enterprises; and consumers who saved and transferred and received money.

Later in the decade, even by the end of 2017, the number of FSPs advanced significantly, to the point where many analysts of Cambodia's financial sector noted that there might be too many FSPs seeking too few customers, particularly at the lower segment of the market. See Fig. 3.3. Analysts noted that such rapid growth might have consequences in creating unhealthy competition, promoting over-indebtedness and prompting the emergence of unsound FSPs that operate illegally and under the radar.[10]

---

[9] Chapter 6 shows an example of how one financial service provider can have a big effect on changing accepted norms of corruption and bribery for the benefit of customers and the broader system.

[10] The topic of the significant growth of unlicensed and unregulated FSPs is taken up in Chap. 4.

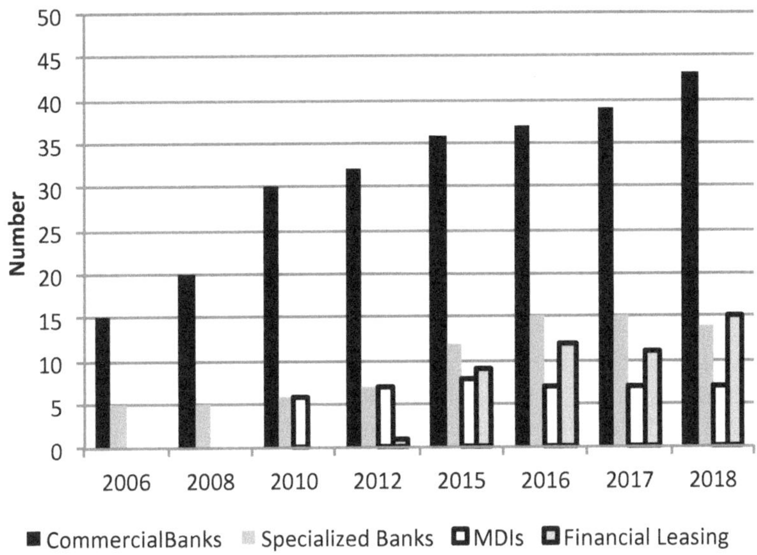

Fig. 3.2 A decade of growth: banks, microfinance deposit-taking institutions (MDIs), and financial leasing
Source: National Bank of Cambodia 2019a, b and Various Years 2008–2018

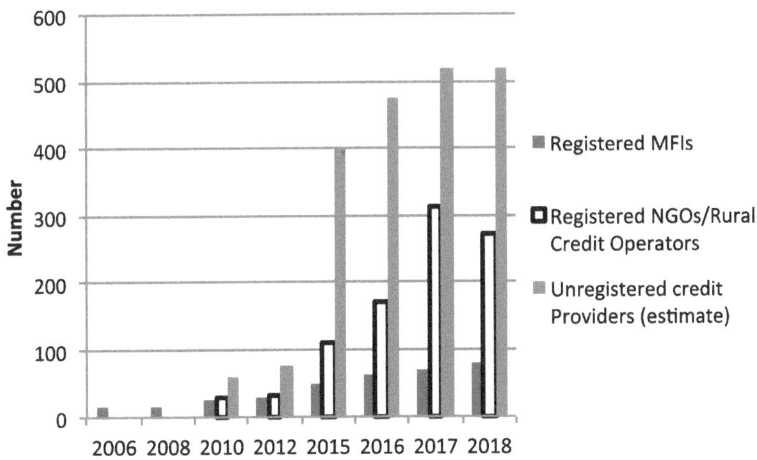

Fig. 3.3 A decade of growth: MFIs and credit providers registered and reporting, not registered and not reporting (National Bank of Cambodia 2019a, b and Various Years)
Source: National Bank of Cambodia 2019 and Various Years 2008–2018

Nevertheless, the growth of the supply side of the market has been impressive, particularly the diversity of the newly established financial enterprises, such as financial leasing companies, and mobile money services. These services are provided by new FSPs in the Cambodian market, as well as by long-standing members of the financial community, such as ACLEDA Bank Plc. that puts a premium on developing new services for the growing market and increasing the savvy of Cambodia's financial consumers.[11]

In addition, the sustained growth of formal financial services providers (FSPs) has directly led to significant improvements in Cambodia's rates of financial inclusion. Much of the growth in customer outreach and geographic coverage is due to the largest MFIs and MDIs, such as AMK Plc., AMRET Plc., Hatta Kasekar Limited, KREDIT Plc., LOLC (Cambodia) Plc., PRASAC, and WB Finance Co., Ltd. (formerly Vision Fund), as well as ACLEDA Bank Plc.

In 2018 banking institutions, including MDIs, dramatically increased their networks to include a total of 1834 branches and 2173 ATMS. According to the National Bank of Cambodia, "this expansion is a result of customers' daily demand for banking operations." The use of credit and debit cards also increased to 102,279 credit cards and 2.1 million debit cards, and "more customers recognize the convenience of electronic banking services and a safer way to settle transactions" (National Bank of Cambodia 2019a, b).

3.3 An Inclusive Financial Market?

Over the past decade, financial inclusion in Cambodia advanced rapidly.

The first global financial inclusion surveys carried out by the World Bank Findex in 2012 (using 2011 data) showed more than 50% of adults worldwide reported having an account at a formal financial institution (bank, credit union, MFI, or any other formally regulated financial institution) (Global Findex Data 2012; Demirguc-Kunt et al. 2012). The survey demonstrated that an extremely low level of the global population actively participated in the financial sector, as a significant number of accounts lay dormant. Further, at the time less than 1% of adults used electronic payments, commonly called mobile money or digital financial services (DFS) (Global Findex Data 2012; Demirguc-Kunt et al. 2012).

The worldwide average financial inclusion rates at the time in 2011 showed that on average 41% of the adult populations in developing economies, similar to the Cambodian economy, had an account at a formal, regulated financial institution (Global Findex Data 2012; Demirguc-Kunt et al. 2012).

Survey results from Cambodia at the time showed only 4% of adults, 15 years and older, owned an account at a formally regulated financial institution and only 1% used mobile money or had a savings account at a formally regulated financial institution. The majority 39% borrowed from family or friends, and 4% used community-based savings mechanisms.

By the end of 2016, financial inclusion rates rocketed compared to the low base of financial inclusion in Cambodia in 2011. See Fig. 3.4 (FinScope 2016) (Box 3.1).

[11] See Chap. 5 for more details on ACLEDA Bank Plc. developments.

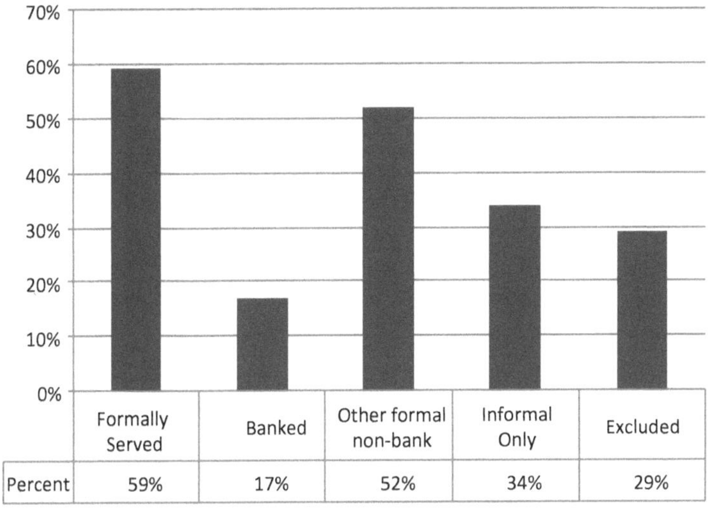

Fig. 3.4 Financial inclusion in Cambodia 2015–2016 (FinScope 2016)
Source: FinScope Consumer Survey Highlights. Cambodia 2015. FinScope 2016

Box 3.1: Financial Inclusion Definition
Financial inclusion means that adults have access to and can effectively use a range of appropriate financial services. Such services must be provided responsibly and safely to the consumer and sustainably to the provider in a well-regulated environment. At its most basic level, financial inclusion starts with having a deposit or transaction account at a bank or other financial institution or through a mobile money service provider, which can be used to make and receive payments and to store or save money. Financial inclusion also encompasses access to credit from formal financial institutions that allow adults to invest in educational and business opportunities, as well as the use of formal insurance products that allow people to better manage financial risks.

Source: Demirguc-Kunt, Asli, Leora Klapper, and Dorothe Singer. April 2017. Financial Inclusion and Inclusive Growth: A Review of Recent Empirical Evidence. World Bank Group Policy Research Working Paper 8040.

3.3.1 How Inclusive Is Cambodia's Financial Sector?

It depends on which survey you look at—Findex or FinScope. One of the two main surveyors, Findex, reports a financial inclusion rate of 4% in 2011 (with 2010 data). The second Findex survey reports a financial inclusion rate that climbed to 22% by 2014, using data from that same year (Demirguc-Kunt et al. 2015) (Box 3.2).

The most recent survey, carried out by FinScope and the National Institute of Statistics (NIS) in Cambodia during 2015–2016, reports 59% of the adult

Box 3.2

Financial inclusion is quantified through survey research as the percentage of the adult population that owns an account (Findex) or has access to or uses an account (FinScope) at a regulated financial institution. Regulated financial institutions include banks and other formally regulated nonbank financial institutions, such as microfinance institutions, credit unions, mobile money services, and other categories of formally regulated nonbank financial institutions, such as microfinance deposit-taking institutions (MDIs) and specialized banks, such as Wing (Cambodia) Limited Specialized Bank.

population in Cambodia, aged 18 years and older, use at least one service, such as savings, checking, credit, or mobile money accounts, provided by a formal financial institution (bank or nonbank) (FinScope 2016). (See Fig. 3.4.)

This means that the financial inclusion rate has increased dramatically from only 4% in 2011–2012[12] and from a more robust figure of 22% in 2014 using 2014 data (Global Findex Data 2014).

How did financial inclusion increase by over 35 percentage points from 2014 to 2015? The difference may be explained by how each survey treated the WING mobile money operation with its 600,000 customers and network of 5000 agents across the country. The Findex survey excluded WING's customers, even though about 12% of adults reported having a mobile money account. The data was "excluded because of a concern that users of a popular over-the-counter transaction service might have incorrectly responded that they used an account when in fact they only made over-the-counter transactions" (Demirguc-Kunt et al. 2015).

By the time FinScope and the NIS completed their survey in January 2016, WING had been operating with a limited specialized banking license for over a year. The National Bank of Cambodia also regulated Wing Limited Specialized Bank. Among Wing's policy changes were registering accounts for their customers, relaunching the Wing Account Card, and fully implementing international banking standards, including the Know Your Customer (KYC) process (Wing 2016).

Had the survey techniques been able to distinguish over-the-counter transactions and accounts, prior to the Findex 2014 survey, then both the Findex and FinScope surveys would have more or less agreed on the depth of financial inclusion rates. Two other differences between the survey instruments likely account for the remaining difference in the financial inclusion rates reported. These differences are age of adults (15+ years for Findex and 18+ years for FinScope) and the timing of the

[12] The Findex survey uses an equivalent definition of formally regulated financial institutions, as does the later FinScope survey (2015–2016). The Findex survey drops the definition of adult to 15 years and older, between Findex Surveys 2011–2012 and 2013–2014, while the FinScope survey defines adults as 18 years and older which is a smaller cohort of the population and also one that is more likely to own or use an account at a formal banking institution than 15- to 17-year-olds, who represent a larger percentage of the population.

surveys, as the numbers of accounts, credit/debit cards, and mobile money accounts increased rapidly during 2015.

3.3.2 Inclusion and Exclusion

By the beginning of 2016, 59% of adults in Cambodia were served by banks and other formally regulated nonbank institutions, such as MDIs and MFIs, including 17% who had an account in a bank. See Fig. 3.4. However, 29% are financially excluded with similar exclusion rates for women (27%) and men (31%) and similar financial inclusion rates for women (60%) and men (57%) (FinScope 2016).

As expected, in rural areas exclusion rates are higher (31%). Yet, 43% of the rural population uses formal financial services due to the advent and expansion of mobile money services and increasing numbers of banks and formally regulated MFIs with operations in rural areas.

While there is considerable growth in the number of FSPs serving the market, this growth is also concentrated among unregistered and lightly supervised MFIs and rural credit operators. See Fig. 3.3. This might be indicative of a weakening of an inclusive financial system as it favors a policy to advance more access to financial services to the detriment of the safety of those services and soundness of the financial system. This potential dilemma is explored later in this chapter.

3.3.3 The Relationship Between Financial Inclusion and Poverty Reduction?

Cambodia's history and low-income status present a financial inclusion success story for the region and globally when compared to other countries with similar income status.[13]

International Poverty Line In 2008, the World Bank came out with a figure (revised largely due to inflation) of $1.25 a day at 2005 purchasing power parity (PPP). In October 2015, the World Bank updated the international poverty line to $1.90 a day. The common international poverty line has in the past been roughly $1 a day (World Bank 2015).

According to the Cambodia FinScope survey 2015, 98% of adults in Cambodia are using or aware of MFIs, banks, and mobile money agents. (See Fig. 3.5.) They are just as aware of, or are using the services of, MFIs and mobile money agents as they are of grocery stores, markets, and public transportation, even though financial services tend to be located further away from the customer than these other services (Lay 2017).

[13] See Chap. 2.

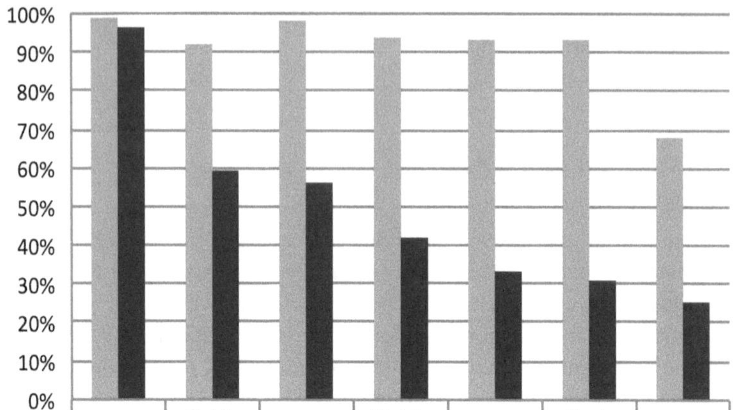

	Grocery Store	Public Trans-port	Market	Mobile Money Agent	MFI	Bank branch/ ATM	Post Office
Urban	99%	92%	98%	94%	93%	93%	68%
Rural	96%	59%	56%	42%	33%	31%	25%

Fig. 3.5 Adults using or aware of financial services and other services (FinScope 2016)
Source: FinScope Consumer Survey Highlights. Cambodia 2015. FinScope 2016

Financial inclusion rates in Cambodia have room for improvement, but great accomplishment is recognized from less than a decade ago when 95% of the population did not participate in the formal financial sector.

Chapter 2 noted Cambodia ranked as one of the most successful countries to achieve the Millennium Development Goal of poverty reduction ahead of the 2015 deadline. According to World Bank research, Cambodia's poverty rate dropped remarkably from 53.2% in 2004 to 13.5% in 2015 and is estimated to fall to 12.5% in 2016 (National Bank of Cambodia 2016a, b; World Bank 2018). See Fig. 3.6.

During that time period, financial inclusion rates in Cambodia's rural and urban areas advanced significantly. By the end of 2017, borrowers in the banking sector (including MFIs) rose from 511,268 in 2005 to almost 2.7 million (increasing a little over five times), and depositors in the system increased from 343,981 to over 4.5 million (rising a little over 13 times) during the same period (National Bank of Cambodia 2017a, b).

Even in 2019, the question is often asked, "Is there a verifiable relationship between financial inclusion and poverty reduction?" And if so, which is the driver? Does financial inclusion advance poverty reduction, or does poverty reduction advance financial inclusion?

What is very clear in Cambodia is that there is an extremely strong relationship between advances in financial inclusion and poverty reduction. See Fig. 3.6.

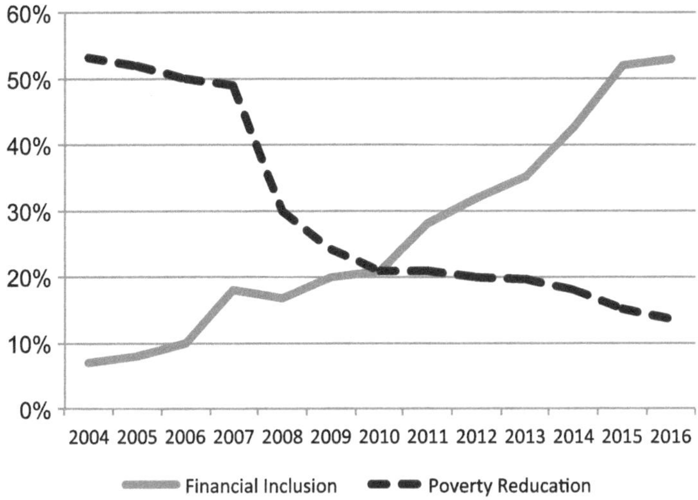

Fig. 3.6 Financial inclusion and poverty reduction. (National Bank of Cambodia 2016a, b)

3.4 The Core Market and the Vital Statistics About Market Expansion

As Cambodia's rates of financial inclusion expanded, new products and delivery methods were developed to serve the growing market. Lessons about customer preferences surfaced as early as 1999. The most astute FSPs listened to customers and learned these lessons well. Among these lessons was that the price of credit is but one factor that influences the demand for the product.

3.4.1 Serving the Market Well

In the absence of a monopoly, the consumer chooses the most valuable service. Cambodian MFIs learned that it was possible to compete in the market based on the quality of the service. They removed the product's hidden costs that are often a higher financial burden to the client than the interest rate alone. This is something that every farmer and small shop owner understands. Those who may be accustomed to bigger deals at more concessional rates often fail to understand how finance works at the bottom of the pyramid.

Mandatory savings products quickly fell into disuse by the same logic. They were risky and costly for the customer. They increased operating costs for the institution. And they did not mitigate risk, as the loan to the customer was relatively larger than the smaller amount of blocked savings serving as the guarantee.

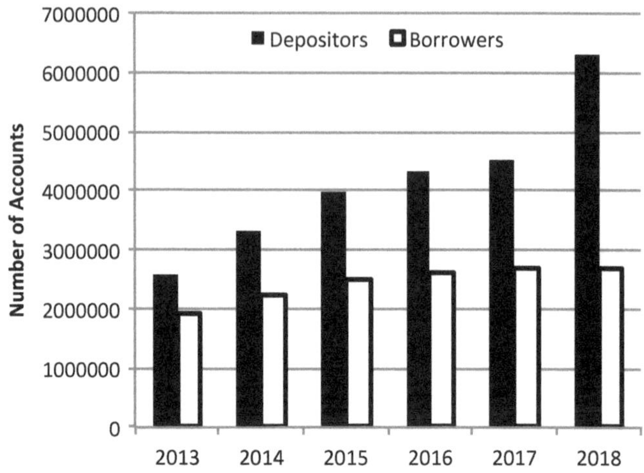

Fig. 3.7 Number of deposit and credit accounts in banks and financial institutions (National Bank of Cambodia 2010–2019)
Source: National Bank of Cambodia (2019a, b)

What the industry was learning in this early stage was really about discovering a workable business model that centered on serving customers well. This lesson is backed by credible evidence, showing customer acceptance and increasing demand for basic products, such as deposits and loans, and, later, digital financial services.

Figure 3.7 shows the increasing number of depositors and borrowers from 2013 to 2018 in the banking sector including customers of microfinance deposit-taking institutions (MDIs) that are permitted to mobilize savings and formally registered lending MFIs and rural credit providers. Figure 3.8 shows the total value of savings and loans within the banking sector, including MDIs over the same period of time.[14]

A closer look at the MFI segment of the financial market reveals similar patterns of rapid growth in both deposits and loans. The NBC reports the following industry average statistics as of the end of 2017. Credit was provided by MFIs and NGOs in 155,087 villages serving 2,144,547 households.

By the end of 2018, the microfinance institutions served approximately 1.90 million borrowers with KHR 22 trillion riels (USD 54,753,600) worth of loans. Microfinance deposit-taking institutions (MDIs) also served 1.75 million depositors by keeping safe KHR 11 trillion riels (USD 27,376,000). The number of depositors in the microfinance sub-sector decreased by 7% in 2016, due to the acquisition of Sathapana MDI by Maruhan Japan Bank during that year.[15] Yet, by the end of 2018,

[14] The banking sector includes MDIs and MFIs, as well as financial leasing companies and specialized banks.

[15] Note; Sathapana Bank figures are included in NBC reports in the banking sub-sector instead of the microfinance sub-sector from the year 2016 onward.

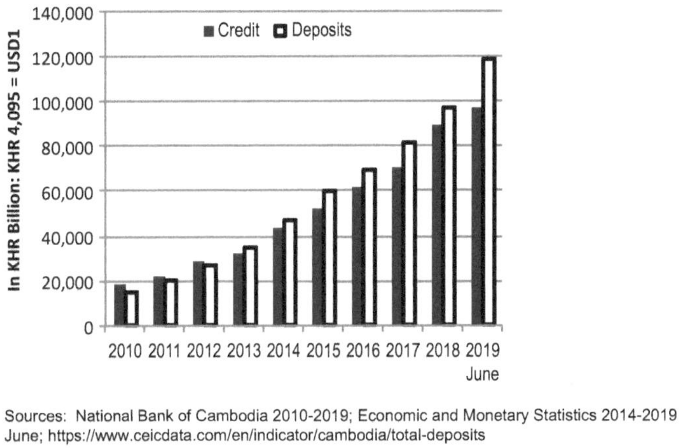

Fig. 3.8 Customer loans and deposits in banks and financial institutions
Sources: National Bank of Cambodia 2010–2019; Economic and Monetary Statistics 2014–2019 June; https://www.ceicdata.com/en/indicator/cambodia/total-deposits

the seven remaining MDIs had almost doubled the number of deposit accounts and the amount of total deposits. See Figs. 3.7 and 3.8 (National Bank of Cambodia 2019a, b).

3.4.2 Creeping Delinquency and Increasing Non-Performing Loans

With continued and rapid growth in the lending portfolio, there is always a concern about increasing over-indebtedness of borrowers that shows up in the non-performing loan portfolio of financial services providers (FSPs). Even while the Cambodian financial sector has a state of the art credit bureau, it is up to the FSPs to follow the regulations, report to the credit bureau, and request information before approving a loan. As noted earlier, a growing number of MFIs operate under the radar.

For several years, increasing competition has been blamed for creating debt stress among borrowers. Competition has also been praised for improving the quality of the service and the diversity of products and supporting micro, small, and large enterprises that have supported Cambodian's growing prosperity.

Interest Rate Caps on Micro Loans Is an interest rate cap a solution to debt stress? Has the interest rate cap led to a more healthy industry for customers and MFI service providers? One indicator that will tell only part of the story is taking a look at the non-performing loan portfolio of MFIs and banks. Figure 3.9 shows the trends in non-performing loans for banks and MFIs from 2010 to the end of 2018. Comparing the performance of each group shows an increasing trend of non-

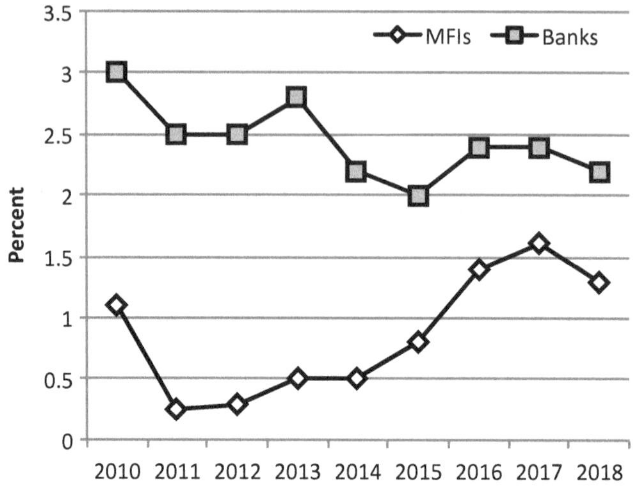

Fig. 3.9 Non-performing loan trend in MFIs and banks (2010–2018) (National Bank of Cambodia. Annual Supervision Reports 2014–2018)

performing loans for MFIs through 2017, with a drop during 2018, while banks have a more nuanced performance from 2016 through 2018. See Fig. 3.9.

The trend in non-performing loans in the microcredit sub-sector of the banking system may tell the story about how an interest rate cap that makes credit cheaper for the micro borrower tempts increased borrowing that the client may not be able to afford nor be able to repay. Such a policy also provides an incentive for an FSP to lend a greater amount of funds at a lower rate to make up for the lower profit margin on a smaller loan. And ability to repay principal of the loan is always a greater problem for a debt-stressed borrower.

Prior to the 2017 18% interest rate cap on micro loans, interest rates on micro loans stood at between 2% and 3% a month on average, depending on the product type, loan size, and the timeframe. The annual interest rate ranged between 25% and 40% per year. In comparison, ACLEDA Bank's interest rates for a 12-month loan in riel, at that time, averaged 15.60% and 10% for a similar loan in USD with a corresponding interest rate on deposits of 7%.[16]

Figure 3.10 presents a history of average lending rates in Khmer riel (KHR) and USD by banks and MFIs from 2005 through the end of 2017. The figure shows how market forces with healthy competition serve the market well in bringing lending rates down without the need for policy measures to do so.

As Fig. 3.10 shows, interest rates—particularly for MFI operations—decreased rapidly from 2005 to 2017 due to "letting the market work," that is, without an interest rate cap.

[16] Rates cited are for 2016, prior to the announcement of the government's new pricing policy on microfinance, as of April 2017. This is discussed in the next chapter.

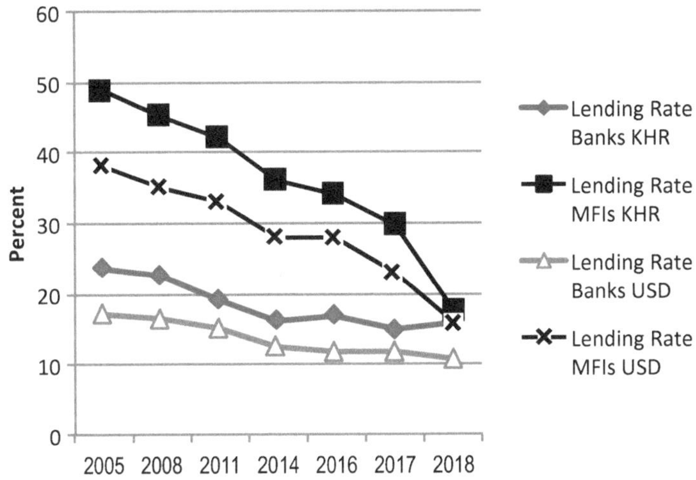

Fig. 3.10 Banking industry-wide average lending rates (2005–2018)
Source: National Bank of Cambodia Annual Report 2018

Chapter 4 takes up the dynamics and the detail of both topics of increasing over-indebtedness, or debt stress, and how the interest rate cap may be a factor in increasing debt stress rather than curbing it.

3.4.3 *The Discovery of an Innovative Business Model*

The discovery of a business model to serve a wide variety of customers with loans, deposit services, and transfers has advanced in Cambodia. Yet that very process of discovery and innovation needs to continue to reach groups of financial services customers that still do not have access to products that adequately meet their financial strategies.

One group of borrowers that experiences such a product mismatch is owners of small and medium enterprises. Loan product design has lagged behind the needs of these increasingly sophisticated credit customers. With a few exceptions, most FSPs that serve the small and microenterprise market still offer standard products developed 20 years ago, with little tailoring to meet customers' needs or enterprise cash flow, particularly for agriculture and small-medium enterprises.

More than ever, this absence of responsiveness to customer's cash flows is tamping down enterprise growth. It also poses risks for enterprises when their cash flow does not match the required loan repayment intervals, as many loan products follow the standard micro-loan design with equal installment payments over the term of the loan (Vanndarong 2016).

3.4.4 The Return on Innovation

"Cambodia is trending digital!" (Duflos 2014). Digital financial services have gained great acceptance among the Cambodian population. There are widespread innovations in fintech solutions to a fast and safe service compared to using cash.

Wing (Cambodia) Limited Specialized Bank is Cambodia's leading mobile banking services provider with the commitment to provide financial inclusion via mobile banking services to unbanked and under-banked people. Wing's operations began in 2009, and the institution is now a countrywide fixture in the marketplace. As of 2017, Wing's "Cash Xpress" agents covered 100% of Cambodia's 163 districts. Wing registered 600,000 accounts, with probably twice as many users, if experience in other countries is applied about multiple users using one account. As registered account users have approximately eight million transactions each month, the assumption about multiple users is most likely (Oliver Wyman and MicroSave 2017).

ACLEDA Unity ToanChet In early 2017 ACLEDA Bank unveiled a new cashless-based e-wallet product that allows customers to use their smartphones for transactions without incurring service fees.

The product, called "ACLEDA Unity ToanChet," is a fintech application that allows customers to transfer funds and pay bills wirelessly on both iPhone and Android devices. "ACLEDA Bank's cashless wallet is finding great acceptance, with 12,000 customers initially signed up for the service at inauguration, which ACLEDA expects to expand within the next five years" (Hor 2017).

Within 5 months, 115,000 registered users engaged with the innovative platform. At that time, Dr. In Channy, ACLEDA Bank's CEO, noted, "I think at this speed, in five years time, there will be at least two million registered customers and they will be part of the new trend of conducting banking services on digital platforms." He added, "I strongly believe that e-banking reaches previously untapped demographics. These include tuk-tuk drivers, taxi drivers, those who sell fish or vegetables, and people living in remote areas" (Saker 2017).

And indeed, by early 2020, 1,330,900 people in Cambodia use the ACLEDA ToanChet application, and over 44,000 people use the ACLEDA ThanChai application in the Lao PDR.

3.4.5 Serving the Market Better

The quantity and quality of basic financial services, such as credit, deposit services, and money transfers and payments, are gradually beginning to serve the needs of the majority. Advances in product quality by innovative financial services providers are still required to tailor more products to the wider diversity of customers and their financial services preferences matching enterprise and family needs.

Just as in the past, leading Cambodian MFIs proved that poor and low-income people in rural and urban areas could contribute to their families and the development of the country. They experimented and found the "return on innovation" an acceptable one. Those leading MFIs are now banks and MDIs.

ACLEDA Bank's inclination for seeking a return on innovation is now widely recognized in Cambodia and the ASEAN region. ACLEDA Bank Plc. along with two other Cambodian banks has been selected by the National Bank of Cambodia (NBC) to implement a Cambodian-Thai QR code-based payment system,[17] which could begin in early 2020. With the signing of an MOU between the NBC and the Bank of Thailand, the two countries aim to "expand cooperation in finance technology and payment services to promote efficiency, the safety of cross-border payment transactions and national currency use." The NBC is currently exploring how to expand the system to neighboring countries such as Vietnam and Laos (ASEAN Economic Community Strategy Center 2019).

The digital age clearly offers opportunity to expand banking services to Cambodia's adult population that is not formally included in the financial system, as well as to expand beyond borders within the region.

3.5 Rules and Norms in Practice

The inclusive growth of Cambodia's financial services market was enabled in large part by the informed actions taken by the National Bank of Cambodia (NBC), an institution with an increasingly strong voice in the evolution of the financial market system. The Law on Banking and Financial Institutions—the regulatory framework that was championed by the NBC—was established in 2000. The framework advanced rapidly, keeping pace with changes in the environment to allow greater benefits from financial services to accrue to poor and low-income people.

From the mid-1990s to the present, the NBC grew into an effective microfinance regulator, a difficult job to get right. They were guided by their desire to build an inclusive financial sector from the very beginning within a liberal framework that promoted safety, soundness, and growth.

3.5.1 The Consultative Process and Product

A consultative process between national policy makers and the financial services providers served to ensure the effective formulation and implementation of the newly established regulations within a reasonable timeframe. Open and honest forums for policy formulation shaped Cambodia's inclusive financial sector as it developed.

[17] **QR codes, or** quick response codes, were first developed in Japan. They are square barcodes and serve as a way to store information in a digital readable optical label.

The process turned the concept of financial inclusion from a nebulous concept in disarray into one that served a concrete purpose with like-minded private and governmental organizations dedicated to building a solid base for change in the underserved and distant segments of the market (Clark 2006).

The NBC has long been an advocate for financial inclusion across the industry as well as a strict supervisor and collaborative partner—quite a difficult role to get right all of the time. The advances in favor of the safety, soundness, and growth of the industry are attributed to an established norm of industry consultation between the NBC and financial services providers that serve the Cambodian people.

Consultations served the industry well since 1998, when a handful of dedicated people were determined to build microfinance in Cambodia. The results of the consultation became their product. Regardless of whether they argued for, or against, any particular action, all parties respected the results of a transparent and well-researched consultative process. These consultations served as a great incentive for all parties to work together to advance a common aim (Clark 2006).

Since that time, the NBC evolved into a "best practice" regulator of microfinance services as noted in the Global Microscope surveys (EIU 2011–2016).

Climbing Up the Ranks In 2012, for the first time, the Economist Intelligence Unit (EIU) ranked Cambodia in the world's top ten countries with the best overall business environment for microfinance (EIU 2012). Cambodia rose to eighth place (from 13th) from the previous Global Microscope ranking in 2011 for the overall microfinance business environment and remained in sixth place for regulatory framework and practices. By 2013 Cambodia rose to sixth place out of 55 countries participating in the annual Global Microscope (EIU 2012–2013).

Later, Cambodia was lauded internationally as promoting financial inclusion by enabling outreach of financial services to poor and low-income people in rural and urban areas. However, by 2016 Cambodia's enabling environment for financial inclusion in the EIU analysis ranking dropped to 30th place out of 54 countries—just a bit above an average score. The steep drop in ranking was mainly due to several weaknesses in supervision, including the increasing number of unlicensed and unregulated lenders (EIU 2016).

Falling Down the Ranks By 2018, the EIU global ranking of Cambodia's enabling environment for financial inclusion changed dramatically, ranking Cambodia 43 out of 55 countries.

In the past, Cambodia served as an interesting model for enabling regulation for many countries including China, Thailand, Sri Lanka, and Vietnam—countries that now surpassed Cambodia in building an enabling environment for financial inclusion. In fact, by 2018 Cambodia's enabling environment landed the country in the bottom 25% of countries participating in the EIU's Global Microscope.

The EIU noted that "the relatively liberal but systematic regulatory environment—until the imposition of the interest rate cap on MFI lending in March 2017—was an important enabler of financial inclusion" (EIU 2018).

The 2017 interest rate cap on microfinance institutions (MFIs) and microfinance deposit-taking institutions (MDIs) has resulted in a decline in the number of borrowers from 1.9 m to 1.75 m (December 2017) at MFIs/MDIs. However, the total volume of loans grew by 25%, reaching US$3.9bn at the end of 2017.[18] This has reignited worries about MDI/MFI clients becoming over-indebted given the limited MFI/MDI staff capacity to conduct credit assessment for high loan amounts (EIU 2018).

While the 2018 Global Microscope noted that digital financial services (DFS) carried a positive view among financial sector participants "as a key enabler (of financial inclusion), money transfer is what currently drives DFS. Mobile money providers are unable to offer savings products and while many financial services providers (FSPs) have been increasing their digital footprints to include the collection of deposits and loans, this is still in its infancy as FSPs struggle with back-end technology" (EIU 2018).

Other concerns that many market participants share are "the number of MFIs and MDIs continues to be a worry … and the recent MFI and MDI surge in refinanced loans has caused alarm amongst various investors concerned about the level of over-indebtedness in the market" (EIU 2018).

3.5.2 *Truth in Lending*

Despite the dynamism of a financial sector, there is always a concern on the part of politicians during electoral campaigns that interest rates are too high and must be capped. The NBC has been able to counter the recurring calls for interest rate caps throughout the last two decades. They provided convincing evidence that interest rate caps tend to favor the elite and disproportionately harm the poor. Instead of a cap on interest rates, they proposed market strengthening regulations and building adequate information services to allow the market to check excessive rates.

One of the cornerstones of this forward-looking regulatory framework was establishing a Truth in Lending Law. The law required all credit providers to calculate interest on a declining balance method.[19] Financial services providers were also required to provide an amortization schedule to each borrower and to explain it, regardless of how educationally deprived that customer was. It was a matter of principle, and the NBC expected transparency in FSP communications and relationships with customers. Compliance was also overseen by the Central Bank.

---

[18] The dynamics of over-indebtedness in the market and increasing loan sizes in MFIs and MDIs are treated in detail in Chap. 4.

[19] A declining balance method calculates interest on the principal outstanding at each payment period; a flat rate continues to calculate interest on the original amount of the loan, even though some of the principal has been repaid. The former is more transparent and is widely used in regulated lending markets. The flat rate is used widely in informal lending markets.

With new pricing transparency—which can only be offered with a liberalized interest rate applied to all transactions—borrowers could compare rates and the quality of services among many providers. Disillusioned with the quick-fix policies of the past and influenced by the IMF in the present, the government determined to let the market work for the sector and the consumers within it.

And, surprisingly, the market worked just as expected.

In the brief period of 10 years, the banking industry-wide average interest rate on lending plunged from 23% on average to 11% for USD and lowered to 16% for KHR.[20] See Fig. 3.10.[21]

Perhaps more remarkable is the steady decline of the average interest rate on micro loans, which are more expensive to offer. Simply put, the costs associated with lending small accounts are higher, and the profit—at the same unit price—is lower. Lending small amounts is less profitable because it is more costly.[22]

While lending rates in both currencies dropped significantly in the past 10 years, deposit rates for both currencies remained in a band between 6% and 7% on KHR for most of the decade and stabilized between 4% and 5% for USD during the same period (NBC various).

The average lending interest rate is more interesting, as a steady decline in both currencies is noted during the 10-year period. Since 2001, when the interest rate on micro loans hovered around 70%, the rate has dropped significantly. Similarly, the interest rate for USD loans decreased from 60% to 28% during the same period (NBC 2016a, b).

By the end of 2018 with the new interest rate cap at 18%, "MFIs loan interest rates fell considerably from 34% in 2016 to 29.7% in riel and from 28% to 23% in US dollars." (NBC 2018a, b, c, d).[23]

3.5.3 *The Precedent for Market Transparency*

According to the NBC, the past 16-year declining trend in the interest rate of microfinance loans was due to the solid performance of five main market mechanisms.

---

[20] These figures are industry-wide averages, including corporate lending (NBC 2015a, b).

[21] According to the NBC reports, as Cambodia is a highly dollarized economy, the NBC is unable to use the interest rate channel to conduct its monetary policy. The interest rates of deposit and credit have been determined by the market mechanism. Figure 3.10 shows a dramatic dip in both KHR and USD. The dip in 2012 and rebound of the average industry lending rate in KHR follow the dip in the USD rate. The NBC notes the decline resulted from the impact that Cambodia experienced due to regional currency depreciation compared to the US dollar, which also diminished the value of the riel.

[22] See discussion of this topic earlier in this chapter in the section "The Vital Statistics About Market Expansion."

[23] Chapter 4 includes a more in-depth discussion of interest rates over time and the effects on the market for loans and savings centered on the interest rate cap on MFI loans as of April 2017.

- First, increasing competition in the market exerted downward pressure on prices.
- Second, improved efficiency in banking operations, particularly among MDIs, decreased operational expenses.
- Third, the traditionally low non-performing loan (NPL) ratio was maintained below 1.5% at its 10-year peak, with the advent of the Credit Bureau of Cambodia (CBC).
- Fourth, increased deposit mobilization from the public enabled a lower cost of funding (NBC 2016a, b).
- And, finally, the Central Bank and the CMA industry association encouraged transparent competition, which strengthened the quality of financial products and services, lowered operational costs, and ultimately lowered the price to consumers.

As depicted in Fig. 3.1, these market players—with banks and MFIs at the core, a savvy and competent regulator and supervisor in charge of setting and enforcing rules, and the support of the CMA industry association and the CBC credit bureau—showed the rest of the world how the market system can work well for poor and low-income people.

The banking authorities rallied around a Truth in Lending Law passed in 2001. The Law was designed to strengthen transparency and market reforms, but not act as an interest rate ceiling, which would undermine the very market reforms they sought to implement. As HE Tal Nay Im, who subsequently became the Director General of the National Bank of Cambodia from 2010 to 2015, said in 2005:

> "It is the government's policy that the interest rate is determined by the market. If MFIs get a license and operate normally, the interest rate will go down, and the interest rate has decreased compared to five years ago. The government cannot fix the rate, and does not want to interfere."
>
> "We want to influence the rate, by influencing the stability of MFIs, fostering competition and strengthening them. We did intervene in the method of calculation, by requiring a declining balance calculation. A flat rate is very heavy for the borrower, and the pricing is not transparent."[24]

3.5.4 Opening the Financial Market to New Entrants

The NBC also allowed market entry for a broad range of organizations to win consumer acceptance in this new and uncharted territory of customer banking preferences in rural or urban areas.

The law did require compulsory registration or licensing for NGOs depending on the size and scope of their lending and savings operations. "Any microfinance operation with sizable banking services was required to submit an application for a

[24] Author interview 2005.

license by December 31, 2002, or scale down its operations and operate only as a small registered MFI with reporting requirements."[25]

Now, almost 20 years later, according to HE Chea Serey, the Director General of the Central Banking Directorate of the NBC, these two policies—truth in lending and opening markets for a range of licensed financial services providers—have been the most important actions taken by the NBC to foster the inclusiveness of Cambodia's financial sector. "They laid the fundamental framework to develop a commercial market system that offered consumers a range of institutional providers," she stated.[26]

Large private banks with foreign or domestic shareholders, wholly owned subsidiaries of foreign banks, community-owned and community-managed organizations, large MFIs, and a few credit unions now operate side by side. At the time prior to the interest rate cap, they charged prices that reflected the prevailing market conditions.[27]

3.5.5 *The Precedent for Experimentation*

The two pillars of the financial system—truth in lending and a range of organizations—made it possible for the NBC to experiment with what would work well in the country. While keen to learn from others, they were determined not to follow an established model that might not work well for the Cambodian people.

And the system continued to evolve due to foresight and willingness to experiment. In 2008, the NBC issued a regulation allowing licensed MFIs to mobilize savings from the public, providing a valuable service to customers, especially in more remote rural areas. The regulation also allowed regulated MFIs to intermediate funds, providing a source of less expensive local funds for the MFI and valuable deposit services for customers.

As a result of the NBC's tradition of a willingness to innovate, the "microfinance deposit-taking institution" (MDI) was born. Establishing the new regulatory status of an MDI enabled Cambodia to reach greater numbers of depositors and savers and higher levels of financial inclusion.

[25] The Prakas on Licensing of Specialized Banks and the Prakas on Registration and Licensing of Microfinance Institutions anticipated three institutional categories: specialized banks, licensed microfinance institutions, and registered microfinance operations. Royal Government of Cambodia (2000) Prakas No B 7-00-06 dated 11 January and "On the Licensing of Micro-Finance Institutions." Royal Government of Cambodia (2002) Prakas No. 7.02-49 dated 25 February. On Registration and Licensing of Microfinance Institutions.

[26] Author interview. 2016.

[27] The interest rate cap on microcredit is discussed in depth in Chap. 4.

3.5.6 *The Importance of Norms*

In any country, formal rules and informal norms may or may not be mutually reinforcing. For example, the formal rules and laws that govern a market may be so widely understood and enforced through fines, loss of licenses, and even imprisonment, that negative behaviors such as bribes and kickbacks that the rules are meant to eliminate actually work.

On the other hand, norms and generally accepted behavior of bribes or kickbacks may be so widespread and practiced with such impunity that any effort to enforce official rules is undermined.

In the most recent Transparency International Global Corruption Perceptions Index 2018, Cambodia ranks 161st out of 180 countries. A country's rank indicates its position relative to the other countries in the index (Transparency International 2017). With a few exceptions, the society has yet to coalesce around principles of fair play and ethical behavior in its nation building process in spite of growing examples of principled and honest financial sector institutions.

Cambodia's financial sector institutions are at a stage of development where formal rules may punish corruption, but this does not prevent the fact that day-to-day business transactions or one's position of importance in the society often requires commonly accepted kickbacks and extra payments.

One example to illustrate how embedded informal norms can be in the society comes from a bank cashier at ACLEDA Bank in the year 2005. Piv Thary, the cashier in ACLEDA's Prey Veng branch, tells a story of customers expecting to pay extra fees despite their feelings that paying a bribe may be just as wrong as asking for one.

> "The customers come with small deposits, or to repay their loans, and they have an extra amount. They push the notes forward, saying, 'This is for you. Do I owe you more?'"
>
> "I tell them, 'No, this is your money. Would you like to deposit that amount too?'"
>
> The customers are astounded. They think, she made a mistake, but they come back, and deposit more. (Clark 2006).

3.6 Supporting Functions

The strength or absence of specialized supporting functions often determines whether a market thrives or fails to survive.

3.6.1 *Capital Markets: The Cambodia Securities Exchange (CSX)*

Capital markets support the growth of the economy and the health of the financial system. Capital markets, such as stock and bond markets, are considered main sources of finance for corporate funding. In Cambodia there are two main capital market instruments in place—stocks and corporate bonds. Both instruments are facilitated by the Cambodia Securities Exchange (CSX) that was launched in April 2012 as a joint venture between the MEF in Cambodia and the Korea Exchange (KRX). See Figs. 3.11, 3.12, 3.13 and 3.14 for recent CSX performance.

The CSX trades both corporate bonds and stocks. "Bonds are essentially an agreement where issuers borrow funds from investors and must repay investors at an agreed rate after a specified amount of time. Governments, companies and many others issue bonds to borrow money for projects" (World Bank 2019a, b). As a bond is a long-term debt instrument, a bond market enables corporations to issue long-term debt to an investor. The investor becomes a creditor and receives interest on the loan for a period of time until the principal is repaid at a pre-established term.

A stock market trades equity securities or corporate shares where the investor becomes an owner of a percentage of the company. The stock market produces both exuberance and gloom. The bond market is generally less subject to highs and lows, as it is based on a fixed price contract between offer of debt and provider of debt.

While still young, the CSX is growing beyond placement of securities of government-owned companies, increasing capitalization and the daily average trading, as well as doubling the number of trading accounts from 2017 to 2018. In addition the percentage of trading accounts with the Mobile Trading System (MTS) has grown to 17% of all accounts, yet 59% of stock orders are placed through the MTS (Cambodia Securities Exchange 2019). See Figs. 3.12 and 3.13.

"Finally groundbreaking developments were made in the bond market, with the listing of the first Riel-denominated corporate bond in Cambodia in December 2018. Hattha Kaksekar Limited (HKL), the issuer and the third largest MDI in Cambodia, offered 1,200,000 bonds in the local currency worth KHR 120 billion, of which 66.7 percent were allocated to International Finance Corporation and the remaining to qualified investors." (NBC 2019b FSR).

Hattha Kaksekar Limited (HKL) is a leading MDI in Cambodia and a subsidiary of the Bank of Ayudhya (Krungsri), the fifth largest commercial bank in Thailand.

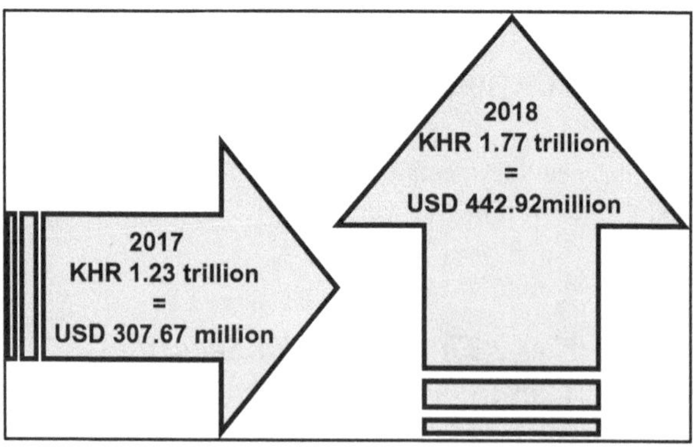

Fig. 3.11 Cambodia Securities Exchange (CSX) market capitalization
Source: CSX Press Release Summary of 2018 Market Performance Statistic: CSX Outperformed in 2018

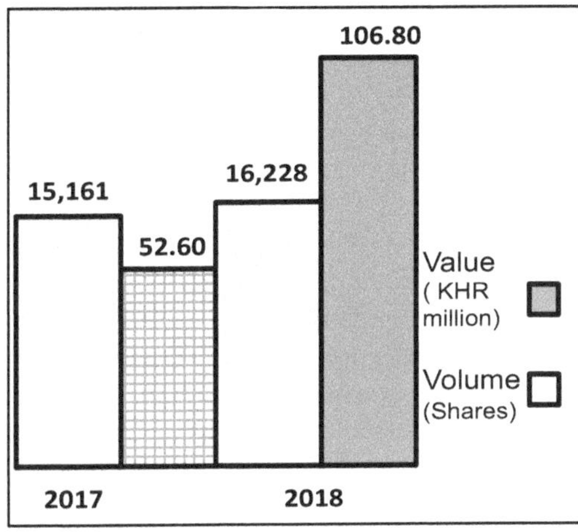

Fig. 3.12 Cambodia Securities Exchange (CSX) growth: daily average trading (2017–2018)
Source: CSX Press Release Summary of 2018 Market Performance Statistic: CSX Outperformed in 2018

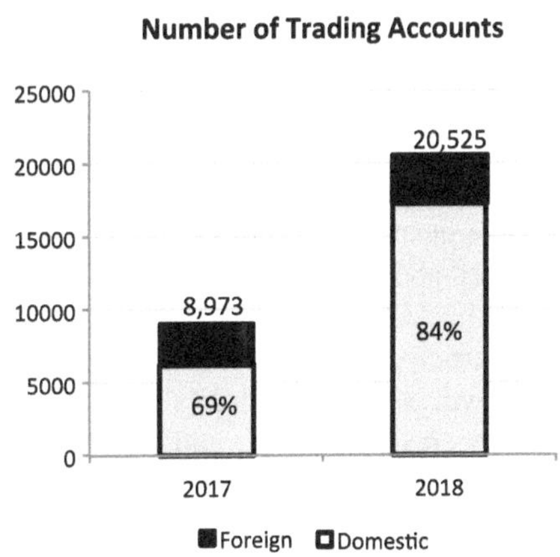

Fig. 3.13 Cambodia Securities Exchange growth: number of trading accounts
Source: CSX Press Release Summary of 2018 Market Performance Statistic: CSX Outperformed in 2018

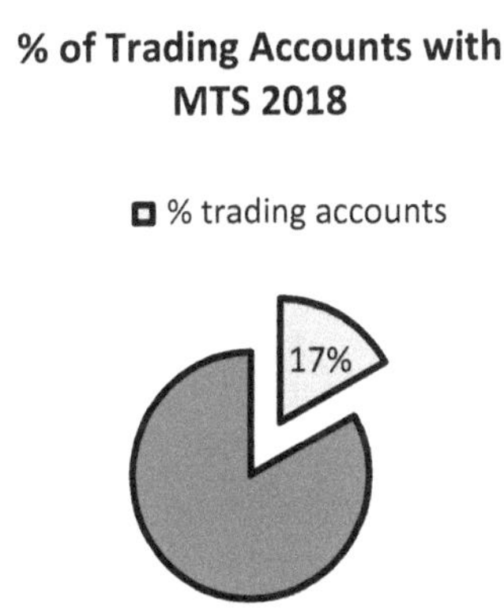

Fig. 3.14 Cambodia Securities Exchange Mobile Trading System accounts
Source: Cambodia Securities Exchange (CSX) Press Release Summary of 2018 Market Performance Statistic: CSX Outperformed in 2018

It was widely reported that even while individuals were interested in purchasing the bonds with an annual 8.5% interest rate and a 3-year maturity, institutional investors purchased the entire amount. This shows both interest and effective demand for local institutional and individual investors interested in Cambodia's financial institutions, particularly those MDIs with solid performance track records and reasonable returns.

Soon after the HKL listing, LOLC followed suit in April 2019 with a bond issue on the CSX. The LOLC issue on the Cambodian bond market included an innovation due to the issue of two types of bonds—a fixed-coupon bond, similar to the HKL issue, and a foreign exchange-indexed bond, which is attractive to foreign investors. Both bond issues were fully subscribed and raised KHR 80 billion (USD 20 million) to support the expansion of LOLC's microfinance and small enterprise lending operations (Khor 2019).

According to the NBC, the CSX notes, "an increasing number of companies, and in particular, financial institutions, are showing interest in issuing and listing their bonds on the stock exchange in the near future" (NBC FSR 2019b). However, there is yet to be a microfinance institution or a bank with an initial public stock offering (IPO) on the CSX.

As the CSX grows, so do the securities firms that serve the secondary market, selling existing securities to individuals and companies. The secondary market is important as it allows the public access, convenience, and efficient and timely transactions in small amounts on an exchange or over-the-counter or mobile transaction as noted above with reference to the CSX's Mobile Trading System.

Using ACLEDA Securities Plc. as an example, there is growth in both awareness and participation in the securities market, from a tepid beginning in 2013 to a spike in growth in 2015 and, finally, in 2018, an extraordinary increase in trading accounts yet a decrease in volume and value. See Fig. 3.15.

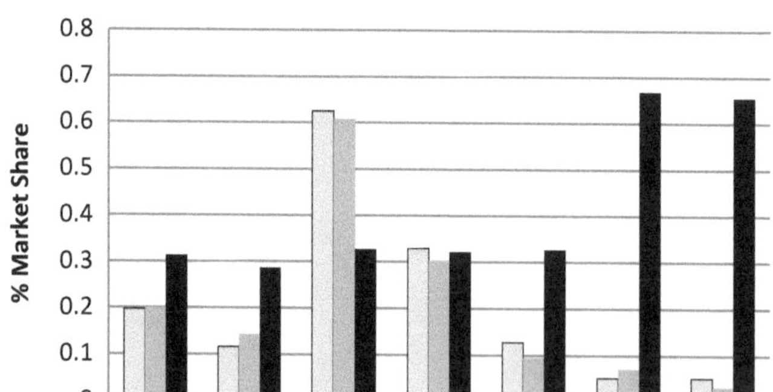

	2013	2014	2015	2016	2017	2018	2019 Aug
Trading Values	0.197	0.116	0.625	0.329	0.127	0.052	0.051616
Trading Volumes	0.201	0.142	0.607	0.302	0.094	0.07	0.031464
Trading Accounts	0.313	0.286	0.328	0.321	0.326	0.668	0.654771

Fig. 3.15 ACLEDA securities market share
Source: ACLEDA Securities. Annual Report 2019

3.6.2 *Information Services*

Supporting functions also include information services, such as credit bureaus that enable lenders to manage risk, and capacity building for providers and customers, such as skills development, business schools, and financial education. (See Fig. 3.1.)

3.6.2.1 Research, Advocacy, and Coordination: Industry Associations

Research, advocacy, and coordination services are offered by industry associations, such as the Cambodia Microfinance Association (CMA) and the Association of Banks in Cambodia (ABC). Industry association services keep financial services providers informed and up to date. An in-depth dialogue and consultative process with the regulators and supervisors have enabled FSPs to achieve tremendous growth in numbers of clients, diversified services, depth of outreach, and the construction of a market infrastructure that serve the retail market and their customers.

3.6.2.2 The Credit Bureau of Cambodia (CBC)

The Credit Bureau of Cambodia (CBC) is one such supporting function that was fostered by a collaborative relationship among industry participants. The CBC's unique ownership structure promotes compliance, use, and information sharing. MFIs and banks are owners of the CBC, along with Equifax Cambodia Holdings Pte. Limited—a subsidiary of Equifax Inc., the internationally known private company specialized in credit bureau operations.

The CBC provides information on individuals and data for market-wide analysis. The information services provided by CBC also enable customers to build a credit history, building a reputation as a good credit risk, which allows better loan terms.

All FSPs licensed by the NBC—MFIs and banks alike—are required to use the CBC for first-time loans as well as for refinancing. This enhances knowledge of credit risk on behalf of the regulated financial services providers that make up the largest segment of the market. It promotes responsible lending, and it reduces the incidence of unintentional reckless lending that could undermine the market, such as issuing multiple loans to one borrower.

Effective credit bureau operations and mandatory compliance for all major financial services providers are often considered the main way to contain systemic risk that could emerge through intentional reckless lending by a few.

Finally, the CBC provides regulatory policy setting authorities and the industry as a whole with data analysis to view an emerging picture of potential over-indebtedness and the degree of danger it may present to the financial system.

Mr. Gabriel Davel, an expert practitioner on systemic crises and their containment, notes in his seminal piece on this subject that an effective credit bureau must cover all credit providers in the market. This is one of the most important features that will detect early warning signs on over-indebtedness that could erode the safety of the financial system overall.[28]

In this regard, the comprehensive, timely, confidential, and governance attributes of the CBC mitigate risk for FSPs and prevent over-indebtedness for customers. System-wide data analyses can serve as early warning signs for any wider systemic stress. One problem that is always discussed in the context of preventing over-indebtedness is whether or not small, registered, but unsupervised lenders use the CBC. The answer is generally no and only very rarely yes.[29]

3.6.3 Financial Consumer Education

Finally, after years of implementing a tight and compelling regulatory framework, allowing growth with safety and soundness, the NBC began a nationwide effort in financial education. The campaign "Let's Talk Money!" is to be followed by another initiative—a comprehensive financial consumer protection charter.

The "Let's Talk Money!" campaign, led by HE Madam Neav Chanthana and her enthusiastic and knowledgeable NBC staff, has recently reinvented itself to become more comprehensive and is designed to promote a lasting effect on Cambodia's next generation.

The "Let's Talk Money!" initiative is now poised to target primary and high school students, with the active advocacy and support of the Ministry of Education (Box 3.3).

Currently primary and secondary schools in Cambodia have no curriculum dedicated to financial literacy, nor do many countries in Europe and the Americas. If this initiative is successful, it will outpace the record of many developed and developing countries in adopting a nationwide dedicated financial education curriculum accompanying students from primary schools through high school.

---

[28] Davel, Gabriel. 2013. Regulatory Options to Curb Debt Stress. CGAP Focus Note 83. Gabriel Davel is the former CEO of the Republic of South Africa Central Bank. South Africa experienced systemic consumer debt crises in the late 1990s and circa 2005.

[29] The topic of proliferation of small credit providers is discussed further in Chap. 4.

Box 3.3: Financial Education and Financial Literacy

What Is Financial Education?	What Is Financial Literacy?
Financial education is the process of building knowledge, skills, and attitudes to become financially literate. It introduces people to good money management practices with respect to earning, spending, saving, borrowing, and investing. The role of financial education is to enable people to shift from reactive to proactive decision-making and work toward fulfilling their financial goals. By broadening people's understanding of financial options and principles, financial education builds skills to use financial products and services and promotes attitudes and behaviors that support more effective use of scarce financial resources. Financial education is a tool to achieve financial literacy and more; financial literacy is essential to both effective consumer protection and effective consumer use of financial products and services.	Financial literacy is "the ability to make informed judgments and to take effective actions regarding the current and future use and management of money. It includes the ability to understand financial choices, plan for the future, spend wisely, and manage the challenges associated with life events such as a job loss, saving for retirement, or paying for a child's education." Of course, financial literacy can mean different things to different people; in some economies, being financially literate might require knowledge of tax codes, insurance requirements, and credit cards, while for people who are "unbanked," financial literacy is more likely defined by concepts of safe and secure savings, budgeting, and wise borrowing.

Source: Cohen, Monique and Candice Nelson, 2011. Financial Literacy: A Step for Clients towards Financial Inclusion. 2011 Global Microcredit Summit. *Commissioned Workshop Paper November 14–17, 2011 – Valladolid, Spain*

3.6.4 Financial Consumer Protection

A comprehensive financial consumer protection law has not yet emerged from deliberations between the NBC and financial services providers (FSPs). Yet, eight FSPs with the predominant market share in Cambodia have been certified in client protection practices by the Smart Campaign,[30] which certifies FSPs as adhering to international standards of client protection. As of April 2017, the leading MDIs and banks in Cambodia that have been certified are ACLEDA Bank Plc. AMK, AMRET, Hatta Kasekar, KREDIT, PRASAC, LOLC, and Vision Fund Cambodia.

A nationwide financial consumer complaints system is a priority for the NBC. Many regulators see a well-run consumer complaints system with widespread coverage as a service that also provides early warning signals of a pending systemic crisis or fraudulent activity in addition to providing customers with a complaints feedback and resolution mechanism.

[30] The Smart Campaign: https://www.smartcampaign.org

On September 27, 2018, the Governor of the NBC signed into law the establishment of a mechanism to resolve complaints by consumers of banking and financial institutions. The law establishes a clear complaints process with timeframes, responsibilities for complaints resolution within the financial institution, and regular reporting requirements.

The system also requires all banking and financial institutions to establish a Consumer Complaint Management Framework that is appropriately supported by dedicated staff, policies, a code of conduct and procedures for annual review, and board-level reporting.

CMA also holds its members responsible to comply with a range of consumer protection practices and responsible behavior toward their FSP counterparts, including prohibiting staff poaching. The self-regulatory approach is collegial, rather than mandatory, as is the ABC code of conduct.

The Cambodia Microfinance Association (CMA) and the Association of Banks in Cambodia (ABC) developed codes of conduct with their membership, and continue to provide capacity building programs to their members, along with data and information services, and coordination and advocacy efforts. The CMA also plays an important role in data collection, advocacy, and bringing innovative topics to members for discussion and consideration.

As a component of its code of conduct, the ABC offers a second-line complaints resolution facility for their members. Overall, the code may need revision to more solidly focus on a range of providers' interactions with consumers to become a true consumer protection charter, yet clauses on transparency and complaints procedures are credible, although as yet untested for a period of time that would allow assessment and changes to implement improvements.

These innovations have supported the banking sector in its giant steps forward in the "flight to quality."

References

ASEAN Economic Community Strategy Center. 2019. Cambodia: NBC selects three banks for pilot QR code system. Available http://aec.utcc.ac.th/cambodia-nbc-selects-three-banks-for-pilot-qr-code-system/ Accessed 30 June 2019

Cambodia Securities Exchange (CSX). 2019. Press Release Summary of 2018 Market Performance Statistic: CSX outperformed in 2018. Available http://csx.com.kh/news/notice/viewPost.do?MNCD=8020&postId=401 Accessed 30 April 2019

CGAP. 2015. A Market Systems Approach to Financial Inclusion: Guidelines for Funders. Consensus Guidelines. Washington, D.C. CGAP: Creative Commons License Attribution CC BY 3.0. Available https://www.cgap.org/sites/default/files/researches/documents/Consensus-Guidelines-A-Market-Systems-Approach-to-Financial-Inclusion-Sept-2015_0.pdf.

Chea, Serey. 2018. Director General of NBC. "The Case of Cambodia in Using Fintech to Promote Financial Inclusion", Presentation at FinTech conference organized by IMF-OAP, the Financial Services Agency of Japan (JFSA), and the Bank of Japan in Tokyo, Japan on April 16, 2018. Available https://www.nbc.org.kh/download_files/news_and_events/news_eng/8150FinancialInclusionandFinTech.pdf Accessed 21 November 2018

Clark, Heather (2006) *When There Was No Money. Building ACLEDA Bank in Cambodia's Evolving Financial Sector*. Springer, Berlin-Heidelberg.

Demirguc-Kunt, Asli, Leora Klapper, Dorothe Singer, and Peter Van Oudheusden (2015). "The Global Findex Database 2014: Measuring Financial Inclusion around the World." Policy Research Working Paper 7255, World Bank, Washington, DC. Available http://openknowledge.worldbank.org/bitstream/handle/10986/21865/WPS7255.pdf?sequence=2%20%20 Accessed 21 November 2018

Duflos, Eric. (2014) Cambodia is Trending Digital! CGAP, Washington, DC. Available www.cgap.org Accessed 21 November 2018

EIU (Economist Intelligence Unit), 2012; Global Microscope on the Microfinance Business Environment 2012. Sponsored by Accion, AfDB, Bill & Melinda Gates Foundation, IDB Invest/IDB LAB, and MetLife Foundation. EIU, New York, NY. Available https://www.ifc.org/wps/wcm/connect/industry_ext_content/ifc_external_corporate_site/financial+institutions/resources/2012+global+microscope+index

EIU (Economist Intelligence Unit), 2016; *Global Microscope 2016: The enabling environment for financial inclusion*; Sponsored by MIF/IDB, Accion and the Metlife Foundation. EIU, New York, NY. Available https://www.centerforfinancialinclusion.org/global-microscope-2016 Accessed 10 January 2018

EIU (Economist Intelligence Unit), 2018; Global Microscope 2018: The enabling environment for financial inclusion; Sponsored by Accion, AfDB, Bill & Melinda Gates Foundation, IDB Invest/IDB LAB, and MetLife Foundation. EIU, New York, NY. Available https://www.centerforfinancialinclusion.org/global-microscope-2018 Accessed 10 January 2018

FinScope (2016) Consumer Survey Highlights. Cambodia 2015. Available https://finmark.org.za/finscope-cambodia-2015-pocket-guide/ Accessed 10 June 2017

Global Findex (2017) World Bank http://www.worldbank.org/globalfindex Accessed 8 August 2018.

Global Findex Data (2014) http://datatopics.worldbank.org/financialinclusion/country/cambodia Accessed 8 August 2018.

Global Findex Data (2012) http://datatopics.worldbank.org/financialinclusion/country/cambodia Accessed 8 August 2018.

Hor, Kimsay (2017) "ACLEDA Taps into E-Wallet Market". *The Phnom Penh Post*, Phnom Penh Available https://www.phnompenhpost.com/business/acleda-taps-e-wallet-market Accessed 8 August 2018

Khor, Jolene (2019) Microfinance Institution LOLC Completes $20m Bond Issue on Cambodia Securities Exchange. MicroMICROCAPITAL BRIEF Available: https://www.microcapital.org/microcapital-brief-microfinance-institution-lolc-completes-20m-bond-issue-on-cambodia-securities-exchange/ Accessed: 30 June 2019

Lay, Sok Heng (2017) The Use of Mobile Phones and Financial Inclusion: Evidence from the FinScope Survey. Available: https://www.nbc.org.kh/download_files/presentation-4th-nbc-conference-with-numbers-sokheng.pdf Accessed 18 July 2018.

Microfinance Index of Market Outreach and Saturation MIMOSA. (2015) Cambodia. Available http://mimosaindex.org Accessed 15 December 2018.

National Bank of Cambodia (2019a) Annual Supervision Report 2018. Phnom Penh. Available https://www.nbc.org.kh/english/publications/annual_reports.php Accessed 10 June 2019

National Bank of Cambodia (2019b) Annual Report Financial Stability Review 2018. Phnom Penh. Available https://www.nbc.org.kh/english/publications/annual_reports.php Accessed 10 June 2019

National Bank of Cambodia (2018a) Annual Report 2017. Phnom Penh. Available https://www.nbc.org.kh/english/publications/annual_reports.php Accessed 20 September 2018

National Bank of Cambodia (2017a) Annual Report 2016. Phnom Penh. Available https://www.nbc.org.kh/english/publications/annual_reports.php Accessed 10 July 2017

National Bank of Cambodia (2016a) Annual Report 2015. Phnom Penh. Available https://www.nbc.org.kh/english/publications/annual_reports.php Accessed 10 July 2017

National Bank of Cambodia (2015a) Annual Report 2014. Phnom Penh. Available https://www.nbc.org.kh/english/publications/annual_reports.php Accessed 10 July 2017
National Bank of Cambodia (2014a) Annual Report 2013. Phnom Penh. Available https://www.nbc.org.kh/english/publications/annual_reports.php Accessed 10 July 2017
National Bank of Cambodia (2013a) Annual Report 2012. Phnom Penh. Available https://www.nbc.org.kh/english/publications/annual_reports.php Accessed 10 July 2017
National Bank of Cambodia (2012) Annual Report 2011. Phnom Penh. Available https://www.nbc.org.kh/english/publications/annual_reports.php Accessed 10 July 2017
National Bank of Cambodia (2018b) Economic and Monetary Statistics, Series No. 297 – 26th Year, July 2018. Available https://www.nbc.org.kh/english/publications/economic_and_monetary_statistics.php. Accessed 20 December 2018
National Bank of Cambodia (2018c) Economic and Monetary Statistics, Series No. 288 – 25th Year, October 2017. Available https://www.nbc.org.kh/english/publications/economic_and_monetary_statistics.php. Accessed 15 October 2018
National Bank of Cambodia (2018d) Supervision Annual Report 2017, Phnom Penh. Available https://www.nbc.org.kh/english/publications/supervision_annual_reports.php. Accessed 15 October 2018
National Bank of Cambodia (2017b) Supervision Annual Report 2016, Phnom Penh. Available https://www.nbc.org.kh/english/publications/supervision_annual_reports.php Accessed 10 July 2017
National Bank of Cambodia (2016b) Supervision Annual Report 2015, Phnom Penh. Available https://www.nbc.org.kh/english/publications/supervision_annual_reports.php Accessed 10 July 2017
National Bank of Cambodia (2015b) Supervision Annual Report 2014, Phnom Penh. Available https://www.nbc.org.kh/english/publications/supervision_annual_reports.php Accessed 10 July 2017
National Bank of Cambodia (2014b) Supervision Annual Report 2013, Phnom Penh. Available https://www.nbc.org.kh/english/publications/supervision_annual_reports.php Accessed 10 July 2017
National Bank of Cambodia (2013b) Supervision Annual Report 2012, Phnom Penh. Available https://www.nbc.org.kh/english/publications/supervision_annual_reports.php Accessed 10 July 2017
National Institute of Statistics of Cambodia, Available on tradingeconomics.com Accessed 15 October 2018
Oliver Wyman and MicroSave (2017) Accelerating Financial Inclusion in South-East Asia with Digital Finance. Asian Development Bank. Manila. Available https://www.oliverwyman.com/content/dam/oliver-wyman/v2/publications/2017/jan/Accelerating-financial-inclusion-in-south-east-asia.pdf Accessed 20 June 2017
Rozas, Daniel (2016) Preventing Over-Indebtedness in Cambodia. MIMOSA (Microfinance Index of Market Outreach and Saturation) Available at www.danielrozas.com Accessed 20 June 2017.
Saker, Jade (2017) "Banks Capitalise on Cambodia's High Mobile Phone Usage". The Phnom Penh Post. Phnom Penh. Available https://www.phnompenhpost.com/.../banks-capitalise-cambodias-high-mobile-phone-usage Accessed 26 June 2018.
Smart Campaign. Client Protection Principles. Available: https://www.smartcampaign.org/about/smart-microfinance-and-the-client-protection-principles. Accessed 8 June 2018.
Smart Campaign. Certified Organizations. Available https://www.smartcampaign.org/certification/certified-organizations Accessed 20 December 2018.
The Springfield Centre (2015) The Operational Guide for the Making Markets Work for the Poor. (M4P) Approach, 2nd edition funded by SDC & DFID. Available https://beamexchange.org/uploads/filer_public/97/53/97533ed8-cfb0-4f06-a87c-3d4ff28b0557/m4pguide_context.pdf Accessed 26 June 2018.
Transparency International 2017. Cambodia Corruption Perceptions Index. https://www.transparency.org/news/feature/corruption_perceptions_index_2017 Accessed 26 June 2018.

Vanndarong, Pen. 2016. The Risk of Discrepancy between MFIs' Product Design and Customers' Financial Requirements. Third Annual National Bank of Cambodia Macroeconomic Conference. Available https://www.nbc.org.kh/download_files/research_papers/english/4864TheRisksofDiscrepancybetweenMFIsProductDesigns&CustomersFinancialRequirements-withdisclaimer.pdf Accessed 18 November 2018

Wing (Cambodia) Limited Specialised Bank (2016) Annual Report. Available: https://www.nbc.org.kh/download_files/supervision/bank_an_rep_eng/Annual-Report-EN.pdf Accessed 20 June 2017

World Bank (2015) FAQs: Global Poverty Line Update. Available: https://www.worldbank.org/en/topic/poverty/brief/global-poverty-line-faq.

World Bank (2018) Cambodia Country Overview. Poverty Continues to fall. Available https://www.worldbank.org/en/country/cambodia/overview Accessed 18 November 2018.

World Bank (2019a) Data. https://data.worldbank.org/indicator/NY.GDP.MKTP.KD.ZG?locations=KH. Accessed 1 June 2019.

World Bank (2019b) 10 Years of Green Bonds: Creating the Blueprint for Sustainability Across Capital Markets. Available https://www.worldbank.org/en/news/immersive-story/2019/03/18/10-years-of-green-bonds-creating-the-blueprint-for-sustainability-across-capital-markets.

World Bank (2015) FAQs: Global Poverty Line Update. Available: https://www.worldbank.org/en/topic/poverty/brief/global-poverty-line-faq

Chapter 4
Cambodia's Financial Market System: Inclusive Dynamics, Impending Crisis?

4.1 Introduction

What type of exuberance defines the Cambodian financial market system? Is it rational? The past 20 years tell a compelling story of inclusive growth in the financial market system in Cambodia. Growth was enabled by policy foresight and the crowding-in of more players in the core market as well as in the support functions of the market.[1] Label this: Exuberance based on rational behavior.

Yet, by 2016 economists and financial sector experts in Cambodia began to express concerns about "irrational exuberance" ruling the day. Concerns surfaced about over-indebtedness, particularly in the microcredit market (MIMOSA 2015; Rozas 2016a, b, c; EIU 2018) and equally with respect to overheated sub-sector credit markets, such as the mid- to high-end property markets and the construction sector (IMF 2018). By the end of 2018, the IMF Mission to Cambodia noted with caution:

> Cambodia's economic outlook is positive, although there are downside risks. Our discussions focused on four areas: managing macro-financial risks, safeguarding fiscal sustainability, supporting inclusive growth, and, addressing governance vulnerabilities.
>
> Bank credit, increasingly concentrated in the real estate and construction sectors, is expected to grow around 20% in 2018. Concerns about credit quality, external funding, increasing concentration in the real estate sector and unregulated lending by real estate developers and high credit growth and growing systemic importance of microfinance institutions (MFI) continue to pose risks to financial and macroeconomic stability.[2]

[1] See Chap. 3, Fig. 3.1, and accompanying text.

[2] According to the IMF Glossary of Selected Financial Terms, Article IV consultation is a regular, usually annual, comprehensive discussion between the IMF staff and representatives of individual member countries concerning the member's economic and financial policies. The basis for these discussions is in Article IV of the IMF Articles of Agreement (as amended, effective 1978) which direct the Fund to exercise firm surveillance over each member's exchange rate policies" (IMF 2006).

© Springer Nature Singapore Pte Ltd. 2020

H. A. Clark, *Beyond Borders, Beyond Banking*,
https://doi.org/10.1007/978-981-15-1687-0_4

A noted microfinance analyst offered another warning, noting how Cambodia's competitive retail microcredit market may have reached a saturation point.[3] As early as 2015, Rozas called for implementing measures to slow down the rapid pace of microfinance institutional expansion. Yet, Cambodia continued to face the same challenge in 2018, and it continued unabated in 2019.

A view of the competitive market is summarized in extensive research by MIMOSA together with the CMA.[4]

> In 2005 when Cambodia's financial sector took off, it was deeply under-developed, and the rapid growth was playing catch up. For over a decade, that worked perfectly well, but what seems clear at this point is that not only has Cambodia caught up with its peers, but for the past several years it has been surpassing them along nearly every possible indicator of penetration and growth.
>
> For institutions that grew up in this environment, the expectations of that growth are now deeply ingrained. Yet it is a mathematical certainty that at some point Cambodia's financial sector will have to slow down. It's simply not possible for credit to grow five times faster than GDP, without at some point hitting a wall.
>
> And hitting the wall will be a lot more painful than hitting the brakes… (Rozas 2016a)

4.1.1 *Five Factors for Concern*

More often than not, from 2016 and increasingly throughout 2018 and 2019, participants in Cambodia's financial system have expressed concern over five factors. These dynamics, if not held in check, may serve to create the conditions for a "perfect storm" in the financial sector. Acting together, such dynamics could combine to undermine the last 15 years of progress made throughout the banking sector, including microfinance.

The center of the perfect storm is in the microcredit sub-sector of the financial system. This sub-sector includes people who can least afford to absorb more risk and the microfinance institutions and banks that serve them.

The five critical factors are:

1. Proliferation of small credit providers at the bottom of the pyramid
2. The system's capacity to absorb more debt nearing the breaking point
3. Interest rate caps fueling expansive borrowing
4. Mergers and acquisitions at the top of the pyramid
5. Taxation Targets

---

[3] Market saturation in this context is best described as follows: "In an increasing number of markets around the world, microcredit has been so successful that the supply of it is catching up with the demand for it. In other words, markets are approaching saturation" (Rosenberg 2011).

[4] MIMOSA, the Microfinance Index of Market Outreach and Saturation, is a tool to measure capacity and saturation levels in markets.

This chapter continues the discussion begun in Chap. 3 by taking a deeper look at each of the five areas mentioned above and their potential to weaken Cambodia's financial system and undermine its inclusivity. Each issue is analyzed by examining the history, the current state of events, and some likely outcomes for the future if no changes are made. Will these areas contribute to the future health of the financial system or serve to destabilize it?

The chapter includes lessons from prior microcredit-led debt crises from selected countries and how they were resolved. It also includes some important lessons from policy makers from these countries who offer advice that they wish was available to them at the time.

4.2 Proliferation of Small Credit Operators at the "Bottom of the Pyramid"

There are a great number of credit organizations entering the Kingdom at a rapid pace.[5] They target customers at the "bottom of the pyramid." While some experts say there are too many players, others claim that small semiformal providers serve communities where formal financial institutions fear to tread or lack the timely delivery of appropriate products most needed by rural households.

Some of the small, local NGOs, rural credit operators and moneylenders are only registered with the National Bank of Cambodia (NBC)—not licensed or regulated by the NBC. These small, mostly rural operators are loosely responsible to report to the NBC on a quarterly basis. While there are light-touch reporting requirements, once registered, there is no ongoing supervision, expectation of compliance with regulations, or enforcement of the rules by the NBC. However, these rules and regulations are applied strictly by the NBC to licensed MFIs and microfinance deposit-taking institutions (MDIs).

Who Are the Small Credit Providers? Generally, small credit providers are not NGOs with a social mission or community-owned organizations as broadly recognized globally and in Cambodia, although there are exceptions. The majority are consumer lenders, and they range from middlemen operating in the agricultural sector to small operators in local markets loaning cash to vendors for a short period of time, such as daily or weekly to ease cash flow problems or consumer lenders offering rent-for-purchase deals for household durables.

As early as 2016, online lenders emerged based on "Peer 2 Peer (P2P)" arrangements or simply offering loans by sending SMS messages through mobile phone

[5] For an estimation of the number of credit organizations, see Chapter 3, Fig. 3.3 A Decade of Growth: MFIs and Credit Providers Registered and Reporting; Not Registered and Not Reporting.

networks or through P2P lending platforms.[6] These lending sources offer quick loans, promising there is no collateral or documentation required. In Cambodia, these lenders have not been licensed by the Central Bank, even though several operators of such schemes have requested NBC recognition. Rather, the NBC has provided warnings to the public about the illegality of these operations and the absence of consumer recourse in cases of fraud or loss.

Big Worries About Small Operators A main concern regarding these small providers—both registered NGOs and Rural Credit Operators—is that they are conferred legitimacy due to the recognition conveyed by the NBC. However, increasing numbers of small lenders continue to operate under the radar. This segment of financial services providers (FSPs) is often held responsible for issuing multiple loans and ignoring the law regarding credit bureau consultation.

Credit bureau consultation for every loan issued or refinanced is a requirement for lenders regulated by the Central Bank in Cambodia. The new type of mobile lenders located only on the Internet and claiming to provide "instant cash" can do so quickly. The NBC has adopted a "Buyer Beware" policy and communicates warnings to the general public through the press and special announcements to the public.

An Innovative Policy for the Time One of Cambodia's most innovative policies for its time—two decades ago—was allowing the emergence of a number of small credit operators in rural areas by removing regulatory restrictions. With fewer regulatory restrictions during the last two decades, this policy and subsequent supportive regulations allowed newly regulated FSPs to join the formal financial system as shown in Chap. 3, Fig. 3.3. The past policy fostered law-abiding financial market dynamism.

In the past 5 years, however, the NBC policy has encouraged increasing numbers of new entrants into the financial market that operate entirely under the regulatory radar as demonstrated in Fig. 3.3 in Chap. 3.

The continuation of the policy unabated—and unsupervised—has had the unintentional and undesirable opposite effect of undermining the sector's law abiding and transparent reputation. For example, it appears to have created an enabling environment for multiple lending to clients under the official regulatory radar. Such a policy could very well result in a greater potential for system-wide over-indebtedness, particularly for the most vulnerable consumers.

A Call to Action Astounded by the growth trends in the number of small NGOs and rural credit providers that emerged by 2016, the NBC began to take steps to

[6]As an illustration, China's online P2P lending platforms have a checkered history. According to research by China International Capital Corporation, experts predicted only 10% of the current P2P lending companies that survived the crisis from 2016 to 2018 less than 200 would still be in business after 3 years (Liu 2018).

counteract potentially damaging effects. In 2015, much to the NBC's surprise, 316 small NGOs and associations came forward to be registered after an NBC circular stating readiness to accept licensing was sent to authorities in one province. The NBC approved registration for only 65 such small operators after an on-site review of who they were and what they did.

Later that same year, the NBC called a moratorium on receiving further applications for microfinance operators or rural credit operator registration. The reason was "in order to ensure the quality, accuracy, and accountability of the licensing role of the NBC" (NBC 2015).

In January 2018 the NBC revoked the licenses of 11 rural credit operators and, earlier in 2017, fined 17 small licensed MFIs for non-compliance with the law. The Cambodia Microfinance Association (CMA) noted that these MFIs were not CMA members. CMA applauded the actions of the NBC as positive developments for the industry, "as organizations that were seriously non-compliant with the law were sanctioned" (Hor Kimsay 2018a, b).

4.3 The System Capacity to Absorb More Debt Nears the Breaking Point

The positive development of ready access to financial services also enabled customers to more easily borrow from multiple sources and in larger amounts. It is still a matter of debate whether or not the majority—or just a small segment of these customers—can afford loans from multiple sources as they bump up against loan limits of one lender and then borrow from another.

This section about the "dynamics of growth" addresses the following questions. Are borrowers able to handle increasing debt from many lending sources at once? Are borrowers able to manage cash flow from many repayment sources? Is the Cambodian form of loan consolidation a good option to prevent further debt stress? Has the interest rate cap in the micro-lending market tended to alleviate the problem of over-indebtedness or contribute to it?

4.3.1 Tracking the Evidence

4.3.1.1 Traditional Measurement Inadequate to Detect Early Warning Signs

The most common standard financial measures for detecting debt stress in the system and for individual credit providers are the portfolio-at-risk (PAR) and loan loss ratios. Financial analysts point out, in situations of rapid and significant growth of the credit portfolio, both of these ratios are less accurate indicators because the bottom half of the equation is growing rapidly, while the numerator grows more slowly. In fact, in conditions of rapid growth, the portfolio may even look healthier than before, hiding even more significant risk.

Experts also note that "when a credit market is growing rapidly, the increased supply of loans and high household liquidity may disguise actual levels of debt stress: defaults may be relatively low for a time, even when debt stress may be reaching unsustainable levels. Regulators are often unaware of the extent of debt stress until it is too late to take preventative measures" (Davel 2013). In other words, "it is impossible to prove that a bubble exists while one is still in it -–the best one can do is point to data that suggests it may be happening" (Rozas 2016a, b, c).

A more reliable measurement using five data points suggests debt stress in the credit market. Traditional financial measures used to detect the early warning signs of a debt crisis are not as accurate in times of rapid and significant growth of the credit portfolios. At these times the analysis is supplemented with other indicators. Five supplemental data points are:

1. Levels of borrower difficulty in meeting financial commitments (using consumer research)
2. Aggressive competition: rapid increases in average loan sizes
3. Aggressive competition: rapid increases in micro lenders' portfolios outstanding
4. The average size of loans outstanding compared to Cambodia's GDP per capita growth
5. Growing incidence of multiple borrowing and multiple sources lending to one borrower

The experience from other countries that have previously experienced significant debt stress that reached crisis proportions is integrated in the discussion on supplemental data points (where relevant) as other country's experience is important even though the circumstances, market, and history may be very different.

This section concludes with a discussion of how the interest rate cap fuels over-borrowing and contributes to debt stress, rather than acting as a policy action to "curb debt stress."

4.3.1.2 Borrower Difficulty Meeting Financial Commitments

Observers of Cambodia's financial system note that a significant number of borrowers may be advancing closer to becoming over-indebted.

FinScope Survey Results in Cambodia (FinScope 2015, 2016)
The FinScope survey conducted in Cambodia in 2015 noted that 35% of respondents expressed that it was *very difficult* to keep up with financial commitments, while 57% noted it was *difficult*, and only 7% found it *easy*.

These findings speak for themselves. By 2015, the level of borrower difficulty in meeting their financial commitments was worrisome. These findings were circulated at least 2 years before the interest rate cap on micro loans went into effect. The effect that such a cap had was to ensure more credit could be obtained at a lower cost (discussed in depth below).[7]

4.3.1.3 Aggressive Competition: Number of Microcredit Loans Outstanding

Cambodia is home to a somewhat unique microcredit market. The market quickly reached a saturation point in a fairly limited market size within 20 years of professional growth within the industry.

Over the past decade, average loan sizes increased as licensed lenders competed aggressively for each other's customers, and the number of unlicensed credit providers operating under the radar expanded tremendously. See Chap. 3, Figure 3.3.

According to financial system experts who have experienced over-indebtedness crises in their own countries, increasing average loan size brought on by aggressive competition among lenders and a significant number of lenders operating under the radar are two early warning signs that the financial system may be reaching unsustainable levels of debt stress (Davel 2013).

One sign that the microcredit market is saturated is demonstrated by analyzing the ratio of the number of MFI loans outstanding to the population of the country (Chen et al. 2010). In Cambodia that number increased above 10% of the population from 2013 to 2017. This measure is considered a marker for market saturation and indicative of asset quality problems brought on by competition. See Fig. 4.1

Cambodia shows a relatively higher figure than several microcredit markets that experienced major credit crises, such as Bolivia, Peru, Mexico, Indonesia, and the Philippines (Loeung and Tep 2018). Cambodia also has a younger population than the comparison group of countries, suggesting that asset quality problems may be higher than the data suggest, as Cambodia's population is youthful and the adult population eligible for credit is a more limited population.[8]

---

[7] A discussion of the effects of the interest rate cap on promoting over-indebtedness is presented in Sect. 4.3 and Sect. 4.4.

[8] The figure is more striking when compared to the adult population. In 2018, Cambodia's adult population above the age of 20 years was only 58.9% of the population or 9,614,808 of a total population of 16.3 million.

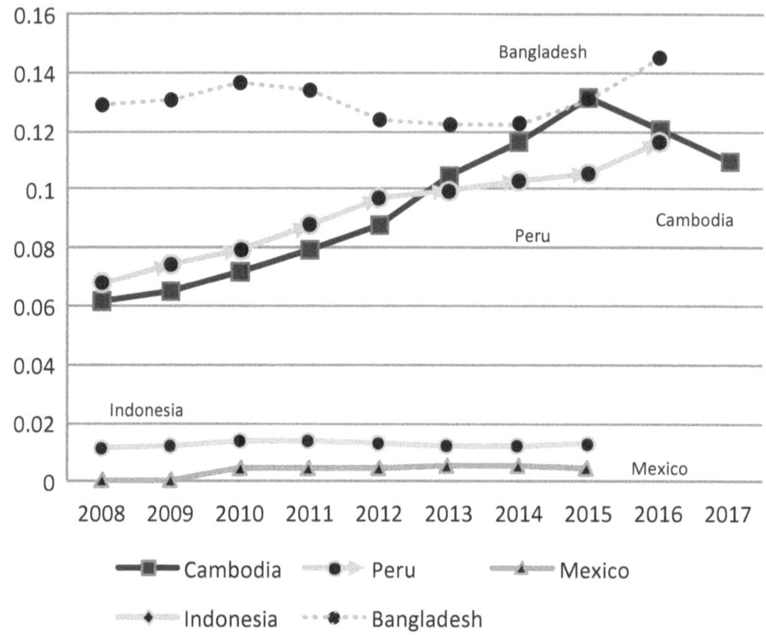

Fig. 4.1 Ratio: number of micro loans outstanding to Cambodian population size and comparison countries
Source: Loeung Sopheap and Tep Bunthoeun (2018)

4.3.1.4 Aggressive Competition: Rapid Growth in Loan Size and MFI Portfolio Size

Recent research of the MIMOSA Project (Microfinance Index of Market Outreach and Saturation) and the Cambodia Microfinance Association reveals that micro-debt in Cambodia has skyrocketed. According to MIMOSA analysis, the average micro-loan size in Cambodia is among the highest in the world, growing from USD 200 to USD 1000 in the decade from 2004 to 2014. And, to date, aggressive competition continues unabated. The average loan outstanding of MFIs in Cambodia increased from USD 328 in 2008 to USD 2429 by the end of 2017 (Loeung and Tep 2018). See Fig. 4.2.

This growth is driven by a number of factors. First, the growing economy and the advancement of technology and business acumen have enabled customers' businesses to start up, develop, and expand. Customer confidence in the banking sector is also a growth factor, as more people use and benefit from a growing and well-regulated banking sector. However, competition within the banking sector and among MFIs and banks that serve the lower segments of the market in a relatively small market has narrowed FSP opportunities to expand to "unbanked" customers.

Finally, many MFIs use loan officer incentive systems that reward quantity over quality. As a result, credit officers increase loan sizes for their existing customers

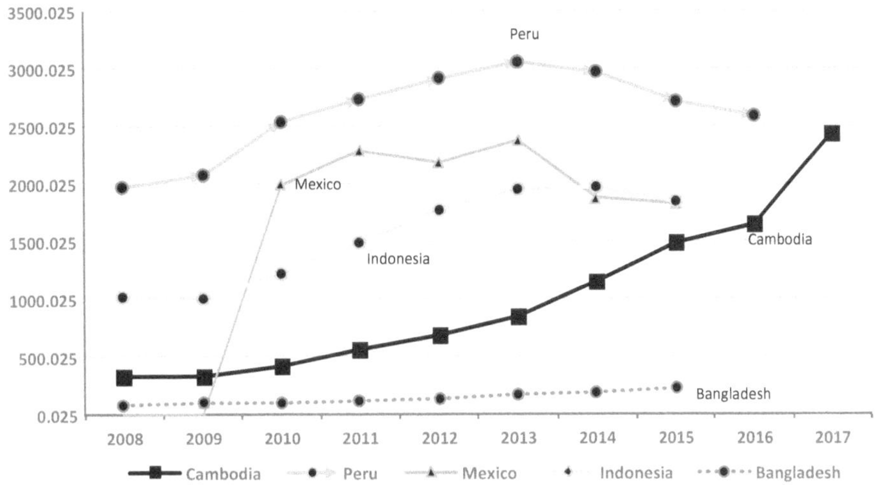

Fig. 4.2 Average loan outstanding: MFIs in Cambodia (2008–2017) and comparison countries
Source: Loeung Sopheap and Tep Bunthoeun (2018)

and recruit new customers, often by poaching them from other institutions with an offer of increased loan amounts. Credit officer incentives need urgent revision in light of the micro-loan context of growing over-indebtedness (Ibid.).

The growth of total loans outstanding averaged 40% for Cambodian MFIs over the 10-year period, 2008–2017. Growth ranged from a high of 79% growth of the portfolio outstanding in 2008 to a low of 3% in 2009 and again in 2016. Growth rebounded in 2017 at 35% after the downturn in 2016. The average portfolio growth figure is higher than for those countries in comparable markets with large microfinance market segments like Peru, Mexico, Indonesia, and Bangladesh. See Fig. 4.3.

The recent and most alarming growth in the MFI sector portfolios is most likely driven entirely by the interest rate cap effective since April 1, 2018.[9]

4.3.1.5 Average Loan Outstanding to GDP Per Capita

The trend in the average loan outstanding to GDP per capita is a critical data point to review as a solid indicator of possible debt stress. Such a data point becomes even more critical when compared to other countries with large microfinance markets, and higher GDP per capita, such as Indonesia, Peru, Mexico, and Bangladesh. The average loan outstanding to GDP per capita issued by MFIs in Cambodia has sharply increased from 43.19% in 2008 to 170.72% in 2017, as shown in Fig. 4.4. This indicates that the growth in loan size is roughly four times the pace of growth in Cambodia's average per capita income from 2004 to 2014.

[9] The effects of the interest rate cap on portfolio expansion are explored later in this section.

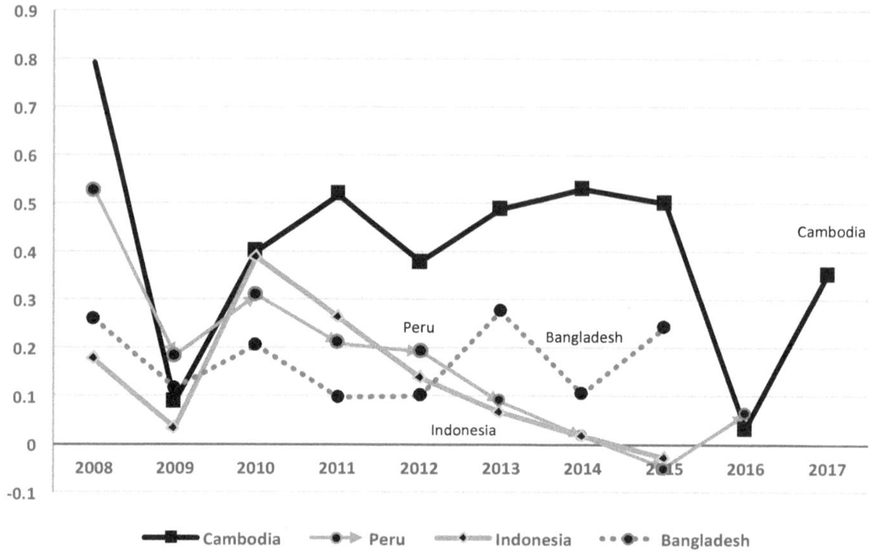

Fig. 4.3 Yearly average % growth of total loans outstanding (2008–2017 year on year and comparison countries
Source: Loeung Sopheap and Tep Bunthoeun (2018)

> A typical microfinance loan in Cambodia has grown from 0.54 of per capita gross national income (GNI) in 2003 to 2.2 per capita GNI in 2014. In other words, loan sizes have grown four times faster than client incomes (MIMOSA 2015).

According to the National Bank of Cambodia, borrowing continues at a high pace. There were 2.69 million people, including 1.75 million microfinance customers, who held the equivalent of USD 3.9 billion in borrowed funds during 2017 (NBC 2018). Loans are growing fast, but by the end of 2017 deposits exceeded borrowing, with 4.5 million depositors entrusting 76,778 billion Riel for the safekeeping of regulated financial institutions.[10]

Even though borrowers and savers are generally two different groups of people in any financial system, the level of deposits is an important indicator of the population's confidence in the banking sector. Despite the growing concerns about over indebtedness in the microfinance sub-sector of the banking system, confidence in the financial system appears to be high.

[10] See Chap. 3 for more detail on total borrowers and depositors and trends over time.

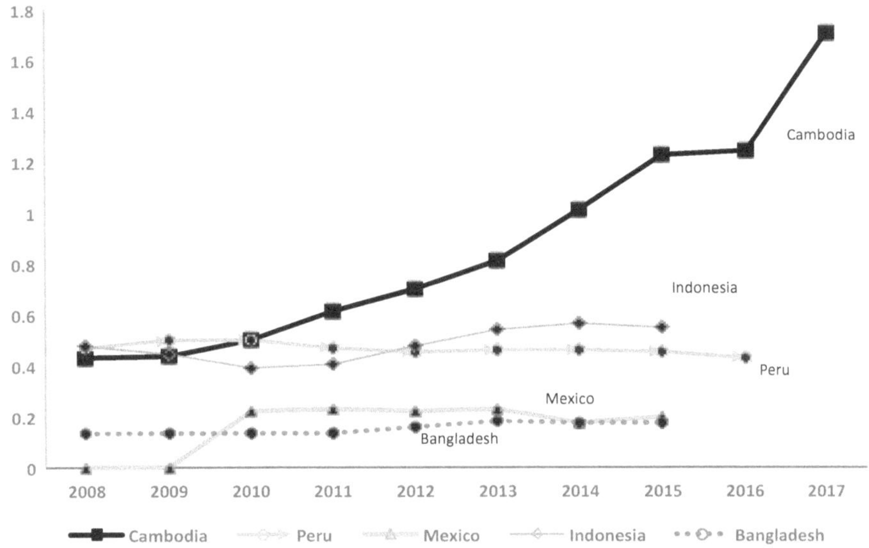

Fig. 4.4 Average micro loan outstanding to GDP per capita (2008–2017) and comparison countries
Source: Loeung Sopheap and Tep Bunthoeun (2018)

4.3.1.6 Multiple Borrowing

Finally, one of the most worrisome data points in any lending market is the incidence of customers borrowing from multiple lenders. Multiple borrowing—if known and tracked— can be a strong indicator of borrower debt stress. Debt crises particularly in the microcredit market, in countries such as in Bolivia, Peru, Mexico, and Bangladesh, began with customers who borrowed from multiple institutions and quickly exceeded their repayment capacity. In some cases, it involved clients who borrowed as many as four to five loans at the same time that they were unable or unwilling to repay (Loeung and Tep 2018).

In Cambodia, even the most conservative lenders indicate that close to 20% of their loan customers have outstanding loan balances with two to five other lenders. In this regard, the Credit Bureau of Cambodia provides an important risk management service in an overheated credit market. This data point could be interpreted in a couple of ways: it may simply indicate the number of borrowers who can afford to borrow from different sources for different purposes. In this scenario, borrowers are working around an MFI's strict loan limits, and they can afford additional debt.

Borrowing from multiple lenders also can be an indicator of debt stress, particularly if the borrower is engaged in borrowing from a new lender to pay off a debt with the current lender. The Bolivians call this behavior "bicycling," and its wide spread use in Bolivia in 1999 was blamed for sparking a nationwide debt crisis that started within the micro and small enterprise credit sector (Rhyne 2001).

4.3.2 The Unique Dynamics of Cambodia's Micro-lending Market

Fortunately, analysts who have been tracking the situation are closer to understanding the dynamics of the current microfinance debt market with the assistance of the Credit Bureau of Cambodia (CBC) data and the Cambodia Microfinance Association's (CMA) Lender Guidelines Project with MIMOSA (Microfinance Index of Market Outreach and Saturation).

The next big step for Cambodian MFIs and retail financial institutions is to put into practice less aggressive growth tactics and place more emphasis on portfolio quality and reasonable and responsible growth. Borrowers may also need additional support from their FSPs and tools to manage growing debt stress. And, the recent research breakthrough, as noted below, may enable financial sector participants to accomplish this goal.

4.3.2.1 A Different Pattern of Over-indebtedness

The CMA MIMOSA research, noted above, discovered a breakthrough in understanding the current dynamics of the Cambodian micro-loan market. The joint CMA-MIMOSA effort was "particularly concerned that frequent refinancing of loans with much larger loans–often by competing lenders 'poaching' clients–was a major reason for both the growth in loan size and for the relatively low level of multiple borrowing" (Rozas 2016a, b, c). The pattern in Cambodia is different than the more common signaling of systemic debt stress or impending over-indebtedness in the microcredit market, when customers borrow multiple small amounts from many lenders.

The research partners learned that some MFI lenders were consolidating the outstanding loans of borrowers who held as many as four or five loans from a variety of lenders. The new lender issued one much larger loan to pay off the customer's existing loan balances from other lenders. In doing so, they provided the customer an incentive to become a dedicated borrower of the new company. In an industry-wide analysis of many MFI reports, these actions look more similar to debt consolidation, showing much larger loan amounts and fewer small loans outstanding.

This practice initially masked[11] the traditional indicator of "multiple borrowing" by customers as a signal of systemic debt stress or impending over-indebtedness in the microfinance market (Rozas 2016c, 2017). In Cambodia, the average loan size was increasing at a time when 93% of borrowers were finding it either difficult or extremely difficult to manage their financial commitments (FinScope 2015, 2016) and loan sizes had grown four times faster than client incomes (Rozas 2016a, b, c).

[11] There was no evidence of regulated lenders ignoring the required credit bureau consultations to detect multiple borrowing or to report new loan activity.

The Importance of Domestic and International Remittances Upon greater scrutiny, the dynamics of loan repayment and the "capacity to pay" assessment also became clearer. Even the most aggressive—but law-abiding lender—would not lend in amounts unwarranted by micro and small enterprise growth. Yet, micro and small enterprise growth or household enterprises did not seem to warrant such dramatic increases in loan sizes. What was happening?

The research showed evidence that over the past 5 years, since 2013, the microfinance market has increasingly come to rely on the growth in both domestic and international remittances to support the growth of microfinance loans. "Domestic remittances have become a major—if not the primary—source of MFI loan repayments, at least in the provinces of Kampong Speu and Takeo that adjoin Phnom Penh. These two provinces are also among the most credit-saturated areas in the country" (Rozas 2016a, b, c).

By the end of 2017, one out of ten people in the Cambodian labor force worked abroad. In 2017, remittances from abroad soared to USD 900 million, equivalent to 4.5% of Cambodia's GDP in 2017 (Chheng 2018).[12]

Even though this new dynamic in loan assessment is heartening to some MFIs and customers, it also means that the repayment of debt is not based on the income from the enterprise the loan is intended to support. Loan assessment of the capacity of the borrower to repay is a fundamental principle that contributed to the success of microfinance. MFIs have developed policies and staff capacity to assess repayment capacity and risk within the micro and small enterprise segments of the market.

The new dynamics within the economy introduce a new risk assessment factor, particularly if the assessment is not adjusted to account for new dynamics. The loan repayment—or default—is dependent on the health of the garment industry, small appliance assembly factories, and the construction sectors within Cambodia, and international remittances sent from Cambodians working abroad, and the health of those economies.

4.4 The Interest Rate Cap on Microcredit Fuels Expansive Borrowing

A Surprise Announcement: March 14, 2017

What happened on March 14, 2017, was not easily predicted; nor was it a surprise for most of the global microfinance industry that always expects heightened political influence on their operations that are considered "low hanging fruit" during an election period.

The headline in *The Phnom Penh Post* on March 14, 2017, read:

MFI loan interest capped.

The announcement was hardly sensational; it was rather blunt and to the point.

---

[12] See Chap. 2 for a discussion of domestic and international remittances and their growth in the past decade.

4.4.1 The Market in Cambodia Worked Well to Lower Micro-lending Interest Rates

Regardless of any political imperative, research from around the world, including Cambodia, shows that liberalized interest rates tend to decrease overtime—and sometimes quite rapidly. This happens when the financial system has two elements. The first element is a credible and enforced Truth in Lending Law (TIL), as there is in Cambodia. The second element is increasingly fair competition in the marketplace.

In fact, most analysts would argue that these two elements are mutually supportive and lead to healthy market growth that benefits customers and financial services providers. The Cambodian market had both of these features and showed how interest rates declined rapidly over 15 years.

Figure 3.10 in Chap. 3 shows how the market interest rate decreased over a 15-year period within the microfinance industry in Cambodia. Table 4.1 shows the approximate dates, the rates, and the reason for interest rate decline in Cambodia over time. This is a lesson in how the market worked in Cambodia. And, in fact, the market worked very well to lower interest rates in Cambodia in recent years.

Most countries would celebrate how Cambodia's market forces worked so well in reducing the interest rate without government intervention. With Government intervention it is expensive to manage both oversight and prosecution of violations. And if the interest rate cap is serious, resources have to be dedicated to ensuring proper oversight at all levels of the system, including informal lenders in rural areas. The NBC recognized it did not have the capacity to supervise small financial

Table 4.1 Micro-lending interest rates decline over time

Date	Interest rate (per annum)	Reason
Prior to 2000	60% +	No competition
		Few providers
		No market sensibility
		High demand for microcredit
2000 TIL (Truth in Lending Law)	Decreased to 48% overnight	Truth in lending law established
2005	48–40%	Competition increases
2010–2015	28–20%	Market coverage increases Competition increases
		Borrowers have more options
2017	18%	Political mandate

services providers in rural areas throughout the country even prior to the surprise promulgation of the 18% interest rate cap on micro loans.[13]

4.4.2 Do Interest Rate Caps Strengthen the Market for Borrowers and Lenders?

Interest rate caps are a very politically popular policy even though experience shows that an interest rate cap below the cost of credit operations has a stunting effect on the market, dulling transparency and heightening deceptive transactions.

Hardest hit is access to the smallest loans for the lower segments of the market—especially in difficult to reach rural areas. Micro loans disappear gradually as they are the most costly for MFIs to manage well. Microfinance institutions withdraw gradually from the rural segment of the small loans market, as they find it more difficult to offer micro loans at the price required by the interest rate cap.

An interest cap below the market rate encourages more people to borrow in greater amounts, simply because the credit is cheaper. As noted above, this is exactly the dynamic that appeals to lenders as evidenced by the larger loan size per borrower within Cambodia's microfinance institutions. In Cambodia's microcredit market where debt stress in the lower segments of the market is already considered a threat, the consequences of the interest rate cap have been to increase over-indebtedness among segments of the microfinance market.

By early 2017, Cambodia was already headed for an over-indebtedness crisis in the lower segments of the market, particularly in rural areas. And, many experts—both local and foreign—were concerned with over-indebtedness in the market at that time, advocating for the implementation of preventative measures. The interest rate cap fueled a smoldering indebtedness crisis in a highly competitive microcredit market by making credit cheaper.

A recent study published by the World Bank noted, "Due to the introduction of the interest rate cap, the number of loans of USD 500 or less declined by 48 percent. Notably, the proportion of households in the first quintile—the poorest— who borrowed from an informal source increased by 5 percentage points in 2017. Meanwhile, microfinance sector lending grew by 53% in the last 3 quarters of 2017 compared to a similar period in 2016. Loan size increased by an average of USD 1,200 and USD 240 for microfinance deposit-taking institutions (MDIs) and MFIs, respectively" (Pimhidzai et al. 2019).

Who Loses Most with an Interest Rate Cap? People with low and erratic incomes who live in remote rural areas will lose the most. Competition is not as robust in rural areas as it is in urban areas, and the products are more expensive to deliver,

[13] See the discussion above in this chapter on Proliferation of Small Credit Operators at the Bottom of the Pyramid.

including maintaining a presence through a branch or a post, or frequent visits by MFI staff.

The interest rate cap is likely to limit growth of new microfinance customers, as these customers are more expensive to serve. Clients who have not yet established a track record or a credit history elsewhere will also lose. The cap penalizes the new generation of clients who are often better positioned to succeed than their parents. As costs increase with perceived higher risk, young entrepreneurs with great ideas and no cash also lose; women financing their children's education lose; and start-up businesses lose.

Experts from Cambodian MFIs say the big losers on the supply side of the market will be the small and mid-size MFIs that legitimately serve the rural areas. These MFIs are not deposit-taking MFIs, so their cost of funds is often high, in addition to the higher costs of rural operations, such as maintaining generators and transportation. These costs are much lower for their urban counterparts, even though other costs are higher, such as rent and salaries.

Finally, the ones who will lose the most are families and businessmen and women who already carry a debt burden, but are not yet over-indebted. They have managed to stay afloat, but for how long?

Who Benefits Most from an Interest Rate Cap? The unregistered illegal money lending operations are the big winners. Most of them remain outside the NBC's supervisory authority. Nor do they follow Cambodia's rules mandating use of the credit bureau, pricing transparency, or industry standards, such as ethical practices regarding preventing over-indebtedness and debt collection practices. When a payment is due to a legitimate MFI, and the borrower does not have the money to cover the principle, she will go to a moneylender to borrow the amount to pay the MFI, at a much higher rate than the cap dictates.

According to industry estimates, there are at least 500–800 such operators that have set up shop in the past decade. It is rumored that there are many new entrants in this market, as a business can easily be established without any legal or regulatory repercussions that fall under NBC authority.

4.4.3 Market Research Around the World

Extensive multi-country research by the Asian Development Bank on the effect of interest rate ceilings arrived at the following conclusions.

> Thus, the repression of financial markets via interest rate restrictions and regulations may be a politically attractive choice, offering freedom from high interest rates for low-income families, but it is rarely an effective one….
>
> Not only does it result in the exclusion of the lowest-income, highest-risk segments of the community, those whom the politicians (and general public) most want to protect, it also

promotes obfuscation and circumvention in financial pricing. The net result is reduced transparency in the market, and the consequent confusion in pricing results in loss of sovereignty for the consumer. To that extent, interest rate repression actually leads to a loss of financial freedom. (ADB 2016)

4.4.4 Interest Rate Caps as a Tool to Curb Debt Stress

From another corner of the world, experience shows that interest rate caps are considered a damaging tool to curb debt stress. Curbing debt stress is an issue of concern to Cambodian authorities and financial sector participants alike.

> Many countries have implemented interest rate controls as part of a package of regulatory interventions to curb debt stress, with the intention to prevent borrower exploitation or to avoid a high interest rate environment that can incentivize over-aggressive lending. However, a simplistic or misguided approach to interest-rate control can do damage to credit supply and can limit access to finance. These disadvantages may well outweigh its benefits in curbing over-indebtedness. (Davel 2013)

> The priority must be to identify and regulate market practices that create incentives that increase the risk of over-indebtedness. This includes practices that reduce a lender's incentive to do an affordability assessment, or elevate fees to a level where they increase the profitability of lending to consumers who are already, or are at immediate risk of becoming, highly indebted. (Davel 2013)

4.4.5 Interest Rate Cap Performance After Two Years of Implementation

A little over 2 years later, it is interesting to see how the predicted trends within the Cambodian microfinance market turned out. In fact, 9 months later, time enough for customers and providers to have felt the early effects of the interest rate cap, the 2017 end of year data in the NBC Annual Report show strong trends in one direction.

According to the NBC's 2017 Annual Report, the total number of people with outstanding microfinance loans decreased from 1.9 million borrowers at the end of 2016 to 1.75 million at the end of 2017. Yet, the total volume of loans in the MFI sector grew by 25% in 2017 (Hor Kimsay 2018a, b; National Bank of Cambodia 2017).

This means that approximately 8% fewer microfinance clients borrowed 25% more money in larger loans in 2017 than during any time during 2016.

According to Cambodian industry experts fewer small loans were offered during 2017, due to the interest rate cap (Hor Kimsay 2018a, b). The average loan outstanding of MFIs in Cambodia increased from USD 328 in 2008 to USD 2,429 by the end of 2017 (Loeung and Tep 2018). See Figs. 4.2 and 4.3.

4.4.6 How Did the Interest Rate Cap Perform as "a Good Tool to Curb 'Debt Stress'?"

In 2018 the Cambodian banking sector moved the NPL ratio down to 2.2% of portfolio outstanding from the previous year when it stood at 2.4% (National Bank of Cambodia 2018, 2019). The NBC's Annual Report notes that nonperforming loans also grew in the microfinance sector during the year 2017, from 1.4% of portfolio outstanding at the end of 2016 to 2% of portfolio outstanding by the end of 2017 and down to 1.3% by the end of 2018. Yet, the worrisome trend in 2018 is a substantial increase in the amount of portfolio outstanding in the microfinance sector— greater than 25% over the end of 2017.

The percentages of NPLs are well within the "safety margin" for the microfinance industry overall. However, the increasing trend in the size of portfolio outstanding and the high rate of nonperforming loans within the non-deposit taking MFI sub-sector—6.5% and 5% for 2017 and 2018, respectively—are causes for increased vigilance. In addition, the rural credit institutions that report to the NBC count over 200,000 loan accounts in 2018, and as a group they carried a nonperforming loan ratio of 11.9% at the end of 2018.

Borrowing from multiple sources has become a trend in the Cambodian microfinance market. This trend requires careful vigilance, particularly as loan size within the microfinance sector increased dramatically in 2017, and portfolio outstanding in the microfinance sector increased by 36% from 2016 to 2017, and again by an additional 21% as of the end of 2018.[14]

While the NPL ratio appears to be decreasing or staying the same, the portfolio outstanding is growing rapidly as noted above. Increasing loan sizes combined with the higher percentage of borrowers already experiencing debt stress—as indicated by increasing total amount of nonperforming loans—are two alarm bells that ought to have gone off long before the interest rate cap made it possible for borrowers to become increasingly over indebted.

As trends in nonperforming loans increase, the microfinance industry is definitely not experiencing less debt stress, nor does it appear to be positioned to do so under the current interest rate ceiling. As predicted, the interest rate cap appears to be promoting more debt stress as micro loans become less available and traditional micro-loan customers are encouraged to increase the amounts they borrow by MFIs and MDIs intent on holding market share in a highly competitive market.

What is clear is that the interest cap on micro loans is either forcing lenders out of the "micro-market," or forcing them to "lend up" to borrowers who may not be able to afford larger loan sizes. Two conclusions about the market's response to the interest rate cap can be drawn at this point in time. First, the interest rate cap influenced the supply of small loans to the market. Because small loans are more expensive to provide, many lenders no longer offered the product to the market. Secondly,

[14] See previous section on increasing average loan size.

the market responded to the cap by issuing larger loan amounts to existing and new customers who already had borrowed and may have been experiencing debt stress. As the evidence shows, the market has responded to the restriction just as experts warned.[15]

The good news is that deposits at MFIs increased dramatically in 2017 and 2018, reaching USD 2 billion at the end of the year. This is a little more than a 35% increase over 2016, and the increase exceeds the lending growth rate during the same time period. This means Cambodians still have confidence in MFIs and the banking sector and that newly found prosperity is being translated into saving for future investment.

4.4.7 *Reversing the Trend*

It appears that an over-indebtedness crisis may have been averted by mid-2019. But, there is no evidence that the conditions have changed substantially that would argue for complacency. The conditions that would fuel such a crisis grow unabated. Financial sector analysts have stepped-up calls for caution among lenders.

They agree on the multiple factors that continue to support an overheated market that may lead to a debt crisis. These factors include cheap credit brought on by interest caps, larger loan sizes, intense competition, loan officer incentives with less focus on portfolio quality and more focus on portfolio growth, eroded capacity for borrowers to repay as evidenced by increasing amounts of nonperforming loans, and the increasing incidence of borrowers having to sell assets to make loan repayments.

4.4.7.1 Market Behavior Prior to the Interest Rate Cap

By mid-2016, prior to the interest rate cap in the micro-market, historical portfolio growth rates in Cambodia slowed far more than the average historic growth rates of over 20% per year. (See Figs. 4.2 and 4.3.) A number of reasons underpin this trend. First, there was a lower demand for credit throughout the economy due to lower rice prices.

Second, several MFIs instituted more prudent policies regarding growth and customer debt stress. During 2016, several MFIs grew more slowly than their historic performance due to lower demand and, more cautiously, due to more prudent policies regarding delinquency (Rozas 2017).

[15] See the results of the FinScope (2015, 2016) survey earlier in this chapter that noted in 2015 that 92% of borrowers participating in the survey expressed that it was very difficult (35%) or difficult (57%) to keep up with financial commitments. This is a good indicator for "debt stress."

At the time, there was no reason to ignore these early warning signs of growing over-indebtedness and debt stress in Cambodia's financial market. The signs seemed credible enough and built on thorough analysis of available data. Reading these signs correctly and action from the MFI industry may have helped to avert a crisis initially.

Going forward, the fundamental question that must be addressed to strengthen the industry is: Can the trend be reasonably reversed without sacrificing access to credit, which is so important to Cambodia's low-income population? In a highly competitive market are MFIs and their new owners, including a number of regional banks, willing to give up market share to avert a crisis brought on by a number of factors, including a policy decree issuing an interest rate cap that lowers the cost of microcredit.[16]

Reversing the trend of over-indebtedness starts with a regulator's dedication to monitor, interpret, and act on the early warning signs of rapid growth in the overall system or segments of it. These signs include trends in the expansion in the number of lenders, rapid growth in loan size or extension of loan terms, increasing rescheduling and refinancing, and increased arrears and default in the system (Davel 2013). The monitoring system should extend to all lenders, including those that operate under the radar, and focus on early warning signs for all segments of the market.

Second, perhaps two of the most important steps to reduce the likelihood of systemic crisis are reducing incentives to over-lend and increasing regulation or prohibition of high-risk market practices, such as abusive debt collections practices. Both practices have the potential to create a systemic crisis. These practices can inspire massive political movements, even when only a small number of people are initially affected (Davel 2013).

Such was the case in Andhra Pradesh state in India. In Nicaragua, the politically inspired "no pago!"[17] movement was the spark that caused street riots and, later, a leading microfinance bank to close its doors permanently (Center for Financial Inclusion 2011).

One main example of an incentive to over-lend and an incentive to over-borrow was found in the US housing market, which created the tipping point for the global financial crisis. Several unsound practices created the conditions for the "bubble to burst": banks lent large amounts of cheap credit that was backed by over-valued assets in a booming housing mortgage market within a weak regulatory environment.

[16] The next section focuses on mergers and acquisitions of Cambodian MFIs.

[17] "No pago!" (I won't pay!)

4.4.8 *Abating a Debt Crisis: Six Important Lessons from Cambodia So Far*

Lessons from MFIs inside Cambodia and beyond its borders in several very different microfinance markets emphasize how a tipping point for an over-indebtedness crisis is easily reached. The conditions that create a systemic crisis are a long period of rapid growth leading to market saturation, combined with other factors that weaken the market, such as intense competition and absence of a credit bureau, or lenders disregarding credit bureau information in the hopes that they will become the borrowers' priority for repayment over other lenders.

The financial crises in the Andhra Pradesh state of India, the countries of Bolivia[18], Bosnia and Herzegovina (BiH), Morocco, Nicaragua, and Pakistan, among others, experienced a microfinance over-indebtedness and repayment crisis after a period of high growth. At the time, each country was an important microfinance market in the respective regions.

Country studies reveal that the global economic recession was not a primary cause of the repayment crises, though it was among the various contextual factors affecting borrowers' repayment capacity. Instead, the case studies reveal that four vulnerabilities within the microfinance industry were responsible for the problems in their respective markets.

The four vulnerabilities were (1) concentrated market competition, (2) multiple borrowing from different MFIs, (3) overstretched MFI systems and controls, and (4) erosion of MFI lending discipline throughout the industry (Chen et al. 2010).

These studies offer early-stage interventions to address debt stress in the system. The big questions for Cambodia are: Will these practices be implemented in time, by "acting early"? Will the Cambodian market "act right"?

First: Ensure a rational and considered national response that can be applied broadly.

As noted earlier in this chapter, curtailing lending may seem to be a rational response for preventing over-indebtedness. However, the results of such a move will be more immediately seen with those borrowers who may be experiencing the most debt stress but are able to recover. Borrowers who are managing multiple loans will experience additional difficulty due to reduced availability of sources of funds to manage cash flow.

It is particularly important for people who are just managing cash flow from multiple lenders to have continued access to credit. This enables them to whittle down debt to manageable levels, before they begin to sell income-producing assets.

While most Cambodian microfinance providers are averse to rescheduling as a practice, there is a time and a place for rescheduling that benefits both the borrower

[18] The microfinance crisis in Bolivia occurred earlier in 1999; however the characteristics of the crisis are similar to others.

and the lending institution. And, Cambodia may reach "extra-ordinary times" when such measures are not only appropriate but also desirable. A policy can be just as restrictive as the organization wants it to be. A prudent organization ensures that a rescheduling policy, or a refinancing policy, is used appropriately, never over-used, and properly and accurately recorded following prudential regulation applied to higher-risk loans.

Second: Consult with other lenders and reduce the competitive barriers to cooperation.

There may also be a time when lenders need to collaborate on debt rescheduling for a borrower who has multiple loans from various institutions. Debt workout is in both the borrower's and the lenders' interests. Monitoring borrower's circumstances and setting up a debt management advisory system through a trusted and independent apolitical system are prudent actions in an overheated market. Some markets with high incidents of default, such as Bosnia and Herzegovina (BiH) in 2008–2009, established debt resolution centers within the private sector to advance mutually agreeable and reasonable plans of action between borrowers and lenders.[19]

Third: A corollary to "don't stop lending" is "don't cap interest rates" below levels that are unsustainable for financial services providers to offer the product to the market.

Setting such unrealistic rates effectively "stops lending" of a particular product—a small loan—to a particular segment of the market, that is, new clients and those who are more expensive to serve. This is generally the segment of the market that can least weather the lack of access to finance and the segment of the market that can least afford to take on larger loan sizes without experiencing debt stress or default. It takes some time for the market to see the effects of an interest rate cap. In Cambodia the market evidence was available by the end of 2017 as existing loans were repaid and new loans were issued in greater amounts or withheld.[20] By late 2018, the initial shockwave turned into an established trend.

Fourth: Lenders need to become more aware of the sources of loan repayment and how to assess them, including the dynamics of change over time.

Domestic remittances have become a major source of micro and small enterprise loan repayments, far from 10 years ago when most MFIs were re-writing their loan assessment policies to fit a growing market with many providers (Rozas 2017). A dramatic change in the sources of loan repayment should also inform MFIs to watch the dynamics of Cambodia's garment and construction sectors—the sources of most

[19] Bosnia experienced significant over-indebtedness in the micro and small lending market during the global financial crisis. One healthy response was setting up a debt resolution center involving multiple lenders in 2008–2009. To this day, the Bosnia and Herzegovina's Debt Advisory Center, an independent association, continues to provide debt counseling and financial education. The Center has become an important feature of the national financial system.

[20] See the previous section on interest rate caps for a more detailed discussion of this topic.

domestic remittances at this point in time. Even though the lender's portfolio is not directly exposed to the health of these sectors, the lenders' repayment is dependent upon them.

Fifth: Reasonable responses by MFIs and banks to an impending crisis are to lower growth targets and correct incentives.

A healthy response is to ensure growth targets are based on timely assessments of the market. Healthy portfolio growth incentives focus on the quality of the loan and portfolio, rather than the size of the loan and the size of the portfolio. Cambodian lenders should ensure these measures are an industry-wide standard way of doing business, far before a market begins to overheat. When these measures are relaxed, the spark is ignited.

Sixth: A healthy financial system consistently relies on the market's supporting functions[21] and requires all retailers to use them.

In this way, all customers and financial services providers—those who are regulated and those who are currently below the radar—are part of a functioning financial system. Financial services providers can ensure a robust financial sector infrastructure through quality participation in the supporting functions—including most importantly the Credit Bureau of Cambodia, the Cambodia Microfinance Association, and its counterpart in the sector, the Association of Banks in Cambodia.

The following advice emerges from Cambodia's recent experience in developing supporting functions to serve the long-term interests of the sector. The supporting functions have also been used to quell actions and help avert an impending crisis:

- Use of the Credit Bureau of Cambodia, including requiring mandatory participation of those providers that fall under the radar and consequences for non-compliance, is the most important first step.
- Consumer education, such as the NBC's "Lets Talk Money" financial education program, is a long-term investment in human capacity. In the short term, it offers borrowers and savers opportunities to learn more about financial services and how to protect themselves in an uneven relationship.
- The adoption of a Financial Consumer Protection Law, accompanied with practical guidelines for the industry, is a step to keep the industry healthy in the future. These could require specific codes of conduct regarding lending practices and acceptable debt collection practices.
- Customer complaints are often a source of information about irregularities that may prompt system-wide problems in the future. It may be prudent to "require that financial institutions establish internal complaints and recourse mechanisms and report complaints data to the regulator" (Davel 2013). As of September 2017, the NBC established a regulation requiring all banking and financial insti-

[21] For a review of the financial market's supporting functions refer to Chap. 3.

tutions under the supervisory authority of the NBC to establish internal complaints and recourse mechanisms and to strictly implement the regulation.[22]
- Finally, building action research partnerships, such as the CMA's Lender Guidelines Project with MIMOSA, allowed all parties to discover a break-through in understanding the current dynamics of the Cambodian microfinance loan market, particularly with respect to over-indebtedness. The research enables them to address the forces driving a potential national level debt crisis in the microcredit segment of the market, and to shore up practices with the objective of averting it.
- When national organizations work in concert with their international counterparts, such as MIMOSA, the Mix Market, and the Alliance for Financial Inclusion (AFI) at the policy level, an independent analysis is informed by experience in many places and under different or similar circumstances. This blended experience can hasten recognition of a problem and provide experience that may be helpful in solving the problem for the health of the industry and for the benefit of the country and its people.

4.4.9 Summary and Prospects

For the next few years, analysts might debate whether Cambodian FSPs implemented strategies that were "too little too late" or "just in time" to avert a looming crisis of over-indebtedness. Currently, as of mid-2019 all FSPs lending in the microcredit market are aware of the bubble—they are in it and they have evidence to prove it. They can try to resolve it as a joint action by the CMA and ABC, or they can continue on their own paths to gain market share.

A report on the Moroccan microfinance crisis of 2009 noted that ending the crisis recommended the following actions to MFIs: stepping up efforts on credit bureau data sharing; maintaining FSP liquidity during a period of crisis; ensuring staff is properly supported, both financially and with respect to management oversight regarding incentive systems that encourage reckless lending; and increasing interest rates to maintain profitability during a crisis (Chen et al. 2010).

In the case of Cambodia these recommendations are also relevant, particularly with respect to healthy attempts to drive down excessive borrowing brought on by low interest rates and ensuring organizational incentives do not promote reckless lending. Even though most of the corrective recommendations from the Moroccan crisis are already present in the Cambodian context, they are worth reiterating.

First, halting new licensing for new microfinance lenders seems to be a very good start in the right direction. Stepping up vigilance of this sector that remains under the radar, for the most part, is a similar early preventative measure of great importance. The legitimate microfinance sector applauds these actions, and the

[22] See Chap. 3, Sect. 3.3.5.3 for more details about complaints and recourse mechanisms and why they are important.

publicity surrounding them shows credible enforcement of the law after such a long moratorium without enforcement.

Insistence on credit bureau consultation should be strengthened, as well as instituting penalties for non-compliance. Ensuring more rigorous analysis of loan applications within the lender's operations, including giving priority to an analysis of the borrower's repayment capacity, is a high priority.

More thorough review and analysis of loan officer incentives to meet a plan that may serve as motivations to be less diligent with respect to loan discipline, such as an analysis of the borrowers' repayment capacity, should be implemented. These actions will enable the industry to verify and respond to credible signs that MFI lending discipline may be eroding throughout the industry.

Finally, the Cambodian microfinance industry, the regulators, and those who provide essential supporting functions must "act early and act right" as the debt crisis further develops. Preventing a crisis, as a viable option, gets more and more distant as the market continues to overheat. The regulator and financial services providers should emphasize planning to actively manage a debt crisis as a practical and worthwhile exercise for all parties involved, including for customers who will be hit the hardest.

4.5 Mergers and Acquisitions at the Top of the Pyramid

The policy of market openness has led to a series of mergers and acquisitions in the Cambodian financial market. This can be assessed as a positive market contribution, as foreign entrants may increase the overall professionalism of Cambodia's banking sector, particularly with ASEAN economic integration tentatively underway.

When the Bank of Ayudhya in Thailand and the Bank of East Asia in Hong Kong entered the market, they brought with them stellar reputations based on a high degree of professionalism and customer value in their home markets. However there are also banks that have entered the market that are owned by companies considered less than upstanding citizens in their own national markets.

There are differing views on the role of mergers and acquisitions (M&A) as practiced in Cambodia in contributing to the overall health and competitiveness of the financial sector. On the one hand, mergers and acquisitions can promote bringing in new systems, advanced technology, more professionalism in the banking sector, and new capacities for a growing sector.

In addition, an acquisition of a local MFI by a well-capitalized foreign bank can enhance macro-prudential measures within the system by meeting capital conservation buffer requirements,[23] for example, and mitigating financial stability risks, which are always concerns of the National Bank of Cambodia.

[23] As part of Basel III, the capital conservation buffer is designed to ensure that banks build up capital buffers outside periods of stress, which can be drawn down as losses are incurred. The requirement is based on simple capital conservation rules designed to avoid breaches of minimum capital requirements (Lekatis 2018).

On the other hand, M&A can have the unwanted consequences of undermining local management, ownership, and governance, affecting the future long-term health of Cambodia's banking system, and particularly the availability of financial services to the lower segments of the market in rural areas.

This section reviews Cambodia's recent experience with mergers and acquisitions and how the experience influences strengthening an inclusive financial market.

4.5.1 The First Merger and Acquisition: Sathapana Limited

The Kingdom's phenomenon of "mergers and acquisitions" started in 2012 with the Maruhan Japan Bank[24] acquisition of a majority stake in Sathapana, a leading microfinance deposit-taking institution (MDI). According to Maruhan Japan Bank:

> The acquisition of a majority stake in Sathapana Limited, one of Cambodia's leading microfinance institutions, positions us as the first ever Cambodian commercial bank to make a direct equity investment in a microfinance institution and, we hope, will contribute towards the breaking down of traditional barriers in the financial markets between the commercial banking and microfinance sectors. (Sathapana Bank 2017))

The microfinance community was surprised and perhaps even shocked at the time. Not so much because the offer was made, since everyone knew how well managed and profitable a business Sathapana was. The shocking part was due to the dilemma it presented: What to think about a company known for serving the gaming and entertainment industry in Japan when it acquired a home-grown microfinance institution in Cambodia that served small, medium and micro enterprises?

Reputational risk became an issue for the Sathapana shareholders at that time, as they were all socially responsible development investors. As responsible investors, they professed a commitment to ethical banking and to the ideal of a "responsible exit."

Several articles at the time questioned the intentions of the acquisition of Sathapana by Maruhan Japan Bank. They underscored the obligations and challenges existing shareholders have when assessing new buyers for the organization to ensure a responsible exit, as follows:

> One example of the challenge of assessing buyers is the case of Sathapana, a Cambodian MFI held by several social and development investors. The outside-the-ecosystem bidder in

[24] Maruhan Bank Japan was registered only in Cambodia. It is a Cambodian local bank with 100% Japanese ownership that began operating in Cambodia in 2008. There is no Maruhan Bank in Japan. Rather Maruhan Bank Japan, registered in Cambodia, is owned by "MARUHAN Corporation of Japan," founded in May 1957 by present Sathapana Chairman Dr. Han Chang-Woo, and is today the leading entertainment conglomerate in Japan" (Sathapana 2019). After the merger, the two institutions would be dissolved to create Sathapana Bank. According to Maruhan Bank Japan, at the time it had only one office globally, and that was in Cambodia. The operation was focused on wholesale lending and was the majority shareholder in Sathapana Limited, the MFI.

> that case was Maruhan Japan Bank (MJB), an existing commercial bank in Cambodia that was already lending to Sathapana and other MFIs.
>
> The bid was financially attractive and brought many strategic advantages. However, one concern that arose was that MJB, is wholly owned by Maruhan Corporation in Japan, whose business includes slot-machine gaming.
>
> To address this concern, the sellers requested a specific legal commitment from the parent company that the scope of its Cambodian operations would remain limited to the banking sector and would not extend into gaming. (Rozas 2014)

The analysts also noted that even though this deal was called a merger, in financial terms it was not. It was a 95.1% acquisition of Sathapana MDI's shares at the time.

Later in 2016, the acquired Sathapana MDI became Sathapana Bank Plc. with an appropriate injection of additional capital from Maruhan Japan Bank (MJB). It seemed only a matter of time before the more expensive and more difficult microfinance and small to medium enterprise finance model might lose its attraction for MJB and its parent company. To paraphrase analysts at the time: How would low-income customers and MSMEs fare within the newly organized Sathapana Bank?

Four years after the initial acquisition of Sathapana MDI, and less than 1 year after the banking license was conveyed, in November 2017, the board announced the creation of a newly branded Sathapana Bank Plc.:

> The new brand: "reflects the continuing evolution of the company to become the leading retail commercial bank in Cambodia as well as its aspirations for the future.... The launch of our new brand identity signals an important phase in the transformation of Sathapana Bank as we seek to appeal to a wider client base while remaining committed to make Cambodian people's lives better through our innovative, digital and tailor-made banking products and services as a commercial bank." (Norihiko 2017)

No one in the responsible finance industry was either shocked or surprised by the rapid transition away from the Sathapana MDI established strategy and customer base: a commercial transformation was more likely to be accompanied by mission drift than not, they believed.[25]

The responsible finance industry in Cambodia was only now becoming aware of what other micro-finance banks learned long before: ownership influences governance, and governance determines strategies, market focus, and staffing patterns. Independent directors on boards of banks and MFIs have gone a long way to strengthening a board's key monitoring function, enhancing corporate and management accountability. Governing boards, particularly the Board Chair, also know that management and governing boards cannot continue to disagree on the basics of the business without tearing the business apart.[26]

---

[25] The next chapter explores how a commercial transformation is not always accompanied by mission drift.

[26] This topic is explored more thoroughly in the Chaps. 5 and 6.

4.5.2 The Next Candidate: Thaneakea Phum Cambodia, Ltd.

The next candidate on the merger and acquisitions list was Thaneakea Phum Cambodia, Ltd. Thaneakea Phum Cambodia (TPC) was the first MFI in Cambodia to be certified in client protection by the Smart Campaign.[27] As a true visionary, TPC was acknowledged globally as an organization dedicated to client protection and customer financial education. Thaneakea Phum gained global recognition for its social responsibility and for trying to make the neighborhood bank model work, both as profit centers and organizations in their own right, legally owned by customers.

In 2014 LOLC (Lanka Orix Leasing Company) from Sri Lanka, and active in the region, acquired a 60% equity stake in the organization. Thaneakea Phum was re-banded as LOLC after its new parent company. DWM a US-based, socially responsible emerging markets fund manager retained a 36.97% stake, and the LOLC staff continue to hold the balance.

In this case the Cambodian CEO, schooled at ACLEDA Bank, leads LOLC just as LOLC brings expertise to the Cambodian market. So far the merger has redoubled efforts of both organizations to responsibly serve low-income people and those who own micro, small, and medium-sized enterprises. In this case, the interests of investors, the MFI, and the clients appear to have been balanced and well considered prior to the sale of the equity stake.

4.5.3 Then It Was Another MFI's Turn: Hattha Kaksekar Limited

Hattha Kaksekar (HKL)[28] was established in 1994, as a food security project for farmers in Pursat Province. Later it grew from a small agricultural lending operation to one of the largest and best run microfinance deposit taking institutions (MDIs) in Cambodia.

The HKL mission "is commitment to long-term social and financial sustainability and improving the income of its clients. HKL provides loans, savings and other inclusive financial services countrywide, in particular to women and low income families in rural areas" (HKL 2017). HKL never drifted from its core mission.

In 2016, The Bank of Ayudhya PCL (Krungsri Bank), which is backed by Japan's Tokyo Mitsubishi Financial Group, acquired 100% ownership of HKL. The acquisition process began in earnest in 2015. At the time, HKL was 60% owned by microfinance investment vehicles (MIVs) and another 20% by the HKL NGO and the HKL Staff Association.

[27] The Smart Campaign is a global initiative with financial leaders to practice financial consumer protection. The Campaign has a rigorous Certification program.

[28] In Khmer, "Hattha Kaksekar" means "Farmer's Hand" or "A Helping Hand for Farmers."

When the investment funds reached their closed-end time limits, it was impossible for the remaining shareholders to purchase the organization and carry out the future plan to become a commercial bank. HKL sought a strategic shareholder with a compatible mission, professional experience, and financial and organizational strength. They presumably found such a partner in the Bank of Ayudhya, which acquired a 100% ownership stake in HKL.

Would the HKL mission and focus change with new ownership? Would the Krungsri-HKL venture continue the HKL focus and mission or change the corporate image to serve the new owner's different brand or a more affluent clientele? HKL acquired a more reliable owner than the multiple investment funds during the merger and acquisition (M&A) process. It still remained to be seen whether or not the new owner would sacrifice the HKL mission and client focus.

Three years after the acquisition process began, the HKL mission throughout 2019 was the same. It emphasized social responsibility, customer satisfaction and client protection indicating that a true partnership had been formed. As Hout Ieng Tong, President and CEO of HKL, noted in early 2018:

> 2017 was a remarkable year for Hattha Kasekar Limited with a well-managed and competitive performance result in loan (both quantity and quality), deposit and other financial services initiatives. HKL has achieved significant milestones in intensive product development, risk management, compliance, collection, business development and staff capacity building, despite a strong competitive environment and prudential regulatory requirements.
>
> HKL is proud to mark the first anniversary of HKL-Krungsri integration, 'Stronger Together' with this achievement. (Hout 2018)

One key lesson that the HKL transformation provides is about the type of ownership that is more likely to emphasize good stewardship of the organization consistent with its core values. It is up to the Board to determine the optimal ownership based on core values and strategic vision well before seeking new owners and, in the case of HKL, well before the MIVs alerted the Board to the time limits and priorities of their investment funds.

In the meantime, the strategic vision to become a full service bank is shared by the management and the new owners. With shared vision between existing staff and new owners, added expertise, and dedication to serving the agricultural sector, HKL-Krungsri has the potential to serve the market well and for a long time to come.

4.5.4 *The Latest Change of Ownership in 2017: PRASAC MDI*

The last change in ownership in 2017 was the largest and most surprising due to the greater size of the PRASAC Microfinance Institution and the timing of the change in ownership only days after the interest rate cap was announced. As of 2017 PRASAC, the largest MDI and one of the most controversial throughout the years was purchased by LOLC Lanka Orix Leasing, with minority stakes held by Bank of East Asia in Hong Kong and a continuing ownership role by the PRASAC Staff Company.

No one can predict the future, but PRASAC is betting on a bright one.

4.5.5 Ownership of Cambodia's Leading MDIs 2012–2019

By late 2018, the last two of three remaining MDIs, with broad outreach and positive returns, were acquired by foreign banks. AMK and Vision Fund were acquired by Shanghai Commercial & Savings Bank, Ltd. (SCSB) Taiwan and Woori Bank South Korea, respectively.

The only MDI with a similar ownership structure to the earlier model of shared ownership among multiple investors is AMRET Microfinance Institution, which also belongs to the global Advans SA Network, a group of financial institutions serving MSMEs in nine countries in Asia and Africa. Advans SA is the majority shareholder in AMRET. Two Development Finance Institutions continue minority ownership roles—the FMO, the Dutch Development Bank and International Finance Corporation (IFC) part of the World Bank Group.

The ownership of Cambodia's eight original microfinance deposit-taking institutions (MDIs) as of end 2019 is presented in Table 4.2.

There are broad insights that can be drawn from the high level of activity in Mergers and Acquisitions in Cambodia's microfinance market from 2014 through 2018.

The Established Trend Is Not Accidental The trend is supported and encouraged by the NBC policy of market openness and a concerted bid to attract well-positioned, quality, banking establishments to the Cambodian market. The NBC has an intentional policy to attract neighboring banks and financial institutions to Cambodia to "professionalize" the banking and microfinance sectors. The NBC is also concerned with capital buffers and increased capitalization that the group of new owners can provide.

The Returns on Equity and Returns on Assets Are Attractive Second, it is clear that the returns present in Cambodia's largest well-run MDIs can be as high as 37% return on equity (ROE) and 5% return on assets (ROA) year over year.[29] These figures are extremely attractive to Asian regional banks, particularly as Cambodia's current economic environment continues predictions of 7% annual growth, while other Asian economies experience lack-luster growth rates.

The Long-Term Intentions of the New Owners Are Not Always Clear Third, it is not clear that the acquisitions, once controlled by new owners, will continue with their microfinance objectives. The strong commitment to the market segment established years ago by Cambodian MFIs enabled millions of poor and low-income women and men, including in the rural areas, to join the formal financial system.

Will the new owners have the same commitment as the early pioneers to inclusive finance, as the NBC hopes? After all, these new owners do not have a

[29] Figures as of 2016, before the interest rate cap on micro-lending became effective on April 1, 2017

Table 4.2 Ownership of Cambodia's leading MDIs 2019

Name	Date of acquisition	Majority shareholder	Ownership stake
Sathapana Bank Plc. previously Sathapana MDI	2012	Maruhan Japan Bank (MJB).	100%
LOLC, previously Thaneakea Phum	2014	LOLC Private Limited	96.97%
		TCP ESOP-LOLC Staff	3.03%
Hattha Kaksekar Limited	2016	Bank of Ayudhya PLC (Krungsri Bank)	100%
KREDIT Microfinance Institution Plc.	2011	Phillip MFIs Pte. Ltd, a member of the Phillip Capital Group, based in Singapore	100%
PRASAC	March 2017	LOLC Lanka Orix Leasing	70%
		Bank of East Asia based in Hong Kong	21%
		PRASAC Staff Company	9%
AMK	August 2018	Shanghai Commercial & Savings Bank, Ltd. (SCSB)	80.01%
		Agora Microfinance N.V.	19.99%
		AMK Staff Association (AMK-SA)	0
Vision Fund (Cambodia) Ltd.	June 2018	Woori Bank	100%
AMRET	2015 subsidiary of the Advans SA Network	Advans SA Network	52.78%
		International Finance Corporation (IFC)	19.99%
		FMO	19.99%
		La Fayette Participations	4.06%
		Botta	3.17%

microfinance focus in their home countries. Or, will the new banking establishments compete with existing Cambodian banks in an already over-crowded urban market to court the emerging middle class that is easier to reach and less costly to serve?

A true test of the new owner's intent may be revealed by their response to the interest rate cap at 18% (discussed above in Sect. 4.3). Will this de-motivate the new owners of MDIs and other established institutions to continue providing financial services to the lower segments of the market in Cambodia? After all, projected profitable business plans prepared for these new investors were based on pre-March 2017 analytics, before the interest rate cap became effective.

What will be the new owners' response to a microcredit market that appears to be overheated? Will the new owners' profit drive come before safety of the larger microfinance sector?

Learning About Transformation: Better Late Than Never It appears that many of the pioneers of Cambodia's new financial sector did not emphasize enough an optimal future ownership structure in their transformation from an NGO to a company and then to a microfinance deposit-taking institution (MDI). An ideal strategy would retain the vision, mission, and human resources to serve the middle- and lower-income segments of the market.[30] Few had a long-term growth strategy that would inform possible future mergers and acquisitions and the effect this change might have on the organization's future ownership and governance.

Developing a More Professional Cadre of Cambodian Bankers The jury is still out as to whether or not the NBC's policy on "M&A" will further develop a more professional cadre of Cambodian bankers. The NBC had hoped the sector and the professionals within it would excel with new banking technology and practices conveyed through foreign bankers. There is perhaps a misconception in Cambodia that a banker from a foreign market is considered more valuable than the homegrown variety. Some foreign bankers believe this; perhaps the NBC believes this as well, given the recent fondness for foreign acquisitions in the Cambodian market.

Before making any judgment about the superiority of foreign bankers, let's consider the experience of Cambodia's homegrown financial sector leaders.

It must be recognized that the growth of the banking system these last 20 years has been built by Cambodia's best and brightest. Banking professionals learned in their own market over time with each subsequent accomplishment better than the last. These leaders prevailed through lean times, and suffered the worst of the bad times. They aspired to be more and rose to the challenges.

They gained acceptance, they played by the rules of the game nationally and internationally. They re-skilled themselves in the concepts and practices of financial intermediation by attending the best educational institutions the world has to offer, such as the Frankfurt School of Finance and Management and Harvard University, among others. They brought knowledge home, and they informed an eager generation of bankers abroad about the significant lessons Cambodia offers to advance financial inclusion.

They created a future for a population devastated by the past. They are recognized beyond their borders as one of the best-managed and most dynamic industries in the world. They catapulted Cambodia's microfinance industry to the top of the global charts. They created—and this must be underscored—a future for a population devastated by the past by means of sustained access to financial services. They used their talents and wisdom to create something new and different in a society that begged for change and the democratization of money.

[30] It is important to note that ACLEDA was the exception to the rule. ACLEDA Bank Plc. consciously preserved its local ownership structure. The next chapter discusses how ACLEDA Bank Plc. has experienced many transitions while emphasizing strategy regarding ownership as market conditions change and an emphasis on retaining majority national ownership.

4.6 Taxation Target

As the financial sector has grown, so has its prominence as a target for more and more taxation. The most recent proclamation intended to apply a value added tax (VAT)[31] of 10% on all primary financial services that do not earn profit on the margin.[32] Such a tax would appear to exempt most deposits and loans, but the 10% VAT would apply to all fee-based financial services, such as transfers and payments, service fees on lending, fees to maintain deposit accounts, credit cards, ATM fees, and the like.

Up to the time of the announcement by the General Department of Taxation (GDT) in May 2017, 1 month after the 18% interest rate cap went into effect, all primary financial services had been exempt from VAT. There is good reason to keep the exemption, as nations with thriving financial sectors and high financial inclusion rates consider such a tax on financial services regressive, inefficient, and damaging to financial inclusion.

A VAT tax is one that is generally paid by consumers for a good or service, not by the providers of goods and services. As a tax on consumption, a VAT tax is considered a regressive and inefficient tax as it disadvantages poor and low-income people who make transactions more often and spend a higher percentage of their income on such taxes than rich people do (Box 4.1).

Box 4.1: A Value Added Tax (VAT)

A Value Added Tax (VAT) is an indirect tax on the domestic consumption of goods and services, except those generally exempt, such as food, medicines, and exports. It is levied at each stage in the chain of production and distribution from raw materials to the final sale based on the value (price) added at each stage.

VAT is not a cost to the producer or the distribution chain members; the end consumer pays the full costs.

VAT on primary financial services is considered an inefficient tax, as it would require large investment by financial services providers to develop specialized IT services to properly support and process the VAT on financial services fees.

Sources: Department of the Treasury. 1984. Tax Reform for Fairness, Simplicity and Economic Growth. Volume 3 Value-Added Tax. Kotoski, Kali and Hor Kimsay. June 7, 2017. "Bank Services VAT Seen as 'Inefficient'." *The Phnom Penh Post*, citing Mekong Strategic Partners and DFDL Cambodia.

---

[31] A value added tax (VAT) is an indirect tax on consumption of goods and services.

[32] Primary financial services that do not earn a profit on the margin are, for example, fee-based financial services, such as money transfers and payments, while financial services that earn a profit on the margin are deposit accounts and loans that earn a profit from interest rates.

It Was Called Munity The timing of the announcement could not have been more unfortunate as another blow to the financial services industry that pays in excess of 30–40% of gross revenue in yearly taxes.[33] The combination of the surprise announcement of an 18% interest rate cap on microfinance loans and an additional 10% value-added-tax (VAT) placed on all fee based financial transactions further demotivated FSPs to serve the microfinance sector of the banking system.

With no other recourse available, the members of the CMA and several members of the ABC active in supporting the microfinance market banded together to form a collective action against implementing such a measure. The CMA and the ABC leadership emphasized that they would have to consult their membership about the effects of such a surprise measure and how they could implement it correctly without a more detailed and clearer definition of which financial services would be subject to the tax (Kotoski and Hor 2017a, b).

In addition, banking sector leaders indicated to the press that, "customers would need to pay a bit more to use financial services. Any additional fees levied on customers should not be viewed as bank-led initiatives, instead it should be noted that it was the government's way of boosting revenue. Please do not confuse that the banks are charging these additional fees," Dr. In Channy said. He added, "The revenue from VAT is for the Finance Ministry, and this will contribute to enlargement of our national budget" (Ibid.).

Tax and finance experts backed the CMA and ABC analysis. Later they lauded the GDT's repeal of the mandate. Experts noted that a VAT tax on financial services penalizes the consumer of financial services and would require banks and MFIs to invest significantly in new IT systems to implement the tax properly and to report on it effectively.

There were few, if any supporters of such a regressive tax on primary financial services, mainly credit and savings. The financial services industry praised the GDT's quick action to withdraw a premature announcement that had no prior consultation with the industry.

The "mutiny" turned into a considered appeal to logic, fairness, and industry consultation.

[33] Calculation made from a sample of 2016–2017 Annual Reports and Audited Financial Statements of Banks and MFIs. The percentage of tax paid includes all withholding tax, income tax, and other taxes levied by GDT. It does not include shareholder taxes on dividends or other taxes shareholders pay to the Cambodian government or their own governments if they are foreign entities.

4.7 Conclusion: Rational or Irrational Exuberance?

Cambodia's modern financial service sector, now past its 20th year of existence, has been characterized by both "rational exuberance," managing sector growth to reach its frontiers, and "irrational exuberance," how to manage growth when the frontiers have been reached and exceeded.

This chapter has focused on a period of "irrational exuberance" by shedding light on the factors behind the sector's emerging debt crisis and urging its stakeholders to "act early and to act right." It also urges financial sector participants to "act right" when the debt crisis in the microcredit sector gains momentum and may spill over into the banking sector as a whole, which is highlighted as a concern by many experts in the sector.

Systemic strengths of stakeholder consultation, combined with decisive and shared actions, were nurtured in the earlier period of "rational exuberance." They also can serve as effective guides for the financial sector through this predicted crisis.

Two questions are front and center and may guide deliberations and actions that will be taken:

> What kind of national financial sector does Cambodia want to build for future generations?
>
> How does financial inclusion of low-income people figure into this vision?

The history of Cambodia's new financial sector, led by microfinance innovators, is full of inspiring examples of dedication and accomplishment. This recent history is contrasted with a financial sector that once required strong measures to push the reluctant domestic and foreign banks along, on their take-off to a "flight to quality."[34]

Cambodia's recent history of financial sector growth has shown the world how the regulator and the industry worked together. They focused on getting the incentives right. They did not rely only on forcing compliance or levying onerous requirements that undermine significant accomplishments, even though these tools often served them well.

Cambodia's financial sector leaders also kept financial inclusion in the forefront of their deliberations. They remembered the times when there was no money, and they were determined to create a financial future for all segments of the population by means of sustained access to financial services.

It may be that these tools of consultation and conciliation have weakened over time, or they may be outdated. Is there an over-reliance on compliance and less attention paid to getting the incentives right? Several industry insiders think so.

The incentives were right in 1999 and 2000 when regulators, financial services providers, and investors came together to discuss the future of the industry as part of an on-going consultative process about the future. Even though some lost and

[34] See Prologue to Part 2.

some won, at least everyone had their say. This was the greatest incentive of all for the industry to participate in discussion, to move forward and abide by decisions in a compliant way.

Financial sector participants relied on a process that most considered fair and just. Perhaps it was not always considered perfect by all players, but enough so that all could agree—even to the shortcomings. Once a process is considered fair and just by all participants, it is the "best of all possible worlds." It lays a foundation for the future; it provides an incentive for the greatest current thinkers participating in the market to go forward. Most important, it provides a platform to inspire future leaders to improve and to progress.

The early industry incentives worked. They jump-started and expanded market-based financial inclusion in Cambodia. And the results over time have been significant. Most important the incentives created more opportunities for expansion and refining products and services to meet a growing, younger, and more prosperous market and a more robust but strict regulatory framework.

Cambodia made immense progress serving its citizens during the last two decades. There is still time for the current generation to do more.

And the next generation is already anticipating great changes and their own contributions.

References

Asian Development Bank (2016) Impact of Restrictions on Interest Rates in Microfinance. Sustainable Development Working Paper Series No. 45 September 2016. Mandaluyong City, Philippines: Asian Development Bank, 2016.

Center for Financial Inclusion (2011) Nicaragua's Microfinance Crisis: Looking Back, What Did We Learn? Available Center for Financial Inclusion. https://www.centerforfinancialinclusion.org/blog/ Accessed 20 July 2018.

Chen G, Rasmussen S, Reille X (2010) Growth and Vulnerabilities in Microfinance. Focus Note 61. 2010. Washington, D.C.: CGAP, February.

Chheng C (2018) Cambodian Cross-Border Labor. Sources Ministry of Labour and Vocational Training, and World Bank 2017. Compiled and designed by Channy Chheng. https://www.facebook.com/photo.php?fbid=102165014895090. Accessed 13 June 2018.

Davel G (2013) "Regulatory Options to Curb Debt Stress." Focus Note 83. Washington, D.C.: CGAP, March.

Department of the Treasury (1984) "Tax Reform for Fairness, Simplicity and Economic Growth. Volume 3 Value-Added Tax." 1984. Available https://www.treasury.gov/resource-center/tax-policy/Documents/Report-Tax-Reform-v3-1984.pdf Accessed 12 June 2017

Economist Intelligence Unit. (2018) Global Microscope 2018: The enabling environment for financial inclusion; Sponsored by Accion, AfDB, Bill & Melinda Gates Foundation, IDB Invest/IDB LAB, and MetLife Foundation. EIU, New York, NY. Available https://www.eiu.com/public/topical_report.aspx?campaignid=Microscope2018. Accessed 10 November 2018.

FinScope (2015) Consumer Survey Cambodia 2015 Presentation. Available http://finmark.org.za/finscope-consumer-survey-cambodia-2015-presentation/

FinScope (2016) Consumer Survey Kingdom of Cambodia 2015 Pocket Guide. Available http://www.finmark.org.za/wp-content/uploads/2016/07/finscope-cambodia-pocket-guide.pdf.

Hattha Kaksekar Limited (2017) Annual Report 2016. Hattha Kasekar Limited (HKL). http://www.hkl.com.kh/en/detail/view/191/34?ctype=article. 2016. Accessed 10 November 2018.
Hout Ieng Tong (2018) CEO Message. Available via HKL http://www.hkl.com.kh/en/detail/view/191/34?ctype=article. Accessed 10 November 2018.
Hor K. (2018a) "NBC Takes Licenses from 11 Lenders" The Phnom Penh Post. Phnom Penh. Available Phnom Penh Post, https://www.phnompenhpost.com/business/nbc-takes-licences-11-lenders. Accessed 5 January 2018.
Hor K. (2018b) "Delinquent Loan Rate Continues to Rise". *The Phnom Penh Post.* Citing the newly published NBC Annual Report. Available Phnom Penh Post https://www.phnompenhpost.com/business/delinquent-loan-rate-continues-rise. Accessed 9 January 2018.
International Monetary Fund (2006) Glossary of Selected Financial Terms: Terms and Definitions. Last Updated: October 31, 2006. 2006 Available via IMF. https://www.imf.org/external/np/exr/glossary/showTerm.asp Accessed 2 October 2018.
International Monetary Fund (2018) IMF Staff Completed 2018 Article IV Mission to Cambodia. Press Release No. 18/371 Available via IMF. https://www.imf.org/external/error.htm?URL=http://www.imf.org/en/News/Articles/2018/10/02/PR18371C; Accessed 2 October 2018.
Kotoski K and Hor K. (2017a) "Tax Pulled After Mutiny" *The Phnom Penh Post*. Phnom Penh. 2017.Available Phnom Penh Post https://www.phnompenhpost.com/business/tax-pulled-after-mutiny. Accessed 8 July 2017.
Kotoski K and Hor K. (2017b) "Bank Services VAT Seen as 'Inefficient'." *The Phnom Penh Post.* Phnom Penh. 2017. Available Phnom Penh Post https://www.phnompenhpost.com/business/bank-services-VAT-seen-as-inefficient. Accessed 14 June 2017.
Liu J. (2018) The rise and fall of China's online P2P lending. Available Technode https://technode.com/2018/08/02/the-rise-and-fall-of-chinas-online-p2p-lending/ Accessed 23 November 2018
Lekatis G (2018) Understanding the capital conservation buffer. Available Treasury.NL http://www.treasury.nl/blog/basel-iii-understanding-the-capital-conservation-buffer/ Accessed 24 November 2018
Loeung Sopheap and Tep Bunthoeun. (2018) Risk Analysis Report on the Over-Indebtedness of MFI Customers in Cambodia. Phnom Penh
Microfinance Index of Market Outreach and Saturation (MIMOSA) (2015) Cambodia November 2015. http://mimosaindex.org/ Accessed 2 July 2018.
National Bank of Cambodia (2015) Annual Report 2015, Phnom Penh.
National Bank of Cambodia (2017) Annual Report 2016. Phnom Penh
National Bank of Cambodia (2018) Annual Report 2017. Phnom Penh.
National Bank of Cambodia (2019) Annual Report 2018. Phnom Penh
Pimhidzai O, Tong K, Anantavrasilpa R, Popovic A, Mel S, Sanchez M, Miguel E, (2019) Microfinance and Household Welfare. Cambodia policy note. Washington, D.C.: World Bank Group. Available http://documents.worldbank.org/curated/en/144661552916327946/Microfinance-and-Household-Welfare-Cambodia-Policy-Note. Accessed 6 June 2019
Rhyne E. (2001) Commercialization and Crisis in Bolivian Microfinance. Development Alternatives Inc., Bethesda.
Rosenberg R. (2011) Is Microcredit Over-Indebtedness a Worldwide Problem? 7 November 2011. CGAP Washington, D. C. CGAP. Available CGAP. https://www.cgap.org/blog/microcredit-over-indebtedness-worldwide-problem. Accessed 28 November 2018.
Rozas D. (2014) The Art of the Responsible Exit in Microfinance Equity Sales. Forum 9. Washington, D.C.: CGAP and Center for Financial Inclusion. License: Creative Commons Attribution CC BY 3.0. Available CGAP. https://www.cgap.org/research/publication/art-responsible-exit-microfinance-equity-sales. Accessed 10 May 2018.
Rozas D (2016a) "Inexorable growth in Cambodia: Like a rolling stone?" Available MIMOSA. http://mimosaindex.org/inexorable-growth-in-cambodia-like-a-rolling-stone? Accessed 10 November 2018.

Rozas D (2016b) Living on the edge in Cambodia – is it worth it? Mimosa Blog January 20, 2016. Available MIMOSA. http://mimosaindex.org/living-on-the-edge-is-it-worth-it/ Accessed 10 Nov 2018.

Rozas D (2016c) Preventing Over-Indebtedness in Cambodia. MIMOSA (Microfinance Index of Market Outreach and Saturation) Available European Microfinance Platform. http://www.e-mfp.eu/blog/preventing-client-over-indebtedness-cambodia. Accessed 23 October 2017.

Rozas D. (2017) Author interview.

Sathapana Bank (2017) Press release November 2017 by Mr. Kato Norihiko, the new Chief Executive Officer of Sathapana Bank. Available Sathapana Bank. https://www.sathapana.com.kh/latest-news/detail/?tx_news_pi1%5Bnews_preview%5D=16&cHash=ee087ed7d8fb578c5d1456871d5127cd. Accessed 13 January 2018.

Sathapana Bank (2019) "About Us". Available Sathapana Bank. https://www.sathapana.com.kh/about-sathapana. Accessed 2 January 2019.

Part III
ACLEDA Bank Plc.: Traditions and Transitions

We expect ACLEDA will become #1, not just the portfolio, or transfers and savings, but because of its transparency and its culture. It will set the example.

Mr. Chea Sok, Chairman of the Board, ACLEDA Bank, Plc. (2000–2014)

Transparency is a growth factor.

Dr. In Channy, President and Group Managing Director,
The ACLEDA Group of Companies

Prologue

The Historical Perspective

Today, the average Cambodian citizen values fair play and respect in the banking system. This expectation develops from increased competition in the lower and middle segments of the market.

The change counteracts decades of authoritarian thinking and the accepted practice of financial services customers allowing others to make decisions for them. Now, consumers recognize they have choices to select a financial services provider that offers value and values them as customers. These subtle but seismic changes are good news for Cambodia, not just for the privileged few but also for the deserving many.

The previous chapters discussed how the shape and tenor of the financial sector evolved as many aspects of Cambodia's economic and political environment influenced its development. The sector has been shaped by the aims of regulatory authorities and the frameworks they chose to advance these aims. The range of financial institutions, the values that they hold, and how they have interacted with one another also have influenced the shape of the financial sector.

Perhaps most importantly, the banking sector's shared vision of inclusivity has shaped how financial institutions treat their customers, their staff, and their competition. The banking sector includes a strong microfinance presence of dedicated microfinance institutions (MFIs and MDIs) and microfinance professionals. Commercial banks, specialized banks, and MDIs possess strong digital capacity as well as physical branches and agent networks in rural and urban areas.

This vibrant and competitive sector focuses on providing basic services for the majority of the population. Today, there are more—and more convenient—options for more people in rural and urban areas to keep their money safe, finance investments regardless of size, and move their money when and where they need to. Those options continue to grow, with the corresponding benefits—and the corresponding risks.

Just imagine, 20 years ago. When the Khmer Rouge was finally vanquished in 1998, most businesses, individuals, and even banks made payments and delivered funds in cash. The roads looked more like footpaths in many places, and sometimes they were completely washed over by floods. Demobilized soldiers—still very much active and armed as independent "highway men"—collected tolls from passing vehicles. Moving large amounts of cash in these conditions required armed delivery men to drive around nervously with large sacks or even truckloads of notes bundled up with rubber bands like half-kilo bricks.

During 2017 alone, Cambodians made over 86 million transactions, through domestic mobile money operations, moving more than 57,185,790 million riel, the equivalent of USD 14,314 billion inside the country without either party ever having to touch a paper banknote. By 2018 mobile transactions through Internet banking and mobile banking services accelerated.

The current picture of the vibrant Cambodian banking sector was not always as it is today. The sector changed dramatically over the past two decades. The greatest changes relied on the dedicated work of a handful of retail banks engaged in microfinance and small enterprise lending. Key among them was ACLEDA Bank Plc., the established ethical banking leader in Cambodia.

Too frequently the history of financial institutions ends with an analysis of progressive balance sheets in closed boardroom conversations. The historical record of Cambodia's financial institutions has been quite different: it has been celebrated in global financial inclusion tallies; and the growing numbers of customers and financial institutions have been admired from afar by other countries, distant financial institutions, and eager students of finance.

Among those who celebrated what Cambodia achieved that others found elusive were those who sought out ACLEDA Bank's openness to ensuring foreign and national organizations could learn from their experience. By the mid-2019, over 142 international organizations from every continent and over 30 countries attended courses offered by the ACLEDA Institute of Business (AIB) and its predecessor the

ACLEDA Training Center (ATC). They came from banks, MFIs, government regulatory agencies, private companies, and non-governmental organizations (NGOs).

Yet, the most important lessons from history often lie hidden in the memories of the organizational architects and those who quietly build a financial sector. They are bankers, teachers, regulators, philosophers, ethicists, managers, lawyers, accountants, businesswomen and men, and high-tech innovators. They are pioneers and protégés. They all share a vision. And, they practice a code of conduct that values transparency, has no tolerance for corruption, and aims to serve their customers well.

The chapters in ***Part III ACLEDA Bank Plc.: Traditions and Transitions*** discuss how one financial sector participant, ACLEDA Bank Plc., led the growth of Cambodia's inclusive financial sector. The chapters address the following questions:

- How do financial sector pioneers go forward and succeed when there is no recent foundation to build upon and little relevant national experience to apply?
- How does an organization build an ethical culture that develops with growth? What principles do they hold; what practices do they follow?
- What are the attributes of an organization and the consultation process with regulators and other financial services providers that contribute to lasting financial sector development? How do both contribute significantly to the development of the entire financial sector?

Part III: ACLEDA Bank Plc.: Traditions and Transitions is divided into three chapters: Chapter 5 Principles and Practices, Chap. 6 Pioneers and Protégés, and Chap. 7 Performance. Combined, these chapters capture important lessons about building a financial institution that serves customers with a broad range of products, builds sector-wide standards and ethical practices, and fosters customer confidence while contributing to national development.

ACLEDA Bank Plc. and microfinance institutions have largely accomplished an abiding 20-year vision of an inclusive financial sector—founded on respect for middle- and low-income customers.

But, the long-term vision for Cambodian society is anchored in the much broader ideals and aspirations of a new generation of Cambodians. Their values extend beyond the banking system.

The new generation values ethical behavior, and they would like to see a lot more of it around them. They would like to see it in their mentors, in their teachers, in their colleagues, and in their leadership. They appear to be ready to work very hard to get it. And, if it costs a lot to get it through hard work, transparency, and integrity, they are willing to pay.

Listen to the voices of the new generation of leaders:

> The new generation likes to work for ACLEDA Bank because ACLEDA Bank is an ethical bank…People in the community like ACLEDA staff because they are well behaved, polite, and consider how customers need to understand the product terms… We feel we are part of Cambodia's development by raising people's income and taking part in the process.
>
> Mr. Sen Sokla, ACLEDA Bank Corporate Secretary

I remember a question from my job interview at ACLEDA Bank: The interviewer asked, 'ACLEDA provides a lot of benefits to staff. But, what does the institution need from you?' My answer: They need my honesty, my creativity and my hard working efforts to achieve ACLEDA's plan.

Mr. Sok Piseth, Head of Information System Audit Department

Deposit and transfer audit work requires strict, rigorous and independent responsibilities. I am very committed to this work. And, I am proud to be able to protect staff and customers from fraud and other risks.

Mrs. Nget Nary, Head of Deposit and Transfer Audit Department

Chapter 5
ACLEDA Bank Plc.: Principles and Practices

We like to advance anti-corruption in Cambodia through our work; every institution in Cambodia can do the same. ACLEDA is successful in this; others outside of ACLEDA can be successful as well.

My beliefs about corruption are based on Buddha's teachings. A person's good acts cannot compensate for the bad acts. You cannot offset accounts.
Chhay Soeun, Chairman of the Board, ACLEDA Bank Plc.

5.1 Introduction

In early 2018, as Dr. In Channy recalled the 25-year history of ACLEDA Bank Plc.—the triumphs and setbacks—he emphasized how values played a dominant role in the bank's vision and growth.

> Our values are at the center of our growth. Our values are based on our beliefs about how we should behave in society and how we should treat others. Over time, these values became rooted in our practices and in our products. Our values are rooted in everything we do…and, everything we don't do.

Over the past 25 years, ACLEDA advanced from a small enterprise development project to a local NGO, to a specialized credit NGO, to a specialized bank, and finally to a commercial bank. Each phase had a specific organizational development mantra that focused the efforts of staff as they built a platform to go forward.

Figure 5.1 illustrates the organizational transformation timeline and the guiding principle that drove the organization to reach the next stage of growth.

The values of ACLEDA Bank's pioneers are well-known in Cambodia and throughout the world. Staff, management, and governing board ethics and values top the list of the reasons why ACLEDA Bank Plc. has been celebrated throughout ASEAN and globally.

Since the beginnings of ACLEDA in 1993, over 25 years ago, the bank's ethos and principles have only strengthened. ACLEDA Bank's principles and practices

© Springer Nature Singapore Pte Ltd. 2020

H. A. Clark, *Beyond Borders, Beyond Banking*,
https://doi.org/10.1007/978-981-15-1687-0_5

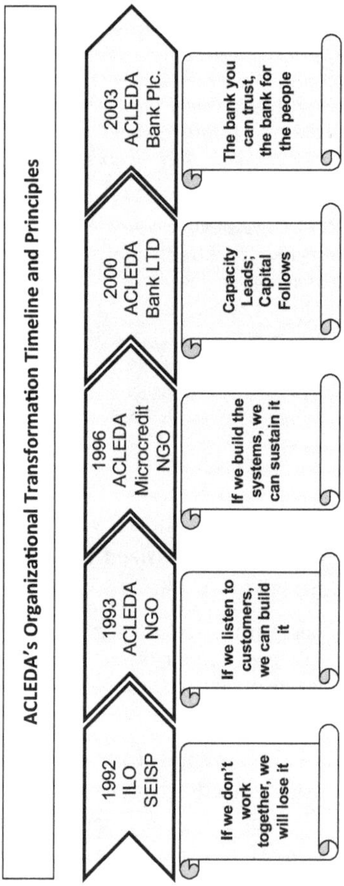

Fig. 5.1 ACLEDA's organizational transformation timeline and principles

serve to attract a new generation of leaders and staff, just as the promise of such an enterprise attracted the early pioneers during Cambodia's tumultuous 1990s.

> "Our culture is now a tradition within the ACLEDA organization. We are recognized for this in Cambodia and the region."
>
> "The *new generation* of Cambodia comes to ACLEDA because they want to belong to these traditions; they hold these beliefs and values, they want to belong to them, they want to improve on them and put them into practice—and they won't give it up." (*Dr. In Channy, President and Group Managing Director*)

It all sounds so easy now. But, ACLEDA's institutional values developed slowly from a strong base and not always smoothly over time. It's easy to think that a like-minded group of people came together from the very beginning, imprinted the values that everyone had to follow, and attracted investments from Development Finance Institutions (DFIs). It's easy to think that later commercial investors came to the table, or even an Initial Public Offering was issued, like several MFIs throughout the world.

But, the seeming ease of these transitions is not the ACLEDA Bank story.

This chapter tells the story of how ACLEDA Bank Plc. was born with fundamental values, in contrast to so many other financial institutions worldwide that are derided for their lack of integrity. It shows how the values and the principles held by individual ACLEDA staff at the beginning eventually became the founding principles of the corporate entity.

The chapter starts with the ACLEDA "pioneers"—the original staff and leadership of what was to later become ACLEDA Bank Plc. The chapter then examines how their business training and small enterprise lending operation could become a value-led business.

Later, the chapter tells the story about how principles and practices strengthened over time and why they were so important at the outset, just as they are equally important today. Finally, the chapter concludes with an initial analysis of how the many value-based traditions of ACLEDA Bank Plc. informed and supported the transitions to new ventures and enterprises that now comprise the ACLEDA Group of Companies.

5.2 The Birth of an Ethical Bank

During the 1990s and the first decade of the twenty-first-century ACLEDA undertook four distinct organizational transformations from a postwar rehabilitation project to a commercial bank. By 2016 ACLEDA Bank Plc. was listed in the top 100 banks in the ASEAN region in "The Bankers Top 100 ASEAN Banks," and it was the first Cambodian bank to be so recognized (The Banker 2016).

In 2017, ACLEDA Bank Plc. jumped to 71st place in "The Bankers Top 100 ASEAN Banks," ranking 17 places ahead of its 2016 placement. It also ranked as one of the top ten banks in five out of six categories, including asset growth, capital growth and strength of capital, and returns on assets and capital.

And, it all started in Cambodia's 1992 UN-led transitional period of chaotic uncertainty with an International Labour Organization (ILO) employment generation project for demobilized soldiers. The Small Enterprise and Informal Sector Promotion Project (SEISP), ACLEDA's parent project, was a roughly drawn small business development, vocational education, and employment generation project for demobilized soldiers.

5.2.1 The Local Economic Development Agencies (LEDAs)

At the heart of SEISP were the Local Economic Development Agencies (LEDAs) that would enable poor and low-income Cambodians to take advantage of economic opportunities through an integrated package of business development, training, and credit. The LEDAs in Cambodia were conceived as independent professional service providers from the start. Yet, there was no design for the future operation of the LEDAs as permanent organizations.

The main objective of the province-based LEDAs was to get something on the ground as quickly as possible. "The creation of employment and additional income had to be realized as soon as possible to improve living conditions, contribute to reintegration and reconciliation, and therefore eventually the consolidation of peace. It was important for the project's supporters to do something urgently for those most affected by the war" (Hakemulder 1995).

5.2.1.1 The Pioneering ACLEDA Staff

Today, 8 of the original 28 SEISP LEDA staff still work for ACLEDA Bank and the ACLEDA Group of Companies. In 1992 they came from all walks of life. They were teachers, government planners, accountants, and mechanics. Most had spent years in the Site II refugee camp on the Thai border; some came from existing government agencies in Cambodia. They were schooled in Cambodia, Vietnam, Thailand, Eastern Europe, and the United States.

The SEISP project staff was not selected based on the depth of their small enterprise skills or their abundant knowledge about informal sector credit. They were recruited because of their potential to contribute, their values, and their business insight. Their attributes and values would serve them well, as they laid down the principles that eventually would become the foundations of ACLEDA Bank.

5.2.1.2 The First Organizational Breakthrough

In 1992, the first breakthrough in organizational development happened almost immediately and through bureaucratic fiat rather than a carefully constructed strategic plan. Technically, the ILO project could not administer a revolving credit fund. The ILO staff approached the national staff and asked them if they had any interest in creating their own organization.

At the time, there were no established procedures for registering an NGO in Cambodia. SEISP staff submitted their application to Cambodia's Supreme National Council and UNTAC and forgot about it, unsure whether this was the correct procedure, or whether they would merit a reply.

Early one day, a special messenger delivered a letter with an official gold-embossed seal. It was a letter from then-Prince Norodom Sihanouk confirming, as President of the Supreme National Council, the official recognition of ACLEDA, the Association of Local Economic Development Agencies, as a national NGO.

With the awe and excitement that recognition by the powerful presents, Channy realized, "Now, we are serious." It was February 1993.[1]

5.2.2 Becoming ACLEDA NGO: The Professional Organization

In Phase 2, from 1993 to 1995, the SEISP Project was in full swing and so was the ACLEDA NGO. The momentum of the ACLEDA organization began to grow based on mutual trust; and staff and management assumed responsibility for that growth. During this three-year period, ACLEDA, working alongside SEISP, would excel and become a leading local NGO providing business development training and micro and small enterprise credit.

ACLEDA was founded as a professional service organization. The next step was logical: ACLEDA had to continue to become a professional organization. The basic tenet came from the staff, and it was reinforced by their actions. See Fig. 5.2 values, practices, and systems of ACLEDA 1993.

Professionalism came from Chhay Soeun, who worked late into the night, and then studied computer technology and English so that he could make sense of the wealth of new information he found on the Internet. It also came from In Channy, who completed his MBA at night and on weekends. ACLEDA's professionalism came from Dr. So Phonnary and Sar Roth, and ACLEDA's Business Development Advisors and Credit Officers, who were listening to their business trainees and microcredit borrowers.

---

[1] For a more detailed account of the ACLEDA Bank history, refer to *When There Was No Money*. 2006. Springer, Berlin – Heidelberg.

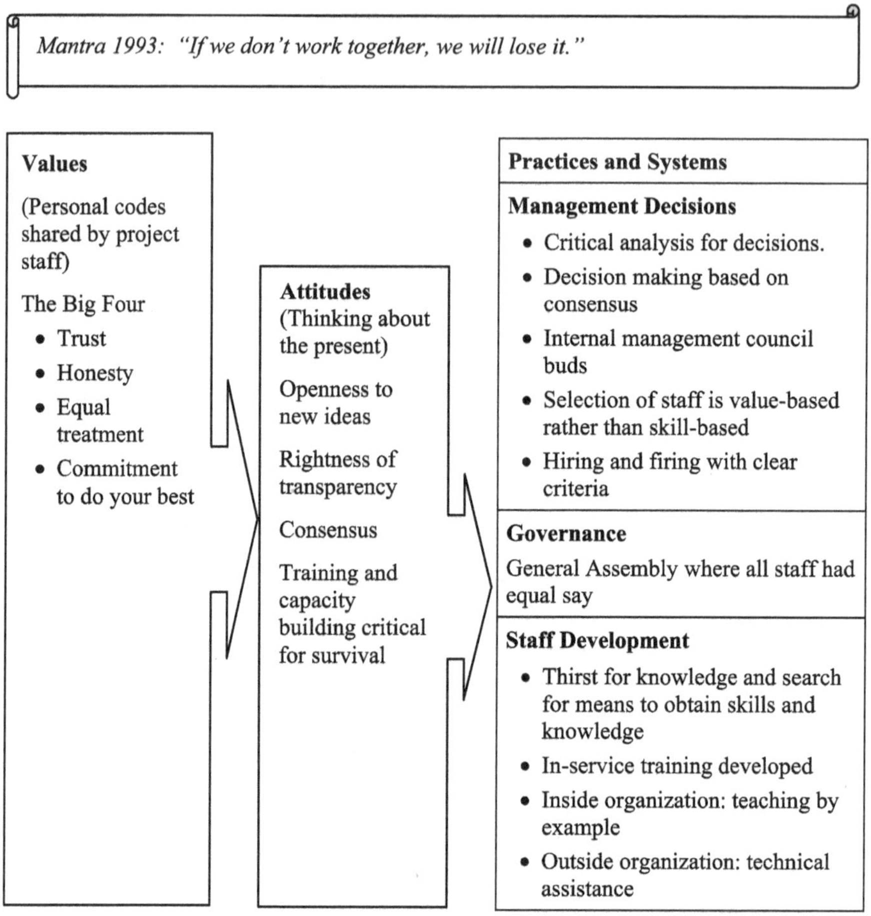

Fig. 5.2 Values, practices, and systems 1993. (Reproduced from Clark 2006)

They were analyzing why none of the project beneficiaries liked the training or the business development services, but everyone wanted the credit.

The desire to continue building a professional organization also came from Roel Hakemulder, the ILO technical advisor. "There was an enormous sense of opportunity – the opportunity to do things in the right way, for once. Especially in Cambodia, where there was such an atmosphere of hope, where people expected a lot from us, where the 'right thing' had been the exception for quite a while, and where I, for one, felt privileged to be there at that time."

> "In your life you get very few chances to do the right thing. It's good to have the chance to do the right thing once" (Hakemulder 2006).

5.2.2.1 ACLEDA's First Corporate Culture

ACLEDA spoke of "professional pride and the opportunity to build a professional organization." The voice of professional pride became for ACLEDA staff an unrelenting mantra: "If we don't do it together, we will lose it." And so emerged ACLEDA's first corporate culture, set from an understanding of the basic concept of trust and equal treatment, not from lofty visionary statements, but from determination. The drive to work together was the only option when so many had lost so much already.

As early as 1993, ACLEDA's mantra summarized what was urgent and important to the organization at the time. The key values were the personal codes of ethics that were shared by the group of people who made up the SEISP project staff: trust, honesty, equal treatment, and a commitment to do your best. See Fig. 5.2.

Their values translated into attitudes of openness to new ideas, the rightness of transparency, no tolerance for corruption, the importance of consensus, and the recognition that training and capacity building were critical to their survival. The values—and the practices that they influenced—took root in the organization in three areas: management, governance, and staff development.

5.2.2.2 Shared Core Values Develop into a Set of Corporate Ethics

ACLEDA's core values emerged from its infancy: honesty, trust, and a belief in one another. In this early phase, ACLEDA created a management group that would become the company's backbone; they found a method of teaching by example to instill an organizational culture.

The organizational culture they developed embraced transparency and enforced "no tolerance for corruption" within the organization. That may seem like a luxury in a postwar environment where bribes facilitate most business transactions and demobilized soldiers carry a variety of weapons to back up their demands. Yet the statement "no tolerance for corruption" was the first and most basic principle of ACLEDA's ethical code. See Fig. 5.2.

Transparency and no tolerance for corruption were the driving forces that linked ACLEDA's core business values of customer service, permanence in the community, and professionalism. ACLEDA Bank staff view transparency as the number one growth factor; expedience was no excuse.

The complete set of values and practices would continue to develop and eventually drive the company. Yet, the values that emerged at the outset remain the backbone of ACLEDA's code of ethics.

"In ACLEDA, we do not tolerate corruption or promote transparency just because of the rules," In Channy explains. "Rules can change. First, there were the beliefs, the principles of how we should behave in society and how we should treat others. Then the rules came, to protect those beliefs" (In 2006).

5.3 The Crossroads: Options for the Future

In the third phase (from 1995 to 1999) ACLEDA advanced from a local NGO providing business training and credit to people affected by war to an NGO specializing in micro and small enterprise credit for those who could make the best use of credit to start or expand a business.

The year 1995 ushered in a crossroads for ACLEDA's organizational growth. It was time to decide among the growing list of options for the future of the organization. Two options for the future became clear. They could continue as an integrated business development organization with a credit component, or they could specialize in microfinance.

By 1996, ACLEDA staff had been listening to their business development trainees for some time. "We knew people didn't like the training, maybe a few and at the very beginning. But everybody wanted the credit. There was business opportunity for them, but no capital. There were business start-ups and growth-oriented businesses for people who were already in business but had no capital to expand. We also knew that vocational training was not our expertise. But, when it came to credit, we knew we could be the best institution in Cambodia" (Sar 2006).

5.3.1 "If We Listen to Customers, We Can Build It."

As a result of a 1996 strategic planning exercise, the third organizational transformation began. ACLEDA decided to become a specialized self-financing microfinance institution. The 1996 strategic plan focused on sustainability. ACLEDA branch managers realized that they would have to generate more income and become more efficient. Most branch managers reluctantly agreed to an increase in the interest rate.

Branch managers returned to their posts with a great deal of trepidation. They had a risky proposition for their customers, a 2% price increase on the small business loan. Customers' reactions surprised even the most anxious branch manager.

When clients were polled about the price increase, the majority agreed, with one condition: "decrease the training."[2] When ACLEDA agreed, customers thought ACLEDA had improved its products.

The mantra for this phase of ACLEDA's growth became "If we listen to customers, we can build it." See Fig. 5.3.

As ACLEDA staff began to practice the model that customers were paying for their salaries, they became friendlier to borrowers and began to devise ways to improve the service. ACLEDA also began to compete with other microcredit providers based on the quality of the service, not so much on price during this period.

[2] For a discussion of the value customers placed on business development training versus the provision of credit, see When There Was No Money (2006).

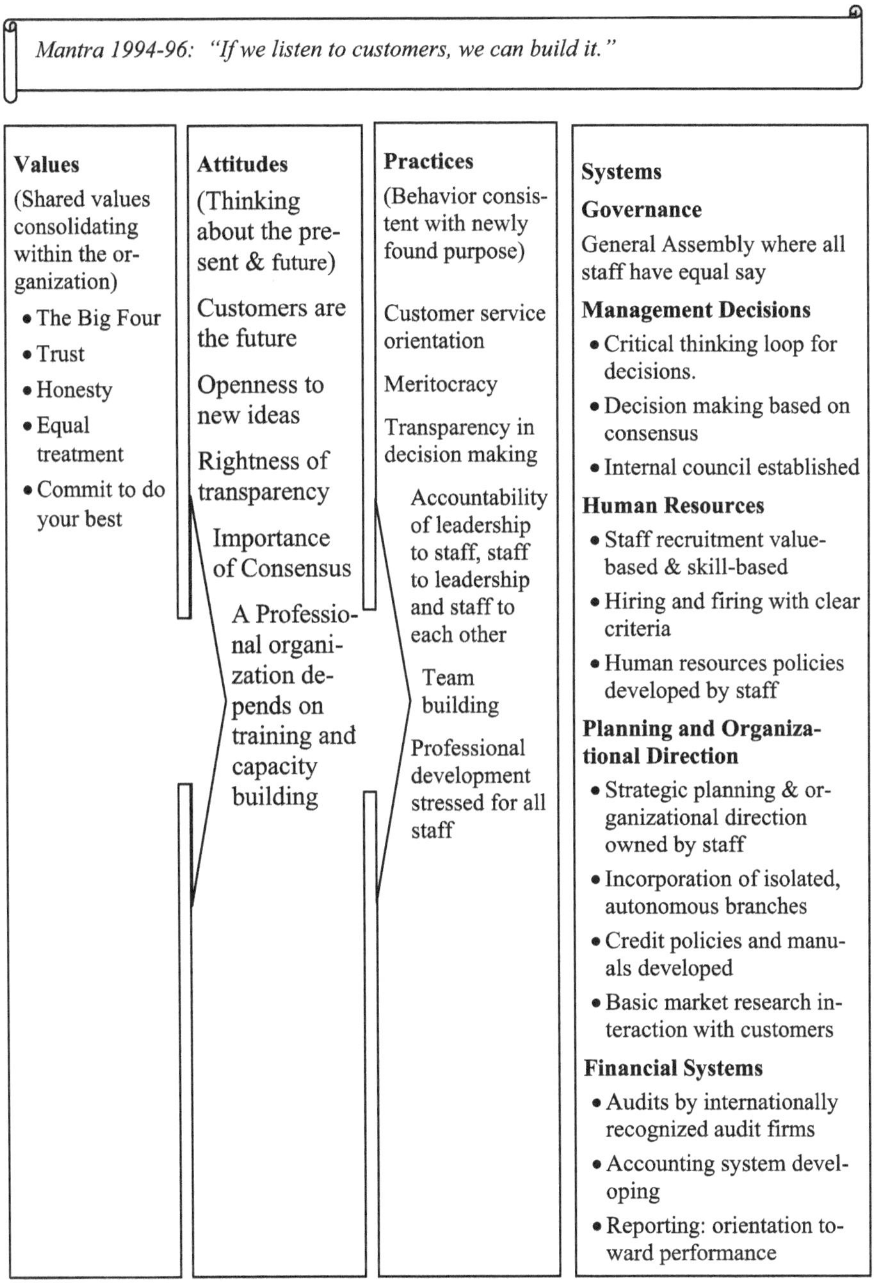

Fig. 5.3 Values, practices, and systems 1994–1996. (Reproduced from Clark 2006)

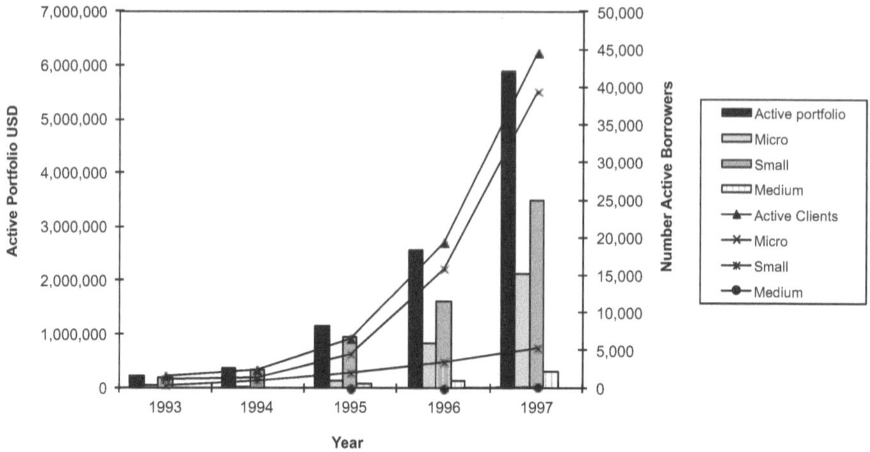

Fig. 5.4 Growth in number of borrowers and portfolio 1993–2000: the early years 1993–1997. (Reproduced from Clark 2006)

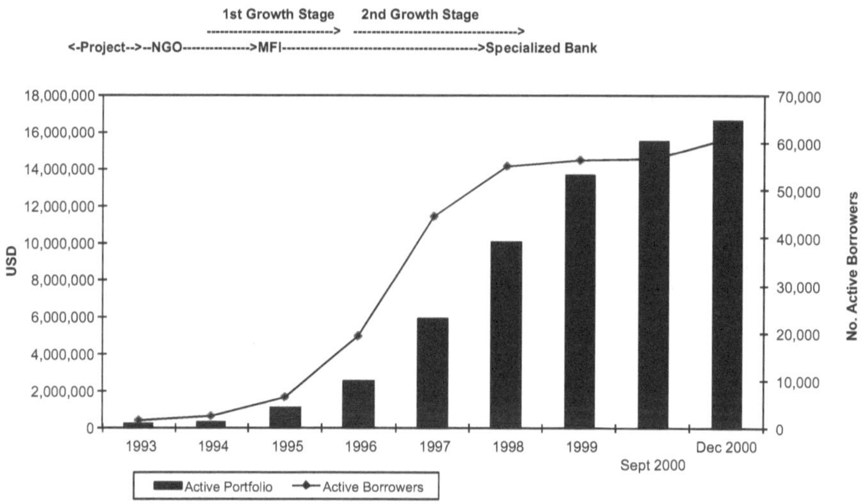

Fig. 5.5 Growth in number of borrowers and portfolio 1993–2000. (Reproduced from Clark 2006)

From 1994 through the end of 1997, ACLEDA's portfolio more than doubled every year, and the number of active loan customers matched this pace as shown in Fig. 5.4. The rapid increase in portfolio size is due to two factors: the large increase in the number of micro loan clients and the growing value of the small business portfolio.

ACLEDA's performance dramatically improved in 1995 when it decided to become an organization specialized in microfinance. With a clear purpose, ACLEDA's portfolio tripled, as did its outreach. See Fig. 5.5. Yet overall, the financial performance continued to show the legacy of a donor project and the high cost of operating in a risky environment where banks fail, exchange rates fluctuate, and the costs of security and neglected infrastructure are very high (Clark 2006).

Within 5 years of the beginning of ACLEDA's small enterprise and credit organization, Dr. So Phonnary's early vision about the ACLEDA MFI providing a quick, friendly, convenient, customer-oriented service was becoming a reality (So 2006). And, it remains to this day. Dr. So Phonnary is now ACLEDA Bank Plc. Executive Vice President and Group Chief Operations Officer.

And, she still listens to customers.

5.3.2 "Understand the Customer, Develop the Product to Suit the Customer, and Provide Excellent Customer Service"

Listening to customers and analyzing their own customer service experience pointed ACLEDA staff in the right direction. They found a unique perspective from their early formation that has lasted to this day. They were learning about how to build a bank when no recent experience existed, and they discovered their key to success—they listened to their customers.

> Based on the keen talent for listening to customers, ACLEDA Bank staff developed the second key principle, "Understand the customer, develop the product to suit the customer, and provide excellent customer service".

> From 1996 to the year 2000, the ACLEDA Microfinance Institution exceeded all expectations. During this period of rapid growth ACLEDA learned how to combine a customer orientation that would produce expansive growth with risk management techniques that would produce sustainable growth. See Fig. 5.6.

> If the mantra during the previous period was, "If we listen to customers, we can build it," the mantra during the growth period added the corollary: "If we build the systems, we can sustain it."

The Third Period Began in 1996 It ushered in the adoption of new systems required for an organization that was growing rapidly within a widely dispersed branch network. The number of customers doubled and then tripled. Staff recruitment kept pace with rapid growth in the number of customers. This phase of growth affirms a clear direction for the organization, as credit policies and manuals were developed and re-designed based on experimentation with products and the product features that appealed to customers.

Staff policies on hiring, review, and firing became more comprehensive and appropriate for a professional microfinance institution (MFI). Strategic plans engaged each staff member and pulled the organization closer together. Even though the first plan may have pushed the organization in too many directions, in retrospect,

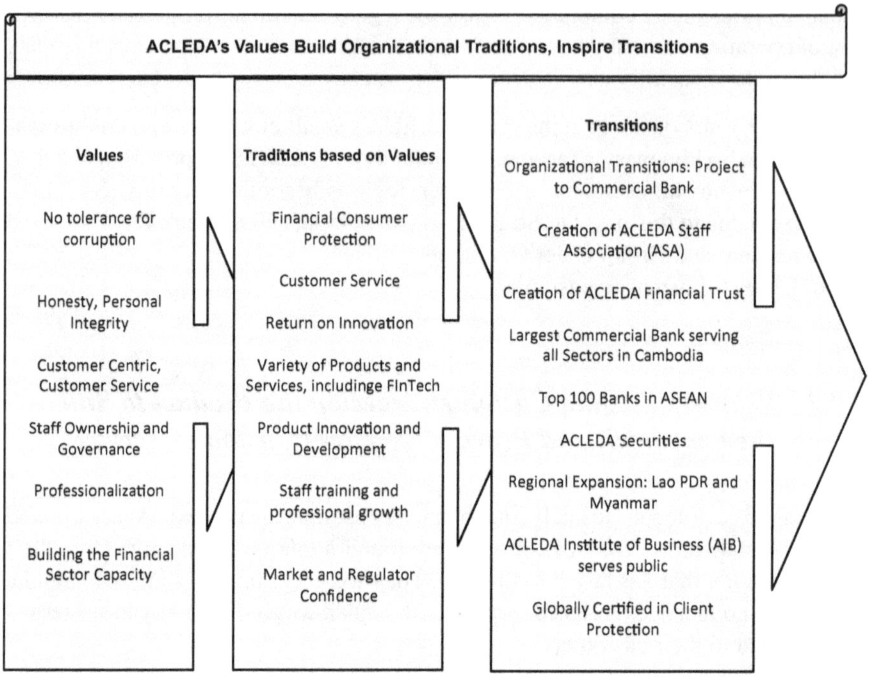

Fig. 5.6 ACLEDA values build organizational traditions, inspire transitions

the planning process, not the plan itself, was the key tool in building a united and consultative team.

Prior to 1996, ACLEDA branches kept only expense records and reported on employment generation and training participation. With the most recent transition, performance-related reporting for a credit operation had to be taken more seriously. As the credit operation became the core business, standardized financial reporting was required from each branch. Compliance was audited by both ACLEDA's internal auditor and internationally recognized audit firms.

ACLEDA's core values were incorporated into the way its pioneers did business. The pioneers passed these traditions on to their colleagues and later to their successors and protégés, establishing another tradition in ACLEDA Bank's history.

The pioneers were also aware that they had set the foundation for ACLEDA to achieve an admirable vision of inclusive growth for which there was no charted path. If this new venture worked, it would be the first time Cambodia could boast of having a financial institution that provided credit in small amounts for the hard-working people of Cambodia, in its small towns, largest cities, and most isolated rural areas.

While no one could predict where this type of banking venture could lead, ACLEDA's pioneers knew they would need more than the combination of values and vision to succeed. And with this realization they found innovation—and the "return on innovation"—as one of their fundamental values and a cornerstone of their culture.

Even their competitors acknowledged that ACLEDA "was always raising the bar and setting the standards and practices for others" (Luchtenberg 2017).[3]

Organizational innovation was more of a necessity than an option for ACLEDA to keep pace with its many transformations in the 1990s. During this time ACLEDA advanced from a project to a local NGO, to a specialized credit NGO, to a specialized bank, and, finally, to a commercial bank.

In 1999, for the first time in ACLEDA's history, all staff had to vote on the future of their organization. ACLEDA's democratic values of staff participation would be put to a test. Would ACLEDA remain an NGO dependent on foreign funding, or would it become an organization that aimed to become self-sustaining in financial resources, human resources, and governance?

For some ACLEDA staff, these new ideas were daunting. They thought choosing a path independent of donors was sure to bring about ACLEDA's demise, even though 2 years earlier, by the end of 1997, ACLEDA MFI broke even. Many staff left in anticipation of that inevitable day when ACLEDA would close its doors. The pessimistic outlook did not correctly foretell the future. Financial performance improved, and the ACLEDA MFI was on its way to reaching the elusive but perhaps attainable goal of a commercially viable microfinance institution.

Dr. So Phonnary thinks back with only a modicum of the frustration she must have felt at the time, "Staff left because they didn't trust themselves to do a good job" (So 2006).

In the staff general assembly of February 1999, an overwhelming majority of staff members voted to approve the five-year strategic plan that called for the transformation of the NGO into a licensed financial institution. The new financial institution would fall under the regulatory framework of the National Bank of Cambodia (NBC). But, it was not until October 2000 that a new board was installed to govern the new entity. The new organization would become ACLEDA Bank Ltd., a specialized bank.

The opportunity to vote on their future ushered in more organizational innovation the principle of staff ownership, governance, and related practices. This new principle became a strong and vibrant centerpiece of the ACLEDA culture. As a result, the ACLEDA Staff Association (ASA) that was established in 1999 became a shareholder of the bank in 2000, along with other shareholders in the new ACLEDA Specialized Bank.

With this achievement, the ACLEDA pioneers became more confident that they could create and coach a new generation of leaders and staff because of—not despite—the new responsibilities thrust upon them by becoming a licensed and regulated bank (Box 5.1).

---

[3]Author interview. 2017 Paul Luchtenberg was previously with World Relief Microfinance in Cambodia, a competitor of ACLEDA during the 1990s. He currently is the Regional Technical Advisor for UNCDF in Southeast Asia.

Box 5.1: Requirements for a Specialized Bank License in Cambodia

A specialized bank is a banking license provided by the National Bank of Cambodia within the Law on Banking and Financial Institutions, promulgated in 1999.

The two defining characteristics of a specialized bank versus a commercial bank are (1) more limited banking activities than commercial banks, generally with a focus on credit or payment and remittances, e.g., and (2) lower minimum registered capital than the amounts required for a commercial banking license.

The Circular on Implementation of Minimum Registered Capital for Banking and Financial Institution, dated 28 June 2016, increased minimum capital requirements for commercial banks from USD 37.5 million to USD 75 million, while the minimum capital of specialized banks increased from USD 7.5 million to USD 15 million.

The NBC also requires both newly established and existing microfinance institutions to have a minimum capital of USD 1.5 million, which is considerably higher than the amount set by the previous regulation at USD 62,500. Microfinance deposit-taking institutions are also subject to new minimum capital requirements to increase their minimum capital from USD 2.5 million to USD30 million.

Sources: Bun Youdy (2018), National Bank of Cambodia (1999, 2016)

5.3.3 *"Capacity Leads, Capital Follows"*

The entire organization would now focus on preparing to become a licensed financial institution, regulated by the Central Bank. All staff dedicated themselves to complete a transition plan that would lead them to develop a regulated, commercial financial institution. New systems were required to shore up current operations and meet the needs of future growth. And, new staff capacities would be required for commercial operations.

The requirements for new systems and staff capacities obliged a new mantra based on existing values. A familiar mantra "Capacity Leads, Capital Follows" took on new meaning with ACLEDA's transformation to a commercial bank. The illustration in Fig. 5.7 shows the platform for growth during this phase and the progressive steps that enabled it.

One of the basic assumptions during the earlier periods, which later proved to be correct, was that attracting additional capital would depend more on the organization's capacity to manage sustainable business operations rather than the ability to disburse massive amounts of credit in line with a quick impact strategy preferred by ACLEDA's donors.

Instead, ACLEDA would follow its long-term strategy of organizational development. They recognized that attracting capital would depend on the staff capacity

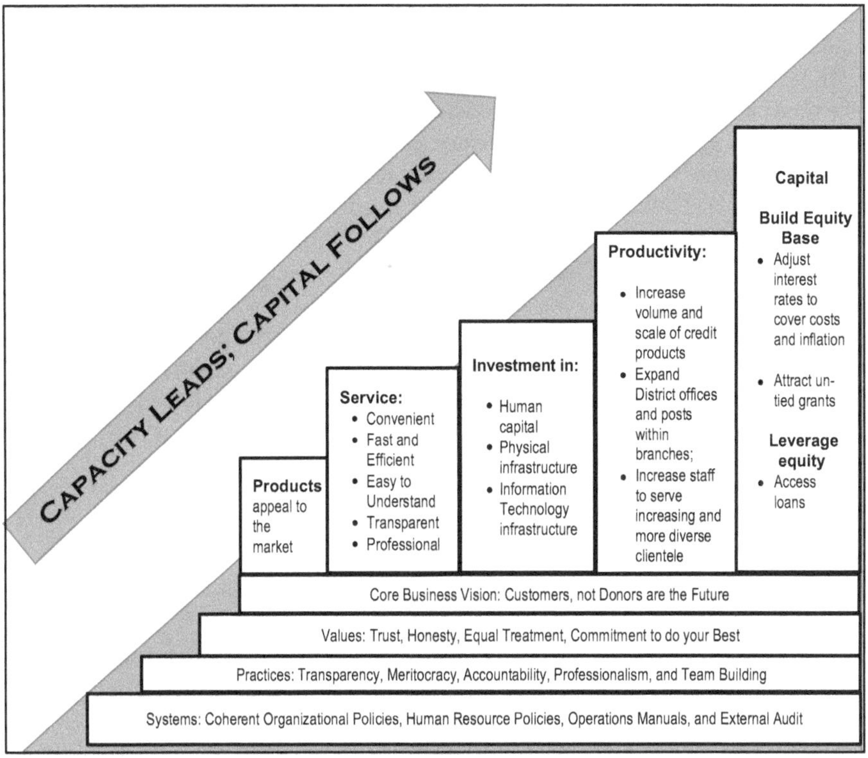

Fig. 5.7 Capacity leads, capital follows. (Reproduced from Clark 2006)

to effectively manage the growing and evolving organization. "Capacity leads, capital follows" had guided ACLEDA through previous transformations and would guide them again through this one.

Another principle, "commitment to do your best," was a fundamental value of ACLEDA staff since the very beginning. They were eager to see it fulfilled.

5.4 The Ethical Bank Emerges

In 2000, ACLEDA was granted a license as a specialized bank by the National Bank of Cambodia. Two years of hard work preparing the organizing documents and association agreements paid off: ACLEDA courted and found shareholders that matched their own values.

The new foreign shareholders included Deutsche Investitions- und Entwicklungsgesellschaft (DEG), the Netherlands Development Finance Company (FMO), the International Finance Corporation (IFC), and Triodos Bank. The ACLEDA NGO and the ACLEDA Staff Association (ASA) joined the foreign investors in boardroom decision-making and with an initial capital infusion combined to produce local ownership of 51%.[4]

In less than a decade, ACLEDA completed its 4th organizational transformation. The transition came and went in 2003 when the current shareholders increased their capital in ACLEDA Bank Ltd, and it emerged ACLEDA Bank Plc., Cambodia's first commercial bank with a countrywide branch network, serving the micro and small enterprise market. While ACLEDA Bank gained a new status, it's original hard-earned values and core culture of transparency remained intact, deepening and expanding to new frontiers within Cambodia and beyond.[5]

These transformations over a decade enabled ACLEDA Bank to offer more products, attract more customers, and grow beyond what seemed possible in 1992. The next two chapters, *Pioneers and Protégés* and *Performance*, explore these facets of ACLEDA Bank's growth and the story of the people who made it happen.

5.4.1 Traditions and Transitions

How do you recognize ethics in banking? You may study ethics or banking. But in the case of ACLEDA, it's the study of bankers who have ethics.

The ACLEDA pioneers developed their banking practice based on ideas and attitudes about how they wanted to treat others in society. Soon an organization-wide culture was established within the bank. The core values centered on "no tolerance for corruption" and "equal treatment" according to capacity, not rank, privilege, or wealth. These beliefs applied to customers and their fellow staff colleagues.

Practices and systems were products of those values, not the other way around. While their strategies and practices changed dramatically over the years, each change was grounded in the set of core values from the beginning that strengthened over time. Good business strategies made the course navigable and accelerated the momentum. Systems enabled ACLEDA staff to see what the organization had accomplished, where it was going, and where it might be possible to chart new courses. But the systems did not dictate the fundamental direction. Values did.

ACLEDA Bank's many value-based traditions informed and supported the transitions to new ventures and enterprises that now comprise the ACLEDA Group of Companies. See Fig. 5.6.

The following section examines those values and how they led ACLEDA Bank Plc. to establish new ventures and initiatives.

[4] See, *When There Was No Money*, Chap. 10 for a detailed review of the initial shareholder structure discussion and decisions. This topic is also discussed more broadly in the following chapters.

[5] The following chapters explore ACLEDA Bank's growth within Cambodia, Laos, and Myanmar. Topics include the foundations of good governance, practices of the board, business ethics, and banking beyond borders.

5.4.1.1 No Tolerance for Corruption

For the most part, the extra tax payments required of every player in the banking sector are now gone. While most other financial organizations paid the extra "tax," ACLEDA staff would wait all day at the NBC, just for a chance to pay only the tax that was legitimately assessed according to the law. ACLEDA's honest behavior earned them the reputation in the broader banking community as an organization with "No tolerance for corruption—no matter how big, no matter how small."

When many MFI NGOs transformed into for-profit MFI companies there was speculation in the banking community at the time about possible scandals and excess benefits going to top executives and staff. Legal experts who knew the banking community well remarked, "No, no, not ACLEDA. They are squeaky clean." From experience, this is something ACLEDA staff, their customers, their investors, their governing Board, and their regulators already knew.

ACLEDA's fundamental value—no tolerance for corruption—became a tradition within the organization, and the broader society acknowledged it. This tradition is responsible for the overall growth of ACLEDA Bank, the trust customers put in its services, and the confidence investors have in their management and growth.

The principle, "understand the customer" is a bedrock tradition of ACLEDA through each of its transformations. The basic principles of developing the product that suits the customer and providing excellent customer service are primarily responsible for the phenomenal growth experienced by ACLEDA from 1996 onward.[6] This tradition continues in ACLEDA Bank Plc. with the continued development of new products including deposits, domestic and international transfers, and electronic banking through ATMs and with online convenience.

5.4.1.2 Technology, Fintech, and Things that Light Up in the Night

The practice of listening to the customer combined with ACLEDA Bank's passion for innovation propelled ACLEDA Bank Plc. into the fintech world. ACLEDA is positioned at the forefront of technology and fintech applications thanks to its culture of innovation and its in-house capacity to deliver. Yet, that wasn't always the case.

The MIS had plagued ACLEDA's operation for years; working on one design or another, they always came up short. But rapid growth made computerization imperative; it was becoming increasingly difficult to manage the growing operation.

As Chhay Soeun, ACLEDA's Former Finance Department Manager and currently Chairman of the Board, said in an interview in 2005 about the origins of ACLEDA's computer systems, "Peter Kooi created a small computer program—"Int-clac"—that was very helpful between the no records period and the Quick Books period."

[6] See Figs. 5.4 and 5.5 and Chap. 7 for more recent growth figures through 2018.

When Terry Mach arrived at ACLEDA in 1995 as the Information Technology Expert, each of ACLEDA's branches had an old desktop computer. One day of the month the computer was lavished with attention as each staff member fought for a turn to pound out their monthly report; on the other 29 days, the computer suffered from neglect and is dust-covered and relegated to a lonely dark corner.

Together with the people who would use the system the most—the branch staff—Terry and the IT team quickly focused in on designing a computer system with the user in mind. "I was concerned about the dust, the humidity, the airflow, purchasing the right hardware, designing the software, writing the program and testing it with those who would use it in the branches. ...And, I kept asking for more money. If you prepare for computerization, you have to be prepared to spend money." More money was not something management wanted to hear at a time when controlling costs was a priority.

"You know, change is a scary thing," says Terry. "It creates more work initially. People have to change their way of doing things, their way of managing things. No one saw the benefit at the time, only the problems. And there were so many problems." Yet, the small computer program integrated branch and center reporting, helping to avoid numerous accounting and recording mistakes, while increasing staff accuracy and efficiency.

The Click Loans and Click Savings programs were designed for speed and accuracy, not for security, as the ACLEDA Bank's GLOBUS system is today. GLOBUS replaced Click Loans and Click Savings as each branch came online.

Regrets? Not in the least. "Information technology leads the business," says Terry. "It changes the thinking, and then the way the business operates changes. People can start thinking about the business, not the calculations. Productivity increases; new products are possible. It's positive for staff, management, the organization and the customers."

In 2017 Terry Mach, now ACLEDA's EVP and Group Chief Information Officer, was working with another group of dedicated ACLEDA staff members on the latest innovation, ACLEDA Unity ToanChet. ToanChet is a fintech application running on a smartphone, enabling customers to access all of ACLEDA Bank's services at any time. The application allows fast, easy, and reliable mobile phone payments between customers and vendors for transactions of any size. It extends access to financial services in the Khmer language as well as English to every village and commune in Cambodia (ACLEDA Bank 2018).

The newest innovation complements others that have been developed recently. In 2014 and 2015 ACLEDA launched ACLEDA Internet Bank and ACLEDA E-Commerce Payment Gateway which enables customers' access to financial services and online payments anywhere anytime.[7]

ACLEDA's customer centric traditions have enabled the organization to smoothly obtain certification for client protection and serve as a trusted product developer for

[7] Chapter 7 on Performance continues a discussion of innovation in product development and the growth it enables.

the rest of the banking community, for example, by establishing convenient tax payment outlets, first on an experimental basis with National Bank of Cambodia support and oversight.[8] And, ACLEDA Bank's customer base continues to grow organically, as the daughters and sons of some of their early clients open bank accounts for the first time.

5.4.1.3 Staff Ownership and Governance

During the deliberations for the transition from NGO to specialized bank, ACLEDA considered the possibility of staff ownership. As Chhay Soeun recalled, the deliberations centered on the following rationale: "When ACLEDA becomes a profitable enterprise, perhaps the shareholders would not want to include others; an exit strategy for shareholders may not include employee shares."

For ACLEDA's leadership, it seemed advisable to mitigate this risk and include employees as owners from the beginning. All employees were included in 1993 as owners of the ACLEDA NGO and its specialization and expansion plan. And, again in 1999 all ACLEDA staff was included to vote on the future of their organization to become self-sustaining in financial resources, human resources, and governance. There was no compelling reason to change the right to ownership now. In fact, to ignore ACLEDA staff history would have been a mistake.

The ACLEDA Staff Association (ASA) was principally conceived to allow all employees to share in the ownership of the bank along with the new foreign investors and to enhance the bank's performance. It was not conceived as an exclusive executive compensation program, nor was ASA's creation necessary to meet the minimum capital requirements for ACLEDA Bank.

And, this is how ACLEDA reaffirmed the value and practice of employee ownership and supported another transition for ACLEDA Bank and for the broader financial sector, if they chose to consider it. In the opinion of ACLEDA's Board, ASA has made ACLEDA Bank stronger and has enhanced the performance of the bank, as well as the performance of the governing board. ACLEDA Bank has offered a unique ownership model for others to study and emulate.[9]

5.4.1.4 Professional Development: A Learning and Teaching Organization

In the 2005 interviews for When There Was No Money, Mr. Tiv Dynare,[10] the chief accountant in the Prey Veng branch said as part of this interview, "We hire them young and train, train, train." In 2005, Mr. Chan Serey, the Director of Human

---

[8] Chaps. 6 and 7 explore other product developments and innovations in banking in more detail.

[9] Chapter 6 discusses the formation of ASA and the thinking behind the birth of ASA in detail.

[10] Tiv Dynare was the chief accountant in the Prey Veng branch in 2005.

Resources, was often quoted by ACLEDA staff when he would tell new ACLEDA staff recruits, "When you are finished with the training, you will be so polite, informed and well-spoken even your parents won't recognize you." In fact, even in 2019, Mr. Chan Serey's saying has become a famous quote around the ACLEDA Institute of Business campus.

Nay Sok Samnang, SVP and Head of Administration Division, says, "New staff come to ACLEDA with basic knowledge and the motivation to learn. They gain experience by working with others, they learn from each other. Later, they become teachers of others." He added, "I like this new staff. I used to be one of them."

Since its inception, ACLEDA focused on capacity building, first out of necessity and then because they saw a greater vision. From the very beginning, this small group of teachers rallied around capacity building as something that was important now and would always be in the future. They embraced educational efforts and knowledge building for all staff, management, and even the Board of Directors.

A highly educated and experienced staff and Board of Directors is the envy of every bank and the banking sector in every country. It promotes a sound reputation and competitive edge for the bank and for the country. Yet, something more than banking was being established in Cambodia by ACLEDA's success and leadership within the banking sector. ACLEDA staff were refining values and molding them into a culture that valued personal and corporate integrity, honesty, and transparency.

Codes of conduct and codes of ethics for the Board of Directors are duly signed. All employees of the Bank are governed by a strict code of ethics which is incorporated into the collective labor agreement and which covers such matters as personal behavior; relationships with colleagues, customers, and regulators; confidentiality; conflicts of interest; acceptance of gifts; money laundering and "whistle blowing." The Audit and Compliance and Risk Committee of the Board of Directors regularly review the codes of conduct and ethics to ensure that they remain relevant and up to date.

At the forefront of ethical behavior, among staff, management, and directors is the organization's incorporation of a strong environment and social sustainability stance along with an annual report on meaningful indictors of responsibility toward staff, the environment, and the community.

5.5 Formalizing the Contribution to Cambodia's Microfinance Sector

Microfinance institutions and, later, microfinance deposit-taking institutions (MDIs) imitated ACLEDA's products and enticed ACLEDA staff to join them. Other CEOs might see this as subsidizing staff development of the competition, but not Dr. In Channy. He has held a brilliant attitude about "staff poaching," an attitude he holds dearly to this day.

> "It's a way that the industry will grow and become more like us. It's good for us. It's good for them. It's good for everyone; no one loses."

And so, an old and time-honored tradition of "capacity leads/capital follows" takes on a new meaning in the context of Cambodia's emerging inclusive financial services market. The "capital" that follows "capacity" is the human capital that inexorably results from ACLEDA's values and traditions.

ACLEDA Bank Plc. has become the incubator for well-qualified, professional, and ethical staff and management teams to serve the Cambodian banking sector. As before, In Channy could not be more pleased. This tradition will be duplicated in Laos and Myanmar whether by design or by accident.[11] It is the inevitable public good that comes from ACLEDA's values and traditions.

The founding of the ACLEDA Institute of Business (AIB) in 2017 formalized ACLEDA Bank's tradition for staff professionalization by serving a growing number of Cambodian under-graduates and associates who have career goals in the banking sector. AIB may revolutionize the higher education sector, just as ACLEDA Bank has done in the banking sector.[12] And both sectors of the economy are looking forward to celebrating the advent of this inevitable day.

With over two decades of dedication to building pioneering organizations, strengthening the financial sector, and contributing to the growth of a country, the ACLEDA Group of Companies continues to represent the future and the promise of future generations.

The best part of ethical banking, as ACLEDA has practiced it, is to see the desired changes that everyone else can see, to make those changes well, to make them first, and, to encourage competitors to do the same.

References

ACLEDA Bank Plc. (2018) Annual Report 2017, Phnom Penh.

The Banker's 2016 Top 100 Association of South East Asian Nations (ASEAN) Ranking Available via http://www.thebanker.com/Banker-Data/Top-100-Asean-Banks-Singapore-stays-strong-but-Cambodia-on-the-rise. ()

Bun, Youdy (2018) Cambodia, The Banking Regulation Review – Edition 9 Available https://thelawreviews.co.uk/edition/the-banking-regulation-review-edition-9/1169667/cambodia (Accessed 8 January 2019)

Clark, Heather (2006) When There Was No Money. Springer, Berlin – Heidelberg

Hakemulder, Roel (1995) Promoting Local Economic Development, International Labour Organization, Geneva

Hakemulder, Roel (2006) quoted in *When There Was No Money*. Springer, Berlin – Heidelberg

In, Channy (2006) quoted in *When There Was No Money*. Springer, Berlin – Heidelberg

Luchtenberg, Paul (2017) Author Interview.

So, Phonnary (2006) quoted in *When There Was No Money*. Springer, Berlin – Heidelberg

Sar, Roth (2006) quoted in *When There Was No Money*. Springer, Berlin – Heidelberg

[11] Chapters 8 and 9 discuss ACLEDA Bank in Laos and ACLEDA MFI in Myanmar.

[12] The ACLEDA Institute of Business (AIB) development is discussed in Chap. 10.

Chapter 6
Pioneers and Protégés

Our corporate culture is very strong to inspire staff to become an effective team. Not just to meet targets, but to develop personally to work in a team, communicate well and aspire to do a good job.
Dr. So Phonnary, Executive Vice President and Group Chief Operations Officer, ACLEDA Bank Plc.

Honesty and integrity drove the organization from the beginning. If any one step were out of line, any hint of corruption, or any doubt that the institution could not deliver, they knew it could fail. The environment was so bad at the time, but the strength of the institutional values and customer demand were the keys to ACLEDA's success.
Claire Van der Vaeren, Former Resident Coordinator, UN Development Programme to Cambodia.

We are employees, but also owners of the bank. This makes us want to work harder, and care for each other. We will do whatever we can to see the bank succeed.
Nay Sok Samnang, Senior Vice President & Head of Administration Division, ACLEDA Bank, Plc.

ACLEDA is a beacon in Cambodia of the way things ought to be.
Anon.

6.1 Introduction

From 1999 to 2017 ACLEDA Bank expanded exponentially. Over the past 19 years, figures show impressive advances, depth, and meaningful growth in the Cambodian market place. In addition, ALCEDA Bank also began to explore other initiatives and investments that fit their guiding ethical principles, entrepreneurial talent, and dedication to innovation and learning.

© Springer Nature Singapore Pte Ltd. 2020

H. A. Clark, *Beyond Borders, Beyond Banking*,
https://doi.org/10.1007/978-981-15-1687-0_6

The previous chapter examined ACLEDA Bank's traditions—its principles and practices—that formed the ethical pillars of ACLEDA Bank's foundation from a project and then growth to become the largest bank in Cambodia by 2016.

Chapter 6 focuses on one of ACLEDA Bank's fundamental traditions—local ownership and governance. This pillar guided the decisions that ACLEDA leadership chose regarding the future ownership and governance structure of the Bank with the formation of the ACLEDA Staff Association (ASA) and the ACLEDA Financial Trust (AFT). This chapter offers a summary of the history and analysis of the ACLEDA NGO transformation. It focuses discussion on why and how ACLEDA planned to include staff ownership as a main principle of the Bank's foundation.[1]

Chapter 7 presents an analysis of ACLEDA Bank's performance over more than a decade of operations. It discusses financial performance and market performance as it ties another of ACLEDA's fundamental values—"listen to the customer"—to innovations and growth in customer services and product development.

Later, ACLEDA Bank made investments in the wider financial market system to enhance transparency. The expansion of ACLEDA's primary ethical pillar—"no tolerance for corruption"—gained momentum outside the organization as the Bank experimented with digitizing corruption out of the market. Chapter 7 discusses this important experiment.

6.2 The ACLEDA NGO: Ownership and Governance

The ACLEDA NGO emerged in 1993, with the transformation of the ILO SEISP project into the Association of Cambodian Local Economic Development Agencies.[2] See Fig. 5.1 in Chap. 5 for a timeline of ACLEDA's transformations from 1993 to 2003.

As an NGO, ACLEDA's General Assembly of all staff served as the ultimate governing body of the ACLEDA NGO. However, branch managers became the most powerful members of ACLEDA, as they comprised the governing board along with the national representative of their national association, ACLEDA. At this point in time, the ACLEDA NGO branches were the former Local Economic Development Agencies (LEDAs) that gave ACLEDA its name—the Association of Cambodian Local Economic Development Agencies. The LEDAs were still the center of the organization.

Looking back now, the first governance system of ACLEDA NGO appears unclear and impractical by any standards of corporate governance. Yet, at the time it had many advantages for both the staff and the leadership of the organization.

The first main advantage of the early governance system was the establishment of a basis for leadership to be accountable to staff, many of whom worked in remote areas, often cut off from communications with the center as well as other branches.

[1] For the detailed history, please refer to *When There Was No Money* (Clark 2006).

[2] See Fig. 5.1 in Chap. 5 for a timeline of ACLEDA's transformations from 1993 to 2003.

The national structure of ACLEDA as an association complemented the decentralization of the LEDAs.

At that point in time, during the mid-1990s, ACLEDA was an amalgamation of the individual LEDAs based in provinces throughout the country. A central point for exchange was considered valuable by both staff and management, even though all of the LEDAs counted on their own branch managers and staff for leadership and management. As such, there was a strong sense of ownership and independence at the provincial branch level.

Staff and management together benefited by exchanging ideas and experience in this uncharted territory of lending credit in small amounts to poor and low-income people in Cambodia. The collegial system of governance also provided valuable and non-threatening peer-to-peer review and feedback. The system provided an opportunity for branch managers to discuss together and receive critical analysis and knowledgeable feedback on what they thought was best for their individual operations, if not for ACLEDA overall.

The system of governance promoted the exchange of experience among the LEDAs by providing a practical mechanism and a central point for administration, management, and peer learning. It also supported branch managers to become better decision-makers, by encouraging and engaging in an analysis of their colleagues' ideas and suggestions.

And, while the staff of Local Economic Development Agencies appreciated the opportunities to learn and exchange ideas, only a few branch managers thought about what they could accomplish together as one united organization.

The organizational system as it was fostered friendly competition among the branches as they implemented exercises that compared performance among branches and discussed, for example, "150 ways to become more productive" as a branch manager and staff training exercise. During one strategic planning workshop, each branch manager expressed a desire to become profitable, but no one knew whether or not they could reach that goal or how. Part of the workshop included a spreadsheet projection and a very active discussion on the 150 ways to become more productive.

6.2.1 A Focus on Sustainability

When the new 1996 strategic plan called for a focus on sustainability, ACLEDA branch managers realized they would have to generate more income and become more efficient. Most branch managers reluctantly agreed to an increase in the interest rate. But, they worried that a price increase would have a negative effect on their customers, whittling down their portfolios as clients sought out other credit operations.

The gamble on sustainability now became apparent to some branch managers. It would lead them to face an impossible situation—a decreasing portfolio and customer base just as they were expecting customers to pay for their salaries through the 2% interest rate hike. If there were no customers, there would be no salaries. Many could see only a spiral of doom.

After a few hours of playing with the figures and various scenarios using the data from each branch, Cheam Teang, the branch manager from Kampot, suddenly jumped to his feet. "I did it!" he shouted pointing to the computer projections. "Yes, yes, I am profitable!" One year later, Cheam Teang's branch in fact, became profitable. It was the first branch to reach profitability in the ACLEDA network. In time others followed, and the Kampot branch never looked back.

Yet, this enthusiastic attitude was not the immediate response of all branch managers. Some were more focused on the spiral of doom and the enticing idea of running their own provincial organizations.

6.2.2 The Benefits and Challenges of Participatory Governance

The participatory governance model prevented an authoritarian governance model from emerging. Instead, the model actively groomed individuals who would become ACLEDA's future leaders. The model obliged all prospective leaders to prove over time that they had the capacity to lead.

Even though the model prevented tyranny, no one foresaw how easily the model promoted revolution.

As an NGO, ACLEDA was familiar with staff ownership and governance issues, including some of the benefits of the model, as well as some of its greatest challenges. In fact, by 1997 as a series of feasibility studies of ACLEDA's transformation from an NGO into a specialized bank began, ACLEDA's experiment with branch manager governance was beginning to go terribly wrong.

The unforeseen drawback of this participatory approach to governance occurred when a small group of branch managers, as heads of the LEDAS—the most powerful decision-makers in the organization—wanted to separate their branches from ACLEDA, their national association, and set up their own independent microfinance NGOs in their respective provinces.

This small group of branch managers reasoned that their branches were the profit centers of the ACLEDA organization. And, they could do much better as independent province-based organizations than by belonging to a national structure. Several branch managers of the LEDAs saw their national association, ACLEDA, as an unnecessary burden.

Growing Tensions Tensions grew during the Executive Committee and Board meetings in January 1999. The meetings were held to discuss business and prepare for the General Assembly meeting that was expected to be a significant one for the future of ACLEDA NGO.

The following month, the General Assembly was slated to discuss and vote on the NGO transformation to formalize the ACLEDA NGO as a Specialized Bank. The creation of the Staff Association, which would allow staff to participate in the new ACLEDA Bank as shareholders, was on the agenda, as was the new ownership and governance model for the entire organization.

During the January Board meeting, branch managers were challenged on their recent decisions to overlook violations of ACLEDA's Code of Ethics. Perhaps the branch managers could see the writing on the wall, when In Channy decided against the decision by the Board to reconsider the firing of a fraudulent credit officer. "We do not keep people who steal." Channy explained.

Another branch manager already felt threatened by ACLEDA's new system of stronger risk management and central control. He thought he would be disciplined for allowing sloppy cash management procedures in his branch, something recently discovered by the internal audit.

Guns on the Table There was an unsettling silence in the boardroom as branch managers shifted in their seats. They saw one branch manager open his bag, just enough to expose a weapon. "I have my gun," he said as he started a long list of criticisms directed at the Internal Audit Department. "No one can do that to me!" he proclaimed, as a second branch manager showed his gun in support.

Vann Saroeun, the Board Chairman at the time and a veteran branch manager who had just completed a comprehensive and very helpful internal audit in Siem Reap, recalls, "They played the gun, and it was terrible."

Channy remembers knowing the meeting would be tense. Prior to the meeting, he asked everyone not to bring weapons. "We knew some people carried guns in those days, and we expected the meeting to be difficult because we were going to discuss business and the future of the NGO," Channy noted as he explained why the announcement was so important at the time. "You cannot have someone with a gun in a meeting where debates are sometimes heated. It is unprofessional in an NGO or a business; it threatens the free discussion of ideas; and, it is against the law."[3]

The last official board meeting of branch managers, and certainly the most dramatic, again saw the majority of branch managers in unity against those who would destroy the organization. The trade-off was clear: retain power to direct the organization, or protect the organization's uncertain future.

Consistent with ACLEDA's past, they chose the future. With approval of the Board Chairman, and the consensus of the Executive Committee, the branch managers who had carried guns to the meeting were fired.

6.2.2.1 Organizational Critical Thinking Advances

As destructive as the participatory governance system later became, it had abundant value by adding to the critical thinking in ACLEDA as an organization. Board members—the branch managers—had to defend their positions on topics ranging from

[3] This section is summarized from *When There Was No Money*.

broad organizational policy to the details of branch management, overall performance, credit product development, and customer services.

Perhaps the most important of all, the General Assembly, as the key decision-making body in the organization, empowered all staff members as owners of the organization.

Staff members became so empowered that the General Assembly of ACLEDA staff, the supreme body of the organization, voted on February 20, 1999, to abolish itself and its governing board.

As Peter Kooi, ACLEDA's technical advisor at the time, recalls, "All the hands went up!"

The General Assembly created and empowered a transition team with full authority to carry out a plan for the ACLEDA NGO to become a commercial bank, including analysis and recommendations for a new ownership and governance structure.

The minutes of the historic General Assembly duly noted, "The assembly finished happily, and successfully at 6:15 PM" (ACLEDA 1999).

6.3 The Origins of ACLEDA Bank Ltd.

The governance system of ACLEDA was melting down well before 1999. It finally collapsed under the weight of ACLEDA's own mounting success. And, it was only a matter of time before the expanding operation exposed weaknesses in all systems.

Advances in operations and management, human resources, finance, MIS, internal audit, and risk management systems later allowed the organization to grow larger. But at the time, a governance structure that established clear roles and responsibilities and the corresponding accountability mechanisms were the remaining obstacles that would allow the organization to grow bigger and better.

The changes proposed were not insignificant, nor would the steps to the next phase of organization be smooth and easy. The imminent end of the NGO held great emotional significance for all ACLEDA staff; it also raised the staff's expectation of greater economic stake in the operation, along with greater financial risk.

From February 1999 to October 2000 when a new Board was finally installed, for almost 2 years, ACLEDA had no formally recognized governance structure from either the NGO world or the business world. The organization was managed and governed by a small core expert transition team who oversaw operations and worked on new bylaws, articles of association, and the shareholder agreements for what ACLEDA Bank would eventually become.

The ACLEDA NGO staff facilitated another major transition that fit their value system. Now, ACLEDA staff was about to take their new responsibilities for wise decision-making about ownership and governance to a whole new level.

So profound was ACLEDA's first transformation in 1993 from an international development project to a local organization, if not in performance, certainly in attitude, that ACLEDA staff barely remembers a time when they were not free to make their own mistakes.

The first transformation, distant though it may be, paved the way for subsequent transformations and sparked a tentative sense that if this were possible, perhaps anything was. If this could happen, perhaps anything could.

Potential to contribute, values, and business insight, the qualities for which the first LEDA staff were recruited, saw them through the first period of transition from a project to a local NGO. Now they harnessed the hard lessons they learned about ownership and governance and put them into a plan for the future of ACLEDA Bank.[4]

6.3.1 *Outgrowing NGO Status*

By the end of 1997, the ACLEDA NGO had grown to serve 44,533 active credit customers with a portfolio just under USD 6 million. The operation was much too large to continue as an NGO, particularly with growth plans determined to reach a mass market. As an NGO, ACLEDA was also prohibited from mobilizing savings deposits, a product valued by many of their customers.

At the same time, an exciting organizational experiment was taking place with microfinance operations in Latin America, the geographical epicenter of commercial microfinance at the time. This future-oriented phenomenon was called "NGO transformation." It suited microcredit NGOs that had outgrown their NGO status, by virtue of their high growth rates, their increasingly commercial operations, and their customer's requests for saving services.

What Is NGO Transformation?

Some authorities argued that NGO transformation was a somewhat romantic label for the legal creation of a new financial company by an NGO that runs a credit operation. A financial institution is created, licensed, regulated, and supervised under the banking laws of the country.

The assets of the NGO are transferred to the new company in whole or in part, in exchange for shares in the new company. But what really transforms during this process is much broader and deeper. The people involved transform; their horizons grow, their relationships expand, and their perceptions about running the business evolve as they leave the donors' protective cocoon and formally enter the world of commerce.

They are now positioned to transform the organization from the ground up, preparing for possible future changes in organizational principles, practices, and culture. They may even prepare to expand the customer base and to meet a different type of competition with new business and market strategies as new opportunities appear. More than ever, they are now positioned to commit to core values, core customers, and core services.

Sources: Brinsden, John (2005) Clark, Heather (2006), Kooi, Peter (2005).

[4] This section is summarized from *When There Was No Money*.

Transformation of NGO operations into regulated financial institutions could increase benefits to poor and low-income people and micro and small enterprises—the NGO's main customers—by expanding outreach to new customers and by offering them new products and services that only a regulated financial institution could offer.

6.3.2 *Counting with Support of the National Bank of Cambodia (NBC)*

As early as the mid-1990s, the National Bank of Cambodia (NBC) expressed a willingness to work with a large number of microcredit NGOs to develop a new regulatory framework that would permit Cambodian MFIs to transform into licensed, regulated financial institutions. In consultation with interested NGO MFIs, and their donors and technical advisors, the NBC set out to develop a broad regulatory framework for the operations of these new organizations.

A 5-year dialogue between NBC and NGO MFI's—detailed in its nature and occasionally derailed by ideology—finally produced the Law on the Licensing of Microfinance Institutions and the Law on the Licensing of Specialized Banks in 1999, which were amended over the years to fit changing circumstances (National Bank of Cambodia (NBC) 1999, 2002, 2006, 2007, 2011, 2018).

The specialized banking license offered by the National Bank of Cambodia mandated limited functions and products, but offered lower capital requirements of USD 4 million, compared to USD 13 million required for a commercial banking license at the time. A newly licensed specialized microfinance bank could be a stepping-stone to a commercial bank license, but the ACLEDA pioneers would have to prove themselves first.

As HE Tal Nay Im, Director General of the National Bank of Cambodia from 2005 to 2010, explained at the time, a specialized banking license was the most appropriate choice for ACLEDA and for any other NGO microfinance operations' intent on transformation.

> "Overall we felt MFIs would benefit from licensing, enabling them to take deposits and to access financing from foreign shareholders, commercial institutions and the Rural Development Bank," she recalls.
>
> "ACLEDA originally requested a commercial bank license, but the first step for them was a specialized bank. They had to gain experience with a commercial operation and deposit mobilization." (Clark 2006)

6.3.3 *Examining Options for Ownership and Governance*

In 2000, ACLEDA's transformation to a licensed, regulated financial intermediary was the first NGO transformation that took place in Cambodia. The transformation was preceded by a 3-year planning exercise, beginning with feasibility studies as early as 1997, which examined every aspect of the transformation process. The plan carefully considered realistic benchmarks for feasibility and reasonable accomplishments. It also considered how to avoid surprises in an atmosphere of uncertainty.

The transition team weighed the advantages and disadvantages of a number of different ownership structures as part of the feasibility study.

One ownership structure—100% NGO ownership—would enable the ACLEDA NGO to transform quickly into a commercial company. Then, with a track record behind them, the new company could seek out investors gradually over time. This structure was later discarded, however, because the transition team thought it would discourage, rather than encourage, investors to come forward.[5]

The discussions about ownership continued with much internal debate about the desirability of attracting foreign commercial investors or investments by development finance institutions (DFIs)[6] and fretting about the advantages and disadvantages of attracting private local investors. The transition team reviewed the experience and lessons learned from prior NGO transformations in other countries. But, they were determined to create the right balance for ACLEDA in Cambodia and not just follow a recipe that worked well in Latin America.

Eventually the transition team agreed that the best ownership structure for the new ACLEDA Bank Ltd. would be to attract investors at the outset, who had a shared vision with the transforming NGO. The team agreed that they would look for investors who would be valued just as much for their capital as for their compatible ethics, expertise in microfinance, banking, and good governance.

6.3.4 Implementing Organizational Change and Financial Mechanisms

In 2000, the ACLEDA NGO transferred its assets and on-lent its liabilities to the new ACLEDA Bank Ltd. In return, the ACLEDA NGO received 44.91% of the Bank's capital of USD 4 million and became the Bank's largest shareholder.

The ACLEDA Staff Association, Inc. (ASA), a holding company, was established to give ACLEDA staff an equity interest in the Bank. ASA Inc. purchased 6.09% of the total Bank shares with their own money. When staff pledged to put their own capital at risk, the ACLEDA Staff Association became the founding commercial shareholder of the newly regulated financial institution.

Foreign investors purchased 49% of the shares in equal amounts. The original foreign investors were three development finance institutions including Deutsche Investitions-und Entwicklungsgesellschaft (DEG, Germany), the International Finance Corporation (IFC, a division of the World Bank), and the Netherlands

[5] Summarized from *When There Was No Money.*

[6] A development finance institution (DFI) is generally a public investment organization and intends to leverage private, commercial participation in the future.

Development Finance Company (FMO). The first private foreign commercial shareholder in ACLEDA was Triodos Bank, an ethical commercial bank in the Netherlands (ACLEDA Bank Plc. 2018).

Today, the financial arrangements seem simple and straightforward. At the time they involved an innovative set of transactions, new laws and regulations, and a group of energetic pioneers from the public and private sector who wanted to see this great experiment succeed in Cambodia. Together they were determined to build a banking system that included poor and low-income people as valued customers.

There was no recipe or playbook that guaranteed success of the Bank or its contribution to an inclusive financial sector. Yet, as with other aspects of the transformation, considerable thought went into the birth of this new organization and the changes that might be accomplished with a new regulatory framework that accommodated microfinance.

6.4 The ACLEDA Staff Association and ACLEDA Financial Trust

6.4.1 Creating the ACLEDA Staff Association (ASA)

The ACLEDA Staff Association (ASA) was created in February 1999. When the ACLEDA NGO transformed into a specialized bank in 2000, it formalized the staff association as a holding company through which the employees of ACLEDA could participate in the long-term growth and value appreciation of ACLEDA Bank.

Through ASA Inc., employees purchased 6.09% of total shares in the newly established ACLEDA Bank Ltd. The former ACLEDA NGO held 44.91% of the total shares in the new Bank, purchased by transferring its liabilities and selling its assets to the newly formed ACLEDA Bank Ltd. Together, the shares of ASA and the ACLEDA NGO combined to reach 51% local ownership (ACLEDA Bank Plc. 2018).

The creation of ASA allowed the ACLEDA pioneers to guard one of their most fundamental values—local ownership and governance—while advancing to new levels of professionalism and clarity about whom they believed in and what they believed.[7]

After a brief consultation visit to Bolivia in 1998 to learn about NGO transformations and how others included employees as owners and investors in their new banks, the ACLEDA pioneers were determined to develop an employee stock ownership initiative for their own transformation that would represent their past history and their aspirations for the future.

With a transformation from an NGO to a commercial entity, there is always a backstory about the origins, growth, and advancement within any organization. The

[7] See Chap. 5 for more detail on corporate values.

story often has to do with ownership and governance, as the organization will change dramatically in these two areas.

No one can anticipate how much change will take place or how fast it will occur. There are factions for and against principles and practices that are sometimes misunderstood or remain unclear, because the experience is limited. The transformation process can easily favor powerful factions within the organization and outside it. So much is uncertain, while so much is at stake.

6.4.1.1 The Thinking Behind the Creation of ASA Inc.

The thinking behind the creation of ASA Inc. centered on the logic of investments and investors. Dr. In Channy felt that creating a profitable enterprise without employee ownership would eventually lead to confusion and disappointment among staff. He reasoned that at some point in the future, the Bank would make a profit, and he posed these questions:

- Why would the initial shareholders want to include others?
- Even if the initial shareholders developed a well-executed exit strategy, why would they want to include staff as owners?
- Would the shareholders see creating a means for employees to participate in the growth of the institution as too burdensome than the simple transaction of one foreign investor selling its shares to another?
- If the shares increased in value, would the staff be able to afford them?

"That's why we were determined to create ASA", recalls Chhay Soeun, who is now the ACLEDA Bank Plc. Chairman of the Board, but back in 2000 he was ACLEDA's Finance Manager.

For ACLEDA Bank's leadership, it seemed advisable to include employees from the beginning, just as they were included as "owners" of building the organization and determining its future. To ignore staff history would not only be a mistake, but it could also inhibit future innovation and organization-wide advancement.[8]

6.4.1.2 Lessons About Structuring Employee Stock Ownership

Four important lessons from this period guided ACLEDA's thinking about how to structure and operate stock ownership for employees as it transitioned from a specialized to a fully capitalized commercial bank.

First, ACLEDA's management thought employee stock ownership could be profitable for employees and healthy for the organization, but it was critical to balance the degree of ownership with concerns about conflict of interest.

[8] This section is summarized from *When There Was No Money*.

Second, the introduction of employee stock ownership needed to prevent a widely dispersed ownership structure that might lead to an unstable capital base. The risk of employees without "deep pockets" had to be addressed.

Third, it was important that the shares should truly be owned by the employees, not subsidized from additional donor capital or transferred to individuals from the NGO as compensation for "sweat equity." Otherwise, management thought, how would the Bank really operate on a commercial basis? And how would the new owners of the Bank treat the employees as investors with equal status if assets were simply transferred to employees and management?

Lastly, the architects of what would become ASA Inc. determined not to separate management from the rank and file in terms of benefits or participation in the governance of ASA. Both management and staff contributed equally to how the organization evolved. The stock purchase and ownership arrangements would be designed to treat all employees equally.

6.4.1.3 Staff Ownership: A Nonnegotiable Position

Through each and every ACLEDA transformation, staff "ownership" has been a nonnegotiable position of ACLEDA leadership: from staff "ownership" of ACLEDA's vision, values, and performance to staff as shareholders in ACLEDA Ltd. and its transition to ACLEDA Plc.

ASA is a unique feature of ACLEDA's transformation that other NGO transformations originally bypassed. Later, several MFIs reconsidered the value of forming a staff association and built one based on their own terms and practices. Staff associations of MFIs served many important purposes. Yet none of them included the unique element of staff association representation on the Bank's governing board that ACLEDA did.

An ASA member is elected from the broader ASA membership to serve on the ACLEDA Bank's Board of Directors and represent ASA's status as an equal commercial investor on the governing board, along with other shareholder representatives and independent non-executive directors of ACLEDA Bank.

Even as ACLEDA teetered under the strain of an outdated governance system, the organization stirred with quiet changes. Within 2 years, the NGO operation would look insignificant in comparison to what the ACLEDA Bank Ltd. would accomplish.[9]

Much earlier, as early as 1995 with the transition from development project to a local organization, the ACLEDA NGO found meritocracy, a learning culture and a determination to become a professional organization. Later, concern about improving performance and the efficiency within all aspects of the operation was added to the foundation.

[9] See Chap. 7 for ACLEDA performance and growth indicators.

Now, the stakes were much higher, and the ACLEDA staff was determined to address the many challenges—and opportunities—that they expected to find. During this third transition from an NGO to a regulated financial institution, they expected to build a bank. And, if the expectations for the future of Cambodia were low, expectations within ACLEDA were high and began to climb.

Most importantly, the people involved in each of these transformations transformed into banking pioneers for a new millennium.

6.4.2 The ACLEDA Financial Trust (AFT)

In 2013 a Financial Trust Law in accordance with the Law on Finance Management was enacted in Cambodia, which introduced the concept of a financial trust to the country for the first time. At the same time, the concept of a financial trust was introduced into the Cambodian legal system. Perhaps not completely understood by those who would be affected by the new law, or those who were required to implement it, the details of the law and subsequent regulations governing the financial trust were finally published in August 2013.

6.4.2.1 The Original Intent of a Trust Law in Cambodia

The original intent of developing a trust law in Cambodia was to introduce a broad-based law that could support a variety of functions supported by trusts, as they are commonly implemented throughout the world.

Supporters of the law ranged from real estate agencies to law firms specialized in estate probate and execution, pension funds, and the philanthropic community that was interested in setting up foundations to allow more permanent and reliable support of good works than continuous fund-raising efforts would allow.

The Asian Development Bank provided technical assistance in support of developing the law in the interests of contributing to streamlining and facilitating development of the many functions within the financial sector that a trust law could support and to analyze and support a broad-based trust law that could support other primary sectors of the economy, for example, pension funds for government and private sector employees.

A trust law would provide the legal framework for a number of financial transactions within and outside the financial system. For example, the trust law could support real estate escrow accounts, private foundations for support of the arts and sciences, university endowments, private trust funds for family inheritances and for people with disabilities, investment vehicles for pension funds, other uses in the private and public sector, and joint private public sector initiatives.

6.4.2.2 The Disappointment of a Focus Only on Microfinance

The trust would be a new type of financial institution in Cambodia, and it was expected to contribute to facilitating a broad range of financial transactions that could improve efficiency and transparency throughout the financial system. Even though the law lays out the foundations, the specific regulations and areas of operation were yet to be defined.

For reasons that are still unclear, the Ministry of Economy and Finance (MoEF) chose to focus narrowly and exclusively on microfinance, and the donor money that may have existed in the organizations after MFI NGOs transformed into commercial entities. Technically the donor funding in most MFIs at the time of their transformation was not donor money, but earned income, as was the case with ACLEDA. The donor money was expensed long ago as a sunk cost of enabling the MFI operation to become sustainable in the long run.

Unfortunately, the trust law has never been broadened beyond the original narrow objective of microfinance nor powered to reach its full potential in the broader Cambodian economy and financial sector.

At the time the Financial Trust Law was promulgated, Dr. In Channy welcomed the trust law as "…a good one that we want. This *Prakas*[10] is designed to examine the operator who uses the trust funds and to see whether it is used for the original intentions of donors."[11]

By the end of 2014, the ACLEDA Financial Trust succeeded the ACLEDA NGO, which was abolished. The ACLEDA NGO was required by the MoEF to register as a financial trust.[12] The AFT however continues to support ASA just as ASA supports the AFT in share repurchase, and the AFT continues as a shareholder in ACLEDA Bank Plc.[13]

6.4.2.3 The Long-Term Objectives of the ACLEDA Financial Trust (AFT)

The long-term objectives of the ACLEDA Financial Trust (AFT) are to:

- Create opportunities for employment and income sources to contribute to Cambodian economic development.

[10] The term "Prakas" is generally translated as a regulation under a wider law.

[11] Dr. In Channy quoted in Phnom Penh Post November 18, 2014, in an article written by Hor Kimsay.

[12] The ACLEDA Financial Trust (AFT) succeeded the ACLEDA NGO under the Sub-Decree No. 476 dated August 26, 2013, on the Financial Trusts of the Royal Government of Cambodia, and the Prakas No. 1041 dated September 26, 2014, on the Management and Monitoring of Financial Trusts of the Ministry of Economy and Finance.

[13] See Sect. 6.5 for more details.

- Promote and support the advancement of the sciences related to economic development including finance and banking and with a focus on financial inclusion and financial literacy.
- Promote economic and educational opportunities for youth and low-income populations.
- Contribute to improved financial services through ACLEDA Bank Plc. and associated entities, in order to stimulate the local economy.
- AFT pursues exclusively the aforementioned objectives. It acts altruistically, does not primarily pursue objectives for its own private commercial interests, and is not affiliated with any political party.

AFT continues to act as one of the shareholders of ACLEDA Bank Plc. that is established under the laws of the Royal Government of Cambodia, to maintain Cambodian nationality of ACLEDA Bank Plc. and to encourage the adherence by ACLEDA Bank Plc. to the original objective of ACLEDA—to support Cambodian micro, small, and medium entrepreneurs.

The former ACLEDA NGO mission was finally complete with the advent and success of ASA Inc., the further development of the ACLEDA Securities Company, and the expansion of the Cambodian Securities Exchange.

Finally, and most importantly, the complete transformation of the ACLEDA NGO to the largest bank in Cambodia was accomplished successfully and with the vision of bringing lasting value to society.

6.5 Summary and Conclusion: The Gamble and the Promise of ACLEDA Bank Plc

Why did ACLEDA staff and management bet on an uncertain future? At the time, Dr. In Channy noted, “We transformed two times before. Each time we improved the operation. Staff trusted management that this third transformation would again make ACLEDA stronger.”

The uncertain future was countered by the promise that what ACLEDA staff and management already had accomplished together was only the beginning of something much better.

They trusted that promise, and they trusted themselves to do a good job.

They defended that promise against those who would divide and destroy.

And, out of the turmoil emerged a leadership and management team whose capacity was matched only by their integrity.[14]

The bank you can trust; the bank for the people

[14] This section is summarized from *When There Was No Money*.

On October 1, 2000, ACLEDA Bank Ltd. opened its doors as a specialized bank. The shareholders included the ACLEDA NGO, the ACLEDA Staff Association (ASA), and four foreign investors: DEG, FMO, IFC, and Triodos Bank.

On December 1, 2003, ACLEDA Bank Plc. was licensed as a commercial bank after the shareholders tripled the Bank's capital to US$13 million.

By 2004 ACLEDA Bank Plc. became the commercial bank with the largest branch network in Cambodia.

By the end of 2016, ACLEDA Bank had become the largest commercial bank in Cambodia by all measures, including its branch network, the numbers and variety of customers using different products, assets and their quality, portfolio and its quality, and deposit mobilization throughout the country, including in rural areas.

The Bank was also recognized as the bank with the greatest number of employees and a national reputation for transparency. By the end of 2018 ACLEDA Bank employed 12,310 staff in 262 branches in all provinces and major towns in the Kingdom of Cambodia (ACLEDA Bank Plc. 2018).[15]

Two important accomplishments within the last 18 years are noted that enabled complete achievement of ACLEDA Bank's original transformation plan in 2000.

First, the idea that ASA Inc. would continue to build lasting employee shareholder ownership has been achieved. As of early 2020, four private commercial investors complement the AFT that holds 26% of the shares in ACLEDA Bank Plc. and ASA Inc. that holds as its principal asset 89,636,246 shares of ACLEDA Bank Plc., representing 25% of the Bank's issued shares (ACLEDA Bank Plc. 2020).

One of the most innovative mechanisms that enabled staff ownership at a greater percentage was due to the officially sanctioned transactions between the ACLEDA NGO and the ASA. This mechanism to transfer shares between ACLEDA NGO and ASA enabled staff to increase their percentage of ownership in the Bank over time.

A share repurchase mechanism ensured the safety of the Bank during lean times or times when other staff investments took priority. But the mechanism continued to work over the years and supported the increasing confidence, viability, and strengthening of ASA.

Second, the idea that international commercial investors would eventually become shareholders of the Bank, replacing the Development Finance Institutions (DFIs) whose job would be done, has been accomplished successfully.

The three original DFIs—DEG, FMO, and IFC—have fulfilled their mandates "to play a temporary role in the market and work toward crowding in market actors, including private investors…. Incentivizing commercial investors to invest in projects with high potential development impact is core to achieving a DFI's mandate, and can be realized when DFIs invest early in new business models or help develop new market segments" (Moretto and Scola 2017).

[15] ACLEDA Bank Website. Accessed May 3, 2018.

The private commercial shareholders[16] that have taken the place of the DFIs over the past decade and are current shareholders of ACLEDA Bank Plc. are the following.

COFIBRED—Compagnie Financière de la BRED (BRED's financial company): COFIBRED is a BRED Banque Populaire's fully owned subsidiary. Given the development of BRED's international activities, it was decided in 2008 to regroup all subsidiaries and participations within a single entity, COFIBRED. COFIBRED's portfolio is made up of more than 45 subsidiaries and participations with a global value of about EUR 1.0 billion, in bank, insurance, e-commerce, and/or financial companies (2017 net profit: EUR 12.4 million). These subsidiaries and participations are located worldwide on the five continents.

SMBC is a top-tier Japanese bank operating globally with total assets of ¥186,202 billion, a Core Tier 1 capital ratio of 15.2% and credit ratings of A (S&P's) and A1 (Moody's) as of September 2017. Through its 440 domestic branches (excluding sub-branches and banking agencies) in Japan and 75 overseas branches (including subsidiaries, sub-branches, and representative offices) all over the world, SMBC provides a broad range of financial services including deposit taking, corporate finance, structured finance, securities investment, money transfer, foreign currency exchange, corporate bond trustee services and custody services, financial futures underwriting, and investment trust sales. "To become a truly Asia-centric institution" has been one of the goals of SMBC's core vision. SMBC has proactively invested its resources in Asian countries with a high growth potential.

ORIX Corporation (TSE: 8591; NYSE: IX) operates a diverse portfolio of businesses in the operations, financial services, and investment spaces. ORIX's highly complementary business activities span industries including energy, private equity, infrastructure, automotive, ship and aircraft, real estate, and retail financial services. Established in 1964, ORIX has also spread its business globally by establishing locations in a total of 40 countries and regions around the world. Through its business activities, ORIX has long been committed to corporate citizenship and environmental sustainability.

Triodos Microfinance Fund, Triodos Fair Share Fund, and Triodos Sustainable Finance Foundation are three investment funds managed by Triodos Investment Management that own shares in ACLEDA Bank Plc. Triodos Investment Management is a 100% owned subsidiary of Triodos Bank, one of the world's leading sustainable banks. The fund's focus is on providing access to financial services for low-income groups and SMEs in developing countries in order to contribute to a sustainable inclusive financial sector. (ACLEDA Bank Plc. 2018, 2019)

In December 2019, ACLEDA Bank announced plans to list on the Cambodian Securities Exchange through a "Peoples' IPO". (ACLEDA Bank Plc. 2019, 2020).

[16] Shareholder profiles are sourced from ACLEDA Bank Plc. Annual Report 2017.

6.5.1 *Preparing to Serve the Next Generation Well*

The ACLEDA NGO was asked by the Ministry of Economy and Finance (MoEF) to transform into a financial trust to pioneer a new type of financial institution in Cambodia that is widely applicable to other sectors of the economy—not only microfinance. As the ACLEDA Financial Trust begins to fulfill its new mission with vigor, enthusiasm, and competence, it aspires to do more and better by broadening the functions of trusts in Cambodia, as envisioned by the original mandate to establish trusts and the law that supports them.

Another transition in the tradition of the ACLEDA Group is advancing. The AFT has reached its final destination, completing its purpose in the financial sector and now takes on a new opportunity to invest in ACLEDA Institute of Business (AIB).[17]

An investment in AIB is in line with AFTs current objectives and long-term aspirations. The higher education sector in Cambodia is an investment-worthy objective that has significant opportunity to make a difference in the lives of thousands of aspiring Cambodian students and young professionals. It is one that is clearly rooted in ACLEDA Bank Plc.'s past and directly related to continuing the Bank's reputation for excellence in the future.

The AFT is eager to participate in the further development of the higher educational sector in Cambodia. On March 30, 2018, the MoEF granted permission for AFT to invest in AIB and "to implement it with great effectiveness." The MoEF further noted that AFT should continue paying the MoEF's annual contribution fee on the trust balance, which is invested in ACLEDA Bank Plc. As such AFT begins to formally embrace the higher education sub-sector while keeping an anchor in the financial sector.

Finally in December 2019 ACLEDA Bank announced plans to list on the Cambodian Securities Exchange through a "Peoples' IPO". As Dr. In Channy affirms, "We always viewed our customers as *builders* of the bank. Listing allows our customers to become *owners* of the bank."

Another chapter of the ACLEDA history comes to a close, just as new opportunities begin to appear on the horizon.

References

ACLEDA (1999) Minutes from ACLEDA's Six General Assembly, February 20, 1999.

ACLEDA Bank Plc. (2018, 2019, 2020) Bank Profile https://www.acledabank.com.kh/kh/eng/bankprofileACLEDA Bank website, accessed 30 April 2018, 3 May 2018, 12 January 2019, 14 February 2020

ACLEDA Bank (2014–2017) ACLEDA Bank Annual Report. ACLEDA Bank Plc. Phnom Penh

Brinsden, John (2005) Author interview on ACLEDA's NGO transformation and principles and practices of NGO transformation

[17] See Chap. 10 for an introduction to the ACLEDA Institute of Business.

Clark, Heather (2006) When There Was No Money: Building ACLEDA Bank in Cambodia's Evolving Financial Sector. Springer, Berlin Heidelberg.

Hor, Kimsay (2014) Finance Ministry demands banks' trust fund details. 18 November 2014 Phnom Penh Post, Phnom Penh

Kooi, Peter (2005) Author interview on ACLEDA's NGO transformation and principles and practices of NGO transformation

Moretto, Louise, and Barbara Scola (2017) "Development Finance Market Development." Focus Note 105. CGAP Washington, D.C.

National Bank of Cambodia (1999, 2002, 2006, 2007, 2011, 2018) Laws Applicable to Banks and Financial Institutions. https://www.nbc.org.kh/english/legislation/laws_applicable_to_banks_and_financial_institutions.php Accessed last 12 January 2019

Chapter 7
Products and Performance

When we started to think about people as customers, our portfolio began to grow. It was only a matter of time before we improved our service to become a quick service, an easy service, a service closer to where the customer lived, and, a service that would always be there. That's what the customer wanted.
Mr. Nay Sok Samnang, SVP & Head of Administration Division, ACLEDA Bank Plc.

When you have no competitor you will sleep. If you see others do as you do, you will wake up and run.
Dr. So Phonnary, Executive Vice President, Group Chief Operations Officer, ACLEDA Bank Plc.

ACLEDA's customers built the bank.
Drs. Peter Kooi, Member, Board of Directors, 2000–Present.

A fast motorcycle turns sharply down a side street in Phnom Penh in 2012. It barely misses a pedestrian. The motorcycle skids to the left and rockets down the street.

The rider is concerned with only one thing—avoiding the police. The police will charge him with a fine and an extra fee for his recently expired vehicle registration tax sticker.

Earlier that week, and even earlier that same day, the motorcyclist tried to pay the fee and secure the vehicle registration sticker. For the past 3 days, he has waited in line just to pay the fee, ensuring a valid registration. Each time he failed to get to the front of the line. Three days wasted, income lost, extra fees paid, frustration, and…still illegal.

Each day, like every weekday in 2012 in Phnom Penh, over 300 motorcycles are parked side-by-side and fender-to-fender on the side street near the Department of Revenue and Taxation. Some are there again for the third day in a row. The motorcyclists line up before 8:00 in the morning and leave at 4:00 in the afternoon when the department closes.

© Springer Nature Singapore Pte Ltd. 2020
H. A. Clark, *Beyond Borders, Beyond Banking*,
https://doi.org/10.1007/978-981-15-1687-0_7

Some of these dedicated taxpayers are lucky enough to work their way to the front of the line. Each motorcyclist who makes it to the front of the line may have paid twice the amount of the legitimate fee for the stamp tax sticker as proof of registration of his or her vehicle.

The crowding near the department is less for cars, but the fee is higher, and it is also matched by an equivalent "extra tax."

7.1 Introduction

The last chapter focused on one of ACLEDA Bank's fundamental traditions—local ownership and governance. This fundamental pillar guided ACLEDA leadership's decisions regarding the future ownership and governance structure of the Bank with the formation of the ACLEDA Staff Association (ASA) and the ACLEDA Financial Trust (AFT).

Chapter 7 starts with a consideration of the investments ACLEDA Bank chose to make in the financial system to enhance transparency in the wider financial market system.

It started with an innovative pilot project, promoted by the Ministry of Economy and Finance (MoEF) and prompted by all those bribe-paying, cued-up motorcyclists, to enhance efficiency and transparency in one primary payment system.

The pilot project provided the opportunity for ACLEDA Bank Plc. to develop a new service by "listening to the customer." Quite unexpectedly, the same service allowed the Bank to expand their primary ethical pillar—"no tolerance for corruption"—to new heights as the Bank experimented with digitizing corruption out of the market.

Lessons about product development—both successes and failures—are presented. These lessons show how both problems and triumphs are not just valuable for organizational learning—but essential for organizational growth.

Chapter 7 concludes with a presentation of ACLEDA Bank's performance and contribution to Cambodia's banking sector over more than a decade of operations. It discusses market performance as it ties together ACLEDA's fundamental value—"listen to the customer"—to innovations in product development and growth in customer services.

7.2 ACLEDA Bank Values Influence the Wider Financial Market System

Since its focus on microfinance in 1995, ACLEDA influenced the way the financial sector worked, particularly through the retail banking system. ACLEDA's influence was also recognized in sector-wide capacity building and influencing informal norms and formal financial sector rules that developed over time.

In 1999 the UN Development Programme (UNDP) and the US Agency for International Development (USAID) chose to support a 3-year USD 300,000 technical assistance grant to ACLEDA, the dominant microfinance NGO at the time. The purpose of the grant was to fund technical assistance in systems development, capacity building, and readiness of the NGO Microfinance Institution (MFI) to take on a new commercial status as a specialized bank (ACLEDA Ltd.).[1]

This experiment, supported by the National Bank of Cambodia, was intended to "show how" such a transition was possible in Cambodia. The hope was that ACLEDA's transformation would lead to other MFI transformations to a legal status in the formal, regulated financial sector. These new entrants would continue to value poor and low-income people as customers and develop the products to serve the entire market, not just the privileged segments.

"ACLEDA was the leader, and everyone else was following," noted Dennis Cengel, the USAID project officer at the time. "They inspired confidence with the banking authorities and among their colleagues." ACLEDA's competitors often noted that "ACLEDA was always raising the bar, it affected everyone's performance" (Cengel 2006).

ACLEDA's performance as an NGO specialized microfinance institution (MFI) was exceptional. If plans to become the first NGO commercial transformation in Cambodia were fulfilled, it would make an important contribution to the development of an inclusive financial sector, one that embraced the majority of Cambodia's population, as worthy customers (Clark 2006).

But in 1998, the IFC—one of the prospective ACLEDA investors—like many other commercially oriented investors battled with the idea that microfinance could be a commercial proposition and that an NGO could in fact transform into a commercial bank. According to Morgan Landy, an IFC advisor at the time, "Over time, IFC people visited ACLEDA and saw how in such a poor country, microfinance could have a large development impact in a very commercial way" (Landy 2006).

Eventually, the positive effects from ACLEDA's commercial transformation would ripple throughout the microfinance community, as all eight of the leading MFIs would seek, and later obtain a microfinance deposit-taking license, a new license issued by the National Bank of Cambodia beginning in 2009. The new license aimed to facilitate commercial transformation, at lower cost than the specialized banking license, but continue to uphold the professionalism of the microfinance industry.

By all counts, any donor would be happy with the stellar return for a small grant for technical assistance for the ACLEDA NGO to transform into to a specialized bank.[2] Other MFIs could now chart their own transformative paths—with NBC's support—as microfinance deposit-taking institutions. This new licensing category for MFI transformation would advance financial inclusion in Cambodia and offer customers a greater variety of products and services. It would also advance the

[1]The decision to transform, the evolution of the ACLEDA MFI, the plan for transformation readiness, and the governance of the transition team are discussed in Chaps. 5 and 6.

[2]For a description and definition of a specialized bank and the minimum capital requirements of microfinance deposit-taking institutions (MDIs), specialized banks, and commercial banks in Cambodia, refer to Chaps. 5 and 6.

professionalization of the microfinance sector and expand the MFIs' reach to new areas with new products.

7.2.1 *The Ministry and the Motorcycle*

The Ministry of Economy and Finance (MoEF), under the direction of HE Keat Chhon, pursued a number of innovations to support the flight to quality of the banking system, as well as wider financial sector market development initiatives.[3]

Some of the least well-known innovations had the greatest impact on the financial well-being of the lower-income segments of the population in Cambodia. One small innovation of the MoEF at the time was outsourcing a public service—payment of vehicle registration stamp tax—to two banks, including ACLEDA Bank. Canadia Bank Plc. also participated in the pilot project.

In 2012 the Ministry of Economy and Finance asked ACLEDA Bank if they would be willing to participate in a pilot project to collect vehicle registration taxes on behalf of MoEF. The proposal to ACLEDA was to issue the vehicle stamp tax registration sticker and collect the payment for motorcycles throughout Cambodia.

Winning innovations in financial inclusion—like this one—often begin with small experiments and limited funding, not big announcements and appropriately large budget allocations. In Cambodia, this small pilot would bring about an array of systemic improvements in the efficiency of consumer payments and advances in eliminating corruption in the payments system[4] for a wide segment of the Cambodian population. Experiments, such as this, with the consensus and buy-in of major market players are the kinds of initiatives that stimulate positive market development nationwide.[5]

ACLEDA Bank's Ready Agreement to Innovate ACLEDA readily agreed to take part in the experiment because the Bank through its extensive nationwide branch-banking network already had access to millions of motorcyclists as customers. It would be good for the Bank and its customers.

And motorcyclists, reasoned Dr. In Channy, were engines of the economy. They were poorly paid, frequently targeted for bribes, and already valued customers of ACLEDA Bank in urban and rural areas.[6] Motorcyclists came to the ACLEDA Bank

[3] See Chap. 3 for advances in the "flight to quality" within the Cambodian banking sector.

[4] A payment system is any system enabling the transfer of funds between parties. For example, when a bank processes a check, it uses a payment system to collect funds from the bank on which the check was drawn and then transfers the funds to the payee's account. In 2018, most payment systems are electronic, and most involve the Central Banks of a country in some way. Financial Dictionary at www.thefreedictionary.com

[5] See Chap. 3 for a discussion of the market development approach to systemic change.

[6] The number of registered vehicles in Cambodia grew by 14% in 2016, with more than 3.2 million vehicles registered, including 2.7 million motorbikes, according to the Ministry of Public Works and Transport. To put this staggering figure into perspective, for every five people you meet in Cambodia, at least one of them probably has a registered motorcycle.

branches during their normal course of business; why not provide another convenient service with the benefit of saved income?

And, if this works for motorcyclists, it could work for all segments of the population.

Participation in this pilot project would be another way for ACLEDA Bank to practice one other closely held principle—no tolerance for corruption. It was a small initiative, but if successful, it might have a large impact on rooting out corruption and promoting transparency in the wider financial payments system. Consumers and business women and men who paid taxes, fees, and registrations just to survive and carry on trade without the ever-present bribes and pay-offs might finally get a break. But just as important, with continued vigilance and investment in IT systems upgrades, this initiative might help increase transparency within the wider financial system.

As a consequence of agreeing to launch the pilot, ACLEDA invested in expanding and enhancing an already sophisticated IT system in order to manage different data and new types of transactions. Developing the new IT system took much longer and was more costly than originally expected. But, when the new system was in place, ACLEDA emerged from the process with a competitive advantage in the market. Most banks did not have the technological infrastructure to deal with massive data, efficient and accurate data processing, and the confidentiality that such a system required.

A small innovative pilot project became the perfect fit for ACLEDA Bank's ethical banking practice. It linked good commercial business sense and shareholder value with innovative products and services for poor and low-income people and all segments of the population.

The value added of this particular service included the possibility to expand transparent payments efficiently to other routine payments as a wider market initiative, not just a pilot effort for motorcycles. Such a small pilot could have a greater effect on digitizing corruption out of the system.

Indeed, that is exactly what happened!

By 2016, four years after the original invitation to participate in the pilot, ACLEDA Bank offered a variety of means for the general population to pay required taxes for all types of vehicles—from the smallest motorbike to the largest commercial transport trucks and 16-wheelers. (See text box.)

ACLEDA Bank highlights benefits and convenience to the taxpayer as follows:

- *Paying tax on means of transportation for all types of vehicles to the government through ACLEDA Bank's Branches conveniently.*
- *Saving you time and money.*
- *Placing a secure payment.*
- *Having a chance to use other products and services of ACLEDA Bank.*

ACLEDA Bank does not charge an additional fee.

Source: ACLEDA Bank Plc. Website.

Today, ACLEDA Bank facilitates customer payments in person at 262 branches in all provinces throughout the country. The Bank also manages an e-payment service, which links customers with utilities companies for water and electricity payments, and bill payment services for the Internet, mobile services, and a variety of other e-commerce companies for both businesses and consumers.

The Bank also links consumers and companies to the General Department of Taxation to pay a variety of taxes easily and efficiently—from those on vehicles to salary taxes, as well as business and investment taxes and payments.

Social accountability advocates in Cambodia note that, even though the government's tax payment process is still very complicated for many citizens, bank-facilitated payments have ensured greater transparency at the point of sale (Sorn 2016).

And, endorsements from motorists using all kinds of vehicles, including motorcycles note, "an expired vehicle registration tax sticker is not a problem—just go to any branch of an ACLEDA Bank or other vendor of registration stickers, purchase a 12 month tax sticker over the counter, and stick it on the bike in a conspicuous position so the police can see it" (Trip Advisor 2018).

7.2.2 Digital Pioneers

ACLEDA's digital payments experiment started by servicing vehicle tax payments off-site from the official tax collection location. It started as a small pilot backed by an innovative idea from the Minister of Economy and Finance who understood the financial system in Cambodia and wanted to improve it.

Creative and competent financial services providers implemented the experiment. The ACLEDA Bank initiative had an impressive impact not only on the original target group but also on the Bank's systems. As a result, positive changes for the entire ACLEDA Bank customer base expanded as new digital products were developed and grew to match increasing customer demand.

Most importantly, this small initiative stimulated broader system-wide change in the payments system of the national financial sector. As such, the system came one giant step closer to a financial system that works for the majority and one that continues to achieve progress toward increasing transparency.

Such a small pilot had a great effect on digitizing corruption out of the consumer payments system and strengthening the financial market system.

And, it all started with one motorcycle.

7.3 Product Innovation: Two Decades of Lessons About Products and Performance

Motorcycles and their registration tax payments are not the only products ACLEDA Bank developed by listening to their customers. ACLEDA pioneered many other products for the Cambodian marketplace since their start with micro and small enterprise loans.

Many of these products, such as insurance and international funds transfers, advanced in the local market through commercial partnerships that ACLEDA Bank Plc. entered into over the years. Western Union was the first commercial partnership in 2001, bringing international family remittances to the provinces. Later, the bancassurance[7] arrangement with Prudential became a most successful market cooperation for both parties to bring access to life insurance to the broader community—a "first" in Cambodia.

Over 25 years, ACLEDA staff and management have learned many important lessons about developing and delivering products to serve Cambodia's people.

Six lessons are highlighted here, which are based on six very different ways that products are developed when the financial institution is interested in keeping or expanding its customer base. Each lesson emphasizes, "listen to the customer," but it also notes that customers can often demonstrate their views about products in very different ways. And, the effective financial services provider attunes its listening to detect and interpret some of the more subtle customer responses to a product.

7.3.1 Lesson 1: Ensure Safety and Ready Availability of Customer Deposits at All Times

Since meriting the specialized banking license in 2002, ACLEDA Bank's first product innovation was developing a safe, reliable deposit service with a decent return on savings. The savings service complemented ACLEDA's primary credit products, the mainstay of the operation at the time.

The importance of voluntary savings to the Cambodian rural and urban population was no mystery, yet at the time, many MFIs still insisted on mandatory savings tied to customer loans. Others insisted that poor and low-income people wouldn't or couldn't save.

An early lesson for ACLEDA Bank was that in times of uncertainty or turmoil, people would come to the branch to pay off their loans and deposit their funds as a means of keeping their wealth and reputations intact. Ensuring safety of savings, as

---

[7] Bancassurance is a business relationship between banks and insurance companies, generally using the bank's consumer network and relationship to offer insurance products to a larger number of people.

well as accessibility of funds at all times, was another lesson that figured into forming the collective ACLEDA mindset.

Later, during times of uncertainty, such as elections, ACLEDA customers tested the availability of their deposits. They were not disappointed. Drawdowns on deposits were readily available in person, in branches, in web-based services, and through the largest ATM network in Cambodia. Reliability of the services inspired further customer trust in the bank, proving once again that depositors want both safety and availability of funds at all times.

See Fig. 7.1 for the phenomenal history of deposits in the Cambodian banking system, highlighting ACLEDA Bank's performance, and Fig. 7.2 for ACLEDA Bank's deposit and credit customer growth statistics.

7.3.2 Lesson 2: Economic Growth Rates Influence the Uptake of Products and Services

Throughout the 1990s ACLEDA financed a limited number of medium-sized enterprises. Over time, ACLEDA Bank added a number of products that were tailored to medium and large businesses and corporations, such as cash management services and payroll services, in addition to credit and deposit services. By 2013 public sector organizations began to see an increasing opportunity to utilize payroll services and other cash management services, pioneered by ACLEDA Bank in early in 2001.

But it was not until later in 2007, when already rising economic growth rates in the country began to further accelerate that ACLEDA's credit product for medium-sized enterprises found greater market appeal. The medium-sized enterprise

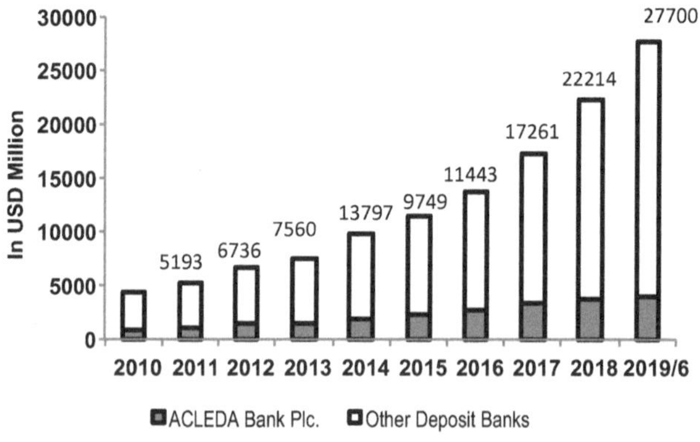

Fig. 7.1 Customer deposits in Cambodia's banking sector 2001–2019
Sources: ACLEDA Bank Plc. annual reports and performance data
https://www.ceicdata.com/en/indicator/cambodia/total-deposits; National Bank of Cambodia annual reports

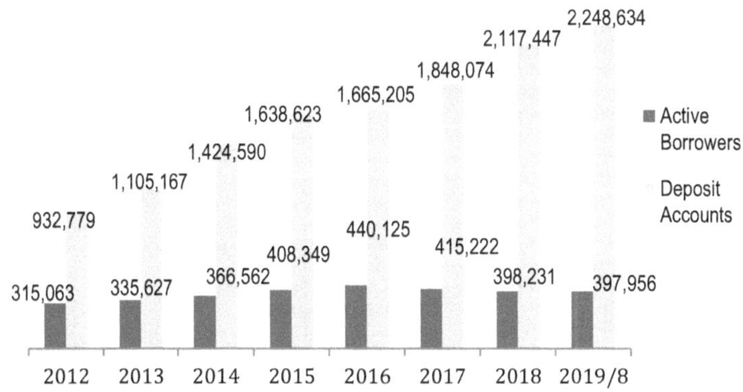

Fig. 7.2 ACLEDA Bank Plc. deposit account growth and active borrowers: 2012–Aug 2019
Sources: ACLEDA Bank annual reports 2012–2018 and achievements through August 2019

portfolio was equal to and then surpassed the value of the small enterprise credit and microcredit portfolios, when compared with the decade before.

On the deposit side, when new regulations were developed to allow strong MFI credit providers to transform into microfinance deposit-taking institutions in 2007, ACLEDA's savings products were emulated in the wider market. The type of savings account and customer electronic access to the account were further enhanced by digital platforms.

By 2017, the picture looked even more robust for ACLEDA Bank Plc., as the retail sector became the largest segment for growth in deposits, with a significant amount coming from first-time depositors. These new customers included employees paid through ACLEDA Bank's payroll service as well as customers in rural areas where ACLEDA continued to open new offices in underserved areas. The expansion of mobile phone and Internet banking services contributed to this growth as well (ACLEDA Bank 2017).

Indeed, by December 2018 ACLEDA Bank had an outstanding loan portfolio of USD 3488 million serving 398,231credit customers, and 2,117,447 deposit accounts valued at USD 3479 million. Credit and savings products were the backbone of ACLEDA's business in 2000 and continue to be in 2019.

See Figs. 7.2 and 7.3 for the history and growth trajectory of ACLEDA's credit products and customer loan accounts.

But, before ACLEDA Bank's performance got to the levels that are reflected in Figs. 7.1, 7.2 and 7.3, ACLEDA, as an NGO and as a small, but growing commercial bank, experimented with several products. Some of these products did not endure after a short debut in the spotlight. Others required modification when the competition entered the market. All products did, however, provide lasting lessons that ACLEDA Bank practices today.

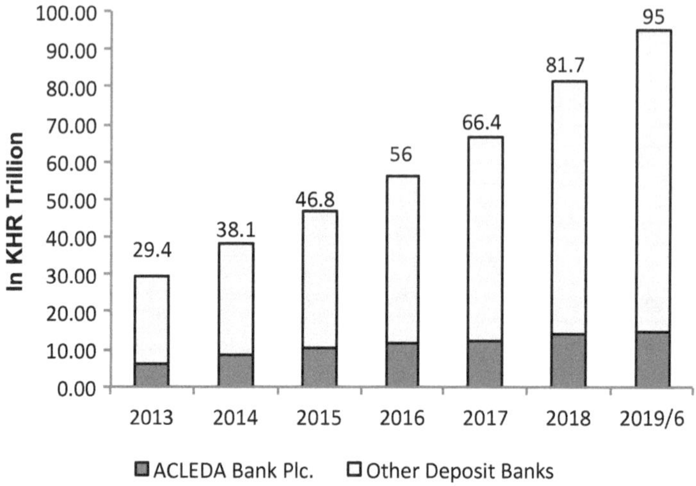

Fig. 7.3 Credit outstanding in Cambodia's banking sector 2001–2019
Sources: ACLEDA Bank Plc. annual reports and performance data
National Bank of Cambodia annual reports

7.3.3 Lesson 3: Match Customer Demand to the Organization's Capacity to Deliver

A third early lesson about ACLEDA's banking operation that was growing more complex each year was that the product offered had to match customer need, translated into customer demand. On the supply side, the product also had to match the organization's competitive advantage in the market place, including the organization's values and expertise.

ACLEDA Bank always valued a direct relationship with the customer and the customer always valued a professional and confidential service from ACLEDA. Just because the competition offered a product and a method of delivering a product, this did not mean that ACLEDA would have an equal competitive advantage to offer the product. In this respect, the experience with community banks is a relevant part of ACLEDA Bank's history.

Community banks, or neighborhood banks had been a main feature of the microfinance landscape in Cambodia since 1991. By 1994, every international NGO involved in microcredit supported community banks in one form or another. While there are no exact statistics for the period, there were hundreds of small community banks supported by international NGOs, directly by international donor projects, local NGOs, and many government agencies, including the Ministry of Agriculture, the Ministry of Women's Affairs, and the Rural Development Bank to name a few.

The banks differed in levels of autonomy of the community and control by the sponsoring agency. Mandatory savings and grouping together of five to six borrowers in a solidarity group, within the larger community bank, were common features of the early community banks. The involvement of local government and community leadership also varied from high involvement, such as assessing and approving loans, to almost no involvement.[8]

ACLEDA originally saw the neighborhood banks as a way to build their portfolio and reach more customers in rural areas in a more cost-efficient way. By late 1995, ACLEDA had established 15 neighborhood banks within its network. That same year, ACLEDA decided not to encourage their development.

In 2003, the chief credit officer in the Siem Reap branch explained how the community banks taught ACLEDA an important lesson about the organization's own competitive advantage in the marketplace. "The methodology didn't work for us," he noted. "Of the eight neighborhood banks originally established in Siem Reap, there was only one left in 1997. It was always the best neighborhood bank and it worked quite well." Three months into 1997, it succumbed to political infighting. "People were fighting about money" (Clark 2006).

Lessons about customer preferences surfaced immediately. On the demand side, customers valued a professional relationship with ACLEDA credit officers and directly with the branch. Customers also appreciated the confidentiality and the safety that the branch service provided, valued features often compromised by the neighborhood bank.

On the supply side, ACLEDA valued a direct relationship with customers and not by building small community banks. The neighborhood banks distanced ACLEDA from the customer, forced people into an arrangement that they did not appreciate, and added unacceptable levels of risk and costs to the borrower and the MFI.

Both the customers and the provider learned valuable lessons about each other. These lessons influenced their future behavior. ACLEDA let the customer choose between the village bank and ACLEDA's regular banking services by providing both. It soon became clear that the customers opted for regular professional banking services over the village banks. But, as long as the ACLEDA-built community banks existed, ACLEDA would continue to support them or help them disband in an organized and satisfactory way to all parties. Out of loyalty and responsibility, ACLEDA supported the last remaining community banks until the last one closed its doors.

7.3.4 Lesson 4: Match Customer Demand for the Product to the Organization's Capacity to Manage the Product's Risk

A fourth lesson about product innovation appeared in 2001, courtesy of the agriculture sector, just a little over a year after ACLEDA had transformed to a specialized bank. The example of product innovation with community banks highlighted the

[8] For a more detailed discussion of community banks refer to WTWNM.

importance of matching a product with an organization's competitive advantage in the marketplace, including its values and capacity to deliver.

This example shows how ACLEDA learned that just because people liked the product and there was immense growth and uptake in the market, it did not mean that the product was one that the organization could deliver or should deliver. The popularity of a product among customers has to match the organization's capacity to manage the product and the associated risk.

7.3.4.1 Features of the Balloon Loan Product Designed for Agriculture

Credit products designed for agriculture have always been a challenge for lending institutions; ACLEDA Bank was no exception. Traditional, un-irrigated agriculture is risky for the borrower and the lender in the best of times. In fact, that is one fairly predictable pattern that makes lenders shy away from financing traditional crop production.

Agriculture credit becomes more risky for the lender when the entire repayment interval for the loan matches the cash flow of the enterprise as it does in a "balloon loan." The repayment is at harvest time, at the end of the crop cycle.

The defining feature of a balloon loan is that principal is paid at the end of the loan term, not at regular intervals throughout the loan term. ACLEDA's balloon loans required regular interest payments throughout the loan term; other organizations required payment of principal and interest only at the end of the loan term. While the first method is relatively less risky than the second, both products tend to be a greater gamble for the customer and the lending institution.

Unlike a working capital loan with regular installments of principal and interest, the repayment schedule of a balloon loan does little to predict the likelihood of the borrower's ability to repay the loan at some point in the future. Even diligent monitoring during the loan period may not reveal any but the most obvious problems, as the ability to repay is generally pegged to a future lump-sum return on investment, such as a harvest.

A balloon loan repayment also requires careful timing. The total repayment must match the harvest, not a week too early before the sale—subverting the very idea of a balloon loan—or a week too late after all of the borrower's other senior debts have already been claimed.

7.3.4.2 A Responsible Product Designed for Agriculture

Originally designed as a reasonable and a responsible product for agriculture, balloon loans were rapidly incorporated into the portfolios of many financial services providers in Cambodia. They held the promise of prosperity for rural areas. It was thought that combining the cyclical nature of risk in traditional agriculture with a balloon loan decreased the uncertainty of default.

And, it did; the unpredictable "if" tended to become the certainty of "when."

In 2001 ACLEDA branches that were heavily invested in agriculture financed by balloon loans showed a serious default rate in the micro portfolio, which represented 30% of the total portfolio, but 80% of the number of borrowers. Without a more rigorous analysis, hasty conclusions could easily have surfaced to close branches in areas deemed unsuitable for lending or to stop the micro agricultural lending business. The easy conclusion was that both were just too risky for a commercial operation.

ACLEDA was determined to dig deeper with a more in-depth analysis of the causes to find a solution that would avoid punishing the customer. In their efforts to detect origins of the crisis, this analysis revealed two other factors, besides the risky balloon loan product, that contributed to the great delinquency crisis of 2001.

First, the number of new staff—most of them credit officers—increased to an all-time high, at a time that called for more experienced staff to support the growing business. By the end of 2001, when the delinquency crisis was in full force, for each staff member who had worked more than 1 year for the organization, there were two who had worked less than 1 year.

Second, expectations for growth were high, with the recently gained status as a specialized bank. Branch incentives were tied to expanding portfolios, increasing numbers of clients, and portfolio quality. However, several branch managers mistakenly emphasized portfolio growth first, intending to worry about portfolio quality later.

Finally, the analysis also revealed that the balloon loan for agriculture, developed out of ACLEDA's virtue for putting its customers first, caused massive delinquency. Just over half of the write-off rate of 10% in ACLEDA's entire micro loan portfolio was attributed to balloon loans. The write-offs for balloon loans during 2001 exceeded the entire outstanding balloon loan portfolio at the end of the year.

7.3.4.3 Resolving the Crisis, Strengthening Management

As ACLEDA began to get the delinquency crisis under control, they deepened the belief that the level of delinquency in a credit operation depends on the organization, not the borrower. The analysis revealed that the deteriorating portfolio quality was primarily a management issue—one that was exacerbated by agricultural lending and balloon loans.

Acting quickly, senior management moved forward in five areas. Strengthening branch management and the credit operation received immediate priority. As management requested and accepted resignations of branch managers and credit officers, ACLEDA redoubled credit management training for all credit staff throughout the entire organization, particularly branch managers.

Second, new policies and procedures were introduced to manage risk without abandoning clients. Third, the regulation for the balloon loan was revised. No more than 10% of the total branch portfolio could support balloon loans. Fourth, new rigorous monitoring systems were adopted, and training in monitoring was redoubled for all credit staff, particularly branch managers.

Finally, the incentive system was revised to tie year-end bonuses to return-on-equity and portfolio quality at the branch level. These changes allowed for a much clearer focus on the return of operations and portfolio quality that is a major component.

By mid-2002 the delinquency crisis abated. By year-end 2003, it appeared to have never happened at all. All branches reported portfolio at risk and write-offs well below the limit ACLEDA had established. The overall portfolio quality—which included agricultural lending and an allowance of 10% of the outstanding portfolio for the balloon loan product—would be the envy of any microfinance institution, or commercial bank. And, ACLEDA Bank Ltd. learned how to put into practice a very commercial operation and redouble absolute loyalty to its customers.

The recovery of bad debt continued, and most—but not all of it—was collected over time.

7.3.5 Lesson 5: Innovation in the Market Is Dynamic; It Encourages the Competition to Work Harder

New market entrants can take market share if their product is more convenient and less costly and provides an equal or better customer service. When ACLEDA moved to design domestic and international funds transfer services, transfer and remittance services were largely new to the national market.

Large funds transfers, mainly official money transfers and international remittances, slowly became available to enterprises, corporations, and government offices a few years after the banking system was reinvented by 1991. When the first commercial bank was reestablished in Cambodia in 1991, the free market economy began to emerge along with the new commercial banking sector (National Bank of Cambodia).

ACLEDA Bank's domestic and international transfers courted a different market than the established one. ACLEDA's market for domestic transfers was comprised of their customer base of entrepreneurs who owned micro, small, and medium-sized enterprises and who worked and lived in both urban and rural areas throughout the country.

Customers for transfers could be served by ACLEDA's wide national branch and rural service-post network, which became the largest bank branch network in Cambodia by 2004.

The transfer service was boosted in 2009 as Cambodia courted the garment industry which continued to establish a greater number of factories. As employment opportunities in the sector grew, the daughters and sons of rural families needed a safe, quick, and convenient way to send a portion of their salaries to rural areas where their families remained. And, ACLEDA Bank's agreement with Western Union allowed families living in Cambodia and those abroad to easily access a safe and reliable international remittance service.

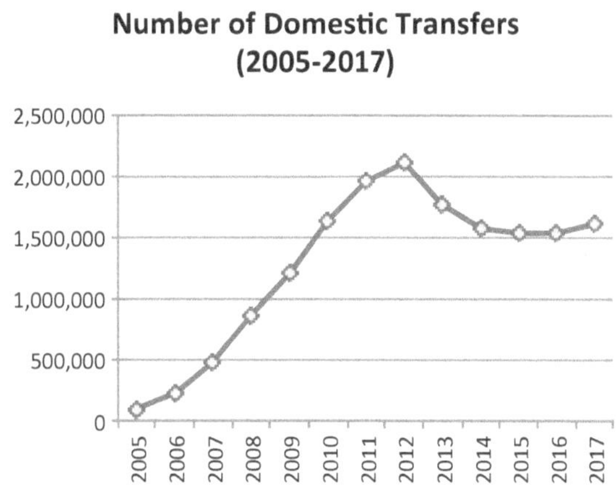

Fig. 7.4 Volume of domestic transfers 2005–2017
Sources: ACLEDA Bank Plc. annual reports and performance highlights 2005–2017

7.3.5.1 Little Competition for a New and Highly Valued Product

Domestic funds transfers grew to become a mainstay of the ACLEDA Bank's services to rural families and their children who worked in the booming garment and construction sectors in the urban areas.

Later, another segment of the market that widely used the service was made up of local banks and MFIs that did not have the technology to transfer funds efficiently and safely or a big enough market for a retail service that would warrant the investment to develop it.

ACLEDA had little competition for this product in the domestic transfer market. Other banks were serving high-end customers. MFIs knew these remittance products were most valued by the lower-income segments of the market, but MFIs did not have the licenses or know-how to provide efficient and safe domestic money transfer services to their customers.

ACLEDA was the only bank with a national network that provided superior domestic funds transfer services. And, they served the market extremely well. As Figs. 7.4 and 7.5 show, the value of domestic transfers doubled from 2013 to 2017 while the number of domestic transfers began to decrease.

Except for a dip in the value—but not the number—of domestic transfers in 2009,[9] domestic transfers grew every year until 2013 when there was a noticeable dip in number, but not the value, of domestic transfers.

ACLEDA's international transfers continued the steadily increasing established pattern. The different pattern in domestic transfers can be explained by two factors.

[9]The year 2009 was a particularly difficult one for all banking transactions worldwide due the global financial crisis and its aftermath, which generally slowed economic activity in every country, including Cambodia.

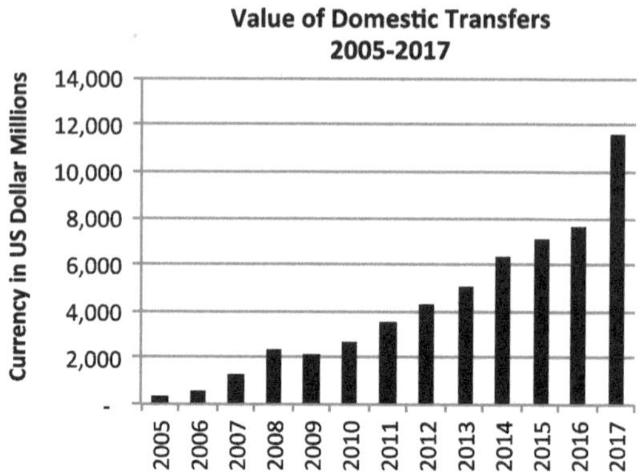

Fig. 7.5 Value of domestic transfers 2005–2017
Sources: ACLEDA Bank Plc. annual reports, and performance highlights 2005–2017

7.3.5.2 The Competition Emerges with a New Model

First, the dip in 2013 can be partially attributed to Wing Cambodia's operations that emerged in the domestic market for small money transfers. Launched in 2009, Wing provided new ways for Cambodians to send and receive money via mobile phones. In 2012, WING also introduced a new product and a new way of providing domestic transfers throughout the country by establishing a nationwide agent network.

In small service shops, in large urban areas, in remote villages, over-the-counter (OTC) transactions were provided to anyone who wanted to send money to anyone else in the country. And, no bank account was necessary.

By 2013, Wing had a booming business, with 100% district coverage nationwide through Wing Cash X-press agents, generally small business owners that qualified to become a Wing agent. Since the introduction of OTC payments in 2012, WING's transaction volume grew from USD 65 million in 2011 to USD 1.5 billion in 2013 and surpassed USD 1.5 billion within the first 5 months of 2014 (Duflos 2014).

Second, in 2013 ACLEDA Bank positioned itself as the provider of choice for funds transfer services throughout the country for local banks, MFIs, and other official and private organizations, which did not have the technology or the legal status to issue funds transfers. As shown in Figs. 7.4 and 7.5, ACLEDA increased the total value of domestic transfers, while the number of transactions decreased and remained near constant for the next 4 years.

WING competed well for ACLEDA customers by offering a product with national coverage and great appeal to a part of ACLEDA's original customer base. Those Cambodians who were based overseas, such as the 3,557 Cambodian United Nations peacekeepers who have been stationed in Africa and the Middle East since 2006, continued to rely on the convenience of international transfers to and from their favored ACLEDA Bank in Cambodia.

7.3.5.3 Lessons About Market Dynamism

There are two main lessons from ACLEDA's experience with fund transfer services, which support the same conclusion: the market for financial services is working well in Cambodia.

First, this example provides an excellent demonstration that innovation in the market place is dynamic. It encourages the competition to work harder, generally resulting in better customer service or segmenting the market so that a variety of capable providers fill the vacuum.

Secondly, the experience shows that entrepreneurial companies develop new business strategies to gain market share when they see an opening in the market. Entrepreneurial companies also develop strategies to recapture market share or diversify their product/market mix, after the competition enters the market place, as ACLEDA Bank did in 2014 and again in 2017. See Figs. 7.4 and 7.5.

The last word on this lesson goes to Terry Mach, EVP and Head of ACLEDA's IT Division, who appreciates innovation and how markets work. "Competition makes you stronger. They attack your weaknesses. You can be the market leader, but you don't have to take the whole market."

7.3.6 Lesson 6: Innovation Is a Mainstay of the ACLEDA Bank Plc. Business Culture

Innovation is often expensive, and it takes time to develop and reach its full potential within a commercial business. There are times when innovation does not yield the anticipated results, so it is also risky. Yet, time and money spent on developing the right product or service, and the technology and staffing infrastructure to support it, are doubly worth the effort. The timing in the market, as demonstrated with the lesson illustrated above, is also extremely important.

Just as the story about the motorcycle and the Ministry demonstrates, ACLEDA Bank ties the traditional return on investment (ROI) to its more subtle foundation, which is the "return on innovation."

The newest product ACLEDA Bank has launched is ACLEDA Unity ToanChet, a fintech application running on smartphones. Customers can complete commercial transactions from anywhere, at any time. The ACLEDA Unity ToanChet application, launched in early 2017, already shows uptake increasing in the Cambodian market. By the end of 2018 ToanChet registered over 115,000 users, and by early-2020 the number of ToanChet users increased over tenfold to 1,330,896 people.

The app serves customers near and far by matching them directly with venders using a mobile phone app, instead of cash-based transaction. Venders such as a tuk tuk driver in Phnom Penh or a mother and her daughter on their way to school find the service valuable, safe, and efficient, just as do customers and retailers in the far-flung province of Ratanak Kiri, or the bustling urban center of Kandal, the agricultural hub of Kampong Cham and the vacation paradise of Koh Kong.

As Dr. In Channy notes, people need something new, and if they are encouraged to develop new ideas for improving their jobs and their own performance, they often do. "ACLEDA Unity ToanChet positions the bank and its customers to prepare for—and participate in financial services of the future" (ACLEDA Bank 2017).

7.3.7 *Technology, Physical Infrastructure, and Human Talent*

For the most part, Cambodia's banking sector mirrors the growth and dynamics of the Cambodian economy. As discussed in Chap. 3, access to a variety of financial services continues to meet the diverse needs of the Cambodian population for deposit services, credit, transfer of funds to and from the rural and urban areas, and international remittances.

Technology New fintech products emerge and show great uptake in both rural and urban areas. Supporting technology has kept up with the developments in the banking sector and makes new fintech products, such as ACLEDA Bank's Unity ToanChet readily available to almost half of the Cambodian population that have at least one smartphone and accessible to the 96% of the population that own a mobile phone (Phong et al. 2016).

Even as the ready application of fintech products in Cambodia provides a glimpse of the future of banking services, the physical services will still make sense when location is convenient; service is helpful, informative, and friendly; and products increase value, safety and utility for the customer.

Physical Infrastructure In 2017, ACLEDA Bank opened additional branches in underserved areas of Cambodia. By the end of 2017, ACLEDA Bank accounted for 30% of the total commercial bank Branches in Cambodia, including 43% of the total commercial bank branches located in the provinces, as shown in Figs. 7.6 and 7.7.

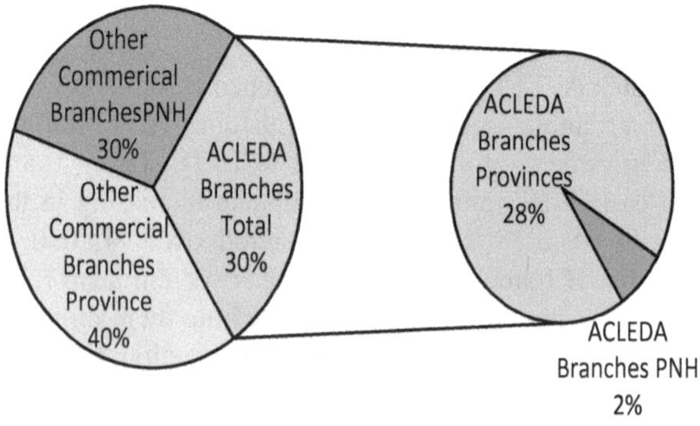

Fig. 7.6 Commercial bank branches in Cambodia 2018
Source: NBC banking supervision report 2018. All figures as of December 31, 2018

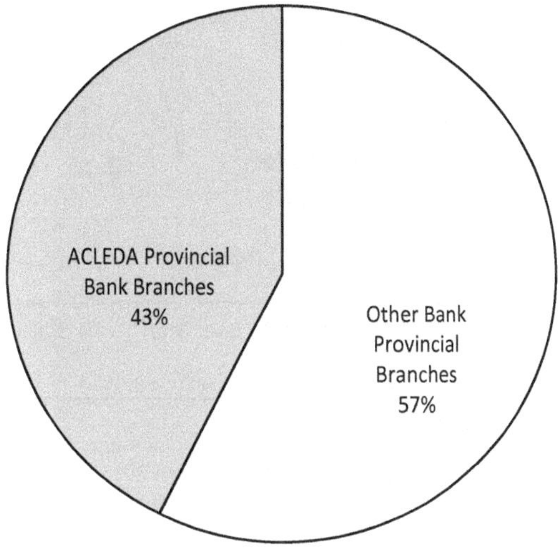

Fig. 7.7 Commercial bank provincial branches in Cambodia 2018
Source: Data from NBC banking supervision report 2018. All figures as of December 31, 2018

The Bank's branch network included 262 branches and outlets in December 2019, maintaining its share of an extensive provincial branch network that is one of ACLEDA Bank's hallmarks of fame.

Human Talent Branch expansion is complemented by staff support in branch operations, market research, and customer services as well as customer assistance for digital services. By December 2018, ACLEDA Bank accounted for 40% of the employment in the commercial and specialized banking sub-sector.

ACLEDA Bank's contribution to the commercial and specialized banking sector employment as a percentage has dropped over the years, even while the absolute numbers of ACLEDA staff have more than doubled, reaching 12,456 staff members since 2008 when 6128 staff worked for the Bank.

See Figs. 7.8 and 7.9 for ACLEDA Bank employment statistics as a contribution to the sector's employment growth rates and within the Bank and the ACLEDA group of companies.

This is a positive sign of the health and resilience of the Cambodian banking sector, as employment in the sector increased from 21,000 in 2008 to 31,445 by the end of 2017.[10]

Even while ACLEDA's absolute contributions to banking sector employment have decreased as a percent of the total, a larger number of commercial and specialized banks increase their own employment contributions to boost the health of the Cambodian economy. And, many well-trained former ACLEDA staff members are enthusiastically recruited by other commercial banks.[11]

[10] Commercial bank and specialized bank employment figures for 2017 from the NBC Annual Supervision Report 2017.

[11] The topic of education and training for the Cambodian banking sector as well as others is discussed later in Chap. 10 on the ACLEDA Institute of Business.

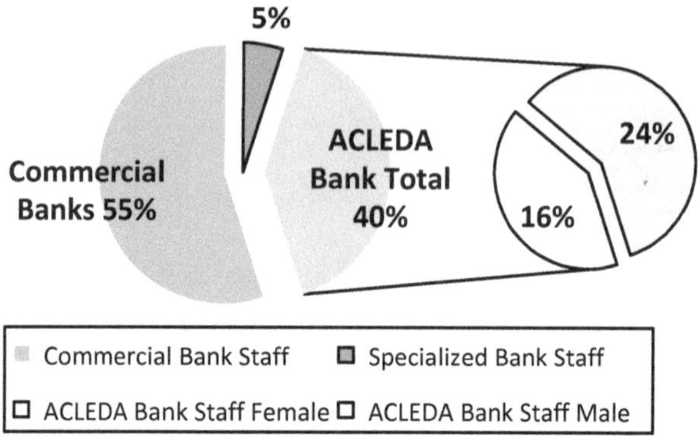

Fig. 7.8 Cambodia banking sector employment 2018
Sources: NBC banking supervision report 2018. ACLEDA Bank Plc. Annual report 2018

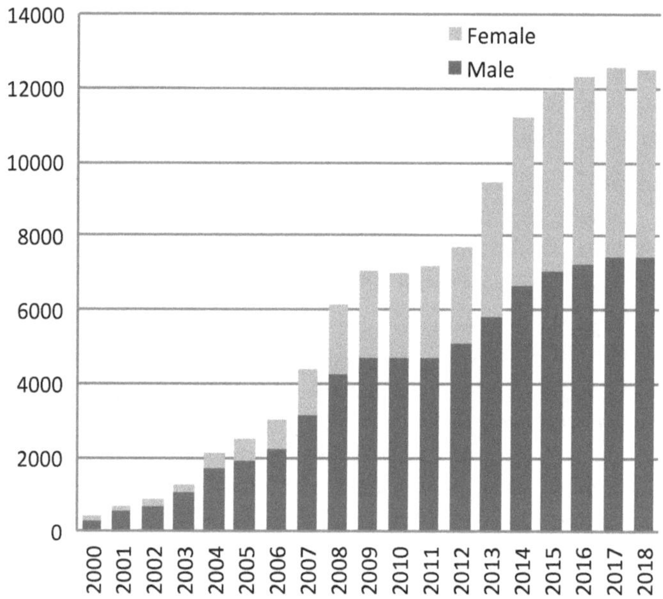

Fig. 7.9 ACLEDA bank staff employment growth 2000–2018
Source: ACLEDA Bank annual reports 2000–2018, and achievements Dec 2018

7.4 Summary and Conclusions

Within a market systems development framework, the core market is influenced by supporting functions, formal rules, and informal norms as explored in Chap. 3. For example, the presence or absence of supporting functions, such as a credit bureau, makes the flow of information between lenders and borrowers more efficient; and, the absence of one makes the flow of information more difficult and any transaction more costly and more risky.

The market system is also shaped by formal rules, such as bank regulations, and informal norms. Informal norms are behaviors that are considered acceptable within society, for example, the presence or absence of corruption in business transactions. Many have argued that informal norms can be even more powerful than formal rules in dictating how a market works. Behavior such as bribery and corruption can allow rules to be broken, ignored, and easily or eventually undermined.

The story of the Ministry and the motorcycle showed how the influence of informal norms can cripple the efficiency of an official, formal financial system that should work efficiently and effectively for millions of people. It also showed how one small experiment had a far-reaching effect on digitizing corruption out of the payments systems for a variety of official and commercial transactions.

Individual financial services providers—market leaders—can influence the way the entire financial market system works.[12] M-PESA's digital finance phenomenon in Kenya, Banco Sol's pioneering microfinance bank in Bolivia, and ACLEDA Bank's "Bank for the People" in Cambodia are only three examples of many others worldwide.

The market works well when new players enter the market, and existing ones are driven to innovate. As this chapter showed, innovations in product development and service innovation can have a fundamental effect on the way the overall financial system operates, as regulators are generally eager to see expansion of safe and sound formally regulated financial services to grow the market and advance financial inclusion within the country. Regulators and Central Banks in Kenya, Bolivia, and Cambodia were supportive of financial inclusion efforts, and they were eager to support advancements in how the financial system worked for the people.

7.4.1 Product and Service Innovations Influence the Market

In Cambodia, product and service innovations widely influenced the way the financial market system works today[13]:

Product and services innovations encouraged other financial service providers to follow the market leader. Following ACLEDA's lead resulted in more competition, lower prices, and expanded services to remaining under-served areas. Other financial services providers emulated or indeed further innovated on the original product or service. This had a positive effect on the financial system, as current customers and many previously excluded customers were brought into the formal system.

[12] For more global information, a good reference is the MIX Market, www.mixmarket.org

[13] For a review of the components of a financial market system refer to Chap. 3.

Second, these product and services innovations increased transparency and transformed norms of behavior in the broader financial system. The innovations showed customers that they had the right to expect transparent banking services for credit, savings, and transfers, even in the lower segments of the market. Most recently and dramatically, they showed how corruption could be digitized out of the public and private payments system.

Third, product and service innovations influenced the formal rules that govern the financial system by providing examples to regulators and rule makers. New types of banking licenses were developed and issued, such as the license for microfinance deposit-taking institutions. Based on MFI performance and demonstrated ability to meet regulatory requirements for mobilizing savings from the public, MFIs began to provide deposit services to a wider variety of customers than commercial banks could reach. Discrete specialized banking licenses for new products and service providers, such as WING's leading domestic remittance operation, were also developed, allowing more expansion and increasing integrity of the system.

Fourth, innovations enriched information flows in the system about the supply and demand of services. Better information encourages competition to emerge, work harder, or merge with others, beginning or completing the life cycle of a company. Better information about products and customer response influenced new products that were developed in response to the market and the demise of products that lost their market appeal. As a result, information flows about the evolution of customer demand and the ability of service providers to respond were strengthened.

Finally, essential support functions to a well-functioning financial system emerged. Innovations at the core of the financial services market stimulated the strengthening of what had been weak support functions in the system. The credit bureau, rating agencies, and specialized audit firms emerged. Capacity building for banking sector employees and job aspirants expanded to serve the national and regional financial services market.[14] Pilot projects emerged about financial education for the general public and discussions center on building a primary school curriculum to create an informed financial services customer base for the future.[15]

In summary, as financial services providers expand product and service innovations, they push system-wide innovation. This innovation, in turn, stimulates discussion of new regulations as new operational, customer-focused, and system-wide safety concerns surface.

As the system pushes ahead and expands, so do new opportunities to advance product innovations and use technology in the financial sector to make fast, safe, convenient, less expensive, and more transparent transactions, delighting customers and regulators alike.

[14] The following chapters discuss regional and national formal higher educational efforts through the ACLEDA Institute of Business and expansion of on-the-job training in Laos and Myanmar.

[15] See Chap. 3 for Cambodia's financial literacy campaign and intentions to integrate financial education into public school curricula.

References

ACLEDA Bank. Highlights 2017. President & Group Managing Director's Report https://www.acledabank.com.kh/kh/eng/fi_presidentreport. Accessed: May 28, 2018, 3:15 PM

Cengel, Dennis (2006) quoted in *When There Was No Money*. Springer, Berlin – Heidelberg

Clark, Heather (2006) *When There Was No Money*. Springer, Berlin – Heidelberg

Duflos, Eric. 2014. Financial Inclusion in Cambodia is Trending Digital. CGAP, Washington D.C. Available: https://www.cgap.org/blog/financial-inclusion-cambodia-trending-digital Accessed: May 20, 2017

Landy, Morgan (2006) quoted in *When There Was No Money*. Springer, Berlin – Heidelberg

Phong, Kimchhoy, Lihol Srou and Javier Sola. December 2016. Mobile Phones and Internet Use in Cambodia 2016. Research Report. The Open Institute, USAID's Development Innovations and The Asia Foundation.

Sorn Sarath (2016). Tax authority sets window for road tax compliance. 23 June 2016. Phnom Penh Post, Phnom Penh

Trip Advisor Advice. https://www.tripadvisor.com. Accessed 12 January 2018

Part IV ACLEDA Bank Plc.: Expanding Beyond Borders, Beyond Banking

"The challenges of very rapid development and growth allow us to think through many policy issues…how to make sure that technology development can benefit many people, not just to generate rapid economic growth, but how to make growth inclusive… using the dividends of high growth and rapidly changing technology… to serve poor and disadvantaged groups of people, and those who are left behind."

"Education defines the future of the country; it decides whether we are going in the right or wrong direction."

HE Dr. Hang Chuon Naron, Minister of Education, Youth and Sport, Royal Government of Cambodia

Prologue

Invitations: Near and Far

On any given day of the working week, the national headquarters of ACLEDA Bank Plc. on Monivong Blvd. in Phnom Penh bustles with customers. After taking a digitized queue slip from a machine near the front door, customers talk with tellers, pay vehicle registration tax, and use ATMs to check balances, withdraw cash, and make deposits. Tellers and cashiers disburse and collect cash; they top up debit cards and mobile phones.

The atmosphere is one of courtesy, efficiency, and confidence. As one regular customer recently reflected: "When I walk into the ACLEDA Bank main lobby, I automatically feel better about the future of Cambodia."

Customer service assistants help improve the customer experience with a kind word, backed by expertise and knowledge. Right now, a customer service assistant is helping a new customer securely navigate an ATM. His colleague confidently directs traffic in front of the headquarters for customers with large or small cars, tuk-tuks, motorcycles, bicycles, and the occasional flock of very brave pedestrians. For those who want to park their vehicle, the multilevel parking lot behind the front building has a digital board at the entrance informing motorists how many parking spaces are available on each floor.

The group of customers in the banking hall represents only a fraction of customers who are online or transacting directly with merchants through ACLEDA Unity ToanChet as they use their smartphones for a variety of ACLEDA Bank services anytime and anywhere.

Behind the scenes on any given floor, accountants tally figures, administrators keep order, and internal auditors review procedures. High-tech experts fix potential system bugs to ensure a smooth experience for the millions of ACLEDA Bank's online customers. These experts devise plans to make operations easier, safer, and more convenient for both customers and staff.

Managers and lawyers prepare final reports for the regulator and supervisor, the National Bank of Cambodia, as credit officers check information they receive from the Credit Bureau of Cambodia.

On a regularly scheduled day of every quarter, the Audit and Compliance Committee of the Board of Directors meets early in the day to discuss the results of financial audits and review internal audit reports, noting and receiving explanations for any unusual trends or incidents. Later that afternoon, the Board's Risk Management Committee meets to discuss strategies to optimally manage potential risk events to ACLEDA Bank, its subsidiaries, and its customers.

Other Board Committees will meet throughout the week. The Assets and Liabilities Committee will deal with new regulations regarding liquidity requirements and other events and issues that affect the Bank's balance sheet management.

The Credit Committee will test the strength of the Bank's credit policy against the monitoring of economic activity in the country and the loan portfolio quality to ensure that any action is taken responsibly and fully complies with applicable laws and regulations.

The Remuneration and Nomination Committee will advise the Board on all matters of Director and executive remuneration. The Committee is prepared to judge changes in the rapidly growing economies of ASEAN and the growth rates of ACLEDA Bank subsidiaries.

From the sidewalk to the boardroom on any given day, the view from within ACLEDA Bank's headquarters is one of a modern banking system—calm and efficient while also dynamic and forward looking.

William Shakespeare's iconic phrase "what's past is prologue"[1] might very well be applied to the experience of ACLEDA Bank: each new discovery from ACLEDA's past—either learned or discovered—has added to the wealth of experience that has informed ACLEDA's future and contributed to charting its destiny.

Part IV of this story is about how past experience has informed ACLEDA Bank's leadership to become the guardians of its future. This part of the ACLEDA history

[1] The quote is from William Shakespeare's *The Tempest*, written between 1610 and 1611. The quote means the past informs the future and allows people to take control of their own destinies.

relates three very different stories of how and why ACLEDA Bank Plc. expanded beyond its borders and beyond banking.

There are three chapters in this section: Chaps. 8 and 9 explore the welcome from neighboring countries that ACLEDA Bank Plc. received to expand banking beyond its borders. These chapters show both the match and sometimes the divergence of intent and actions between the host and the guest. Chapter 8 tells the story of how ACLEDA Bank Lao began and grew with great aspirations, but also with difficulties.

Chapter 9 tells the story of ACLEDA MFI Myanmar Co., Ltd. and the ACLEDA pioneers' experience going back to their roots in microfinance.

Chapter 10 explores how ACLEDA expanded beyond banking into Cambodia's higher education sector. To some this appears to be an anomaly; to others it appears as just another step to reach the dream of the original ACLEDA Bank staff—a group of teachers with high ideals.

The three chapters combined show how the ACLEDA pioneers in foreign lands and different sectors of the Cambodian economy welcomed new challenges in pursuit of building something of value for the country and its people. As they set about creating new operations, they resolved problems and came to terms with differences. Sometimes cultural norms—influenced by custom—and financial sector rules issued by law and regulation emerged quite unexpectedly, creating challenges. Each chapter considers how the pioneers combined their knowledge, expertise, and agility—their past as prologue—to build better organizations in Cambodia and beyond its borders.

The new generation of pioneers, just like the ones who built ACLEDA Bank in Cambodia, learned as much about their own beliefs and knowledge as they taught others. As they worked with their counterparts in neighboring countries and in both the banking and education sectors of the Cambodian economy to build new organizations, they focused first on building a solid base. That base served to develop innovative products and services that would expand benefits to their target markets—banking customers and students of higher education. At the same time, these efforts aim to improve the overall health of the banking and education sectors in the countries where they work.

Chapter 8 focuses on ACLEDA Bank Lao. The chapter examines the welcome invitation to ACLEDA Bank Plc. from the Bank of Laos (BoL) in 2007. The offer was to build a microenterprise and small business bank that would operate widely in the Lao People's Democratic Republic (the Lao PDR). The welcome to set up ACLEDA Bank Lao could easily have read, "Come As You Are!" Both Laotian officials and ACLEDA management were eager to accept the welcome and work together on this new venture; the common sentiment on both sides of the offer was, "They are just like us."

If ACLEDA Bank, Plc. was successful, it would be an innovation in the Laotian context—the first national level microenterprise and small business bank capitalized with private funds. And, if there was one—among many other areas of expertise—that ACLEDA Bank, Plc. could share with its neighbors, it was microenterprise and small business lending, cash flow, and deposit services. Both parties were eager to establish a lasting partnership.

Chapter 8 examines the thinking behind the invitation and the first experience for ACLEDA Bank with setting up an operation in a neighboring country. It tells the story about how the initial assumption— "just like us" —turned into "well, maybe not so much like us." It also shows how the ACLEDA pioneers combined their expertise and new experience to build a more vibrant organization from one that experienced persistent challenges in its early years of operation.

Chapter 9 focuses on ACLEDA MFI Myanmar Co., Ltd. The chapter explores the second ACLEDA expansion in ASEAN to the Republic of the Union of Myanmar in 2012. The invitation to set up ACLEDA MFI Myanmar Co., Ltd. could easily have read, "Come As You Used to Be!"

When Myanmar opened its doors to the world in 2011, after 50 years of isolation, the government was eager to develop a financial sector that worked for poor and low-income people through appropriate microfinance products and easily accessible microfinance institutions. In this way, ACLEDA also received a rare gift from the Republic of the Union of Myanmar. The gift was an opportunity to rediscover ACLEDA Bank's roots and re-experience the original promise of microfinance that was fulfilled in Cambodia some 20 years before.

The ACLEDA Microfinance Institution (MFI) opened its doors to customers in early 2013, with two branch offices. By December 2018 ACLEDA MFI Myanmar had expanded to nine branches and sub-branches. Chapter 9 also shows how ACLEDA MFI Myanmar incorporated lessons from ACLEDA's first expansion to Laos.

The lessons from ACLEDA MFI Myanmar, considered as a "shining star," are focused on setting up and building a new institution in Myanmar with a relatively untrained, but highly educated youthful population. Lessons also come from how to work effectively in a challenging regulatory environment with restrictions on lending and deposit rates. As a bonus to ACLEDA's regional institutional learning, some of the lessons learned in Myanmar challenged ACLEDA Bank Cambodia's views about who makes a good credit officer and why.

Chapter 10 considers ACLEDA Bank's most recent expansion beyond the boundaries of banking and the financial sector. The chapter centers on a new venture, the ACLEDA Institute of Business (AIB), which is now firmly situated in a new sector of the Cambodian economy—the higher education sector.

The invitation to ACLEDA Bank Plc. to enter the education sector came from the Ministry of Education, Youth and Sport (MoEYS) in Cambodia that welcomed ACLEDA's expertise in business and finance. Yet, ACLEDA's invitation to join the club of institutions of higher education was met with stiff resistance from existing higher educational institutions. This most recent invitation from ACLEDA Bank's future colleagues might have read: "Please don't come at all!"

Chapter 10 tells of the story of AIB's advances and why it adds value for students. But most importantly it shows how AIB contributes to the higher education system in banking and finance in Cambodia and beyond its borders and benefits from the experience in Cambodia, the ASEAN region, and elsewhere around the world.

This chapter also highlights the "dream." AIB is the collective dream of the ACLEDA Bank Plc. pioneers. This group of teachers, turned bankers for over a quarter of a century, never lost their vision.

Chapter 10 explores the precursors to AIB: the ACLEDA Training Center (ATC), the ACLEDA ASEAN Regional Microfinance Center (AARMC), and the ACLEDA International Visitors Center. Each organizational innovation influenced the way AIB would develop, just as Cambodia's higher education sector gave ACLEDA Bank Plc. the original rationale for improving skills, competencies, and technological innovation.

Among many short-term goals to enhance the income-generating enterprises of poor and low-income individuals, the ACLEDA Financial Trust (AFT), ACLEDA Bank Plc., and the ACLEDA Banks and MFI throughout the region work toward long-term goals.

The AIB complements these goals with the original promise of the "group of teachers" turned into bankers.

They vow that the next generation will not be left behind, but will excel beyond boundaries.

This chapter considers the education sector in Cambodia, its stage of progress, and how "one small bank might just make a great big difference."

The "past is prologue"; the future is beyond borders and boundaries.

Chapter 8
Building ACLEDA Bank Lao Ltd.

In the middle of difficulty lies opportunity.
—Albert Einstein

Twenty-five kilometers from Nadeang village in early 2017, Mrs. Somchay waits for a taxi that will take her to the ACLEDA Bank Lao Ltd. Xaybouly Service Unit in Savannakhet Province. Mrs. Somchay is a lively woman in her mid-forties and a mother of four children. Like many of her neighbors, her two sons work in Thailand and send regular remittances back home. Her two younger daughters share a room with a family in Vientiane where they attend secondary school. She sends them money to pay for their room and board, along with a small extra allowance.

Mrs. Somchay considers herself lucky as she has a job producing embroidered cloth for a small handicraft enterprise located in Savannakhet Province. She has never earned the minimum wage of LAK1.1 million (USD117)[1] a month, even though more than 64% of the Laotian population does.[2] Mrs. Somchay is proud of what she has achieved without an education, but she is also determined that her daughters *will* have one.

A private taxi, owned by a more prosperous man in the neighboring village, carefully rounds the bend in the dirt road on the way to ACLEDA Bank Lao's Xaybouly Service Unit, a little over 30 kilometers away. The round trip will cost the travelling party—Mrs. Somchay and her three neighbors—about LAK 50,800, equivalent to USD 6. It may seem like a small amount to pay, but when compared to the minimum wage that was recently established, the amount seems to be quite a financial burden just to manage money and keep it safe.[3]

[1] LAK stands for Lao Kip the currency of the Lao People's Democratic Republic. The exchange rate to USD was 8567 in January 2019, according to www.xe.com/currencyconverter the ACLEDA Bank Lao (ABL) website.

[2] The minimum wage increased from LAK 900,000 (USD108 in May 2018) to LAK1.1milion LAK (USD132 in May 2018).

[3] This is a common way of sending and receiving money in rural Laos (Tiwari and Coupienne 2014).

© Springer Nature Singapore Pte Ltd. 2020

H. A. Clark, *Beyond Borders, Beyond Banking*,
https://doi.org/10.1007/978-981-15-1687-0_8

Today, Mrs. Somchay will deposit the cash her son sent with a friend travelling from Thailand. She will make an easy transaction in ACLEDA Bank's Xaybouly Service Unit to convert the Thai currency into Lao Kip and deposit half of it in her savings account. She will send most of the other half of the money with her friend who will travel to Vientiane in a week and give it to her daughters.

Mrs. Somchay could only dream of the day when she could just send the money to her daughters directly or when her sons could transfer funds directly into her account from Thailand. It would save her a lot of money, it would be a lot safer, and then she could dedicate more of her time to embroidery. Little did she know that the day was just around the corner.

ACLEDA Bank Lao Ltd. (ABL) celebrated its 11th anniversary in July 2019. As of January 31 2020, ABL serves 33,378 active borrowers and manges 128,074 deposit accounts through 38 branches and offices that offer a range of financial services. ABL's financial services include the mobile banking service and the mobile phone application ThanChai that Mrs. Somchay dreams about.

Over the past 11 years ABL has had to weather a number of challenges. Some were brought about by the Lao PDR's growth and financial sector dynamics. And, some were associated with the growing pains of a start-up business, ACLEDA's first regional expansion beyond its borders.

The 11-year journey has been full of highs and lows worthy of this label: "The tenacious ABL and its great turn-around story." To fully appreciate this journey, the reader needs to understand the Lao context. It is as follows.

8.1 The Lao People's Democratic Republic (Lao PDR) Today

8.1.1 The Lao PDR: A Brief Profile

The Lao Peoples Democratic Republic (Lao PDR) is a landlocked country, sharing borders with its neighbors—Cambodia, China, Myanmar, Thailand, and Vietnam. Until recently Laos was considered one of the poorest economies in the world. Impressive growth rates in gross domestic product (GDP) and foreign direct investment over the last decade have advanced its global economic standing. Over the last decade, Laos sustained an average GDP growth rate of 7.8%, relatively higher than its neighboring countries, but on par with Cambodia (World Bank 2018).

Today the Lao PDR is considered a lower middle-income country,[4] with declining, but still high, poverty rates. By the end of 2017, annual gross national income

[4] As of July 1, 2016, the World Bank defines **low-income economies** as those countries with a GNI per capita, calculated using the World Bank Atlas method, of USD 1025 or less in 2015. **Lower middle-income economies** are those with a GNI per capita between USD 1026 and USD 4035. World Bank Development Indicators

(GNI) per capita reached USD 2270, and GDP per capita climbed to USD 2457. This is considerably higher than only 5 years ago when GDP per capita hovered at just under USD 1600 and was one of the lowest in Southeast Asia (World Bank 2018).

8.1.2 Growth and Growth Sectors of the Economy

According to the World Bank, economic activity remained strong, with the Lao Statistics Bureau estimating the GDP growth rate at 6.9% in 2017 (Najdov et al. 2018). Even though 2017 marked the fourth year of a gradual decrease in the GDP growth rate, economic expansion remained robust and on par with the best performing regional peers, as shown in Fig. 8.1. GDP growth is expected to further moderate in 2018 due to a number of factors, including the external environment and the recovery from the severe flooding of 2018. Growth is projected to rebound slightly in 2019–2020 driven mainly by the industry and services sectors of the economy. See Fig. 8.1 (Najdov et al. 2018).

Mountains, rivers, and jungles isolate many areas of the country, making the Lao PDR breathtakingly beautiful as a vital tourist attraction. Tourism contributed 4.2% to the Lao PDR's GDP in 2017 and was expected to grow by 3.8% in 2018 (WTTC 2018).[5] The topography also supports electricity generation, which contributed roughly 23% to the country's GDP in 2017, increasing dramatically since 2010. Growth was driven mainly by industry that contributed 3.4% to GDP growth in

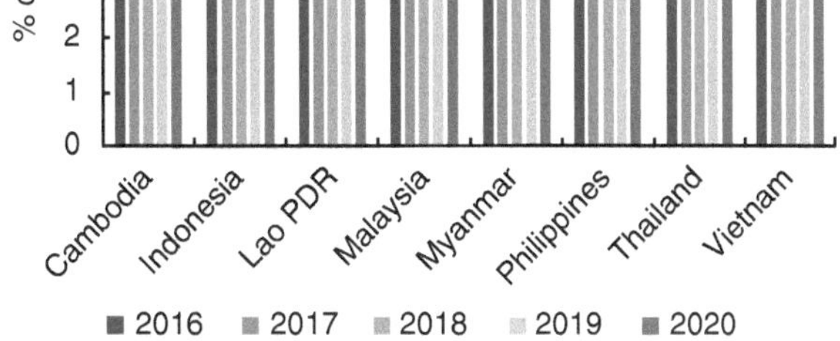

Fig. 8.1 Regional GDP growth and projections. (Reproduced from Najdov et al. 2018)
Source: World Bank East Asia and Pacific Economic Update October 2019

[5]According to the World Travel and Tourism Council, travel and tourism directly and indirectly accounted for 11.9% of total employment in 2017. The Council's estimates for indirect contributions of travel and tourism to the economy are higher in 2018 (World Travel and Tourism Council 2018).

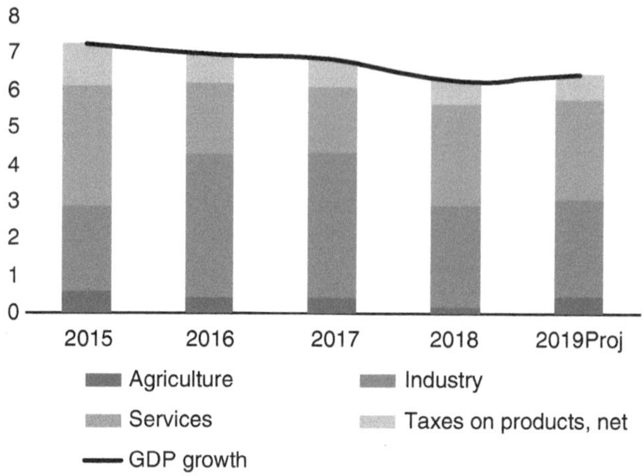

Fig. 8.2 Contribution to GDP growth and projections. (Reproduced from Najdov et al. 2018) Source: Lao Statistics Bureau and World Bank staff estimates)

2018 and the services sector—including tourism—which expanded its contribution to 2.2% of GDP growth. See Fig. 8.2.

Electricity, mainly exported to China and Thailand, figures as a main source of GDP growth and export earnings—along with manufacturing and other non-resource exports that continue to replace falling exports of metals and minerals. In fact, "non-resource exports have risen rapidly in recent years, with their share in total exports increasing to reach slightly over 50 percent of total exports for the first time in the last decade" (Najdov et al. 2018; Davading et al. 2019). See Fig. 8.3.

The same topography that supports the energy sector has historically made it difficult for the growth of commerce and widespread productive agriculture because of a weak communications infrastructure and access to markets. Still, agriculture is one of the main sources of employment in the Lao economy and a growing source of exports, as shown in Fig. 8.3. In fact, of the 4.3 million adults who live in Laos, 78% of them are involved in farming (Jefferis 2015).

8.1.3 Poverty

Lao PDR achieved its poverty-related Millennium Development Goal (MDG) by halving the national extreme poverty rate over the past decade. Poverty in the country was reduced from 33.5% in 2003 to 23.2% in 2013 (World Bank 2015a, b).

Income distribution within the country is reasonably equal, with a Gini coefficient of 0.36, but inequality has risen slightly in the past decade. The annualized income gains of the bottom 40% of the Lao population are considerably lower than their regional peers. See Fig. 8.4.

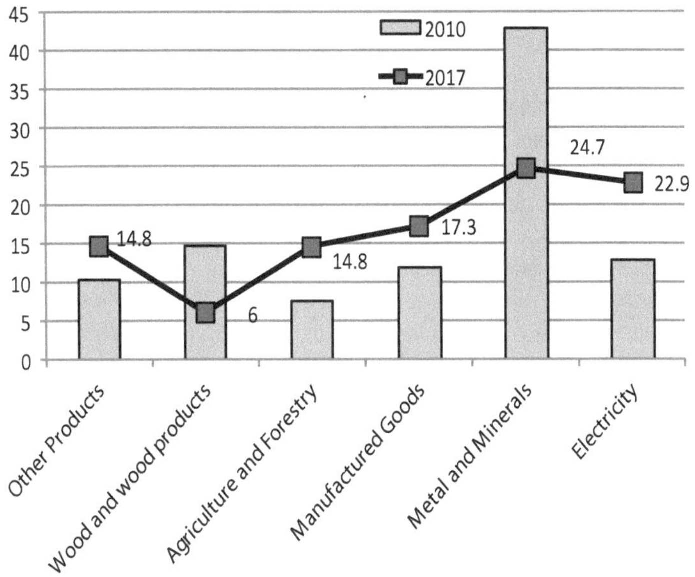

Fig. 8.3 Share of non-resource exports 2010–2017. (Reproduced from Najdov et al. 2018) Sources: Ministry of Industry and Commerce; BOL; trading partners' customs data; UNCOMPTRADE; and World Bank staff estimates)

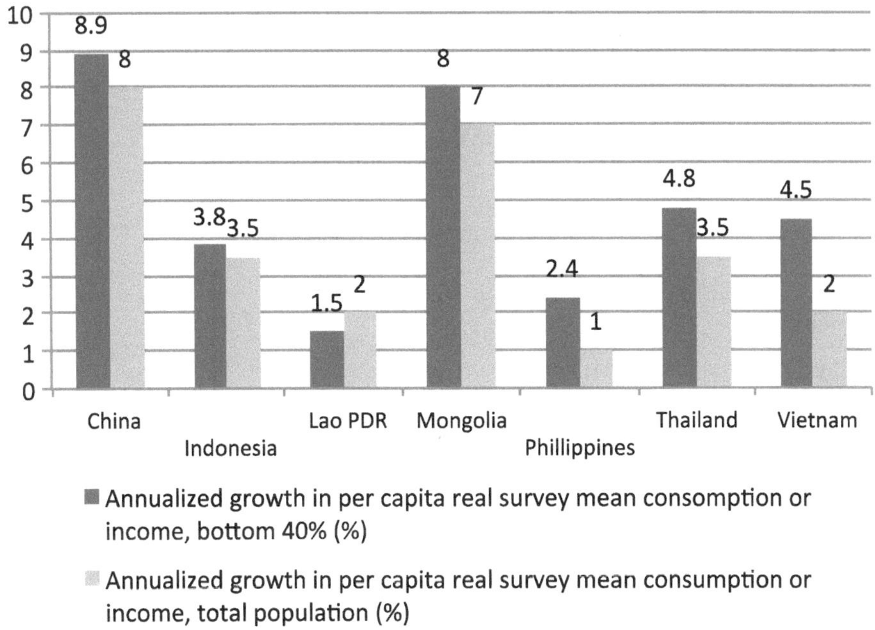

Fig. 8.4 Poverty decreased but inequity remains a challenge
Sources: World Bank Poverty Data; EAP Economic Update October 2017; Najdov et al. 2017

According to the United Nations, "The progress in poverty reduction varies by location, ethnicity, education and occupation of household heads. One-third of the population in upland areas is still below the poverty line. The growth in consumption has benefited the richer quintiles more than the poorer segments of the population, and the rural-urban gap remains significant" (United Nations 2015). And, "there is a strong correlation between poverty and ethnic groups that traditionally have dwelt in remote rural areas" (Jefferis 2015).

Access to education and health services is poor in rural areas that are often isolated due to rivers and streams flooding at certain times of the year. "Due to their remote location, ethnic minority populations have comparatively less access to markets and public services, such as health, education, agricultural extension and communication and road infrastructure. The central government's attempts to improve the living conditions in rural areas has led to substantial changes in the livelihood of the affected population, but much remains to be done" (Jefferis 2015).

Poverty has declined substantially over the past two decades, but still remains high, hovering around 19%.[6] Past growth patterns, where growth was largely driven by natural resources and mineral extractive industries, had a limited impact on poverty reduction and job creation (World Bank Lao Economic Monitor 2018; Najdov and Phimmahasay 2016). The current growth pattern showing a gradual change away from natural resources toward manufacturing and commercially oriented agriculture and renewable forest resources could be expected to contribute more dramatically to poverty reduction.

The agriculture and manufacturing sectors have potential to generate greater employment opportunities, when linked with a skilled labor market and promotion of commercially oriented agriculture linked with smallholder farming households (Ibid.). In addition, agro-processing, tourism, and trade are sub-sectors that generally have significant potential to create jobs requiring a range of skills and gender neutral positions—from highly skilled jobs to lower skilled positions for the next generation.

8.1.4 Southeast Asia's Techno Boom

Throughout Southeast Asia connectivity is growing at an impressive rate. Connectivity is important to mobile banking and overcoming time, space, and cost constraints to manage money, especially for isolated populations.

According to techinasia.com all key digital indicators in Southeast Asia made notable advances in 2017, with mobile Internet use and social media use gaining the

[6] This estimate is based on prior income trends and growth rates. Since the last expenditure and consumption survey, the poverty rate is estimated around 19%. The last expenditure and consumption survey was completed in 2012. The results of the next one are due in 2019 (World Bank).

Table 8.1 Internet and mobile use in Cambodia, Lao PDR, and Myanmar, comparison with Singapore

	Population (millions)	Internet users	Active social media users	Mobile Phone Connections
Cambodia	16.60	9.7 million (58%)	9.7 million (58%)	21.24 million (128%)
Lao PDR	7.22	3.10 million (43%)	3.10 million (43%)	5.68 million (79%)
Myanmar	54.23	22 million (41%)	22 million (41%)	68.24 million (126%)
Singapore	5.83	5.14 million (88%)	4.60 million (79%)	8.56million (147%)

Source: We Are Social 2020 Global Digital Report January 2020

most. More than half of Southeast Asia's population uses the Internet, with the number of Internet users in the region growing by more than 30% or 80 million new users in 2017 alone. Mobile Internet use appears to be driving much of this growth, although mobile Internet penetration has not quite hit the halfway point yet. By the end of 2018, the current pace of growth suggests that the halfway milestone will be passed, as most new Internet users in the region are now "mobile-first and, often mobile-only" (Kemp 2019).

Given the diversity of economic development in Southeast Asia, it's not surprising that digital connectivity is not evenly distributed across the region's 11 countries. Brunei leads the region in terms of Internet penetration, with Singapore close behind at 88% in 2019.

At the other end of the scale, less than one-third of the local population in Laos, Myanmar, and Timor-Leste had access to the Internet in 2017. However, all three of these countries posted strong digital growth in 2019, with users in Laos up an impressive 83% from the previous year. Cambodia, which was also at the lower end of the regional rankings, posted strong growth as Internet users continued to grow, reaching 58% of the population by January 2017 (Kemp 2019). See Table 8.1. Internet and Mobile Use in Cambodia, Lao PDR, and Myanmar, comparison with Singapore.

Mobile phone usage is by far the most popular means of communication in Southeast Asia. Cambodia still ranks ahead of the regional average when it comes to mobile broadband connectivity. Laos posted double-digit, year-on-year growth in mobile broadband penetration rates since 2017, even though less than one-third of all mobile connections in Laos are 3G or faster.[7]

According to the latest figures in 2019, mobile and Internet usage in Cambodia, Lao PRD, and Myanmar expanded (We Are Social 2020). Cambodia ranks ahead of the regional average when it comes to mobile broadband connectivity. Both Cambodia and Laos posted double-digit, year-on-year growth in mobile broadband penetration

[7] This is the definition of "broadband" according to the GSMA's classification. The Global System for Mobile Communications Association (GSMA) is a global trade body that represents the interests of mobile network operators worldwide with approximately 1200 mobile operators as members. Website: www.gsma.com

rates from 2017 to 2019. Lao PDR and Myanmar both have higher mobile penetration rates in 2019 with the number of mobile subscriptions compared to the national population reaching 91% in Lao PDR and 101% in Myanmar. See Table 8.1.

8.1.5 *The Business Environment*

According to the World Bank's Lao Economic Monitor (LEM), "increasing regional integration and a broadly favorable commodity price outlook provide opportunity for the non-resource sectors to grow. Greater ASEAN integration and favorable external environments open opportunities for reviving tourism, and building manufacturing and agro-processing. Readily available and affordable electricity, combined with good access to Thailand's infrastructure could be helpful in attracting investment" (Najdov et al. 2018).

However, boosting growth outside of the resource extractive sectors will need improvement in the business environment. Lao PDR dropped to 141st place in the 2018 Ease of Doing Business rankings from 139th in 2017. The country lags behind regional peers, particularly on starting a business, getting credit and electricity, protecting minority investors, and resolving insolvency. For example, the time it takes to start a business in Lao PDR requires eight procedures over 67 days. While this is better than in Cambodia, it is still much longer than in Thailand (five procedures within 4 days) and Vietnam (nine procedures within 22 days).

Most firms participating in the 2016 Ease of Doing Business survey in Laos reported that informal practices are the biggest obstacle. According to the survey, informality involves unevenly enforced regulations and inadequate business registration to avoid costs and the complexity of the formal system, tax evasion, and a culture of non-compliance or bypassing the regulations (World Bank Group, Doing Business (2018a-d, 2019)). See Fig. 8.5.

Informal practices, tax rates, and a poorly educated and under-skilled workforce are the top three obstacles reported in the 2016 Doing Business Survey. However, firms in the special economic zones (SEZs), and outside of the zones alike, find lack of skilled labor a critical constraint. According to the 2016 enterprise survey, 13% of firms reported the lack of skilled workforce as the biggest obstacle compared to 7.3% in East Asia and the Pacific on average and 5.4% on average among lower middle-income countries (World Bank, enterprise surveys 2018).

8.1.6 *The Demographic Dividend*

Lao PDR is set to benefit from the "demographic dividend" to the economy. Lao PDR has one of the youngest populations in the region. Nearly 60% of Lao PDR's population is estimated to be less than 25 years of age. Projections also show a rapid increase in working-age population. However, the full benefits of the demographic

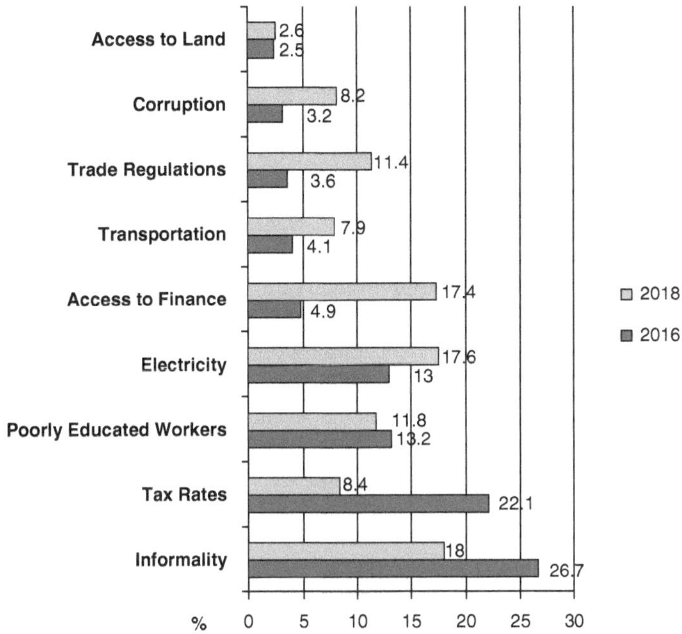

Fig. 8.5 Business practices that hold back progress: enterprise survey
Sources: Enterprise Surveys, World Bank 2016, 2018, and Doing Business in Lao PDR:8 Constraints to Productivity, World Bank 2018

dividend will be realized only if new jobs are able to keep pace with the growth of the working age population and only if young women and men are better equipped with the appropriate skills and knowledge (United Nations 2015).

According to the United Nations Country Analysis Report, even while Lao PDR has achieved universal coverage of primary school enrolment rates, the primary education survival rate remains low.[8] "Secondary enrolment has improved, although it remains low because of the low primary survival rate. Disparities are prominent in education, more so for the secondary level. The quality of teaching and learning outcomes are inadequate, and need to be addressed by significantly improving teacher quality, teacher training programs and teacher distribution" (United Nations 2015).

The issues of job creation and quality skills-based education and knowledge for Laotian young adults become all the more critical with the move toward regional integration (United Nations 2015), as other countries in the region set priorities to invest in educating the next generation.

[8]The primary education survival rate is the rate at which students go on to secondary school from primary school.

8.2 The Lao PDR Banking Sector

Similar to Cambodia, the financial sector of the Lao PRD was somewhat buffered from the global financial crisis in 2008. Banks in Laos were not widely exposed to the international financial system, and the Lao Securities Exchange only opened its doors for business much later in January 2011.

However, by late 2008, just as ACLEDA Bank Lao Ltd. was beginning operations, gross international reserves[9] held by the Lao PDR declined by 5% within a 2-month period. At the time, real GDP growth of 7.5% in the Lao PDR was expected to remain fairly strong, and it did. Throughout the crisis and through 2017, real GDP growth remained above 6.8% per year, topping out at 8% in 2013.

GDP growth did slow down during 2008 and 2009 due to the prevailing global economic recession and the faltering demand and prices for the Lao PDR major commodity groups, such as energy, metals (gold and copper), and major agricultural commodities, such as coffee, rubber, and maize (Najdov et al. 2018).

8.2.1 Retail Banking in the Formal Financial Sector

In 2015 Dr. Phon Narin, ACLEDA Bank Lao's second Managing Director and CEO, noted with admiration—as well as concern—that "Almost a decade ago Laos had only 12 banks. However, the situation changed dramatically after the Law on Commercial Banks was promulgated in 2006. Since then the number of banks has soared and, at the end of the third quarter in 2015, there were 40 commercial banks, including significant regional newcomers, and 142 licensed microfinance institutions in Lao PDR" (ACLEDA Bank Lao 2017).

State-owned commercial banks (SOCBs) continued to dominate the banking sector in 2019. Their share of total assets in the banking sector increased to 43.5 percent, as one SOCB was recapitalized in 2016. However, since 2012 the share of SOCB's total assets in the financial system declined from 55.6% to 43.5%.

According to the Lao Economic Monitor, this reflects a growing share of banking sector assets in foreign bank branches. Their share reached 28.3% by the end of 2017. Private banks and joint-venture banks (banks owned by SOCBs together with foreign banks) have maintained their shares of banking sector assets of around 18% and 10%, respectively (Najdov et al. 2018).

The highly competitive market place for financial services was occupied by more than 42 private and state-owned commercial banks with 96 branch offices, 494

[9] International reserves are a country's "external assets"—including foreign currency deposits and bonds held by central banks and monetary authorities, gold, and SDRs.

services units, and 1156 ATMs as well as "more increasingly aggressive licensed microfinance institutions" (ACLEDA Bank Lao 2017).

By the end of 2017, the banking sector continued to crowd in more microfinance institutions than commercial banks. Microfinance institutions (MFIs) expanded rapidly in 2017. The total assets of MFIs reached about USD 450 million in July 2017, up by 11% year on year and reaching almost 3% of GDP.[10] According to the Lao Microfinance Association, 123 MFIs—19 deposit-taking MFIs, 74 non-deposit-taking MFIs, and 30 savings and credit unions—had been licensed or registered by BOL and served roughly 247,000 clients and had a little over 62,000 active borrowers, a total loan portfolio of about USD $88 million. As of the end of 2016, there were 102 licensed MFIs working in all provinces of the country (Lao Microfinance Association June 2017).

Banking sector assets at the end of 2017 reached around 87% of GDP (LAK122 billion or USD14.8 billion), similar to a year earlier when banking sector assets reached 87.5% of GDP. According to the World Bank's Lao Economic Monitor, the year 2017 "may have marked the end of the period of rapid deepening of the sector, as indicated by the low level of change in banking sector assets that had increased dramatically from 62.3% of GDP in 2012. No new banking institutions entered the market, while slowing deposit growth and low profitability limited the ability of the banks to increase their assets' size. Still, compared to other countries in the region and at similar level of development, Lao PDR's banking sector is substantial" (Davading et al. 2019; Najdov et al. 2018).

In summary, in 2017–2018 in the formally regulated banking sector, credit growth in the economy decreased, and the stalled entry of new banks resulted in more modest expansion of the banking sector.

8.2.2 Retail Banking in the Informal Sector

Village banks and village funds are both new innovations and long-standing traditions in the Lao informal retail-banking context. There are important differences in the two models. Village banks are part of the informal financial sector, while village funds are disbursement mechanisms used by the formal public sector to support a variety of purposes for village development. Village level banking has been an important feature of the rural financial landscape for decades, but the two models are often confused. See Box 8.1.

[10] For discussion of GDP growth, see Sect. 8.2 of this chapter and growth rates reported in Lao Economic Monitor.

Box 8.1: Village Bank or Village Fund?

What are village banks?	What are village funds?
Village banks are specialized informal (unregulated) community owned and managed saving and credit organizations, often, but not exclusively, located in rural areas. Village banks intermediate their members' deposits to other members who borrow.	**Village funds** have been promoted by the government and donor agencies in Laos for decades. They support a variety of productive and social purposes, in remote rural communities. Sometimes they have included credit and savings services.
Village banks that are supported by the AFP project[11] are member-based organizations that operate in a specific village with an average of 75 members. Village banks are authorized by the provincial authorities and recognized by the district village authorities, which gives them a semi-formal status.	Village funds have been used by national government agencies as transfer mechanisms from the national government to local government leaders to foster a variety of village development initiatives, such as medical supplies, emergency procurement of food, and stock-raising for vulnerable people.
An elected committee from the community is responsible for running the village banks. The committee's duties comprise the decision on new credit applications, record keeping, updating of member passbooks, and accounting for cash and accounts administration.	Village leaders, party members, and mass organization officials are generally appointed to advisor roles and on management committees. Villages for whom the funds are intended often do not make the distinction between a village fund, offered by the government to serve a specific purpose such as emergency medical supplies, and a village bank, designed to be a permanent source of finance and safe savings for members of the community.
Credit and savings services have a less robust track record in village funds than through specialized village banks. The funds often fail to provide access to permanent financial services for a number of reasons, mostly due to mismanagement from lack of capacity, theft, and lack of active participation among both savers and borrowers. Studies note that there is a risk of committee members monopolizing the benefits of the village fund and the borrowing rights.	
Sources: GIZ. 2015. Assessing financial literacy in rural Laos. Access to finance for the poor is supported by GIZ, *Deutsche Gesellschaft für Internationale Zusammenarbeit*—German Corporation for International Cooperation ILO 2007. *Meeting the Challenge: Banking As a Solution*	

A particularly strong model of village banking most recently established in Laos is supported and supervised by Lao MFIs and savings and credit unions (SCU) located in the regions in close proximity to the village banks. In this way, formal sector retail-banking organizations act as network support organizations (NSO) to village banks. NSOs provide technical assistance, capacity building, and advisory

[11] AFP (Access to Finance for the Poor is supported by GIZ, *Deutsche Gesellschaft für Internationale Zusammenarbeit*—German Corporation for International Cooperation)

services, contributing to the village bank's sustainable operations. They can also on-lend funds to strong village banks in the case of liquidity shortages.[12]

Village bank operations vary, but village banks usually hold monthly banking days in local temples, community halls, or private homes to collect loan repayments and savings deposits from members. The village bank generally has a committee of members who oversee operations and record transactions.

A glimpse of history from AFP-GIZ files shows that one village bank had 447 members by 2015. The bank had also constructed its own building. When the bank was founded in 2010, many villagers were suspicious of the concept and especially worried if their savings would be safe. Today, the Head of Village Bank Committee says, "During our first year we only had about 70 members; they started with small savings of 10,000 Kip[13] per month. One year later, members received an annual dividend of 13%" (Roesler and Fischer 2016).

"Today, after six years of successful operations, the Village Bank has clearly earned the trust in the village. Almost all of 194 member families have two or more member accounts. Some members save as much as 100m Kip with the village bank," says the Head of the Village Bank Committee. He also notes that, "without our Network Support Organization we would not be here today. Several times they prevented us from making wrong decisions and they helped us to stabilize our operations and build necessary capacities."

Not all village banks work in this way, although they may serve many isolated communities in rural areas. Village funds and village banks are ubiquitous in rural Laos. The Lao countryside is littered with more failed village banks and village funds than those that are still operational. One of the clearest village fund evaluation statements noted: "But overall, the project faltered within a year due to poor management and insufficient funds generated subsequently to meet villagers' demands. Many villagers saw the loans as free money and they were not compelled to repay" (ILO 2007).

8.3 Access to Financial Services and Financial Inclusion

The proportion of adults using at least one regulated financial service in Lao PDR was only 47% according to the United Nations Capital Development Fund (UNCDF) sponsored Making Access Possible (MAP) diagnostic and the FinScope Survey in 2014. Only 12% of adults used more than two types of formal financial services. A further 28% of adults use only informal services and 25% are totally excluded

[12] This model is supported by the Access to Finance for the Poor (AFP) program. GIZ and the Bank of the Lao PDR (BOL) jointly manage the AFP program.

[13] 1 USD = 8400 Kip as of mid-2018.

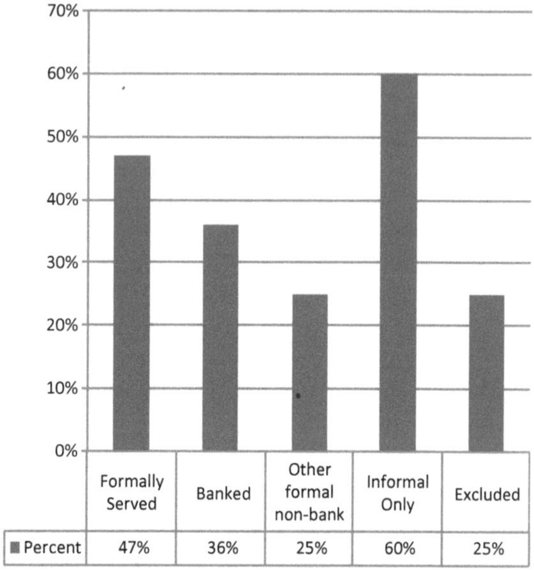

Fig. 8.6 Financial inclusion—adults using formal finance. (Reproduced from FinScope 2014)

(Jefferis 2015). See Fig. 8.6 and 8.7 for a more detailed view of how adults in the Lao PDR use differentiate between formal and informal providers for different products, such as savings, remittances, and credit.

The reported proportion of adults using unregulated financial services is relatively high at 61%. Many adults, 33% of the total, use both formal and informal financial services. Informal financial services provide a complementary channel to those who use formal financial services and also extend services to those who do not use—or have no access to formal products (Jefferis 2015).

Even though access to finance is quite deep, with reasonably high financial inclusion, it is not very broad. The FinScope survey showed that only 29% of adults use more than one formal financial product category (i.e., savings, credit, insurance, and payments), while 17% use only one formal service, and 28% only use informal products (Jefferis 2015).

ACLEDA Bank Lao Ltd. (ABL) in this context has the potential to reach customers who are familiar with financial services in areas that are underserved with formal financial services. As such, and given the relatively small market, ABL competes with commercial private and state-owned banks as well as licensed MFIs and informal financial services providers.

Perhaps most noticeable from the FinScope survey in Lao PDR are the dramatic results showing the proximity of the population to services, which is strikingly different from Cambodia. The report notes that the physical outreach of banks through branches and service points is limited to urban areas and district centers. Further, it is unlikely that it will be economically viable for banks to extend their physical networks significantly beyond this. Non-branch channels will be needed to reach

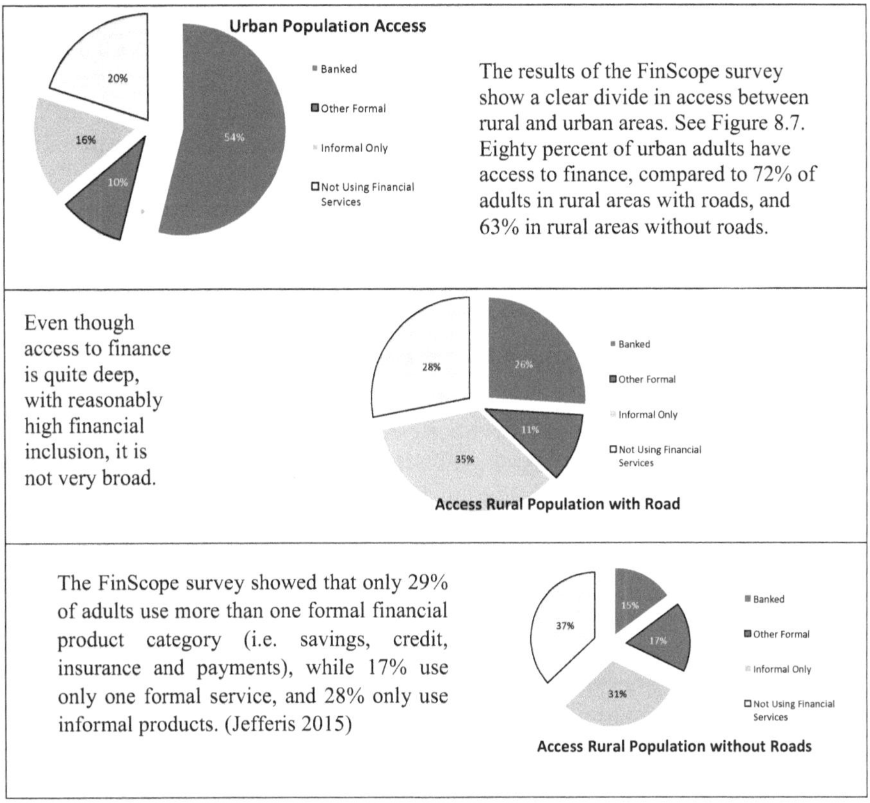

Fig. 8.7 Financial inclusion—the rural-urban access divide. (Reproduced from FinScope 2014)

rural customers, as most of the population does not live in close proximity to formal financial service providers.

To access formal banking services, customers travel to district centers, which is convenient for some, but can be expensive and difficult for others. The survey indicates that banks are more accessible to non-farm and non-urban people than either high-income or low-income farmers. Farmers, regardless of their income levels, appear to have the least access to formal banking sources, including ATMs, of all income groups represented in the survey.

Technology may help to fill the gap. Even though technology-based provision of financial services is at an early stage in Laos, access to digital services has increased dramatically in the past 4 years.[14] The use of technology and the Lao population's apparent acceptance of new ways to bank show that there is potential to extend

[14] See the previous section on Techno Boom.

banking beyond physical branch-based services. As broadband connectivity becomes more available and as more people upgrade to smartphones, it's likely that Lao PDR will experience the same evolution as other markets, and users will upgrade to smartphones as mobile broadband becomes available.

These future possibilities reaffirm ACLEDA Bank Lao's expansion to underserved areas and the potential customer base that makes up 63% of the population living in rural areas. This vision that was once thought to be unimaginable now appears to be within reach.

8.4 Regulatory Environment for the Banking Sector

Even while the Lao financial sector is often characterized as one with a liberal regulatory environment, over the past 2 years, the Bank of the Lao PDR (BOL) has progressively set a range of regulations that can best be described as very conservative. In response to the increasing competition and concerns with bank safety and soundness, the BOL increased the compulsory reserve ratio for banks. Later, articles for the establishment of a commercial bank were amended to require banks to have sufficient funds and total assets of not less than USD 5 billion. These changes may exert market pressures on smaller banks.

In the highly dollarized Lao economy, the BOL also imposed stricter controls on currency exchange operations and the use of foreign currencies in an effort to promote the use of the Lao Kip. As a result credit growth moderated throughout 2017. While lending to commerce increased over the 2-year period through December 2017, total borrowing and borrowing of other sectors dropped dramatically (World Bank 2018).

8.4.1 Interest Rate Caps

Perhaps one of the most difficult regulations for microfinance and commercial banks serving micro, small, and medium-sized enterprises was the cap on interest rates for both deposits and loans. Accompanying the interest rate cap on lending was a 4% net-weight gap between deposits and loans.

In 2015, the BOL sought to reduce loan interest rates as a means to stimulate economic activity in the country, particularly in the small and micro segments of the economy. This major change for the banking sector resulted in dramatic decrease in the number of deposits obtained and loans issued by commercial banks in a short period of time. By the end of 2017, the Lao Economic Monitor reported some revealing results about how the intended stimulus package worked out in practice.

Prior to 2014, Lao currency deposits attracted interest rates averaging 10% per year. They fell to an average of 7.7% per year by the end of 2015 when the cap went into effect. The trend of increasing dollarization of the deposit portfolio continued with foreign currency deposits growing by 15.3%, compared to 6% for local currency deposits. This reflects the continued implementation of the interest rate caps on Kip deposit and lending rates as well as some currency substitution following the adjustment in the effective exchange rate of the Kip.

The World Bank expects the "authorities will continue to manage the exchange rate within the +/− 5 percent band [...as it may provide...] the authorities with greater flexibility and lower pressures to intervene in the market to stabilize the Kip. It appears that the recent reduction in the policy rate and application of interest rate caps has had limited positive impact on stimulating credit growth and lending to small and medium size enterprises (SMEs). Given recent trends in lending and weakening loan-portfolio, credit growth could further ease" (Najdov et al. 2018).

8.4.1.1 Interest Rate Caps and Spreads on Lending and Deposits

While there is no cap on foreign currency deposit rates, as of late 2017 lending rates in foreign currency are capped at 3 percentage points above the respective deposit rate. Earlier, the spread was 4 percentage points.

As of January 2018, the cap is set at 5.6%, slightly down from 5.7% earlier. Further, bank's average weighted lending rates are capped at 3 percentage points above the lending rate.

While other countries have also used caps, the low ceilings in Lao PDR could be especially restrictive, according to the Lao Economic Monitor. "The application of the cap on the average weighted lending rate of commercial banks (meaning that individual loans could carry higher interest rate as long as the average rate for the bank is below the cap) provides some opportunity to price-in different levels of risk-exposure; however, this is unlikely to be sufficient. For example, caps are also applied in Cambodia; however, these are set at around 20 percent, providing sufficient room for banks to adequately price risks" (Ibid.).

8.4.2 Banking Sector Capitalization, Restrictions, Credit Growth, and NPLs

Even though the retail-banking sector overall is well capitalized, there are other challenges, such as some state-owned banks and some privately owned banks do not meet the minimum regulatory level for capital to risk-weighted assets of 8%. And, others have been recapitalized recently.

By 2018 a restriction on foreign currency lending contributed to lowering credit growth in the overall economy. According to recent performance reports in the banking sector, non-performing loans (NPLs) also trended upward, even though the official figures may be understated due to a 2017 regulation that loans related to public investment projects should not be treated as NPLs.

The profitability figures for the sector are also low when compared to retail-banking sectors in the region. For example, return on equity for the sector in the Lao PDR was 7.7% compared to 8.7% in Cambodia,[15] 9% in Thailand, and 13.6% in the Philippines. On a more troubled note, the World Bank's Lao Economic Monitor also considers that more banks are reporting losses in 2017 than they did in 2016.

Inflation is expected to pick up; however, further fiscal consolidation, moderate credit growth, and gradual recovery in commodity prices are likely to keep inflationary pressures moderate and within the government's target of less than 5% (World Bank 2018).

In summary, even though there are some warning signs present in the current environment, the Lao financial sector has some positive attributes, which may continue to strengthen financial soundness throughout the system. Three key systemic financial soundness indicators applied to selected financial sectors across the region during 2018 show that the Lao PDR is improving soundness, while risks of increasing NPLs remain relatively high and profitability throughout the Lao banking sector is comparatively low compared to peers in the region.

8.5 Regulation Promoting and Inhibiting Financial Inclusion

Without the ability to price risks, banks are unlikely to take them.

As noted earlier under the section on the regulatory environment, banks are left little flexibility in pricing credit. Inability to price for risk is one of the major financial regulatory barriers to increasing financial inclusion rates throughout the country. This is especially true for inclusion of rural residents and for low-income people without a financial history, defined as access to and previous use of formal financial institutions.

Unanticipated Effects of Inability to Price Risk Generally, artificially low interest rate caps on loans do not favor financial inclusion, despite the political statements surrounding such actions. With low interest rate caps come an array of unanticipated effects on customers and their lenders. First, banks and MFIs that are subject to the interest rate cap are likely to offer only higher loan amounts to customers who are easier and less expensive to serve.[16] Financial institutions are also

[15] This figure reflects performance before the interest rate cap went into effect in Cambodia in April 2018.

[16] For a more detailed discussion of the effect of the interest rate cap on increasing loan size to customers who are easier and less expensive to serve, see Chap. 4.

likely to increase the loan period, thereby avoiding the higher costs of frequent loan appraisal and renewal, and may start charging higher upfront fees if permitted by the regulation.

The combination of these factors has a dampening effect on any efforts lending, and savings establishments would otherwise make to reach new customers in underserved areas. The dampening effect is reinforced when the customers require small loan amounts or when they only have enough excess funds to make small deposits. Customers without an established financial history are also more expensive to serve, as they are considered more risky.

Regardless of the size of the loan or the deposit, there is a fixed cost that a financial services provider has to serve any customer, so there is always an incentive to lend up and chase more prosperous clients. See Chap. 4 for a discussion of perverse incentives that a low interest rate cap presents, including additional debt made available beyond a borrowers' ability to repay.

Financial Inclusion Rates Can Be Improved In the Lao PDR 25% of the population do not have any access to financial services, and 60% of Lao adults use informal financial services, such as village banks. Most village banks are not formally regulated bank institutions, and they often operate with limited oversight and support.[17]

In the Lao PDR, the people who are most excluded from formal financial services are the two lowest income quintiles (41% of people in the lowest Quintile 1 and 29% of people in income Quintile 2). Forty-six percent of people who have no formal education are also excluded, as are the 37% of potential customers who live in rural areas without roads (FinScope 2015).

The most costly customers for financial services providers to serve are poor, uneducated, and isolated rural people. Even though interest rate caps are politically attractive, they set up additional barriers to increased financial inclusion with policies that cap interest rates below a financial institution's price for risk and cost. In addition, new customers are more expensive and more risky for financial services providers to serve than existing ones.

"Credit provision is limited, and is the least-used financial product," noted the MAP Lao Synthesis completed in 2015. The findings are still relevant today with respect to the barriers to credit provision for small enterprises in rural and urban areas. Sometimes credit is the least used financial product because people fear debt, but other times it is because credit is simply not available for investment.

Other requirements that reduce financial inclusion and make it more difficult and therefore more expensive to lend to the lower segments of the market include

[17] See Box 8.1 for more details on how village banks and village funds operate.

requiring documentation that does not exist or is difficult and expensive to produce, such as formally registered land titles used as collateral.

Banks still tend to focus on collateral-based lending and have not developed cash flow or payroll-based loan products. Loan maturity tends to be short (5 years or less), and some banks have concerns about the effectiveness of legal processes for loan recovery, even when there is collateral, which only adds to perceived risk.

Collateral-based lending tends to favor the middle class, as they have assets to pledge. Yet, in both Cambodia and the Lao PDR, land is the favored collateral for lenders. In the Lao PDR this practice excludes poor and low-income people from formal bank lenders, as the government requires a formal land title to secure the pledge, which few low-income people have.

Commercial credit provision is inhibited by restrictions on loan-deposit spreads, which make it difficult to price for risk. A substantial proportion of credit is provided as state-subsidized "policy loans," notably to farmers. Although there is no robust data on this type of lending, there appear to be low repayment rates. Easy access to subsidized credit, combined with weak follow-up on repayments, is thought to have undermined the "credit culture" and makes it more difficult for commercially focused credit providers to enter the market (Jefferis 2015).

The credit information system is weak even though there have been planning meetings in 2018 about establishing a credit bureau, using IFC expertise in this area of financial sector supporting infrastructure.[18] A credit information system through a credit bureau owned by retail financial institutions is a positive contribution to the democratization of the financial system. It is one positive intervention promoting inclusive finance, as all borrowers regardless of income, location, or formal educational status can establish good credit histories.

8.6 Invitation: "Please Come As You Are!" - A Welcome to Build ACLEDA Bank Lao, Ltd.

Just as the global financial crisis of 2007–2008 threatened economies throughout the world, ACLEDA Bank Plc. was preparing the inauguration of its first subsidiary operation in Lao PDR. Two years after the initial welcome by the Bank of Laos, the opening of ACLEDA Bank Lao Ltd. (ABL) was celebrated with good wishes and dedicated preparation to ensure a quality operation. The shareholders, the board of directors, management, and staff were eager to establish ACLEDA Bank Lao and proud to open its doors on July 8, 2008.

[18] See Chap. 3 for a discussion of financial sector supporting functions.

Today, ACLEDA Bank Lao Ltd. offers a wide range of banking products and financial services to corporate and retail customers through a variety of delivery channels. ACLEDA Bank Lao offers banking services to a large rural and urban customer base of small and medium-sized businesses. The expansive branch network serves most of the country from the majestic hills of Luang Prabang to the intriguing mountains of Attapeu and the bustling commercial centers of Savannakhet and Champasak Provinces.

As of the end June 2019, ACLEDA Bank Lao Ltd. managed a network of 39 branches, including 25 district offices throughout the country. Branches are complemented by 41 ATMs, 81 points of sale (POS) that are accessible with an ACLEDA Bank card, and ACLEDA ThanChai, a convenient smartphone banking application that allows customers access to banking services anytime, anywhere. The popularity of ACLEDA ThanChai fintech application is growing with 30,904 using the application to ease payments, check account balances, and other banking transactions.

After almost a decade of experience serving the market of small and medium-sized enterprises, by the end of June 2019, the value of the loan portfolio reached **USD 128 million** lent to 32,546 active borrowers, **53% of whom are female**. See Fig. 8.8.

Total savings and deposits topped USD 99,898,000 with **120,494** deposit accounts (ACLEDA Bank Lao 2019). See Fig. 8.9.

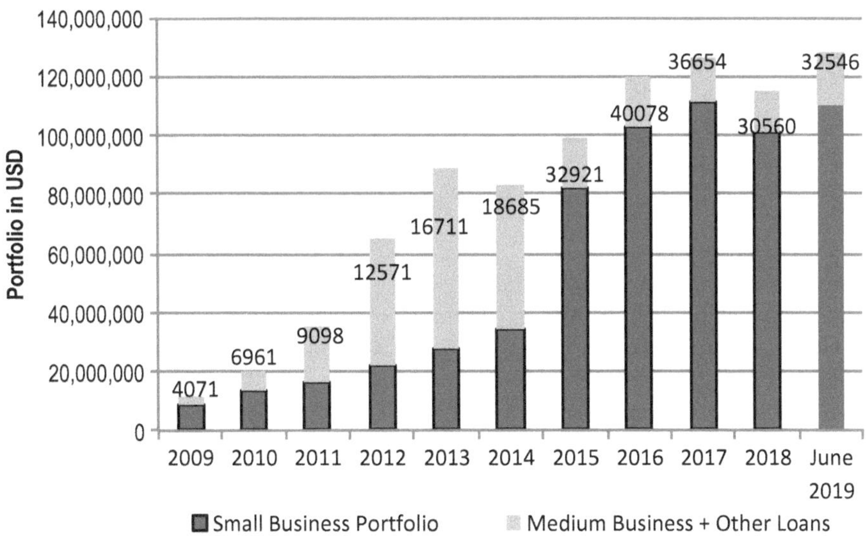

Fig. 8.8 Loans outstanding and number of active borrowers 2009–2019
Source: ACLEDA Bank Lao, Ltd. Annual Reports and Performance 2008–June 2019
Note: Portfolio converted to USD at prevailing exchange rate at the time

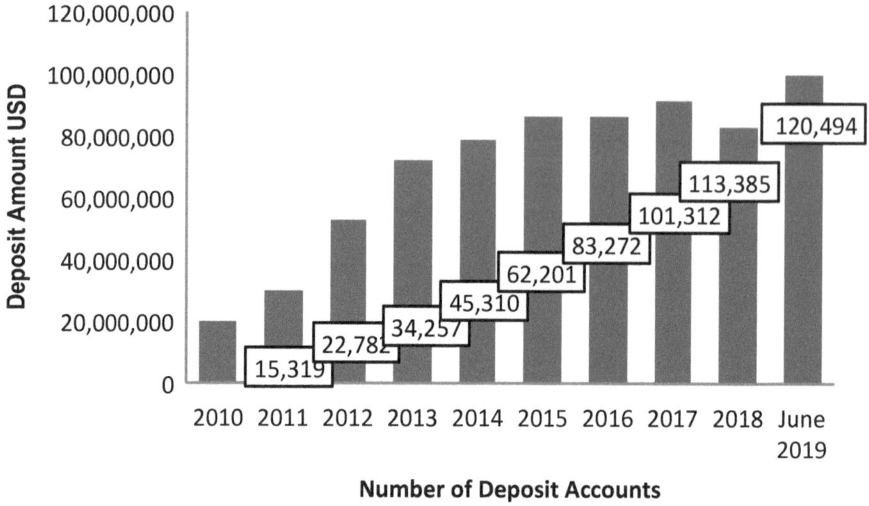

Fig. 8.9 Amount of customer deposits and number of accounts 2010–2019
Source: ACLEDA Bank Lao, Ltd. Annual Reports and Performance 2008–June 2019
Note: Deposit amounts converted to USD at prevailing exchange rate at the time

Domestic and international transfers and cash management services continued to grow along with ACLEDA customers' businesses. Domestic funds transfers experienced robust growth, more than doubling the number of transfers within the country over the past 3 years. By June 2019 ABL's total assets stood at USD 159 million managed by 1009 staff.[19]

8.6.1 The "Highs and Lows of ABL Performance"

The solid ABL performance by mid-2019 wasn't always the case. Shortly after the initial honeymoon in 2008, ABL experienced creeping delinquency due to a number of factors, including the weakening business environment as well as internal control and staff capacity issues.

By 2010–2011, along with many other financial institutions in Lao PDR, including banks and MFIs, losses accumulated due to the rising number of defaults in the changing business environment, as government cut back on outside contracting. Small and medium-sized businesses with established government contacts and work orders were hit particularly hard as were the banks that served them.

[19] Detailed performance indicators over a decade of growth are presented later in this chapter. Total assets are posted as of end 2017.

Later, a variety of financial sector regulations put in place from 2013 to 2017 took a toll on all retail-banking operations in the country. ACLEDA Bank Lao was no exception. All banks operating in Laos adjusted operations to comply with new regulations regarding foreign currency lending, interest rate caps on loans, and mandatory interest rate spreads between deposits and loans.[20]

These circumstances presented a difficult environment for even the most expert banking operations and the people who managed them. Yet, ABL's CEO and Managing Director, Dr. Phon Narin, and his intrepid team were determined to prove that the ACLEDA Bank model could provide the small business owners of Laos—their neighboring countrymen and women—honest and transparent services to finance their businesses, secure their future with safe savings services, and conveniently move their money from place to place.

The first welcome to set up operations in Laos was offered by the Bank of Laos based on the appropriateness of the ACLEDA Bank business model of providing credit, deposit services, cash management, and transfer services to the micro, small, and medium-sized enterprise market. And, ACLEDA Bank Lao, with its resolute and experienced board of directors and management team was not about to give up easily, if at all.

They searched for a solid plan and meticulous execution to turn around their banking operation in Laos so that it could achieve the original dream of the ACLEDA Bank Plc. founders.

What follows relates the ABL turnaround story of how they lost the way and how they found it once again.

8.6.2 A New Kind of Bank

ACLEDA Bank was a new kind of bank in the Lao PDR. As the Bank's welcome to the country from the Laotian government anticipated, they would create a small enterprise bank that would cover all provinces and extend to small towns and rural areas. Their credit operations would finance small, micro, and medium-sized enterprises in all sectors of the economy, services, industry, and agriculture.

They used operating principles that adhered to international standards of governance. They aspired to ensure all ACLEDA staff members were well trained, and they expected them to excel not only in their technical specialties but also to practice high ethical standards and develop a robust customer service mentality.

[20] See the pervious section of this chapter for details on the regulatory changes and how they affect the financial sector.

ACLEDA Bank's experience of harnessing technology and making it work for people without access to financial services was particularly attractive for a mountainous country where travel was difficult, expensive, and often dangerous.

ACLEDA Bank integrated concepts of Environmental and Social Sustainability (ESS) into all of their operations and reported regularly on "people, planet, and profit" to their board of directors and their shareholders. In practice, this meant developing and adhering to a strong mission statement, developing guidelines and practices as well as the systems that would support action, and reporting on progress. Environmental and Social Sustainability in banking was new to Laos. If ACLEDA were to achieve their ESS goals, it would ideally demonstrate an exceptional example to the banking sector in Laos and perhaps inspire replication and adoption by others. See Box 8.2 for ACLEDA Bank's Environmental and Social Sustainability mission.

Within the overall ESS guidelines, the key principles of ACLEDA Bank Lao's corporate social responsibility policy were enhanced with staff input as follows:

> "ACLEDA Bank Lao Ltd. is an "equal opportunity" employer. Apart from those jobs that involve a higher physical risk (e.g. guards and messengers) appointment to all positions at every level is based entirely on merit regardless of gender or physical disability
>
> A high level committee under the Chair of the Board is tasked with the responsibility of setting and monitoring the Bank's moral and ethical standards and respect for human rights.
>
> In consultation with its staff, the Bank developed and will continue to review: social policies concerning: codes of conduct, human resources management, health and safety, external relations, freedom of association and the right to collective bargaining."

All ESS policies are published on Lotus Notes so that every staff member has free (and paperless) access to the most up-to-date versions.

The first welcoming for ACLEDA Bank Lao was inspired by the many visits and exchanges between Lao and Cambodian policy makers and retail bankers who participated in the ACLEDA AARMC International Visitors Program.[21] The inspiration to expand regionally was further stirred, while AARMC training staff began to design and deliver retail bank and MFI training programs in Laos. In many ways, these training programs, supported by KFW, served as a 3-year introduction to the later welcoming of ACLEDA Bank's expansion to the Lao PDR.

Later the excitement surrounding the expansion to a neighboring country may have caused the ACLEDA pioneers to err on the side of positive thinking instead of confronting the brutal facts inherent in the start-up of any new business.

The pioneers saw a neighboring country very much like their own, extending a warm, open, and honest invitation to set up a small and medium enterprise bank nationwide. With the enthusiasm that such recognition and invitation brings, some

[21] See Chap. 10 for capacity building investments made by ACLEDA Bank Plc.

Box 8.2: Environment and Social Sustainability (ESS)—"People, Planet, and Profit"—Environmental and Social Sustainability Mission Statement

ACLEDA Bank is committed to achieving strong, sustainable financial returns while respecting the environment and community within which we live. We subscribe to the concept of the triple bottom line ("people, planet, and profit") reporting and are constantly developing indicators for measuring and reporting on our performance and impacts on the society and the environment and to implement a reporting structure based on the guidelines of the Global Reporting Initiative.

The key elements of ACLEDA Bank's ESS mission are:

To provide a framework of guidelines within which ACLEDA Bank can operate in a sustainable manner so that our impact on the environment, society, and the community in which we operate is managed in a responsible way.

To continue to introduce energy efficient systems into our buildings and to manage sensibly our energy usage where we operate.

To honor the society in which we live and actively work to promote an inclusive culture, embracing not just shareholders and staff, customers, and business partners but respect for the individual within our community.

To recognize that supporting the community is not just morally sound but good business as well—our "good health" and prosperity are naturally interdependent.

ACLEDA Bank fully subscribes to international conventions, which prohibit the provision of credit to, or otherwise support any activities, which might harm the environment, be morally repugnant or jeopardize human rights. In particular, the Bank has in place policies that forbid involvement with exploitative forms of forced or child labor, trade in weapons and munitions, gambling, casinos, brothels, regulated wildlife or wildlife products, and production or trade in radioactive materials or significant volumes of hazardous chemicals.

ACLEDA Bank monitors paper usage, energy consumption—electricity, gasoline, diesel and lubricants, water, motorcycle and vehicle business travel.

ACLEDA Bank Lao Ltd.'s corporate culture is built on respect for the society in which we operate and an inclusive approach to our stakeholders embracing not just shareholders and staff, customers, and business partners but the community at large. In addition to the environmental programs mentioned above, the Bank observes a policy of equality in all our dealings with the public in general and customers and staff alike.

Above all, ACLEDA Bank Lao Ltd. has practiced from the very beginning "zero tolerance" of corruption both internally and externally, and transgressions are dealt with summarily.

more optimistic views may have prevailed over greater caution and more careful study.

In retrospect, more careful study may have laid a more solid foundation to start up a new operation, even though it would not have changed the final decision to green light the entrance into the Laotian market. Nor would further study have prevented some of the most challenging regulations for commercial banks to support financial inclusion efforts, particularly in rural areas. Many of the most restrictive regulations and practices were established after the start-up of ABL.

Additional research may have provided a more intensive focus on the expansive budgets required to build branches and increase their outreach. The further resources that were required to build human capital and for investment in staff development, training, and mentorship to develop ACLEDA Bank Lao as an institution worthy of its founder might have been better understood.[22] Such actions may also have prevented some of the upheaval and doubt about staff capacity and performance that later came in 2009–2012 and again in 2014–2015. Understanding these influences may have set ABL on a more stable course much earlier.

Perhaps the ACLEDA pioneers did not recognize just how different they were from most banks in their own country, in neighboring Lao PDR, in the region, and, indeed, globally.

8.6.3 Growing Pains of a New Start-Up: ABL 2008–2011

> ACLEDA Bank Lao Ltd.'s vision is to be a commercial bank providing superior financial services throughout Lao PDR.
>
> Our mission is to provide small and medium entrepreneurs with the wherewithal to manage their financial resources efficiently and by doing so to improve the quality of their lives. By achieving these goals, we will ensure sustainable benefits to our shareholders, our staff and the community at large. We will at all times observe the highest principles of ethical behavior, respect for society, Lao law and the environment.
>
> Source: ACLEDA Bank Lao Ltd Website, Vision and Mission.

Setting up a commercial bank from scratch is not an easy task, even if the developers are from a neighboring country and have set up a bank before. On the one hand, there is always the risk that the big vision and knowing how to deliver state-of-the art products and services in one context may make the effort even more burdensome in another context. On the other hand, that same vision may make the new operation soar to greater heights.

Perhaps the pioneer architects in Laos may not have fully appreciated that ACLEDA was a different kind of bank, and the environment in the Lao PDR was a different kind of environment with only very few similarities. Some of the major

[22] The next chapter tells the story of the founding of ALCEDA Microfinance Institution Myanmar (AMM) and how lessons from ACLEDA Bank Lao Ltd. were usefully applied.

differences started with the country's different economic and political system. The Lao PDR embraced a state-led market economy. The banking sector was dominated by state-owned banks that fulfilled the state's purposes at the retail level and were more dependent on government budgets than earning potential. There was almost certainty of government-granted recapitalization of state banks in case of difficulty.

Outside the banking sector, special concessions were provided to government-led investment projects and enterprises, including different reporting requirements and the possibility of recapitalization through state-owned banks.

In comparison, Cambodia boasted a market-led economy. The banking sector for all intents and purposes encouraged the development of private sector retail banks and favored competition and innovation, as long as increasingly strict regulations and prudential reserve ratios were met.

Compared to Cambodia, the consumer market for financial services in Laos was small and at least somewhat served by two of the largest state-owned banks, including the Agriculture Promotion Bank and Banque Pour Le Commerce Exterieur Lao Public (BCEL), two state-owned banks with extensive geographic coverage throughout the country and wide consumer acceptance.

Similar to Laos, many populations in Cambodia also were isolated by geography and far from banking services, but Cambodian government priorities at the time were to ensure major highway connections were built throughout the country. In fact, in the early days of ACLEDA Bank Plc. operations in Cambodia, ACLEDA literally "followed the road" as it was built, as an intentional bank-building and market development strategy.

In Lao PDR there were few roads, and many villages are simply isolated from other parts of the country. During the rainy season, isolation increases.[23] In many areas of the country, local ethic languages predominate, making it more difficult to communicate over the distance.

From an institutional perspective, over a 10-year period, ACLEDA Bank Plc. (ABC) benefitted from a gradual development experience from a project to an NGO to a specialized bank to a fully fledged commercial bank. Even though this strategy would not be necessary or beneficial to either party in the Lao PDR, organizational evolution allowed ABC to innovate with products and services and customer acceptance, gradually over time.

This gradual growth also promoted a cultural expansion within the hallways and the cubicles of the organization. ACLEDA Bank Plc. staff and management changed during this period too, as they experienced what worked well, recognized what only

[23] See the very touching story on video, "The Difference a Bridge Can Make" produced by the World Bank in 2017a, b. http://www.worldbank.org/en/news/video/2017/04/12/the-difference-a-bridge-can-make

needed to be tweaked for small improvements, and knew from experience what was built to fail.

But perhaps the biggest issue that no one really anticipated, or prepared for, was that ACLEDA Bank expectations were precisely to build a new kind of bank in Lao PDR. And their expectations of themselves and their expectations of others were very, very high.

8.7 ACLEDA Bank Lao Ltd.: Year-on-Year Performance

ABL operations improved year on year, with some sudden and dramatic downturns, generally due to a series of unexpected events. Ready with a 3-year, break-even plan approved and used as a guide, ABL board, management, and staff were energetically optimistic at the outset of Bank operations in 2008. Later, the optimism took a more cautious turn. Each 2-year period seemed to present unexpected growing pains for the experienced ACLEDA Bank pioneers, as the notion of "just like us" continued to be challenged.

ACLEDA Bank Lao Ltd.'s long-term strategic priorities from 2008 to 2019 varied little as a tribute to the founding team. The yearly priorities were modified based on the level of achievement, new regulations, and considerable learning in a new environment. But they always focused on expansion to new customers by providing tailor-made financial services to small business enterprises.

A long-standing priority—from the outset and to this day—was developing a customer service culture within the Bank. Two focus points of the customer service culture were articulated early. They are to ensure personal accessibility for all ABL customers and to increase ABL services as the market expanded by adopting the best practices of the parent company, ACLEDA Bank Plc. in Cambodia. ABL also prioritized understanding and responding to customer needs by providing a comprehensive range of financial innovations as customers moved up the wealth ladder.

Although not within sight in 2008, the ABL pioneers saw upgrading financial technology (fintech) applications and branchless technology solutions as important ways to more conveniently serve the small business customer, particularly in the rural areas of the country. Later, in 2015 when electronic banking services (EBS) and fintech solutions were in sight for implementation, additional strategic priorities came online.

8.7.1 Bumps in the Road: The Early Years 2008–2011

During the first 6 months of operations in 2008, and into the year 2009, ABL reports showed growth trends in line with the 3-year plan, and no significant issues were reported. But Dr. Narin and his senior staff noted some very worrying trends as early as 2008 primarily associated with new staff hires.

Key among these worrying trends were new staff's inexperience within a "best practice" banking institution. The accepted practice by loan officers in Laos was to request "commissions" for approving loans or "the kindness of the customer"—behavior that was against ABL's Ethical Code of Conduct. And, there were early signs of high staff turnover after bank training.

Early in 2008, the Governance Committee of the Board of Directors—the keeper of ACLEDA's corporate value of "zero tolerance" for corruption—conducted a study with the internal auditors. The purpose of the study was to "assess the rapid growth of our staff, particularly new employees, on working practices and ethical behavior within the Bank and monitor the effectiveness of the training and counseling program as a means of maintaining the organization's standards" (ACLEDA Bank Lao, Ltd. 2009).

During this same 6-month start-up period, the Risk Management Committee of the Board—charged with monitoring portfolio quality and compliance with the approved credit policy and applicable laws and regulations—had noted that portfolio quality was "excellent." And, it was. But, it was too early in lending operations to detect the underlying risk of inexperienced staff.

By late 2009, with only 2 years of operations, the portfolio grew tenfold from USD 1,113,000 at the beginning of the year to USD 11,960,000 by December 2009.[24] Accompanying the increase in portfolio was a rise in the portfolio at risk (PAR). Even though the focus throughout 2009 was to maintain high loan portfolio quality and liquidity, loan portfolio quality issues surfaced once again during 2010. This was attributed to staff inexperience.

The decline in quality lending opportunities had a material impact on slow earnings in the first half of 2010, even though the operation appeared to improve during the second half of the year. See Fig. 8.8 for a history of portfolio growth.

Dr. Narin spent days and nights analyzing the reasons for the delinquency and designing measures to stop it. One common practice in Laos in both banks and MFIs was for credit officers to ask for and accept commissions directly from the borrower without knowledge or agreement of the banking institution's management. Such a practice was often called "the kindness of the customer."

Dr. Narin reviewed the internal audit department's study and then mounted a public promotional campaign about ACLEDA Bank's products and policies. He sought to reverse the trend in delinquency and tell the public that ACLEDA Bank never charged commissions. He wrote notices in newspapers, spoke to relevant authorities, and appeared on television.

Another reason for high delinquency, he surmised, was attributed to high staff turnover in the context of ABL's rapid growth and increasing staff needs. Total ABL staff numbered 246 by the end of 2009, a twofold increase over the prior year. By the end of 2010, ACLEDA Bank Lao employed 399 staff members—a 50% increase over the prior year. See Fig. 8.10 for ACLEDA Bank Lao staff growth over a decade.

[24] The figure cited is the portfolio size, net of provisions.

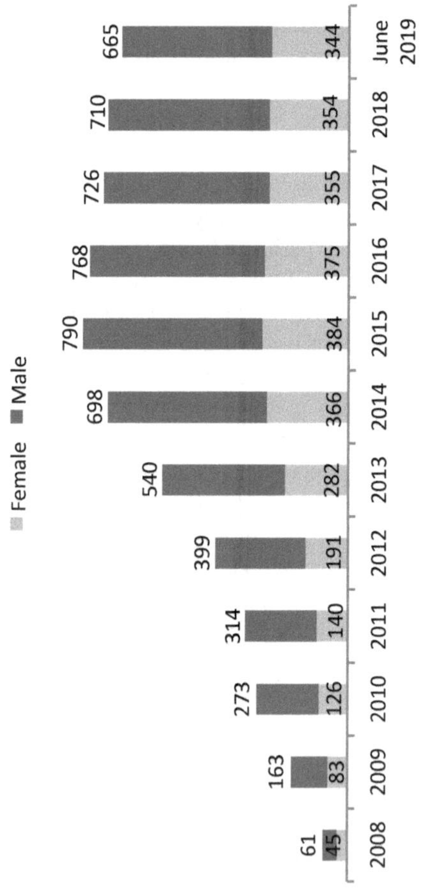

Fig. 8.10 Staff ACLEDA Bank Lao Ltd. 2008–2019
Source: ABL Annual Reports and Performance 2008–2018; Monthly Performance Achievements

At the time of start-up, ABL underestimated the resources that would be required to recruit, train, mentor, and retain professionals who could meet ABL standards. Higher-than-expected staff turnover surfaced by the end of 2009. By 2010, turnover was 5.6%, and it later increased to 13.5% in 2011.

Training and capacity building efforts at all levels of the new organization had to be broadened and accelerated. ABL embarked on a program to develop the managerial skills of new senior Lao staff through training and mentoring so that they could take over from the seconded Cambodian management team according to plan.

To ensure this program's success, ABL placed even more emphasis of dual control in operations until the time new Lao staff were ready to assume full control. Within less than 2 years of operations, over 1000 career development, refresher, and induction training programs were held for staff. Once the tradition was established, it continued.

With the rapid growth, growing delinquency, emphasis on staff development, and concern about the unexpected growing losses in 2010, the initial rollout of 15 ATMs that same year appeared almost as a footnote in the Annual Report of tumultuous 2010.

Later, ATMs proved to be a popular service in Laos, and by mid-2018 the Bank had placed 41 ATMs throughout the country. The ATM service is linked to the ACLEDA Bank in Cambodia allowing cardholders of either Bank to access their funds in the other's country at any time.

Almost as a vow of determination, but with a bit of caution and apology, ABL's 2010 annual report noted, "Given the extreme unpredictability between the starting up phase and the second year, we are satisfied that the decisions taken have kept the Bank sound and well able to cope with the challenges of 2011. We are targeting 2011 as the year when we will achieve sustainable monthly profitability."

And, surprisingly by the end 2011, ABL made its first annual net profit of USD1.2 million.[25]

8.7.2 Good Practice and Good Fortune

The good fortune was attributed to the continued strong performance of the Lao PDR's economy. The good practice was due to the operational reviews undertaken by management and staff from 2008 through 2011. The Bank's revenue increase was attributable to higher net interest and non-interest income as well as the improvement in the operating expense ratio from an unacceptably high 92.3% in 2010 to a mediocre 57% in 2011, but trending in the right direction.[26]

[25] The net gain in 2011 contributed to the coverage of net losses from 2008 through 2010 of USD 4,823,000.

[26] An excellent on line Glossary of economic and financial terms is https://www.economist.com/economics-a-to-z

As the Lao economy remained robust, the loans outstanding in all sectors exceeded ABL targets, climbing 81.7% in 2011 compared to 2010. By the end of 2011, over 9000 micro, small, and medium-sized enterprises borrowed USD 35,427,000 to support and expand their operations.

During 2011, ABL also began to replace Cambodian consultants who had been seconded to Laos to work with and mentor Lao managers. That same year, local branch managers led all ABL branches, and Lao managers took their places on the Executive Committee of the Bank together with the four remaining Cambodian consultants. The succession plan of training, mentoring, and localization of talented Lao managers was working for ACLEDA Bank Lao Ltd.

It was a celebratory time. After all, ABL confronted and addressed numerous challenges with the start-up banking operation in Laos.

8.7.3 Smooth Sailing?: The Latter Years 2011–2018

From 2011 to 2013, ABL got down to business. Each year was better than the previous one. All performance figures met expectations. Finally the ABL pioneers—both Cambodian and Laotian—could offer the public a well-managed bank of standing with customers and regulators.

The Bank grew because it treated customers with respect and courtesy and designed products and services that met their business and family requirements. In 2013, as evidence of considerable efforts, ACLEDA Bank Lao Ltd. received a certificate of appreciation from the Lao government for doing the "Best Job and Excellent Results" over a period of 5 years (2008–2013). ACLEDA Bank Lao Ltd. was one of only two private commercial banks to receive this certificate of appreciation from the government.

On February 2, 2013, the Lao PDR became the 158th member of the World Trade Organization (WTO). Accession to the WTO provided the Lao PDR with more market opportunities by diversifying its list of trading partners; it would also enable higher gains from trade and enhance investor confidence. The accession to the WTO appeared to be the right time for ABL to launch trade finance for services, particularly in exports.

Facilitated by ABL, foreign buyers could deal directly with ACLEDA Bank Plc. in Cambodia that had already built up a comprehensive network of correspondents around the world covering 459 branches in 57 countries, including some of the biggest names in international banking. This arrangement allowed ACLEDA Bank Lao Ltd. to reach out to more customers, facilitate Laos' external trade growth, and open doors to new international trade relations.

Within the country, the ABL branch office network expanded from 28 to 41 offices, mainly in rural districts now represented in almost every province in the country, except for Phongsaly in the extreme north and Houaphan in eastern Laos. All offices were provided secured online connections, and the total staff at the end of the year numbered 822, an all-time high and an increase of 39% from 2012.

And, Performance Was Robust Throughout 2013…

In 2013 the ABL loan portfolio grew 34.99% and loan disbursements increased by 15.28% when compared to 2012. However, the Bank's PAR ratio increased from 1.96% to 3.37%—a definite warning sign. The increase in the PAR rate was attributed primarily to the economic slowdown in Lao PDR at the end of 2013 and some identified weaknesses in the Bank's credit management that had been reviewed and adjusted.

And, Then Came 2014…

As the ACLEDA Annual Report for the year noted, 2014 was a difficult one for banks in Lao PDR. The necessity of the government to make cost savings to ensure a more balanced budget had a negative effect on certain business sectors. Moreover, the enforcement by the Central Bank of prudential standards with respect to the provision of loans in foreign currencies caused banks, including ABL, to carry an excess of liquidity in foreign currency on the balance sheet. This diminished the earnings potential of the Bank. It was estimated that it would take the Bank almost one year to gradually reduce its assets in USD and move toward a balance sheet mainly in Kip.

In addition, the decline in public contracts to the private sector had a negative impact on some small and medium enterprises, just as it did on ABL's loan portfolio quality. Now experienced in these fluctuations and unexpected events, the Bank set aside more reserves to cover possible losses on loans outstanding. The increase of these reserves and the cost of keeping substantially higher levels of liquidity in foreign currency than normal led to a negative result in 2014.[27]

Perhaps invigorated by the challenges of the new restrictions, ACLEDA Bank Lao Ltd. saw several advantages. They took measures to improve liquidity and expand the loan portfolio in local currency, by expanding the number of active borrowers among small businesses.

By 2015, the number of "Small 1" loan clients grew by 112.16% and "Small 2"[28] loan clients by 50.49% of active loan clients compared with the end of 2014. The value of small loans in the outstanding portfolio grew, showing adherence to mission. "Small 1" loans grew by 87.26% and "Small 2" loans by 50.67% of the gross loan portfolio outstanding. For the first time in 2015, female borrowers made up more than 50% of the loan clients, if just so, at 50.16% of the total borrowers.

Everything was finally working very well.

And Then Came the Results of Year 2015…

ABL's 2015 plan to make up for the losses accrued in 2014 hit a huge regulatory obstacle. As noted earlier in this chapter with the discussion on regulations, the

[27] For more detail on the new regulations influencing the 2014 market for financial services in Laos, see the previous section on the financial sector regulatory environment.

[28] Small Loans 1 and 2 support small enterprises. The loans carry different amounts and terms, requirements, and flexibilities, for example, individual loans or group loans.

BOL mandated an interest rate ceiling on lending and an even more demanding requirement of a spread between loans and deposits. Looking back, it is surprising that the USD1.6 million loss in 2015 was not even higher.

2015 was another difficult year for all banks in the Lao PDR. Commercial banks in Laos were mandated to lower their interest rates for both deposits and loans in line with a decision made by the Bank of the Lao PDR, which sought to reduce loan rates and thereby to stimulate economic activity.

Since the lower interest rate was announced, the number of deposits mobilized and loans issued by commercial banks dropped significantly. Contrary to the intended purpose of the requirement, there was no uptick in economic activity or boost in domestic productivity. Lao currency deposits attracted interest rates averaging 10% per annum at the end of 2014, which then fell to an average of 7.7% per annum by November 2015.

A New Change in Policy Encouraged ABL to Innovate More…
In 2015, ABL's retail deposits grew by 10% to USD 86.17 million. This growth was mainly led by first-time depositors such as factory employees paid through the popular payroll service offered to companies by ACLEDA Bank Lao Ltd. With the opening of new service posts (a minimalist branch), savings accounts also increased from new customers. An important factor in the growth of deposits was the continuing development and expansion of the Bank's automated delivery system. At the end of 2015 it comprised 45 ATMs and 100 POS terminals throughout the country with 24,136 cards issued.

By the end of 2017, ABL had 2 years of solid performance. Performance during 2016 and 2017 finally made up for the considerable losses of 2014 and 2015. In fact, the performance of 2017 was the most robust year yet for ABL and 2018 followed in that tradition.

See Fig. 8.9 for a history of ABL's growth in total deposits and number of customers (ACLEDA Bank Lao, Ltd 2017).

8.8 Lessons

ABL experienced difficulties throughout 2012 to 2018. A number of problems put a strain on growth in customer outreach and profitability. They included lending to enterprises with government contracts and loans linked to government contracts. Staff fraud mainly involved credit officers but included other staff as well. Staff fraud was mostly, but not exclusively, in the form of accepting commissions from borrowers, a common practice in Laos. But this practice was against the ACLEDA Code of Conduct and a practice that ABL could not abide despite its prevalence within the country.

Interest Rate Caps and Limits on the Deposit Rate Are Restrictive Low interest rate caps on loans took away the financial institution's ability to assess and then price risk. Uncertainty and directives with little notice for full compliance were issued. The most damaging directive was issued on September 11, 2013, as a BOL regulatory decision. It restricted commercial bank lending to only the currency of the borrower's income. This meant that the BOL required disbursement in LAK to the majority of ACLEDA clients. And, the regulation was effective immediately.

Loans to enterprises with government contracts also contributed to deteriorating performance, as did staff fraud that contributed to a USD 270,300 loss for the 10-year period. The amount of the fraud was much higher than the year before for every year during the 10-year period, except for 2013. However, amounts of staff fraud were recovered from staff over the 10-year period from a high of 98% to a low of 3% was returned each year, reaching a total recovery rate of 28% over the 10-year period.

Loans to private enterprises with government contracts also contributed their share of losses to ABL when the government cut back on outside contracting of small and medium enterprises beginning in 2013. The total NPL for this category of disaster was approximately USD 1.2 million over the 10-year period.

Fortunately most of these challenges did not appear All at once When an analysis is done of which factors hurt the ABL enterprise the most, it comes down to two—a BOL regulation hastily implemented by directive and fraud by staff. Even though the liquidity crisis was severe, it was resolved within a year. Lending to government enterprises had a severe effect on increasing the NPL and default rate, as many enterprises that serve government contracts do not expect to repay loans in a timely manner, or had their contracts cancelled by government during the lending period in 2014.

Of all the difficulties managing a small enterprise bank in Laos from staff fraud to lending to enterprises with government contracts, the most difficult financial challenge ABL faced was due to the BOL regulation regarding currency restrictions, hastily announced with expectations of hasty implementation.

ABL faced a surplus in USD and Thai Baht, but a shortage of Lao Kip (LAK). This mismatch severely decreased the loan portfolio outstanding. Month by month the portfolio decreased as a result of the liquidity crisis due to currency mismatch and inadequate advance notice of the pending regulation. The portfolio outstanding decreased from USD 91.59 million in October 2013 to 83.17 million in December 2014, a decrease of USD 8.42 million, at a time when the portfolio should have been expanding with experience in the market.

As a result, the net profit after tax showed a negative 22.56% change from 2012 to 2013, and a whopping negative 284.20% change from 2013 year end to 2014. The year 2013 is also remarkable for defaults on small enterprise loans greater than USD

10,000 when 51 borrowers defaulted and USD 2.6 million was classified as in default or in arrears. As a result ABL increased loan loss reserves adding to expenses.

In fact, in its challenging history to date, the period from 2013 through 2015 was the most difficult for ABL financially. The resilience of ABL showed in its recovery from many challenges throughout its history from staff fraud to high NPLs of private enterprises with government contracts. However, the most devastating and expensive blow to ABL's viability was due to the currency mismatch and inadequate time to meet new government requirements without incurring a loss. ABL did not see recovery of its rock-solid operation rebound until 2016.

8.9 Epilogue: 2019—A New Beginning

The new CEO and Managing Director of ABL, Dr. Svay Hay, recognizes both the potential and the challenges of ACLEDA Bank Lao Ltd. that are likely to develop from 2019 onward. He has followed the evolution of ABL from his post as Director of ACLEDA Securities, Plc. in Cambodia.

And, Dr. Phon Narin returned to Cambodia as the Director of the ACLEDA Institute of Business,[29] a position where he can distill his experience in the Lao PDR for the next generation of aspiring bankers in ASEAN who are eager to hear about the challenges and potential of a most inviting country.

And the Beat Goes on…

On the second floor of modest office buildings in many rural and urban areas in Lao PDR a process of transformation is underway. Almost every day new and current customers speak to ACLEDA Bank Lao representatives, who tell them about a new option available to manage their accounts. ACLEDA ThanChai is a mobile application, which enables customers to take advantage of ABL's banking services, anytime, anywhere.

Using their smartphones outfitted with the ThanChai mobile app, customers can now send and receive funds to the bank accounts of their family members in locations throughout the country with no additional fees at ACLEDA Bank Lao. When they realize how this simple mechanism saves so much of the family budget, new customers decide to take a chance and try it out, along with 44,376 other ThanChai mobile app users in the Lao PDR and supported by ACLEDA Bank Lao Ltd.[30]

[29] Chap. 10 is devoted to The ACLEDA Institute of Business.

[30] Figures as of February 2020.

References

ALCEDA Bank Lao, Ltd. (2019) Achievement as of January 31, 2019. Available http://www.acledabank.com.la/la/eng/bp_achievement. Accessed 14 February 2019

ALCEDA Bank Lao Ltd. (2017) Annual Report. Available http://www.acledabank.com.la. Last accessed 13 February 2019

ACLEDA Bank Lao Ltd. Vision and Mission. Available http://www.acledabank.com.la/la/eng/bp_vision_mission. Last accessed 13 February 2019

ACLEDA Bank Lao Ltd. (2009) Annual Report 2008. Available http://www.acledabank.com.la. Last accessed 13 February 2019

Davading, Somneuk; Phimmahasay, Keomanivone; Kularatne, Chandana; Nghardsaysone, Konesawang; Hoppe, Mombert; Phounvixay, Vidaovanh; Masaki, Emiko; Mbuya, Nkosinathi Vusizihlobo; Pimhidzai, Obert; Danchev, Plamen Nikolov; Phommalangsy, Phouvanh. 2019. Lao PDR Economic Monitor: Macroeconomic Stability Amidst Uncertainty (English). Washington, D.C.: World Bank Group. Available http://documents.worldbank.org/curated/en/818841549314902040/Lao-PDR-Economic-Monitor-Macroeconomic-Stability-Amidst-Uncertainty. Last accessed 14 February 2019

FinScope 2015. Results from FinScope Consumer Survey Laos 2014. Available https://finmark.org.za/finscope-consumer-survey_laos-2014/. Last accessed 13 February 2019

GIZ. 2015. Assessing Financial Literacy in Rural Laos. Available https://www.giz.de/en/downloads/giz2015-en-assessing-financial-literacy-rural-areas-laos.pdf. Last Accessed 17 February 2019.

International Labour Organization (ILO). 2007. Meeting the Challenge: Banking As a Solution. Available https://www.ilo.org/wcmsp5/groups/public/%2D%2D-asia/%2D%2D-ro-bangkok/documents/publication/wcms_099876.pdf. Last accessed 13 February 2019

Jefferis, Keith (2015) MAP Laos Synthesis Note. Cenfri, FinMark Trust and UNCDF MAFIPP. Available http://mafipp.org/wp-content/uploads/2016/11/161031-MAP-Lao_Summary-Synthesis-note-4th-draft-biblio-Eng.pdf. Last accessed 13 February 2019

Kemp, Simon. 2019. Digital Around the World in 2019. Available: https://wearesocial.com/global-digital-report-2019. Latest Accessed 14 February 2020

Lao Microfinance Association. 2017. Annual Report 2016. Available https://www.laomfa.org. Accessed 18 June 2018.

Najdov, Evgenij; Davading, Somneuk; Phimmahasay, Keomanivone; Ngardsayson, Konesawang; Hoppe, Mombert; Zorya, Sergiy. 2018. Lao PDR economic monitor: safeguarding stability – an ongoing agenda: thematic section – how can farmers get more for their rice and consumers pay less? (English). Washington, DC: World Bank Group. Available http://documents.worldbank.org/curated/en/418261529002464394/Lao-PDR-economic-monitor-safeguarding-stability-an-ongoing-agenda-thematic-section-how-can-farmers-get-more-for-their-rice-and-consumers-pay-less. Latest Accessed 14 February 2019

Najdov, Evgenij; Phimmahasay, Keomanivone. 2016. Lao Economic Monitor, May 2016: Challenges in Promoting More Inclusive Growth and Shared Prosperity. World Bank, Washington, DC. © World Bank. Available https://openknowledge.worldbank.org/handle/10986/24372 License: CC BY 3.0 IGO.

Najdov, Evgenij; Davading, Somneuk; Phimmahasay, Keomanivone. 2017. Lao PDR economic monitor: lowering risks and reviving growth (English). Washington, D.C.: World Bank Group. http://documents.worldbank.org/curated/en/677161512735183133/Lao-PDR-economic-monitor-lowering-risks-and-reviving-growth

Roesler, Rene and Dennis Fischer. 2016. Financial Inclusion in Laos and the Evolution of Village Bank Pung. Available https://www.giz.de/en/worldwide/41279.html. Last Accessed 17 February 2019,

Tiwari, Akhand and Francois Coupienne. Understanding Customers' Behaviours and Needs. Digital Financial Services in Lao PDR. Research Highlight. July 2014. United Nations Capital Development Fund (UNCDF). Available

United Nations. 2015. Country Analysis Report: Lao PDR Analysis to Inform the Lao People's Democratic Republic – United Nations Partnership Framework (2017–2021). Available

UNCDF. 2014. Making Access Possible Program. Available http://map.uncdf.org/lao-peoples-democratic-republic

We Are Social (2020) Global Digital Report 2020. Available https://wearesocial.com/global-digital-report-2020. Accessed 14 February 2020.

World Bank Group. Doing Business 2019: Training for Reform Economy Profile Lao PDR World Bank, Washington, DC Available http://www.doingbusiness.org/content/dam/doingBusiness/country/l/lao-pdr/LAO.pdf Last accessed 13 February 2019

World Bank Group. 2018a. Doing Business in Lao PDR: Constraints to Productivity. World Bank, Washington, DC. © World Bank. Available https://openknowledge.worldbank.org/handle/10986/29384 License: CC BY 3.0 IGO."

World Bank Group. 2018b Doing Business 2019; World Bank, Washington, DC. © World Bank. https://openknowledge.worldbank.org/handle/10986/30766 License: CC BY 3.0 IGO."

World Bank Group. 2018c The World Bank in Lao PDR. Overview. Last updated September 2018. Available http://www.worldbank.org/en/country/lao/overview Accessed 15 February 2019

World Bank Group. 2018d. Economy Profile of the Lao People's Democratic Republic. Doing Business 2019; World Bank, Washington, DC. © World Bank. Available https://openknowledge.worldbank.org/handle/10986/30766 License: CC BY 3.0 IGO." Last accessed 14 February 2019

World Bank Group. 2017a. Lao PDR Economic Monitor, December 2017: Lowering Risks and Reviving Growth. World Bank, Washington, DC. © World Bank. Available https://openknowledge.worldbank.org/handle/10986/29030 License: CC BY 3.0 IGO." Last Accessed 13 February 2019

World Bank Group. 2017b. 2016 Lao PDR Enterprise Survey: Country Highlights. World Bank, Washington, DC. © World Bank. Available https://openknowledge.worldbank.org/handle/10986/28475 License: CC BY 3.0 IGO."

World Bank Group. 2016. Lao PDR Enterprise Survey. Country Highlights Lao PDR 2016 Available http://www.enterprisesurveys.org/~/media/GIAWB/EnterpriseSurveys/Documents/CountryHighlights/Lao-PDR-2016.pdf Accessed 15 July 2018

World Bank. 2015a. Poverty in Lao PDR: Achievements and Challenges. December 2015. Available http://www.worldbank.org/en/news/video/2015/12/10/poverty-in-lao-pdr-achievements-and-challenges. Last accessed 24 January 2019

World Bank. 2015b. Lao PDR poverty policy notes: drivers of poverty reduction in Lao PDR (English). Washington, D.C.: World Bank Group. http://documents.worldbank.org/curated/en/590861467722637341/Lao-PDR-poverty-policy-notes-drivers-of-poverty-reduction-in-Lao-PDR. Accessed 15 July 2018

World Bank. World Development Indicators. GNI per capita ranking, Atlas method and PPP based. Available https://datacatalog.worldbank.org/dataset/gni-capita-ranking-atlas-method-and-ppp-based. Accessed 15 July 2018

World Travel and Tourism Council. 2018. Travel and Tourism Economic Impact 2017 Laos. Available https://www.wttc.org/-/media/files/reports/economic-impact-research/countries-2018/laos2018.pdf. Last accessed 24 January 2019

Chapter 9
Banking on the Future: ACLEDA MFI Myanmar Co. Ltd. and the Evolving Financial Sector of the Republic of the Union of Myanmar

Success does not just happen. It is designed.
—Author Unknown

As 2012 drew to a close, 22 recent university graduates and newly recruited young professional bankers went back to their home villages in the Republic of the Union of Myanmar. They needed to complete one of the many steps required to get a passport.

Some took the 5-hour bus ride on the divided highway to the outskirts of Naypyidaw, the new capital city of Myanmar. Others carefully swerved in and out of traffic on a motorcycle taxi to the suburban neighborhoods of Yangon. Four young women shared a taxi to Bago, 3 hours away. No one used a mobile phone to call the family; no one had a mobile phone.

Together, they were about to embark on a journey to Cambodia that would change their lives.

This cadre of young micro-bankers from ACLEDA Microfinance Institution (MFI) Myanmar was traveling from Yangon to Phnom Penh to attend a course of instruction at the ACLEDA Training Center (ATC),[1] now licensed as a Higher Education Institution by the Ministry of Education, Youth and Sport in Cambodia as the ACLEDA Institute of Business (AIB). The course was an induction course to ACLEDA Bank's world of banking.

As promised, the 45-day course of instruction was more than sitting in a classroom and calculating ratios. It covered the stuff of micro-bankers' dreams—and nightmares! On offer was all the experience accumulated from over 25 years of building the largest bank in Cambodia and one that has been rated in the top 100 banks in ASEAN for the past 5 years.[2]

---

[1] The ACLEDA Training Center was licensed as a Higher Education Institution by the Ministry of Education, Youth and Sport and renamed the ACLEDA Institute of Business (AIB) on January 25, 2016.

[2] *The Banker's* yearly survey ranks the top 100 banks in the ASEAN region against standard banking ratios, such as Tier I capital growth, asset growth, return on capital, return on assets, cost to

© Springer Nature Singapore Pte Ltd. 2020

H. A. Clark, *Beyond Borders, Beyond Banking*,
https://doi.org/10.1007/978-981-15-1687-0_9

The course would also expose most of these aspiring young bankers to a foreign country for the first time. They would hear the history of ACLEDA Bank Plc. and how and why it evolved from a project, to a microfinance institution, to a bank. They would meet seasoned professional bankers from ACLEDA Bank Plc. and the experienced professors and trainers of the ATC who never forgot their own journeys in building ACLEDA Bank and their contributions to the evolution of the Cambodian financial sector.

Mr. Min Aung and his fellow classmates—20 young women and another young man—were off on an educational adventure of a lifetime. The training would enhance their capacity to perform well in their jobs, at or above the standard of excellence required by Mr. Kim Bunsocheat, Managing Director & CEO of ACLEDA MFI Myanmar Co. Ltd. (AMM).

The course filled the minds of 22 lucky people with talk about ethics and how to implement client protection principles.[3] The course showed them how experienced credit officers treat clients and demonstrated excellent customer service provided to borrowers and savers, as well as their fellow staff.

Equally important, they met legends in the field of microfinance and banking for the people. Through decades of experience, these experts helped the newly recruited bankers from Myanmar understand ACLEDA's ethical Code of Conduct and why it is important to the business and to society, as they began their own professional banking journey.

Later, these newly minted young bankers would become attractive to the recruitment officers of AMM's MFI competitors in the increasingly competitive MFI landscape in Myanmar. But for the moment, the induction training served to put the new recruits, who had been selected for their management and banking potential, on the pathway to becoming competent international experts within the growing ACLEDA Bank Group of Companies.

In 2017, AMM's Legal Department Manager & Company Secretary, Mr. Min Aung, noted how much he was impressed with the care and dedication his new employer had given to educational techniques and ensuring knowledge combined with practical technical skills and application. He recalled how the faculty of what would become the ACLEDA Institute of Business designed a special legal curriculum for him to supplement the main course. It was a special 3-day practicum to prepare for the business of banking in the Myanmar country context, including application of legal frameworks, litigation, and contracts law, among other topics.

Later, Mr. Min Aung said about the experience, "It was very good company," referring to ACLEDA Bank Plc., the ATC faculty, and his fellow classmates. It was an unforgettable experience.

---

income ratio, and pretax profit growth. https://www.thebanker.com/Banker-Data/Banker-Rankings/Top-100-Asean-Banks-Indonesia-on-the-rise. *The Banker* is a service from the Financial Times Ltd.

[3] See Box 9.1 for a brief description of the client protection principles.

9.1 The Rebirth of ACLEDA Microfinance

ACLEDA MFI Myanmar Co. Ltd. (AMM) celebrated its seventh year anniversary on February 8, 2020.[4] As of the end of January 2020,[5] AMM served 103,191 active micro-borrowers and holds 164,341 savings accounts on behalf of borrowers through 14 branch and sub-branch offices in the Yangon and Bago Regions in the Republic of the Union of Myanmar (AMM 2018a, b).

Despite difficult circumstances, ACLEDA MFI Myanmar Co., Ltd. maintained its position as a market leader in terms of assets, loans, deposits, and profitability almost since the outset of start-up to expansion. Plans are also in place to expand the branch network to other regions and states, particularly in rural areas (AMM 2018a, b).

Over the past 5 years, AMM reinvented the steps of the ACLEDA Bank Plc.'s founders, by tracing the Bank's original roots as a microfinance institution in a new context. AMM entered the microfinance sector in Myanmar, a new country with different regulations, almost 25 years after the founding of its parent company, ACLEDA Bank Plc. And, true to its microfinance origins, AMM began serving a similar group of customers with credit and saving services.

Mr. Kim Bunsocheat still held the knowledge and the skills of how to make microfinance work for its customers and for the MFI. He would never forget his previous position as a group loan officer and, later, as a small enterprise loan officer.

As the Manager of the Poi Pet Branch, a very successful branch of ACLEDA Bank Plc.'s network in Cambodia, he quickly brought the branch to profitability and higher levels of growth while focusing on the customer. He knew how to teach his staff to work with group guarantees and the techniques of lending without collateral, two fundamental principles of microfinance.

It requires much more expertise to assess the character of a borrower than it does to assess the value of that person's collateral. These critical lessons were emphasized under Mr. Nhem Chamroeun's credit consultancy with AMM's credit officers, and Mr. Yim Bunnarith's consultancy in human resources for all staff training and mentoring.

Mr. Kim, and AMM's Financial Consultant and CFO Mr. Moeurng Rotha spent the early part of their careers in ACLEDA Bank Plc. branches as credit officers. They were specialists in the finer points of customer service appreciated in villages and urban areas whose residents and entrepreneurs are poor and low-income men and women and whose literacy may be limited. Mr. Kim's dynamic staff would rediscover this knowledge, pass it on to their new colleagues, and together apply these techniques to make microfinance work well for customers in Myanmar.

---

[4]ACLEDA MFI Myanmar Co. Ltd. (AMM) is a wholly owned subsidiary of ACLEDA Bank Plc. It obtained its operating license from the Myanmar Microfinance Supervisory Committee (MMSC) on February 8, 2013. The Grand Opening of ACLEDA MFI Myanmar Co. Ltd. (AMM) was held at the AMM headquarters and branch in Yangon on March 25, 2013.

[5]The Fiscal year in Myanmar runs from April 1 to March 31. The Government of Myanmar changed the fiscal year from April–March to October–September starting from fiscal year 2018/2019 (i.e., beginning October 1, 2018).

Box 9.1: The Client Protection Principles

The smart Campaign is a global effort to unite financial leaders around a common goal: To keep clients as the driving force of the industry. The client protection principles were developed with microfinance institutions, banks, international networks, regulators, banking, and microfinance associations, among others. The principles represent a global consensus on what constitutes fair treatment of clients and the practice of good ethics and smart business:

- Appropriate product design and delivery.
- Prevention of over-indebtedness.
- Transparency.
- Responsible pricing.
- Fair and respectful treatment of clients.
- Privacy of client data.
- Mechanisms for complaint resolution.

Source: The smart campaign https://www.smartcampaign.org

ACLEDA Bank Plc., AMM's parent company, certified in the global client protection principles, ensured together with AMM leadership that the principles became a central part of AMM's customer focus and operating methods (see Box 9.1 The Client Protection Principles).

The environment in Myanmar also brought an array of tests to meet the microbankers' skills. New lessons, admirable performance in the face of significant challenges, and the remarkable satisfaction of a growing customer base are all part of the AMM story.

AMM created its own organizational lessons as it weathered a number of challenges particular to microfinance and specific to the context of Myanmar. And, as with AMM's sister bank,[6] ACLEDA Bank Lao, some of the challenges they met were associated with the growing pains of a start-up business.

The ingenuity and skills of the AMM staff and leadership steered the way for developing solutions to many challenges. Yet, the AMM team had one great advantage. They studied the lessons from ACLEDA Bank Lao Ltd., ACLEDA's first regional expansion beyond its borders in the Lao PDR. When they applied these lessons to their own circumstances, they found them suited to growth with quality and adapted them to a new environment.

Along with difficulties also came remarkable customer acceptance and surprising growth in Myanmar's competitive environment for microfinance. Those lessons have gone down in the history of the ACLEDA Bank Group of Companies, and they are recorded here for the future.

[6] A sister bank, or sister company, is a company owned by the same parent company. Sister companies have the same parent company, but they may operate separately from other sister companies owned by the same parent company, as they do in the ACLEDA Group.

To fully appreciate this journey, the reader needs to understand the context in Myanmar. A brief portrait of the economy and the financial sector follows.

9.2 The Republic of the Union of Myanmar Today: An Overview

The Republic of the Union of Myanmar, long isolated by distance, politics, and internal unrest, opened the country and its economy to the rest of the world in 2011. Years of isolation and a repressed economy impoverished the population of a once rich and leading nation in Southeast Asia.

Myanmar is still considered one of the poorest economies in the world even though impressive growth rates in gross domestic product (GDP) and foreign direct investment over the last 5 years have advanced its global economic standing.

According to the World Bank, over the last 5 years, Myanmar's average real GDP growth rate was 7.3%, relatively higher than its neighboring countries except for the Lao PDR and on par with Cambodia. See Fig. 8.1 in Chap. 8, which includes GDP growth for select countries in the region, including Myanmar.

In 2015, the World Bank reclassified the Republic of the Union of Myanmar as a lower middle-income country.[7] Poverty rates among the population of 53.8 million people in 2018 remain high, but have been declining. By the end of 2018, annual GDP per capita climbed to USD 1571, 15% higher than only 3 years previously when GDP per capita averaged USD 1266, and was one of the lowest in Southeast Asia (World Bank 2018a, b, c).[8]

9.2.1 *The Economy: Overall Performance and Growth Sectors*

According to the World Bank's Economic Monitor, the Myanmar economy performed better in 2017/2018 with modest growth and partially reversed the deterioration experienced in 2016/2017. The economy experienced a broad-based increase in real GDP growth to 6.4% in 2017/2018 up from 5.9% in 2016/2017. Inflation decreased to 5.5% in 2017–2018. For most of 2017, the exchange rate of the USD to the MMK was stable (Mishra et al. 2018).

By the second quarter of 2018, macroeconomic volatility in Myanmar increased, even while growth in East Asia and Pacific region was still in line with expectations at 6.4%.

[7] As of July 1, 2016, **low-income economies** are defined as those with a Gross National Income (GNI) per capita, calculated using the World Bank Atlas method, of $1025 or less in 2015. **Lower middle-income economies** are those with a GNI per capita between $1026 and $4035.

[8] The World Bank GNI per capita ranking is based on the Atlas method and purchasing power parity (PPP).

> The Myanmar Kyat (MMK) depreciated significantly by 18% against the U.S. Dollar from April through October 2018, with increased volatility. Depreciation was triggered by global factors, such as the possibility of faster-than-anticipated monetary policy normalization in the United States, but also by domestic factors, such as continued reliance on FDI flows for financing the current account deficit and a thin foreign exchange market which means that few and relatively small transactions can significantly move the exchange rate. (Beck et al. 2018)

The MMK to the USD is also worth less than 40% of what it was 6 years ago (XE 2018).

Inflation declined to 6.1% in January 2019 from a peak of 8.8% in October 2018 as the exchange rate stabilized and fuel prices fell. But fuel and food prices pushed inflation up again to 7.9% in March. Inflation is expected to accelerate from 5.5% in 2017/2018 to 8.8% in 2018/2019, driven by exchange rate pass-through and rising food prices. However, Myanmar's economic outlook is positive with growth projected to further accelerate to 6.7% by 2020/2021 (Beck et al. 2019).

The economy continued to be driven by growth in the services sector and strong performance in the industrial sector, especially manufacturing with a focus on garments. The services sector, including tourism and banking, continued to grow, despite a slight slowdown likely due to decreasing tourist arrivals and banking sector uncertainties (World Bank 2018a, b, c).

See Fig. 9.1 Sector contribution to real GDP growth 2018–2019.

Myanmar's main export is natural gas, dwarfing the remaining items in its export basket, including rice, wood and forest products, rubber, garments, and jade and gems. During 2016/2017, rice exports reached record highs and continued to access new markets, and garment exports continued to rise. Gas exports were robust

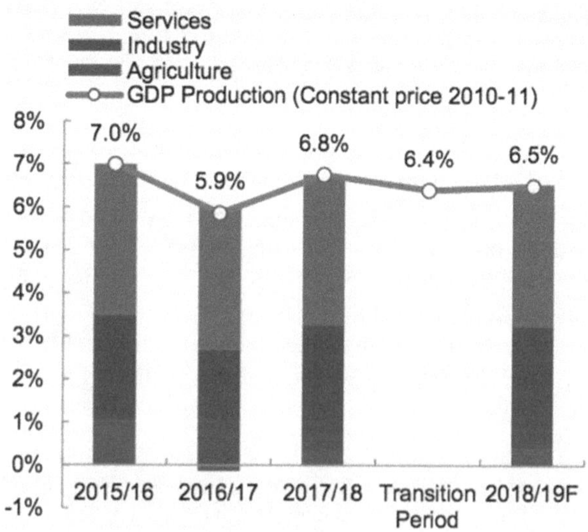

Fig. 9.1 Sector contribution to real GDP growth (Reproduced from Beck et al. 2019)
Sources: Ministry of Planning and Finance, World Bank staff estimate, Myanmar Economic Monitor: Building Reform Momentum 2019

during the year with the increase in global gas prices, offsetting declining production from maturing fields (World Bank 2018a, b, c).

Manufacturing activity accounts for 75% of the industrial sector of Myanmar's economy. It is estimated to have grown by 11% in 2017/2018, supported by strong food processing performance and an increase in the external demand for garments. Employment increased in manufacturing and construction following these expansionary trends.

Foreign direct investment (FDI) in manufacturing grew over 65% in 2017/2018 compared to 2016/2017, accounting for about one-third of total FDI commitments, compared with just 17% in 2015/2016. In addition, the World Bank's survey of business conditions notes that easing credit conditions to the manufacturing sector also helped boost its growth.

The service sector contribution to growth increased slightly and grew by 7% in 2017/2018, down from 8% in 2016/2017 and an annual average of 9% in the previous 2 years. Financial and telecommunications services performed well, although growth in wholesale and retail trade services fell. And, growth in the tourism sector remains underdeveloped by lack of promotion, poor infrastructure, high costs, and, recently, concern over the humanitarian crisis in Rakhine state. The overall forecast for 2018/2019 is still lower than 2017/2018. See Fig. 9.1.

At midyear 2018, the two major risks identified for the Myanmar economy by the Myanmar Economic Monitor were external risks from uncertainty in global trade policy and with commodity prices and the limited progress in addressing the humanitarian crisis in Rakhine state that could affect business sentiment and thereby weaken the economy's performance (Beck et al. 2018). By 2019 the downside external and domestic risk assessment continued and with additional factors, such as the slowdown of growth in China, trade tensions, and higher oil prices, as well as the continued Rakhine state crisis (Beck et al. 2018).

9.2.2 *Poverty*

According to the recent Myanmar Ministry of Planning and Finance-World Bank joint poverty analysis, poverty in Myanmar has declined from 48.2% of the population in 2004/2005, to 42.4% in 2009/2010, and further to 32.1% in 2015. However, the analysis notes that poverty remains substantial, especially in rural areas where people rely on agriculture and casual employment for their livelihoods (Myanmar Ministry of Planning and Finance; World Bank 2017a, b).

Similar to other countries, poorer households in Myanmar are more likely to be solely engaged in agriculture and, within agriculture, in casual labor activities. Poverty among farming households is strongly linked to low agricultural incomes, reflecting small plots of land and limited irrigation resulting in a heavy reliance on the main monsoon crop (Myanmar Ministry of Planning and Finance; World Bank 2017a, b).

Thirty-eight percent of the rural population is estimated to be poor compared to 14.5% of the population in towns and cities. This means 15.8 million people live below the poverty line, and 13.8 million of this number live in the rural areas.

Poverty in Myanmar is also geographically disbursed: the coastal, hills, and mountain regions have a higher number of the poorest people, while 65% of Myanmar's poor people live in the dry zone and the delta regions, the most populated regions in the country.

Access to basic infrastructure and services remains a challenge in both rural and urban areas. Only one-third of the population has access to the national electricity grid, while road density remains low at 219.8 kilometers per 1000 square kilometers of land area.

Poor access to electricity is considered a main constraint for businesses that are not located in the special economic zones. But, access to electricity can have a major generational influence on closing the poverty gap and paving a way for a more prosperous future.[9]

9.2.3 Human Development Index

The Human Development Index (HDI) and accompanying reports supported by the UNDP "explore who has been left behind in human development progress—and why" (UNDP 2018). The HDI is a summary measure for assessing progress in three basic dimensions of human development: a long and healthy life, access to knowledge, and a decent standard of living.

Myanmar's HDI value for 2017 is 0.578 positioning the country at 148 out of 189 countries and territories. Myanmar ranks 148 out of 189 countries worldwide in human development, according to the 2017 Human Development Index (HDI) statistical update for Myanmar (UNDP 2016a, b). Myanmar's global ranking puts the country in the medium human development category, together with Cambodia, which ranks 14 out of 189 countries and the Lao PDR with a rank of 139. See Table 9.1 for country HDI indicators and values (UNDP 2018).

Table 9.1 Myanmar's Human Development Index (HDI) and component indicators relative to selected countries in the East Asia and Pacific (EAP) region

	HDI value	HDI rank	Life expectancy at birth	Expected years of schooling	Mean years of schooling	GNI per capita (USD)
Cambodia	0.582	146	69.3	11.7	4.8	3413
Lao PDR	0.601	139	67	11.2	5.2	6070
Myanmar	0.578	148	66.7	10	4.9	5567
EAP region	0.733	–	74.7	13.3	7.9	13,688
Medium HDI countries	0.645	–	69.1	11.5	6.7	6849

Source: UNDP (2018) Human Development Indices and Indicators: 2018 Statistical Update: Myanmar

[9] For an inspiring story about poverty, opportunity, and the role of electricity, see, "Turning on the Lights in Rural Myanmar" produced by the World Bank in June 2017. http://www.worldbank.org/en/news/video/2017/06/29/turning-on-the-lights-in-rural-myanmar

Myanmar's GDP per capita still ranks as one of the lowest in Southeast Asia, and poverty and human development indicators lag.

Even though Myanmar growth rates have declined in the last 3 years, the country has the potential to regain its position as one of the fastest-growing economies in the East Asia and Pacific region and globally. With its large population and productive lands, it is well positioned to meet development challenges, as reforms in the business and financial sector continue to advance.

9.2.4 *Doing Business in Myanmar*

Small firms dominate the private sector in Myanmar, even though a few large manufacturing firms employ a significant number of people. Data from the Myanmar Business Survey shows that 36% of firms in Myanmar have one or two workers, while 72% have five workers or fewer. The median is three employees.

In addition, the survey excludes most informal firms, which represent 83% of the 22 million people employed in the country, according to the most recent release of the Labor Force Survey (Myanmar Business Survey 2015). The surveys indicate that micro and small businesses dominate in all sectors of the economy, while large firms across all sectors offer more employment opportunities.

See Fig. 9.2: Size of firms by industry, trade, and services and Fig. 9.3 for the percentage of total workers employed by size of the firm.

The Government of Myanmar set an ambitious target to improve Myanmar's ranking in the World Bank's Doing Business report by bringing Myanmar within the top 100 countries in the ease of doing business ranking from its current ranking of 171 out of 190 countries.

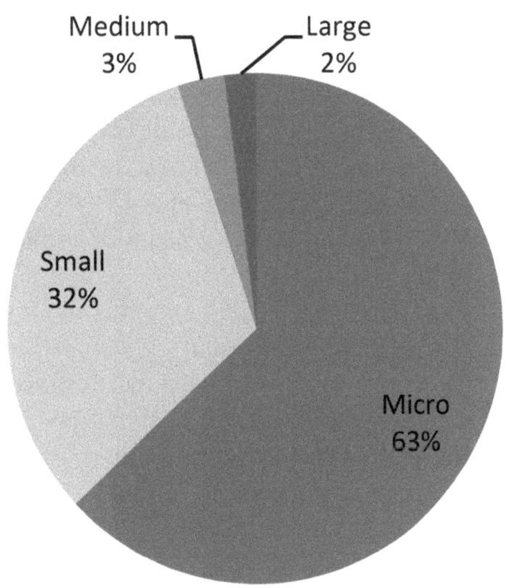

Fig. 9.2 Number of firms in industry, trade, and services by size (%). (Reproduced from Mishra et al. 2018)
Source: Myanmar Economic Monitor: Growth Amidst Uncertainty (2018)

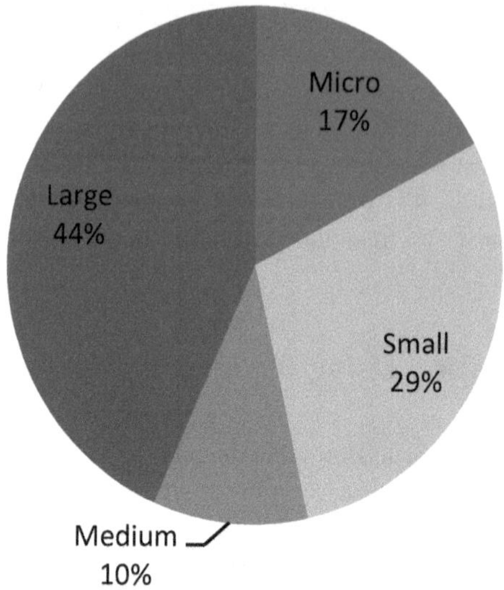

Fig. 9.3 Workers employed by firm size (%). (Reproduced from Mishra et al. 2018)
Source: Myanmar Economic Monitor: Growth Amidst Uncertainty (2018)

As noted in the previous chapter, the Doing Business report measures policies (regulations and procedures) along the ten indicators affecting the life cycle of domestic companies, such as starting a business, getting a location and constructing a facility, getting financing, paying taxes, trading across borders, and dealing with contracts or disputes.

Experience in many countries over time suggests that improvement in the Doing Business indicators are associated with increasing the size of the formal private sector, more job creation, and more inclusive private sector growth.

Firms in both the manufacturing and service sectors found it easier to access credit in 2017/2018 than in 2015/2016. Analysts note that this may in part be attributable to the growth in the non-banking (e.g., microfinance) sector (World Bank 2018a, b, c). They note "despite sluggish overall credit growth, there were signs of progress in financial access of SME activities. In Q1 2018/19, SME credit grew by 80 percent (y-o-y). This was driven by increasing lending to SME activities in manufacturing, labor-intensive businesses, retail, wholesale and enterprises focused on providing services" (Beck et al. 2019). See Fig. 9.4 for the results of the Enterprise Survey showing the percentage of firms reporting credit is more easily available in 2018.

However there is still a long way to go when it comes to the ease of getting credit as noted in the World Banks's Doing Business Report for Myanmar in 2019. The analysis determined the weak performance on the ease of getting credit as mainly due to the lack of a credit information system, coverage of a credit registry, credit bureau coverage, and the legal rights with respect to collateral, secured transactions, and insolvency procedures, among others. See Box 9.2.

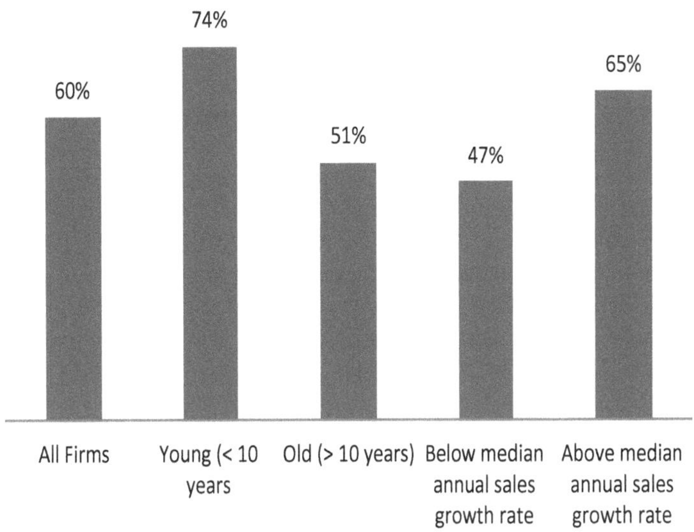

Fig. 9.4 Enterprise survey: percent of firms reporting credit more easily available in 2018 than in 2016. (Reproduced from Mishra et al. 2018)

Box 9.2: Doing Business Report: Myanmar 2019

The ranking of economies on the ease of getting credit is determined by sorting individual scores for getting credit. These scores are the sum of the scores for the strength of legal rights index and the depth of credit information index. Myanmar showed no improvement in its overall ranking in the World Bank's latest ease of doing business index. Myanmar's ranking remains the same as it was in the 2018 doing business report, at 171st. It also remains the least favorable ASEAN member country in which to conduct business, according to the 2019 report.

The ease of doing business score captures the gap of each economy from the best regulatory performance observed on each of the indicators across all economies in the *Doing Business* sample since 2005. An economy's ease of doing business score is reflected on a scale from 0 to 100, where 0 represents the lowest and 100 represents the best performance. The ease of doing business ranking ranges from first to 190th, the number of economies included in the report.

Source: World Bank (2018a, b, c) Doing Business 2019: Training for Reform: Myanmar Economy Profile

Since 2013, Myanmar has implemented eight positive reforms as measured by Doing Business, including reducing the stamp tax duty on registering property, making it less costly. Myanmar has also made starting a business easier by reducing the cost and the processes required to register a company. Reducing the documentation required for exports is also a new innovation.

See Fig. 9.5 for Myanmar's 2019 Doing Business Scores and Fig. 9.6 for Myanmar's 2019 Doing Business Rank compared to other selected EAP Countries and the EAP regional average.

Despite some important progress, particularly with the introduction of credit information sharing regulation, the Doing Business 2018 report shows that Myanmar's overall performance on ease of doing business lags behind the average for East Asia and Pacific (EAP) economies in most areas. Myanmar's overall ranking in Doing Business 2018 was 171st out of 190 countries globally and 24th out of 25 economies in the EAP region (World Bank 2018a, b, c).

Even while credit restrictions for firms appear to have eased as indicated in Fig. 9.4, rising input costs and slow progress on improving the business climate remain. In addition, more firms are concerned with the constraint in finding suitably qualified employees, particularly in administrative, financial, and managerial positions, perhaps as a tribute to the expanding number of these positions along with the growth of the economy.

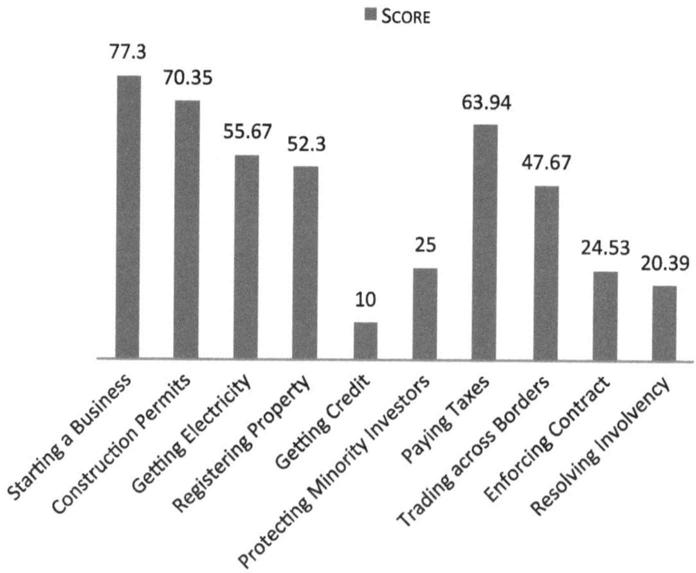

Fig. 9.5 Ease of doing business scores on doing business topics—Myanmar. (Reproduced from World Bank 2018a, b, c)

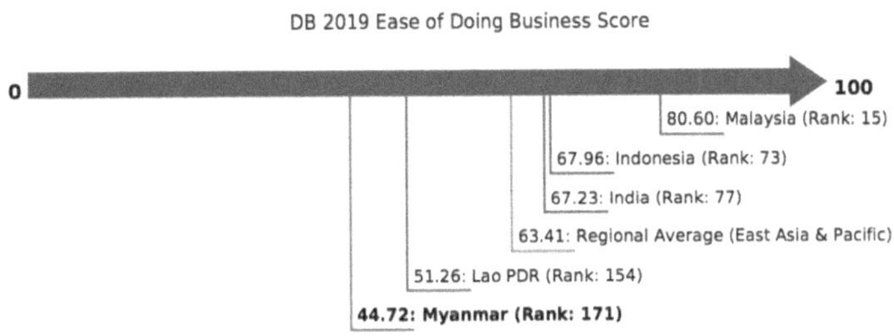

Fig. 9.6 Ease of doing business 2019 Myanmar Rank with other EAP countries, World Bank 2018. (Reproduced from World Bank 2018a)

Myanmar's new reforms are yet to be tested, but they are all aimed toward building a robust private sector and a financial sector that supports growth and minimizes risk.[10]

9.2.5 *Southeast Asia's Techno Boom: Focus on Myanmar*

As noted in the previous chapter on the Lao PDR, throughout Southeast Asia Internet and mobile connectivity are growing at an impressive rate. Connectivity is important to mobile banking and overcoming time, space, and cost constraints to manage money, especially for isolated populations.

With the recent liberalization of the telecommunications sector, mobile and Internet penetration has increased significantly from less than 10% in 2014. Myanmar's mobile subscription penetration rate at the end of 2019 was 105%, up from 93% in 2017, and up 83% from the previous year. See Table 8.1 in Chap. 8: Digital use in SEA, featuring Laos, Cambodia, and Myanmar.

According to Techinasia.com,[11] all key digital indicators in Southeast Asia made notable advances in 2019 with mobile Internet use and social media use gaining the most. "These numbers don't tell the full story in Myanmar," notes Techinasia.com.:

> When we first started compiling our reports on digital use in Southeast Asia five years ago (2012), Facebook was still blocked in Myanmar. Since these restrictions have been lifted, however, social media use has skyrocketed to the extent that Facebook now records 14 million users in the country.
>
> What's more, more than six million of these users only joined the platform in the past 12 months of 2017, delivering year-on-year growth in social media users of 84% —one of the highest growth rates in the world.[12]

---

[10] Important financial sector regulations and reforms are discussed later in this chapter.

[11] Kemp, Simon. 2017. The full Guide to Southeast Asian's digital Landscape in 2017

[12] ibid.

Fintech can be a solution for access to financial products for a wider segment of the population, but it also needs to be accompanied by exceptional customer service and financial literacy to have the greater catalytic effect on customer financial well-being and development that are the main aims of an inclusive financial system.

As ACLEDA Bank Plc. has found in launching ToanChet in Cambodia and ThanChai in the Lao PDR, the fintech applications are used first by customers to save time and money in making payments and remittances. Later customers expand their usage to manage their household finances and their businesses.

It may be that Myanmar could leapfrog the intermediate step of ATMs and go directly to more convenient, safer, and more streamlined mobile banking services.

9.3 The Financial Sector

Recent regulatory reforms aim to strengthen the financial sector and to support a more vibrant financial industry. New reforms and directives in the financial sector aim to improve the business climate, ease access to credit for all segments of the market, ensure banks in Myanmar are able to meet international standards, and enhance banking sector learning. The uptake of the directives will depend on the ease of implementation by financial services providers in Myanmar.

While the microfinance sector grows, the Central Bank of Myanmar (CBM) is also pushing forward with important reforms that aim to improve access to banking services in the lower segments of the markets, as well as advance foreign investment in the local market.

Within the past 3 years, microfinance institutions have grown to reach a ready market for credit and deposits. As of January 2019, MFIs in Myanmar served five million clients, and the total loan portfolio of the sector grew by 60% in 2018/2019 to reach approximately 1.3 trillion kyats (approximately USD 0.8 billion). The total MFI paid-up capital also increased over the same period (Beck et al. 2019).

Three main CBM directives target the lower segments of the market and access to capital for local banking establishments and increasing. First, by January 2019, the Central Bank of Myanmar (CBM) allowed banks to lend at 16% interest rate ceiling for uncollateralized loans. The new ceiling—that is higher than the previous 13% ceiling for collateralized lending— is thought to be favorable for expanding access to finance for SMEs.

The second aspect of the new ruling allows borrowers to pledge collateral other than assets already approved and listed by CMB. As with the 13% previous interest rate ceiling for collateralized loans, the new 16% interest rate ceiling for non-collateralized loans must cover all charges the borrower must pay for the loan, such as service changes and additional fees. The 16% ceiling for non-collateralized loans can be applied to installment loans as well as term loans with a lump sum repayment.

The directives increasing the interest rate ceiling for non-collateralized loans, broadening of the types of assets that can be pledged as collateral, and allowing the flexibility to apply to both installment and balloon loans should promote further access to credit for a broader segment of the population.

On the financial institutional front, the CBM is positioning to redouble efforts to ensure local banks are well-capitalized and have opportunity to enhance banking expertise, more effective customer services, and institutional practices.

As noted in the Myanmar Economic Monitor, "The CBM issued a notice inviting foreign interest of up to 35 percent equity investment in local private banks. On January 29, 2019, as part of its reforms aimed at boosting capital levels and activity in the financial sector, the CBM issued a notice that will allow foreign banks to take stakes of up to 35 percent in domestic private banks.... There are 13 foreign banks that opened branches in Myanmar since 2013, when the banking sector opened to foreign participation. More recently, the CBM has indicated an openness to allow 100 percent foreign bank subsidiaries to set up in Myanmar" (Beck et al. 2019).

These topics are taken up in more detail in the section below.

9.3.1 Financial Inclusion

A Making Access Possible[13] (MAP) diagnostic and field study during 2018 found a significant increase in financial inclusion from a prior MAP diagnostic, 5 years ago, in 2013. The key finding is that adults with access to at least one formal financial product increased from 30% in 2013 to 48% in 2018.

This signifies a healthy increase in the country's financial inclusion rate within the 5-year period. The progress also supercedes the target set to reach 40% of the population with formal financial services within the 5-year time span. These figures roughly translate into six million more adults with access to formal financial services than those with access in 2013. Similarly, the percent of the population who use "informal services only" fell by 30% from ten million in 2013 to about seven million adults by 2018 (DaNa Facility 2018).

The 2018 MAP study also linked the significant increase in rural uptake of formal financial services to high growth levels of financial services customers in the microfinance and cooperative sectors. These two sectors are fueling nationwide growth of financial inclusion in both rural and urban areas. A greater number of formally regulated financial services providers, as well as the diversity of products they offer, continue to have a positive effect on financial inclusion rates.

In addition, the MAP study notes that 17% of adults have access to more than one financial service. This is also attributed to the increased activity of MFIs and cooperatives that are formally regulated, as they can offer savings services to their borrowers. Low, but encouraging uptake in mobile money, at about 2% of the adult population, is an early sign of acceptance of new ways of banking.

[13] Making Access Possible (MAP) is a survey undertaken by FinScope, an expert survey organization, specializing in financial inclusion. In Myanmar, the Department for International Development (DfID) in the UK and UNCDF support this effort.

The Rise of Fintech Mobile phone penetration has recently expanded to reach significant numbers of the population.[14] This is an encouraging sign that financial services customers may quickly adopt fintech applications, if offered by accessible and trusted financial services providers and accompanied by strong orientation with overtones of financial literacy.

Regulators are particularly concerned about consumer protection safeguards, as fintech products and services are perceived to be more vulnerable to fraud and theft. Most regulatory environments have not yet developed a full range of provisions and protections that would ensure a comfortable margin of safety and soundness about fintech applications for both consumers and the financial system.

In reality, fintech applications are no more vulnerable to fraud and theft than physical services, such as cash and credit cards, for example. However, the scale of the fraud is likely to be greater, the fraud is likely to be accomplished more quickly, and, there is greater unlikelihood of rapid detection by consumers who tend to be unfamiliar with safeguards. In addition, consumers often have no recourse for any frauds that may have been committed.

Regulators and financial services providers are more cautious with fintech products and services because there is less experience with them and less knowledgeable customers are more vulnerable. There is good reason to be cautious, particularly if there are no safeguards, no "financial tech literacy," and no consumer recourse in place.

9.3.2 Retail Microfinance: A Big Part of the Financial Sector in Myanmar

The retail-banking segment of the financial sector in the Myanmar is increasingly diverse and competitive, even though there are restrictive policies and regulations that tamp down healthy levels of financial inclusion. While the banking sector sleeps, the microfinance sector appears to thrive, despite the difficult regulations that limit sustainable growth and outreach.

A New Financial Institutions Law With respect to banks, in 2016 the government issued a new Financial Institutions Law, which aims to bring Myanmar's regulations into line with the core principles on banking supervision issued by the international Basel Committee on Banking Supervision, Basel I the first set of banking regulations issued by the committee in 1988. Basel II, and now Basel III, is the current international standard. However, the banking sector in Myanmar faces significant challenges in the transition to comply with international standards (World Bank 2018a, b, c).

As many experts in the financial system note with respect to bank lending products in the Myanmar economy, the introduction of more compliant products as well

[14] See the section on Southeast Asia's Techno Boom.

as more suitable products for enterprises and consumers will entail the banking sector's shift away from reliance on overdrafts backed by real estate as their main product. However, a shift to term lending—a more suitable product for enterprises and consumers—requires risk assessment, which also entails banks' ability to assess risk required for the investment and of the borrower.

The Myanmar Economic Monitor notes that plans to upgrade the financial sector legal, regulatory, and supervisory framework are pending. However, "there is a general understanding that if banks are to effectively play their role in domestic resource mobilization, financial intermediation and inclusion it is mandatory that these institutions move onto a more solid footing. But given the somewhat 'unique' structures and practices that banks in Myanmar have adopted … it is not expected that the actual transition to a more modern, transparent financial system will be painless" (Mishra et al. 2018).

Yet the consumer of financial products is ready to take advantage of an array of safe and sound financial products and services. And, microfinance institutions appear to be at the forefront of product innovation. They are also working with the regulator to ensure safe product design and competent microfinance institutions to bring new products to a segment of the population that has not yet been reached.

As Mr. Kim Bunsocheat, Managing Director and CEO of AMM, said in 2015, "The financial sector is the lifeblood of any country's economy. Myanmar has emerged as a new frontier market. Only three in ten Myanmar adults have formal access to credit, deposits or other financial services, such as insurance and remittances. Small businesses are aggressively seeking capital, with demand for micro credit out stripping supply by four times." (Box 9.3).

Box 9.3: A Quick Synopsis: Making Finance Work for All

"A sound, efficient, and inclusive financial system can play a critical role in creating and sustaining a market-based economy and ensuring inclusive growth in Myanmar. Myanmar's financial system is small, shallow, tightly held and vulnerable. It significantly underserves large parts of the private sector and general public.

The reform agenda necessary to develop a "fit for purpose" financial system in Myanmar runs both deep and wide, even as recent changes have yielded significant gains. On the one hand, the financial sector needs to move on to a more solid footing; on the other hand, it needs to significantly expand outreach and the range of available instruments.

A stable solution therefore requires complex and simultaneous reforms. Policymakers have to implement a realistic, minimally disruptive, clearly articulated roadmap that is also sufficiently transformative so as to carry the benefits of more effective financial services to the general public."

Source: Mishra et al. 2018. Myanmar Economic Monitor: Growth Amidst Uncertainty

9.3.2.1 Microfinance Continues to Grow as a Significant Part of the Financial Sector

Microfinance plays a large role in the retail financial sector. MFIs are regulated by the government's Financial Regulatory Department (FRD) and supervised by the Microfinance Business Supervisory Committee (MBSC).

As of March 2018, there were 176 licensed microfinance institutions including 5 international NGOs, 22 NGOs, 39 foreign companies, 3 partnership firms, and 107 local companies. ACLEDA MFI Myanmar Co. Ltd. (AMM) with its operational network in 13 branch offices and one sub-branch is among the 180 microfinance companies operating in Myanmar by early 2020 according to the Myanmar Microfinance Association.[15]

In the retail-banking sector, there are 4 state-owned banks, 77 financial cooperatives, 29 private banks, 13 foreign bank branches, and 48 representative bank offices. The Myanmar Agricultural Development Bank and a large network of cooperatives serve rural areas, even though people in rural areas are still on average quite distant from the nearest bank or cooperative branch.

According to Making Access Possible (MAP) 2018, credit and savings with MFIs and cooperatives mainly drove the significant increase in rural uptake of formal services outside of banks. The increase in access to formal financial products in this category doubled since the prior MAP survey in 2013.

Nevertheless, distance continues to be a significant barrier to accessing financial services in rural areas. The average time it takes for rural clients to reach banks, ATMs, or mobile money operators is over 1 hour, while MFIs can be reached on average in rural areas in 43 minutes compared to 24 minutes in urban areas. In contrast, the time it takes for urban customers to reach MFIs is equivalent to the time it takes customers to reach a bank, mobile money operator, or ATM (FinScope 2018).

The sheer number of retail-banking institutions, including such a high number of MFIs, would suggest a robust level of financial inclusion. The current vision of such substantial financial inclusion is reduced by a number of factors. The small size of most MFIs and the localized operating areas designated for MFIs limits their outreach.

The widely dispersed population and distances among population centers limit the outreach of both banks and MFIs. In spite of this, financial inclusion has accelerated in the past five years and exceeded expectations, increasing access from 30% in 2013 to 48% by 2018, beyond the targeted 40% increase in financial inclusion expected within this timeframe.

Yet, there is generous room to increase customer outreach and institutional performance.

[15]According to the Financial Regulatory Department (FRD) announcement, there were 176 licensed MFIs operating in Myanmar as of March 2018. By early 2020 the Myanmar Microfinance Association noted 180 microfinance companies operating in the country.

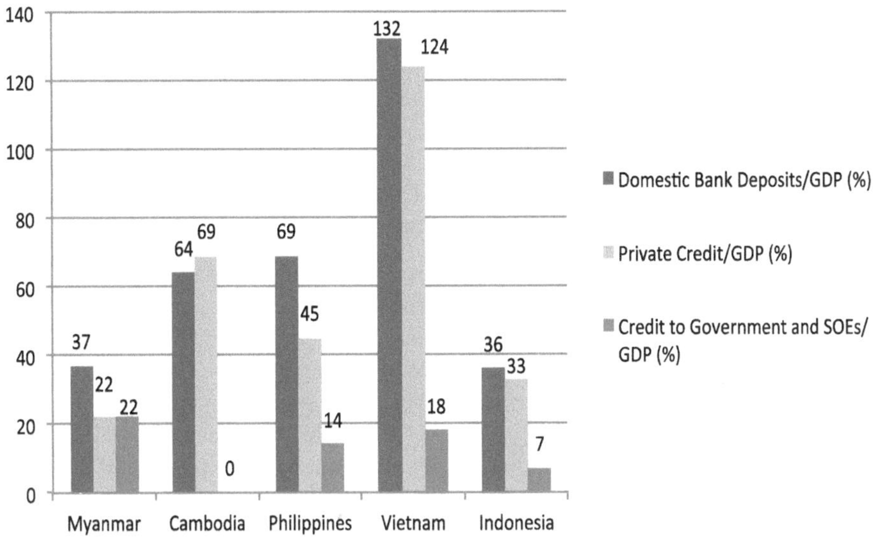

Fig. 9.7 Financial depth: Myanmar and ASEAN comparators. (Reproduced from Mishra et al. 2018)
Source: Myanmar Economic Monitor: Growth Amidst Uncertainty

9.3.2.2 Key Indicators and Trends, Policies, and Promises

Key sector-wide indicators show Myanmar's financial sector lags behind several countries in the region. See Fig. 9.7: Financial Depth. There is abundant potential for the Myanmar financial sector to grow. "The system currently mobilizes only 37% of GDP by way of deposits in the banking system and lends only 22% of GDP to the private sector. It is worth noting though that in 2011 at the point when Myanmar launched its reform agenda, the ratios were 15% and 7%, respectively" (Op Cit. Mishra et al.).

Savings Services Are Limited, Demand Is Great As of March 2018, the 176 MFIs that have been issued licenses in Myanmar to provide microfinance services serve approximately 1.45 million clients. Over 85% of Myanmar's microfinance clients are women. To date, only one type of MFI license has been issued in Myanmar.[16] While the license allows MFIs to mobilize savings, provide credit, accept remittances, and sell insurance, the only services currently permitted are loans and savings.

The savings services come with several penalties for the MFI and may provide an incentive for customers who only want to save their money, to borrow instead.

[16]This figure does not include cooperatives, even though they were once included in this category and do provide microcredit products to their customers.

MFIs can offer deposit services only to those who borrow from the MFI. This topic is discussed in more detail in the section: "The Journey Begins."

Use of Informal Finance Has Not Decreased Access to formal financial services is improving for all market segments. But, the increase in outreach of formal financial institutions—banks and MFIs—has not been even across the country. There are many rural areas that are not served or underserved, even though the government places a premium on increasing access to financial services in rural areas.

While access to formal financial services is increasing dramatically, the use of informal moneylenders has not decreased. The 2018 MAP survey indicated that the use of informal loans from unregistered sources, such as moneylenders, has not decreased in the past 5 years since the last MAP survey in 2013 (FinScope 2018).

Local moneylenders also serve family needs for small amounts of money for household expenses or emergency purposes. And, while loans from informal sources are delivered at a premium price, they are delivered quickly. The purpose of the loan is rarely an issue nor is the timing of the disbursement to the borrower.

Not many MFIs or banks can compete with informal lenders at this stage of their development. As MFIs expand in Myanmar and banks become more consumer-friendly, they may begin to offer products in a way that competes with informal finance that many people use, regardless of their income. Such competition is likely to reduce informal finance usage, but unlikely to eliminate it entirely.

Financial System Supportive Infrastructure Is Growing Finally, one of the most important new initiatives in the wider financial sector is one aimed at improving access to credit information. The government adopted a regulation allowing the establishment of credit bureaus. Credit bureaus have a proven robust effect on improving the MFI or bank's knowledge of the customer's credit worthiness while also reducing risk and costs for the credit operation and for the overall financial system. The credit bureau in Myanmar is expected to be operational by late 2019 (Htin Lynn Aung 2018).

When the credit bureau is owned or partially owned by the industry, as it is in Cambodia, sector-wide use of this valuable resource tends to improve.[17] The first credit bureau in Myanmar, Myanmar Credit Bureau Limited, received its license on May 22, 2018. It is a joint venture between the Myanmar Bank Association and Singapore's Asian Credit Bureau Holdings and supported by the World Bank's International Finance Corporation (IFC).

Creation of a credit bureau and sound operations are essential steps to increase the supportive financial sector infrastructure helping SMEs without collateral overcome obstacles in accessing financial services. Such services will also assist lenders to better assess borrower creditworthiness. The services of this new facility should

[17] See Chap. 3 for more information on why the credit bureaus are important to the health and soundness of the financial sector, using the credit bureau in Cambodia as an example.

help lenders improve their own risk assessment procedures by incorporating credit bureau consultation as part of the loan assessment process.

In the long term, the credit bureau will contribute to a healthy financial sector that includes a range of borrowers from micro to large enterprises and in the process expand financial inclusion.

9.4 Banking on the Future: The Journey Begins

There is one major difference between ACLEDA's expansion into Myanmar and the first expansion to the Lao PDR. In Myanmar ACLEDA has been prevented by policy and regulation from taking on the role of financial intermediation between savers and borrowers. Yet, AMM has been able to accomplish considerable achievements in Myanmar, despite the lack of financial intermediation.[18]

The first section of this chapter discusses four important regulatory barriers that prevent a more healthy advancement of AMM to serve more customers, including those who live in underserved rural areas. The chapter then turns to the lessons of ACLEDA Bank Cambodia (ABC) and ACLEDA Bank Lao (ABL) that helped and informed the successful development of the new venture—ACLEDA Microfinance Myanmar. Following these lessons, the remarkable performance of AMM, despite significant barriers, is presented. Next, there is a brief discussion of why AMM is considered a "shining star" in the ACLEDA Bank Group of Companies. The chapter concludes with wise words of advice from AMM staff.

9.4.1 Regulatory Barriers to Financial Inclusion

AMM operates a licensed and regulated MFI following financial sector regulations issued by the Central Bank of Myanmar (CBM). These regulations tend to restrict the AMM operation—and those of other MFIs that have the qualifications and experience to operate as microfinance banks.

At the outset of operations, regulatory barriers made it difficult for AMM to operate sustainably, making enough profit to reinvest in expanding the business and serving more customers.

First and foremost, AMM is prohibited from intermediating funds between savers and borrowers. AMM is only permitted to mobilize deposits from borrowers, which somewhat defeats the purpose of borrowing in the first place and leaves customers who only want to save with no formal means to do so.

Adding to this dilemma, and second on the list of four regulatory restrictions, is the amount of savings that an MFI is permitted to keep safe for the borrower. A

[18] See the Glossary for a definition of financial intermediation.

maximum of 5% of the loan amount is permitted as a compulsory deposit, which often acts as a very small guarantee. At the time of AMM's start-up, a maximum of 10% of the loan amount was permitted as an extra voluntary deposit.

The third restriction is the spread between interest rates on deposits and loans. At the outset in 2012, there was an interest rate ceiling on loans of 30%. To make matters more difficult for the micro-banker, there was also an interest rate floor on deposits of 15%.[19]

Given the high costs of operation—due to poor infrastructure in rural areas and inflation—the interest rate spread between deposits and loans was unlikely to produce financial results to ensure sustainability of the operation any time soon, unless, of course, there was a way to leverage capital from outside funding. Controlling costs was particularly difficult, as all MFIs were required to lend 50% of the portfolio outstanding and outreach in rural areas.

Finally, to complete the circle and make matters more daunting for the micro-banker, there were restrictions on both local and foreign borrowing and investment. In 2014, the Microfinance Business Supervisory Committee (MBSC) issued directives that local MFIs could only borrow from the Myanma Economic Bank (MEB).

International MFIs, such as AMM, could not borrow from local banks and could only borrow up to USD three million through an international loan.[20] AMM was fortunate since it could rely on generous paid-up capital from its parent company, ACLEDA Bank Plc.

Later in 2014, three international financial institutions that were historically important to the ACLEDA Group became shareholders of AMM. They were the International Finance Corporation World Bank Group (IFC), KfW, and COFIBRED, a subsidiary of Banque Populaire. Today, AMM is a fully owned subsidiary of ACLEDA Bank Plc.

9.4.2 *The Experience of Parents and Sisters*

The combination of the four regulatory restrictions, mentioned above, ensured a difficult time for any MFI to become sustainable. Yet, after the first year of operations, AMM earned a small net profit—far from sustainability—but surprising given the circumstances, the timing and the regulations. The first year's performance held out the hope that the operation might survive, but not thrive or expand, given the regulatory restrictions. With such a difficult regulatory environment, it is a wonder that AMM earned any surplus after the first year of operations (AMM 2014).

---

[19] According to the Microfinance Law and Directives, December 2011, for compulsory deposits a minimum of 15% interest per year was required and for voluntary deposits a minimum of 10% per year.

[20] Myanma Economic Bank (MEB) is a government-owned development bank. Myanmar had one of the highest levels of restriction for foreign direct investment on the insurance and banking sectors (OECD 2016).

Looking back at the ACLEDA family history, it took 6 years (from 1993 to 1999) for ACLEDA Bank Plc. in Cambodia to cover all costs as a microfinance NGO, even though that was a different time and place.

ACLEDA Bank Lao Ltd. had many highs and lows before the confidence of sustained operations arrived in 2016, 8 years after start-up. The Bank was shored up throughout this 8-year period with continuous efforts by ACLEDA Bank Plc. to maintain solvency and build and rebuild to attract a growing customer base.[21]

How did AMM reach operational breakeven in such a short time? Mr. Kim says simply, "We limited expenses." Limiting expenses was a viable strategy during the initial years of operation. Yet, AMM also knew that limiting expenses in later years after start-up could also limit expansion, postpone staff development and training, deteriorate customer service, and age operational systems beyond repair.

It also appeared that Myanmar's microfinance regulator understood these same principles.

9.4.2.1 Lessons from ACLEDA Bank in Cambodia and ACLEDA Bank Lao

ACLEDA MFI Myanmar Co. Ltd. had the benefit of experience from ACLEDA Bank Plc. in Cambodia and ACLEDA Bank Lao as it prepared to enter the Myanmar market and the associated policy and regulatory environment. Several important lessons from their sister bank, ACLEDA Bank Lao, served to limit mistakes as well as energize growth. In addition, the regulatory timing—if not the regulations themselves—aided in AMM's development.

The First Lesson The regulator in the Lao PDR made entry easy, but with every successive year—until 2014—there was another regulatory surprise that negatively affected operations. These changing rules turned ABL's hopeful climb to profitability and expansion into large deficits. The surprise announcements with little lead time for implementation were even more detrimental as they prevented planning within the organization to counter additional restrictions.

In Myanmar the situation could not have been further to the opposite end of the spectrum. The regulatory environment for MFIs was so restrictive at the beginning there was little room to make it even more so. Yet, with each successive 2-year period, regulations loosened, particularly vis-à-vis increasing loan size and openness to new products, including fintech products and agricultural products.

The regulator in Myanmar also freed up MFIs to access finance from abroad. However, the distance between floors on deposits and ceilings on loans remained intact. This is one of the most difficult regulatory barriers for a retail microfinance bank.

[21] See Chap. 8 for a briefing on ACLEDA Bank Lao Ltd. in the Lao PDR.

The Second Lesson The regulator in Myanmar began an open dialogue with MFIs as the country's financial sector opened to licensing MFIs. As the conversation began and progressed, and more experience was gained, there was more openness to proceeding along a path to which each party could agree. This time the lesson from the parent, ACLEDA Bank Plc. was instructive.

The early experience of microfinance in Cambodia was bolstered by extensive collaboration with the regulator, who carefully listened to microfinance practitioners and allowed for reasonable flexibility to try out new ways to reach an extensive market of poor and low-income people with credit and savings. AMM's and Mr. Kim Bunsocheat's collaborative experience with the regulators in Myanmar was very similar to ACLEDA Bank's experience in Cambodia since 1996. Practitioners and policy makers worked together for the development of the sector as a whole (Kooi 2018).

In contrast, ABL was thrown regulatory surprises by the authority once every 2 years of operation. Especially burdensome was a restriction on currency (requiring ABL to hold onto expensive dollars) ensuring ABL remained illiquid until the dollars could be legally repatriated.

Even though the problem was eventually resolved by ABL, it postponed the organization's objective to become a sustainable operation within 3 years. The dilemma appeared to be a lack of communication between the authorities and the retail-banking sector, which did not allow each party to plan as appropriate to its enterprise. See Chap. 8 for more details.

9.4.2.2 Progress Continues in Myanmar

In October 2017, The Microfinance Business Supervisory Committee (MBSC) in Myanmar issued an official letter to revise the loan size from MMK 5,000,000 to up to MMK 10,000,000.[22] Earlier in 2016, MFIs were permitted to borrow funds from foreign institutions to accommodate larger loan sizes and to somewhat compensate for the lack of intermediation of funds between borrowers and savers, as well as to support the growing, but underserved small and medium enterprise (SME) market.

The MBSC was aware of many low-income businesses that were interested in borrowing from ACLEDA MFI and the revision letter offered the ACLEDA MFI quality opportunities to expand its operations, if and when they could secure a capital infusion from foreign institutions.

Additional regulatory revisions were also helpful to all MFIs. Even though the cap on the total amount of compulsory deposits remained in place, the limit on voluntary deposits was removed, as long as the depositor remained a loan customer of the MFI. In addition, new products, such as hire purchase for farm equipment, were approved; and, MFIs were permitted to handle remittances, as long as the MFI applied to and was approved by the regulator.

[22] This is equivalent to USD 3251 and 6500 using January 2018 exchange rates.

Finally all MFIs, locally owned or foreign owned, were permitted to borrow from abroad or locally.

To this day, the financial regulator, FRD, and supervisor, MBSC, remain engaged with MFIs on consultation as well as compliance in a context of rapid expansion of the MFI market. Contrast this with Cambodia's financial sector regulators who understood the importance of dialogue at the outset but were unable to sustain it over time as the MFI market grew.

The Myanmar Microfinance Association plays a continuing research and advocacy role in the consultative process and engages with a concerned regulator. The latest consultative process in Myanmar saw several bottlenecks to progress and profitability loosen. Further, client protection principles were adopted focusing on fair treatment, responsible pricing, preventing over indebtedness, and protecting client data.

There is an openness to offering new financial products that are important to microfinance and small businesses, as well as to the general population. These new products on the microfinance horizon in Myanmar are balloon loans for agriculture, micro-insurance, remittances, and mobile money.

The Third Lesson given to AMM from ABL in the Lao PDR comes from ABL's experiment with consultants sent from ACLEDA Bank in Cambodia. The ACLEDA Bank Plc. consultants' job is to shore up the newly founded operation and mentor staff. The consultants were recruited for their knowledge, technical expertise, and experience working with and mentoring others.

The lesson from ABL that AMM applied was to take as much time as needed for mentoring and coaching new staff to become effective. They understood that a training course conveys knowledge, but management skill and technique requires time and coaching in different situations and sometimes involves difficult situations. AMM continues to keep consultants in key positions until Myanmar staff is ready to fill them.

And they will be ready, very soon.

9.4.3 AMM Performance

AMM performance over the last 6 years is shown in the five figures below.

From the outset, AMM created a foundation for growth and then fulfilled the promise. First and foremost AMM invested in staff, as shown in Figs. 9.8 and 9.9. The one strategy that serious companies pursue above all others: they know that ensuring customer growth depends on well informed and highly performing staff. Even though AMM staff turnover was considered high at 25% during the first 5 years, the financial sector has gained well-schooled graduates, courtesy of ACLEDA.

As shown in Figs. 9.8 and 9.9, since its inception AMM has trained 460 staff members, most of whom are women, and their percentage in the AMM operation continues to grow. Yet, AMM's staff training is greater than it appears. The current

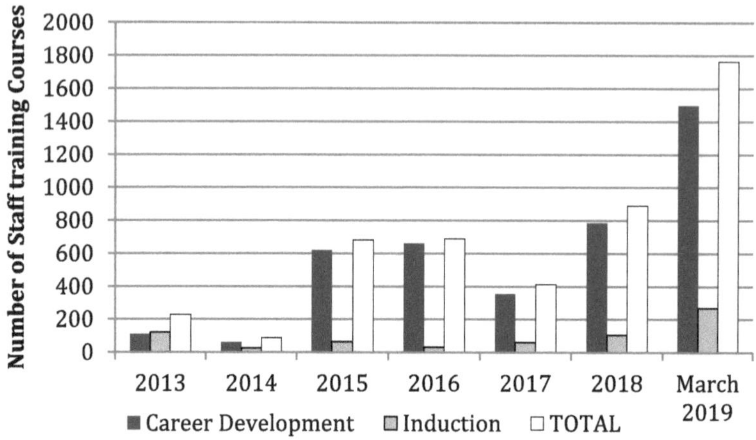

Fig. 9.8 AMM staff training: career development and induction courses 2013–2019
Source: ACLEDA MFI Myanmar Annual Reports, Achievement and Environmental and Social Sustainability Report 2012- March 2019

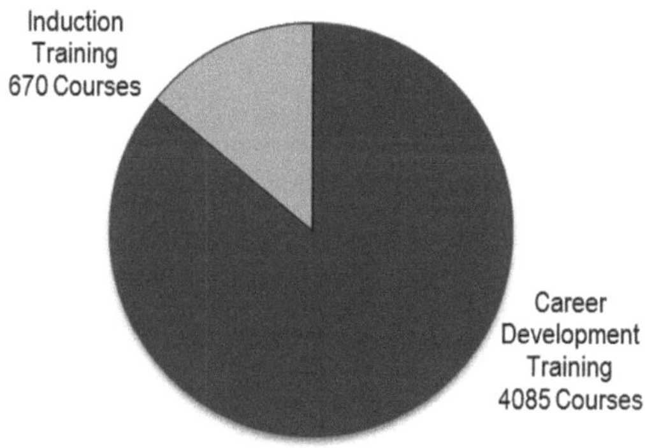

Fig. 9.9 Total AMM staff training courses 2013–2019
Source: ACLEDA MFI Myanmar Annual Reports, Achievement and Environmental, and Social Sustainability Report 2012–March 2019

statistics do not count for over 180 experienced staff members who have left the organization but now work with other MFIs and banks. Every year from 2014 through 2018, the staff attrition rate averaged 24% per year, but it continued to decrease from a high of 27% in 2015.

AMM vows to continue investing in building management and staff capacities by providing regular training and workshops. Even though they know they are likely to continue training the competition. They follow the sage advice of Dr. In Channy, who continues to advocate for capacity building in the financial sectors of the countries where ACLEDA Bank works. He has always held an enlightened attitude about "staff poaching"—an attitude he holds dearly to this day. (Fig. 9.10).

As Dr. In Channy is fond of saying "It's a way that the industry will grow and become more like us. It's good for us. It's good for them. It's good for everyone; no one loses."

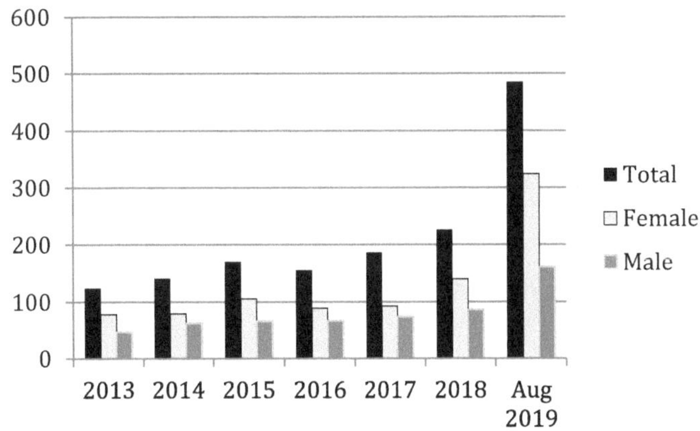

Fig. 9.10 AMM staff number and gender (2013–2019)
Source: ACLEDA MFI Myanmar Annual Reports, Achievement Reports 2012–August 2019

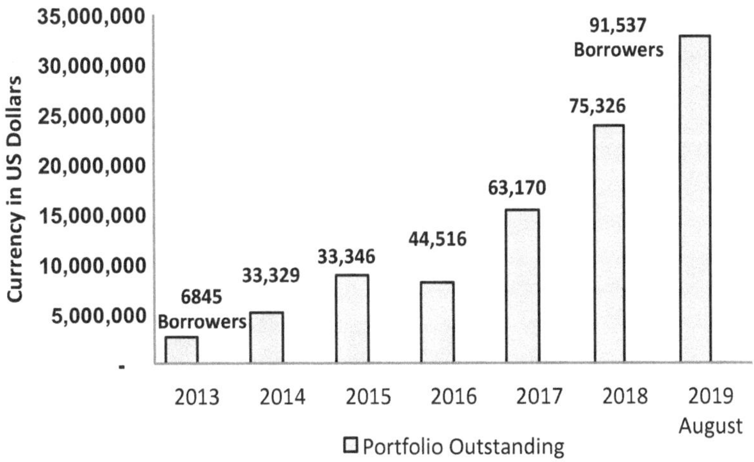

Fig. 9.11 AMM borrowers and portfolio outstanding (2013–August 2019)
Source: ACLEDA MFI Myanmar Annual Reports and Highlights 2012–2019

As a result of excellent staff and their attitudes toward borrowers, AMM's customers increased. See Figs. 9.11 and 9.12. This growth trend was accompanied by an increase in the portfolio outstanding and the number of loans, in addition to an increase in deposits—both mandatory and voluntary.

The uptake in the number of depositors and the amount of deposits shown in Fig. 9.12 is notable and based on the regulators easing of restrictions as discussed in the section on regulatory barriers to financial inclusion.

Within the last 3 years, AMM expanded the number of branches and upgraded sub-branches to serve more customers with more services. See Fig. 9.13 ACLEDA Microfinance Institution (AMM) Branch Development 2013–2019.

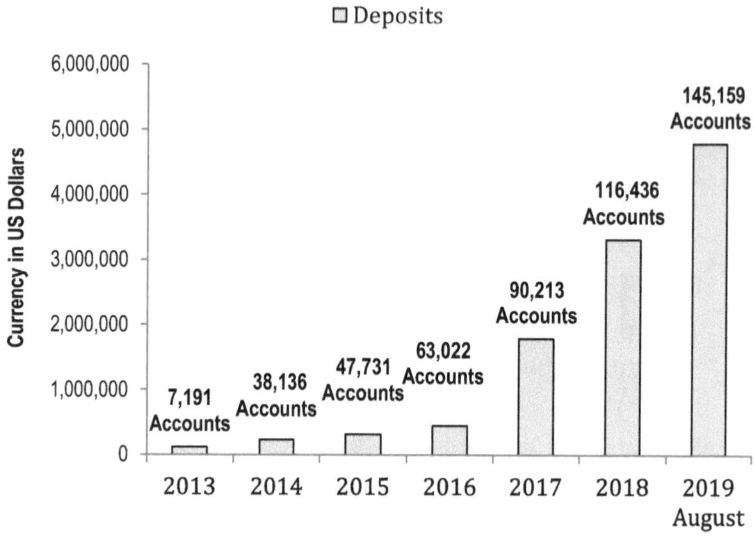

Fig. 9.12 AMM customers with deposit accounts and balances (2015–August 2019)
Source: ACLEDA MFI Myanmar Annual Reports and Achievement 2012–2019

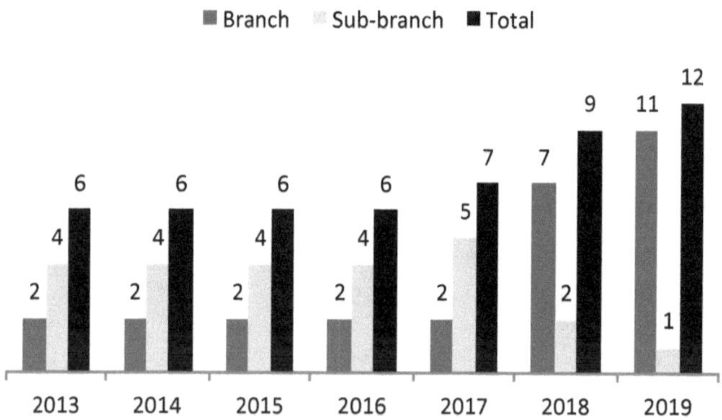

Fig. 9.13 ACLEDA Microfinance Institution (AMM) Branch Development 2013–2019
Source: ACLEDA MFI Myanmar Annual Reports and Achievement 2012–August 2019

AMM provided credit to a credit-starved market in a competitive environment. Even with considerable restrictions on interest rate spreads between deposits and loans, as Fig. 9.14 shows, a reasonable net profit after tax was possible.

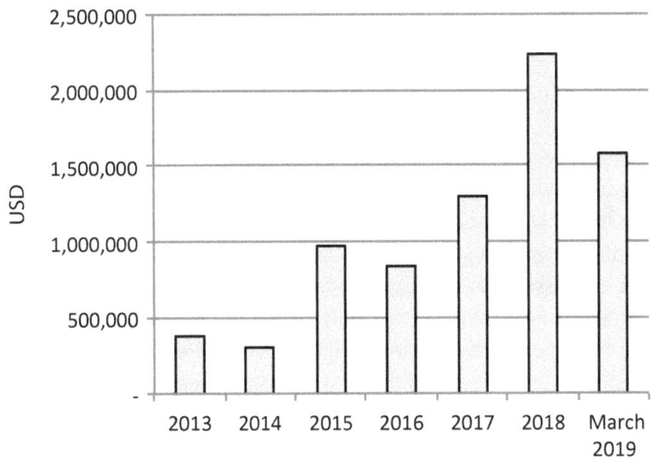

Fig. 9.14 AMM net profit after tax (NPAT) 2013–2019
Source: ACLEDA MFI Myanmar Annual Reports and Financial Results 2012–2019

9.4.4 Behind Great Numbers Are Great People

ACLEDA MFI Myanmar Co. Ltd. and its parent company ACLEDA Bank Plc. are experienced participants in rapidly advancing financial sectors. They know that there are times to opportunely introduce new products and services that the population or main segments of it—will readily accept. They also know the risk of advancing too rapidly. They consider careful analysis of outreach, uptake figures, and risk ratios.

The AMM and other MFI's rates for non-performing loans (NPLs) continue to be extraordinarily low, as demonstrated by AMM's NPL rate of an average under 1.5% over the 5-year period of business operations.

Besides ensuring an affordable loan amount and a valuable client selection process, such a high performing loan rate appears to be because most loans are made to groups rather than individuals. This is consistent with global experience with small group lending, but group lending with the group guarantee is not a requirement for high repayment rates and low delinquency.[23]

In the Myanmar context, there is strong social pressure to repay any debt. Cultural factors, such as people's reluctance to take on more debt than they can afford, are also likely to play an important role. Another factor the borrower considers is the knowledge that if a loan is not repaid, the only alternative for future borrowing will be much higher-priced moneylenders who charge up to 20% per month—far more than the maximum rate charged by MFIs of 2.5% per month.

[23] See Chaps. 7 and 8 for many other causes of high delinquency and/or high repayment rates that have little to do with group guarantees.

9.4.5 A Shining Star

ACLEDA MFI Myanmar is considered the "shining star" of the ACLEDA Bank Group of Companies. Many ask why. It is considered a star with great potential and one that is loved by a new generation of aspiring Myanmar micro-bankers and their customers for how it values them, as well as for the future it offers them.

Within the ACLEDA Bank Groups of Companies, it is considered a star because of its performance and its contributions to microfinance practitioners and for advancing the discussion on the regulatory framework in Myanmar.

As of early 2020, AMM employs a staff of 504 micro-bankers who were coached and mentored by 5 consultants from ACLEDA Bank Plc. in Cambodia. Not all the young professionals who attended the first courses at the ACLEDA Training Center in Cambodia in 2012 and 2013 are still with the company today. But five of them continue contributing to microfinance in Myanmar through the efforts of AMM. They are in management positions within the company, and they have a bright future.

Although unintentional—but not entirely unexpected—another contribution that AMM is proud of is its contribution of skilled and highly trained professionals to the vibrant microfinance and banking sector in Myanmar. Since its first year of operation through FY 2016, staff turnover in AMM averaged over 24% a year and lowered to around 21% in 2017 and 2018.

Such a contribution is costly, but building a financial sector requires investment and mentoring of human resources. ACLEDA Bank Plc. is accustomed to the phenomena of its competitors search for professionally well-developed talent.

Now, 8 years since AMM's start-up in Myanmar, it seems prescient of the authorities in Myanmar to have issued an invitation to ACLEDA to, "Please, come as you were." It was also perceptive for ACLEDA Bank Plc. to accept such an invitation with open arms.

While microfinance may be seen by some as a step backward in time, the invitation requested ACLEDA to "Come as you used to be," instead of the high-powered bank that you are. ACLEDA leadership recognized the opportunities and responded to a calling that is demonstrated by AMM's commitment to mission and performance. Rather than revisiting the past, AMM forges a future for a new generation of bankers and customers.

It is really something significantly new and exciting.

Today a cadre of Cambodian and Myanmar experts in micro-banking operations, marketing, management, financial reporting, law, regulation, and governance work together, turning their good intentions into a lasting contribution to serve the people of Myanmar with financial services and to support the evolution of the financial sector.

9.4.6 The Last Word

The last words on microfinance in Myanmar go to the AMM managers and staff—the future leaders of the financial sector in Myanmar. Listen to them:

Ms. Nan Poe Sandy Thway, AMM Marketing Department Manager, notes with the understanding that only a marketing director can turn into practice, "There are three things customer service officers and credit officers should always do:

> It is important to remain calm and never to lose your temper when you are dealing with a customer problem.
> Always talk slowly and politely so that the customer will understand and want to listen.
> And, it never hurts to smile; it costs you nothing."

Ms. Nan Poe Sandy Thway started her career with ACLEDA MFI Myanmar from the early days in 2013 as a Cashier in the Yangon Branch and worked her way from the Operations Department to a Marketing Officer to her current position.

The Credit Department Manager is Ms. Htet Htet Khaing. She joined ACLEDA MFI Myanmar Co., Ltd. in early 2014 as a Credit Officer and was promoted to be Credit Department Manager the following year. As she explains:

> "I studied in the AIB classroom and in the field, I learned a lot in the university, and from AIB, but everything I know about credit and borrowers comes from my customers."
> Question: "And, who was your best customer?"
> Answer: "Most of them are the best customers."

As Ms. Su Sandy Win, AMM's Finance Department Manager says,

> You learn a lot in the classroom, but what you learn that really improves your own and your company's performance is learned on the job. If the organization provides a good environment, then both the staff member and the organization benefits, and each one of them benefits sooner.

Ms. Su Sandy Win has never worked with ACLEDA Bank Lao, but this lesson is also the most important gift that ACLEDA Bank Lao gave to ACLEDA MFI Myanmar.

And, ACLEDA MFI Myanmar learned the lesson well.

References

ACLEDA MFI Myanmar Co. Ltd. (2018a) Annual Report 2017–2018

ACLEDA MFI Myanmar Co. Ltd. (2014) Annual Report 2013–2014

ACLEDA MFI Myanmar Co. Ltd. (2018b) Achievement as of December 31, 2018. Available http://www.acledamfi.com.mm/mm/eng/pr_achievement. Accessed 14 January 2019.

Beck, Hans Anand; Rahardja, Sjamsu; Myint, Thi Da; Nair, Arvind; Guo, Fang; Reungsri, Thanapat; Maw, Aka Kyaw Min; Kessler, Martin Dov Alfred. 2019. *Building Reform Momentum (English)*. Myanmar economic monitor. Washington, D.C.: World Bank Group. http://documents.worldbank.org/curated/en/326771560523871008/Building-Reform-Momentum. Accessed 11 July 2019.

Beck, Hans Anand; Rahardja, Sjamsu; Myint, Thi Da; Nair, Arvind; Guo, Fang; Maw, Aka Kyaw Min; Reungsri, Thanapat; Kessler, Martin Dov Alfred. (2018) *Myanmar Economic Monitor: Navigating Risks (English).* Myanmar Economic Monitor Washington, D.C.: World Bank Group. Available http://documents.worldbank.org/curated/en/986461544542633353/Myanmar-Economic-Monitor-Navigating-Risks. Last Accessed 12 January 2019.

DaNa Facility (2018) New Financial Sector Research finds Strong Growth in Myanmar Financial Inclusion. http://www.danafacility.com/new-financial-sector-research-finds-strong-growth-in-myanmar-financial-inclusion/ Accessed July 21, 2018.

Htin Lynn Aung (2018) "Credit Bureau to Be Up and Running Within Next 12 months". Myanmar Times (12 Dec 2018) Available https://www.mmtimes.com/news/credit-bureau-be-and-running-within-next-12-months.html. Accessed 16 January 2019

FinScope (2018) Making Access Possible Myanmar 2018 Launch Presentation: Naypyidaw, Myanmar. June 19, 2018 Available http://www.finmark.org.za/wp-content/uploads/2018/07/FS-Myanmar-2018-Launch-Presentation.pdf

Kemp, Simon (2017) The Full Guide to Southeast Asian's Digital Landscape in 2017. Available https://www.techinasia.com/talk/full-guide-southeast-asia-digital-landscape-2017. Accessed 10 May 2018

Kooi, Peter (2018) Author interview.

Mishra, Deepak K.; Mohib, Saiyed Shabih Ali; Beck, Hans Anand; Myint, Thi Da; Nair, Arvind; Zaourak, Gabriel Roberto; Reungsri, Thanapat; Kessler, Martin Dov Alfred. (2018) *Myanmar Economic Monitor: Growth amidst uncertainty (Vol. 2): main report (English).* Washington, D.C. World Bank Group. Available http://documents.worldbank.org/curated/en/111271527015535987/main-report

Myanmar Business Survey (2015) Referenced in MEM Growth Amidst Uncertainty, World Bank, May 2018.

OECD (2016) Multi-dimensional Review of Myanmar: Volume 3. From Analysis to Action **In series:** OECD Development Pathways. Published on June 23, 2016 Available: http://www.oecd.org/countries/myanmar/multi-dimensional-review-of-myanmar-9789264256545-en.htm

World Bank. 2018a. Doing Business 2019. Training for Reform. Economy Profile Myanmar Available:.http://www.doingbusiness.org/content/dam/doingBusiness/country/m/myanmar/MMR.pdf. Accessed 3 January 2019

World Bank (2018b) Gross National Income per capita 2017, Atlas method and Purchasing Power Parity. Available https://data.worldbank.org/indicator/ny.gnp.pcap.cd

World Bank in Myanmar: Overview. Last updated October 2018. Available http://www.worldbank.org/en/country/myanmar/overview Accessed 19 December 2018

World Bank (2018c) World Development Indicators Available: https://datacatalog.worldbank.org/dataset/gni-capita-ranking-atlas-method-and-ppp-based. Last Accessed 15 February 2019

World Bank (2017a) An Analysis of Poverty in Myanmar (English) Washington, D.C.: World Bank Group. Available http://documents.worldbank.org/curated/en/829581512375610375/An-analysis-of-poverty-in-Myanmar. Last Accessed 19 December 2018

World Bank (June 2017b) "Turning on the Lights in Rural Myanmar" produced by the World Bank in June 2017. https://www.worldbank.org/en/news/feature/2017/06/29/turning-on-the-lights-in-rural-myanmar Accessed 8 July 2018

UNDP. 2016a. Human Development Report: Briefing Note: Myanmar. Available: http://hdr.undp.org/sites/all/themes/hdr_theme/country-notes/MMR.pdf Accessed 15 July 2018

UNDP. Human Development Index 2016 Available http://hdr.undp.org/en/countries/profiles/MMR Accessed15 July 2018

UNDP. 2016b. Human Development Report 2016: Human Development for Everyone. Briefing Note for Myanmar Details of indicators and their importance are found at: http://hdr.undp.org/en and http://hdr.undp.org/en/countries/profiles/MMR; http://hdr.undp.org/en/countries Accessed15 July 2018

UNDP. 2018 Human Development Indices and Indicators: 2018 Statistical Update: Myanmar. Available http://hdr.undp.org/sites/all/themes/hdr_theme/country-notes/MMR.pdf Accessed 12 July 2019.

XE 2018 Available https://www.xe.com/currencycharts/?from=USD&to=MMK&view=1Y Accessed 15 January 2019

Chapter 10
ACLEDA Institute of Business: A New Generation of Bankers

From month to month new students enroll, existing students continue, and AIB gains more trust from the student body and Cambodian society
Dr. Phon Narin, Managing Director, ACLEDA Institute of Business

We also teach participants how to transfer knowledge to their colleagues.
Mr. Chhan Ponloeu, President & CEO of ACLEDA Training Center Ltd. 2011–2016, Managing Director 2016, ACLEDA Institute of Business

We train, you gain.
ACLEDA Training Center (ATC) tagline 2008–2018
Created by Mr. Tauch Ngam Youra, Vice President & Head of Public Relations Department, ACLEDA Institute of Business

Long, Long Ago…
ACLEDA Bank built the foundation of the ACLEDA Institute of Business (AIB) years before they bought the land, drained the swamp, drove the pilings into the ground, and poured the concrete.

The faculty and staff of AIB's predecessor, the ACLEDA Training Center (ATC), knew what the campus should look like long before the construction crew welded the steel girders into place and put up the walls for each building on campus.

Before they worked with architects and construction contractors to identify priorities, they knew their priorities: state-of-the-art classrooms and study facilities; dormitories to accommodate students from rural areas or overseas; open, green public spaces to relax and clear the mind; and sports facilities to expend youthful energy.

Long before AIB received its license as a higher education institution, the ACLEDA Institute of Business (AIB) dominated the imaginations of the ACLEDA Bank Plc. founders. These thought leaders dreamed about excellence in banking with high ethical standards; they dreamed about a integrating a quality professional

© Springer Nature Singapore Pte Ltd. 2020

H. A. Clark, *Beyond Borders, Beyond Banking*,
https://doi.org/10.1007/978-981-15-1687-0_10

education in ethical banking into the financial and educational sectors in Cambodia and beyond its national borders.[1]

Their vision was grounded in ACLEDA staff training programs that were piloted and revised over the last 20 years. The perfection of the course curricula was based on feedback from over 560,000 course participants[2] through the many transitions of ACLEDA Bank's in-house training department to the ACLEDA Training Center for the banking industry in Cambodia, in the ASEAN region and globally.

Long before the first AIB architectural blueprint was approved, ACLEDA leadership understood that its inclusive financial services approach would require an innovative business school. The institution would emphasize ethics in business together with an ethical approach to customer service. They intended to teach the full range of ethical practices, including relations toward customers, staff, competitors, regulators, government authorities, as well as transparent business practices from the boardroom to the smallest point of customer service, whether it was face-to-face or virtual.[3]

By adopting the global client protection principles and becoming certified in their consistent implementation, ACLEDA Bank Plc. promotes international banking standards for financial consumer protection.[4] ACLEDA Bank Plc. considers these standards a hallmark of their customer relationships and values the set of standards as a cornerstone of ethical banking.

As of the beginning of 2019, the Smart Campaign had certified nine financial institutions in Cambodia in client protection practices and standards, including eight MFIs and MDIs. ACLEDA Bank Plc. is the only commercial bank in Cambodia that has been certified. (Smart Campaign website).

For the ACLEDA pioneers, high standards were prerequisites for advancing ethical banking, even though Cambodia's legal and regulatory frameworks did not yet require such a comprehensive set of high standards for a financial services providers' relationship with customers.

ACLEDA's vision for the new generation of bankers incorporates ethics and technical excellence into every aspect of finance and banking to guide the next chapters of Cambodia's growth and development. And AIB prepares young people to excel in their future careers as ethical bankers (Box 10.1).

---

[1] The generally accepted definition of ethical banking is that it encompasses any bank, financial institution, or system that operates based on values driven by environmental and social responsibility. For a summary history and discussion of ethical banking, see, Callejas-Albiñana et al. 2017.

[2] From 2000 to 2018, ACLEDA Bank held a variety of courses for Bank staff, Cambodian MFIs and banks, overseas visitors, staff of Lao PDR and Myanmar subsidiaries, and students and the general public in Cambodia, including MSEs (micro and small enterprises). The details are presented later in this chapter.

[3] See Chaps. 5 and 6 for a full discussion of the origins, development, and history of ACLEDA Bank's ethical banking practices.

[4] See Chap. 3 for a discussion of Smart Campaign Client Protection Principles and Certification in Cambodia.

Box 10.1: The Smart Campaign

Smart Campaign certification in client protection provides an independent, objective seal of confidence that a financial institution is doing everything it can to treat its clients well and protect them from harm.

"Certification represents a rigorous standard of practice in customer protection... We have been happy to collaborate to support this common aim."

Source: Smart Campaign website: www.smartcampaign.org/certification

The next sections of this chapter explore the fascinating history of the ACLEDA Institute of Business (AIB), the people who built it, and the reasons why. The chapter reviews AIB's stages of development—from its origins as the Training Division of ACLEDA Bank Plc. in 2000 to the present day. ACLEDA Institute of Business was certified and licensed by the Ministry of Education, Youth and Sport (MoEYS) in early January 2016.

But before those stories are told, the Higher Education sub-sector in Cambodia and the changes and challenges that are featured in the Ministry of Education's Policy on Higher Education Vision 2030 require an introduction. The Vision 2030 Policy on Higher Education has been in place since 2014. The education sector is briefly reviewed to set the context for a better understanding of the higher education sub-sector within it.

10.1 Higher Education in Cambodia

The Cambodian government recognizes the important role that higher education plays in the development of Cambodia's future in ASEAN and globally. The Cambodian population will benefit from the significant opportunities offered by growing regional integration and globalization when the educational sector is designed to keep up with technology, educational standards, new management methods, and creative thinking and problem-solving techniques.

Unfortunately, education in Cambodia—from preschool to university—is plagued by a series of interrelated problems that lead to undereducated and poorly prepared secondary and higher education graduates.

In 2013, one veteran participant in the higher education sector noted:

> A situation analogous to the economic crisis is being created. A 'bubble' is forming of university graduates with worthless degrees. Intense competition has led to the existence of risky and exotic educational products, where capacity to pay is more important than academic ability. As a result, many institutions are offering 'subprime' degrees: degrees that have little actual value, due to a variety of factors—including, selection of students with low capacity, teaching by unqualified faculty, minimal evaluation, and corruption. (Ford 2013)

10.1.1 Strategy and Expenditure

The Ministry of Education formulated the "Cambodian Higher Education Vision 2030" in an effort to unify priorities and develop a clear road map to bring Cambodia's higher education initiatives and institutions to a higher level. Vision 2030 supports adapting and conforming to global and regional trends while ensuring development of future human resources that will contribute to development nationwide.

The strategy links the lofty ideal of equitable access to higher education as well as much more practical efforts to improve the quality of instruction, the quality of instructors, and, by applying accreditation, clear standards and evaluation to both. The core mission to nurture and produce graduates who will become economically competitive, as well as socially responsible, is emphasized and redoubled.

As discussed in Chap. 2, Cambodia ranks 124th out of 137 countries in Higher Education and Training, Cambodia's poorest performance in any pillar of the World Economic Forum Competitiveness Index (World Economic Forum 2017). This ranking placed Cambodia's higher education and training below all 22 Asian countries that participated in the index.

By 2018, Cambodia's position in higher education and training fared little better, ranking 121st out of 140 countries participating in the Index. Cambodia's score of 40 in the higher education and training pillar placed it well below the East Asia and Pacific average of 70. Yet there were small improvements in staff training, the quality of vocational training, and digital skills among the general population. Meanwhile, Cambodia's competitiveness scores decreased for the skill sets of graduates and the ease of finding skilled employees (World Economic Forum 2018).

These results are also fairly comparable to the low general Cambodian government expenditure on education.[5] Historically, the highest value for government spending on education over the past 16 years was 2.6% of GDP in 2010 and 2.02% in 2013, while the lowest value was 1.26 of GDP in 1998 (UNESCO, World Bank 2018).[6]

The 2016 expenditure on education still falls short of internationally recommended minimums (World Bank 2018). With less than the suggested minimum of expenditure on the overall educational budget, the MoEYS has been obliged to prioritize (Sem and Hem 2016), entailing a process of elimination covering which items in the MoEYS budget are funded adequately and which continue without budget support from the government.

[5] Definition: General government expenditure on education (current, capital, and transfers) is expressed as a percentage of GDP. It includes expenditure funded by transfers from international sources to government. General government usually refers to local, regional, and central governments (UNESCO).

[6] As a comparison, the average OECD nation spent $9313 per young person. As a share of its economy, the United States spent more than the average country in the survey. In 2010, the United States spent 7.3% of its gross domestic product on education, compared with the 6.3% average of other OECD countries (UNESCO).

In addition, the 2018 Human Development Report Statistical Update notes from 2012 to 2018 Cambodia's government expenditure on education[7] as a percentage of GDP averaged 1.9%. Cambodia's contribution of GDP to education is the lowest in the Southeast Asian region and well below the average of all countries participating in the 2018 Human Development Report (UNDP 2018; World Bank 2018).

Nevertheless, in the 2019 national budget, the Ministry of Education is slated to receive the largest share of the national budget approved by the National Assembly in November 2018, which allows for a greater share of spending as a percentage of GDP in 2019 (Chea 2018). Perhaps the tide is turning toward greater investment in education from primary school to higher education.

In an increasingly competitive world, the opportunities to advance, or even to stay in the same competitive position, are dependent on quality higher education and training. This is particularly the case for countries, like Cambodia, that rely to such a great extent on only a few industries in the private sector to fuel economic growth. These industries are mainly supported by foreign investment and vulnerable to competitive pressures from other producing countries.

The priority of investing in higher education becomes even more striking when combined with the results of the World Economic Forum 2017–2018 Executive Opinion Survey that indicated the top two most problematic factors for doing business in Cambodia were corruption and an inadequately educated workforce, in that order.[8] These two problematic factors for doing business in Cambodia topped the list during the prior year as well.

The case for investing in education, and particularly higher education, is rarely challenged outright. Rather, the low investment priority given to the education sector is often framed in terms of other areas that are assigned greater importance for government subsidy. The Asia Pacific Human Development Report cites a more realistic rationale for priority setting, with the following statement:

> Without appropriate interventions, today's educational inequalities will become tomorrow's inequalities in wealth and human development. (UNDP 2016)

10.1.2 A Long and Difficult Journey

Higher education in Cambodia has traveled a long and difficult journey. As noted in a Cambodian government report, "In Cambodia, the development of the higher education sector after the end of colonialism met serious challenges, especially during civil war, and the Khmer Rouge period when education was totally abolished" (MoEYS 2014).

[7] Definition: government expenditure on education—current, capital, and transfer spending on education, expressed as a percentage of GDP.

[8] See Chap. 2 for a more detailed analysis of World Economic Forum Competitiveness Index for Cambodia.

During this period, university students, graduates, their mentors, professors, and guardians were considered "all the wheat that grows among the rice plants."[9] They were specifically targeted for execution during the Khmer Rouge reign of terror from 1975 to 1979.[10] The complete destruction of many of Cambodia's institutions during this period—including the education system—left subsequent governments the difficult task of giving priority to specific sectors of the economy.

And, within those economic sectors, the ailing budget required setting specific and urgent priorities for rebuilding and designated budget support. The educational sector was not a high priority, and within the sector, higher education was a lower priority.

According to the MoEYS, "During the 1980s and 1990s, Cambodia did not prioritize higher education as it sought to rebuild the entire education system with a focus on the provision of basic education for the entire population throughout the country" (MoEYS 2014).

The first university to reopen its doors after the Khmer Rouge years was the Royal University of Phnom Penh in 1979. But it was only in the late 1990s that the increased number of graduates from secondary school led to an increased demand for higher education. Limited government budgets consequently led to limiting the number of student enrollments that such budgets could support. The limitation of such a desirable good also had an impact on whose children received the chance to attend university and those who did not, regardless of aptitude or scholarly achievement.

> To cope with this demand—and inequity—a policy initiative was introduced, based on the principle of public private partnership. Under this policy, the first private higher education institution (HEI), Norton University, was established in 1997 (MoEYS 2014).

Since that time, the number of private universities increased substantially, especially during the mid-2000s. The number of public HEIs increased from 8 in 1997 to 39 in 2014. By mid-2018, more than 70 of Cambodia's 119 institutions of higher learning were private (Amaro 2018). Fee-paying classes were also introduced into the public HEIs, which up to that time were supported only with government budgets and/or through donors.

As a result of greater demand and more spaces available for prospective students, the higher education landscape in Cambodia transformed dramatically. It moved

---

[9] For narratives from the period, see Dith Pran. 1999. *Children of Cambodia's Killing Fields: Memoirs by Survivors*. Yale University Press. New Haven.

[10] "More than three quarters of all university teaching staff and a phenomenal 96% of students were massacred by the Khmer Rouge," according to Chealy, C (2006). Cambodia. Cited in Higher Education in South East Asia (pp.13–31). Bangkok: UNESCO Asia and Pacific Regional Bureau for Education. Cited in Williams, James, Kitamura, Yuto and Keng, Sopcheak. 2014. *Higher Education in Cambodia: Expansion and Quality Improvement.* Williams J.H., Kitamura Y., Keng C.S. (2016) Higher Education in Cambodia. In: Kitamura Y., Edwards D.B., Sitha C., and Williams J.H. (eds.) *The Political Economy of Schooling in Cambodia. International and Development Education.* Palgrave Macmillan, New York. Chealy, C. 2005. "Cambodia." In *Higher education in South East Asia*, pp. 13–33. Bangkok: UNESCO Asia and Pacific Regional Bureau for Education.

from serving only the elite to extending broader mass access to higher education. The principle worked as long as the considerable challenge could be met by secondary schools able to produce competent graduates—graduates who could pass both the final exam for high school graduation and the higher education institution's entrance exam.

The number of students in higher education increased from nearly 10,000 in the early 1990s to more than 200,000 in 2013. By 2017, the gross enrollment rate in tertiary education was 13.14%.[11]

The gross enrollment rate reflects a dramatic increase in Cambodia's higher education student body since 2008, especially among women.[12] In 2008 the gross enrollment rate in tertiary education was 6.18% for women and 12.05% for men. By 2017, the gross enrollment rate in tertiary education was 12.17% for women, almost double, and 14.07% for men, showing a 2% increase in 2017 over 2015, but a significant decrease from the gross enrollment for men in 2011 of 18.24% (UNESCO 2018).

At the beginning of the 2017 academic year, just over 201,300 students were enrolled in both private and public Cambodian Higher Education Institutions.

10.1.3 A Refreshing Vision Keeps the Main Goal Insight

The MoEYS Policy on Higher Education Vision 2030 is as refreshing as it is inspiring. It is also ambitious.

The policy aims to transform higher education to universal access and also as a high-quality human development resource that positions Cambodia and her graduates in expanding regional and global markets. The current state of the educational system in Cambodia requires every bit of the inspiration, ambition, and resources that have been pledged to support future generations that have been neglected for some time.

It is no secret that the higher educational system continues to fail its graduating students on a regular basis. Yet, this phenomenon starts long before a student reaches the higher education institution of her/his choice. As the MoEYS Vision 2030 notes, what is required is a complete renovation—as if the only resources that mattered are the students, their professors and instructors and the great pursuit of excellence in knowledge.

[11] The gross enrollment rate is the number of students enrolled in a given level of education, regardless of age, expressed as a percentage of the official school-age population corresponding to the same level of education. For the tertiary level, the population used is the 5-year age group starting from the official secondary school graduation age (UNESCO 2018).

[12] In 2008 the gross enrollment rate in tertiary education was 6.18% for women and 12.05% for men. By 2017, the gross enrollment rate in tertiary education was 12.17% for women, almost double, and 14.07% for men, showing a 2% increase in 2017 over 2015, but a significant decrease from the gross enrollment for men in 2011 of 18.24% (UNESCO 2018).

Table 10.1 MoEYS figures for 2016–2017

School level	Percentage of repeaters per year	Percentage dropout per year
Primary (grades 1–6)	6.6% students a year	4.6% dropout
Lower secondary (grades 7–9)	2.5% repeat each year	17% dropout
Upper secondary (grades 10–12)	2.8% repeat each year	19.4% dropout

Source: MOEYS statistics and indicators 2016–2017

But, a difficult journey continues for some. A review of 2016–2017 educational statistics shows that the long and difficult journey to achieve much higher rates of educational attainment continues. See Table 10.1.

According to Dr. Hang Chuon Naron, Minister of Education, Youth and Sport, and Anne Lemaistre, former UNESCO representative in Cambodia, "Despite the success made by the MoEYS in terms of access to primary education level which stood at 93.5% for the 2016–2017 school year, only 55.7% of eligible students have enrolled in the lower secondary level, and, only 25.1% of the eligible students have enrolled in upper secondary levels" (Hang Chuon and Lemaistre 2017).

The 2017 Cambodia Socio-Economic Survey (National Institute of Statistics 2018) covers school enrollment among many educational statistics. It shows the low level of education attainment among the population aged 25 and above. The figures show that 20.7% have no formal education, 36% have some education, and 22% have completed the primary level of schooling. Only 16.7% have completed secondary education level.

After completion of higher secondary school, students are ready to take the national exam, which is the final test of whether they receive a passing grade for their high school education and obtain their secondary school diploma.

In September 2018, the MoEYS announced the results of the national exam for all high school seniors across the country. Out of 115,268 Grade 12 students who sat for the national exam, there were only 75,059 students who passed the National Examination 2018 (Bacc II). This is equivalent to 65% of all Grade 12 students in 2018, compared to 63.8% of all Grade 12 students who passed the exam in 2017. See Fig. 10.1.

According to the MoEYS press release, the following achievements were reported among the 115,268 high school seniors taking the exam, 50% of who were female. The press release reported that 40,209 students failed the exam, while the vast majority of high school graduates who passed the exam received an "E" grade which signifies the lowest passing grade. See Fig. 10.1 passing grades and Fig. 10.2 exam performance of the most recent high school graduates, September 2018.

The current performance shows a very discouraging barometer for employers who will increasingly need the educational system to prepare young people for jobs in more competitive industries. As shown in Fig. 10.2, there is a huge gap in numbers between those who passed with an "E" grade or a "D" grade and those who attained at least a "B" grade.

The low levels of innovative learning techniques designed to develop creativity among graduates will continue to be problematic as they enter the workforce or continue on to seek higher education. The long and difficult journey will continue

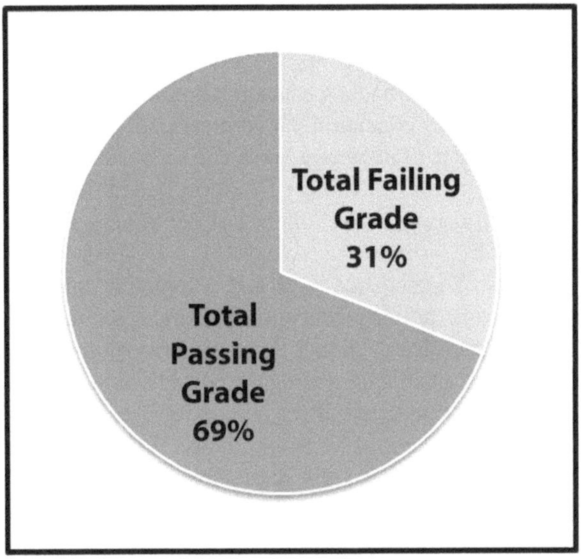

Fig. 10.1 High school graduation exam passing grades (2019)
Source: Ministry of Education as reported in the *Khmer Times* September 9 Mom Kunthear

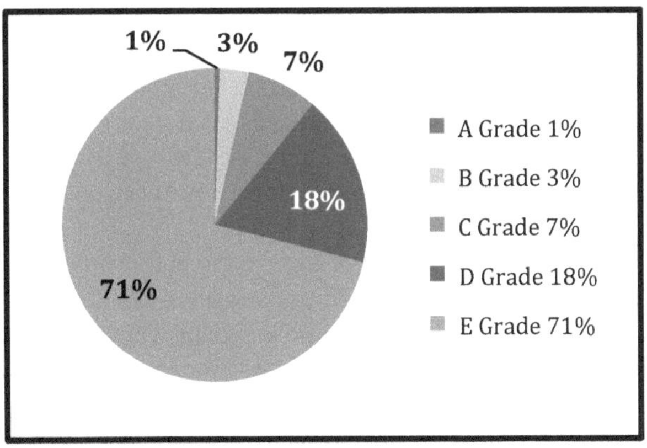

Fig. 10.2 High school students graduation exam performance 2019 passing grades
Source: Ministry of Education as reported in the *Khmer Times* September 9 Mom Kunthear

for the foreseeable future even with more public resources allocated for the re-invention of Cambodia's education system.

While few students become high school graduates, they are also rarely prepared to enter the work force or continue schooling. The low quality of instruction from primary school to higher education institutions relies on methods of instruction and curriculum content that is rarely supportive for meeting the future requirements of the labor market or developing the intellectual creativity to contribute as partners in global and national innovation and development.

10.1.4 Stumbling Blocks: Access, Quality, and Composition

The major achievement in Cambodia's educational system is the movement toward 100% enrollment in primary education. Government spending on primary education has increased, mainly to build new schools and renovate deteriorating ones that do not have adequate physical and sanitary facilities. In addition, literacy rates have improved in the youthful population, often, but controversially attributed to the investment in preschool.

Still, the low levels of attendance rates and completion rates indicate that the intention to ensure a basic primary education (through six grades) must go much beyond bricks and mortar. The National Strategic Development Plan 2014–2018 clearly cites the enormous challenges facing the educational sector as follows: "The education sector lags and concerted effort is required for improvement. Principal problems include the low quality of learning, limited learning infrastructure, insufficient well-qualified teachers, not fully implemented quality assurance systems, and few quality institutions of higher education" (RGC 2014).

Teaching resources are stretched beyond capacity to deliver quality, averaging 1 teacher for every 43 students in public primary schools. Cambodia's pupil to teacher ratio in primary school is the poorest in the ASEAN region (MoEYS 2017).

The high dropout rates among primary and secondary students are not the only factors that influence the educational level in Cambodia. The dropout rate among teachers is also high. About 2000 teachers in Cambodia have dropped out of teaching each year since 2012. These are significant numbers, given that MoEYS takes on only around 5000 new teacher trainees each year (Sem and Hem 2016). And, the lack of teachers continued to accelerate each year from 2015 to 2018, while the net enrollment rates for students in both primary and secondary school have continued to grow.

By 2018, the estimates of teacher shortages in the national public school system include a shortage of 4040 teachers at the primary level and 1309 at the lower secondary level. This is compounded by the problem that even when the teaching roster is fully staffed, a lot of official teaching time is lost due to teacher absence and attention to activities in the classroom other than teaching and learning. Also teachers, especially in the rural areas, work on the family farm during planting and harvest time or undertake additional job (Sem and Hem 2016).

One underlying problem that continues is "ensuring that civil service pay and non-material benefits are sufficiently competitive to attract, retain, and motivate professionals of various key skill sets." For example, a 2014 study finds that "the best students are not attracted to teaching" and that "most teacher trainees scored in the E, D, and C ranges on the Grade 12 exam" (Tandon and Fukao 2015).

Even if better professionals were to be attracted through the salary increases or additional incentives, performance monitoring and citizen feedback mechanisms in Cambodia are weak and need to be strengthened for actual improvements in efficiency and quality of public service delivery to materialize (Tandon and Fukao 2015).

The Ministry of Education, Youth and Sport (MoEYS) acknowledges that "the long and difficult journey" will continue up to and beyond its Higher Education Vision 2030. The forthright and focused framing of the challenges and opportunities in higher education in Cambodia as written in the MoEYS policy statement is as follows:

> A major challenge for the coming years will be to address the mismatch between the needs of the labor market in terms of skills, critical thinking ability and knowledge and the current products on the market. This will require better understanding of the labor market, better coordination and links with industry and better information for students so they can select appropriate courses."
>
> "Maintaining high quality programs, internationally acceptable certification within an affordable pricing structure is also a challenge. Further work and increased resources will be required to ensure that more talented students from disadvantaged backgrounds can access higher education through scholarship programs or possibly student loan schemes. (MoEYS Website 2018, 2020)

10.2 ACLEDA Institute of Business: The Dream

Within the higher education sector, the ACLEDA Institute of Business (AIB) created a realistic vision of a brighter future for Cambodia's poorly trained university graduates, who often complete their courses with the minimum academic knowledge required. Yet, it is widely acknowledged that there is an "alarming mismatch between education and employment" (MoEYS 2014).

Many university graduates are less accomplished in employable skills and poorly prepared to implement self-management, creative thinking and problem-solving, and the communication skills required to join the professional workforce and excel in their positions. Further, "there are concerns about the quality of higher education provision across the country" (MoEYS 2014).

Early on, the founders of AIB were determined to ensure graduates entered and excelled in the working world—and an increasingly competitive employment marketplace. Each graduate would be equipped with excellent banking skills, strong capacity and communications skills to serve the customer well and fairly, and finely honed business ethics that would become the foundation of a successful career in finance and banking regardless of the employer.

From the beginning, ACLEDA's founders, a dedicated group of teachers turned bankers, planned to deliver a specialized course of study that was not offered anywhere else in Cambodia. Indeed, it was only rarely offered outside of Cambodia. They designed a curriculum that focused on knowledge, skill, and practice. Subjects range from the fundamentals of banking and finance to the heights of expertise in high finance.

Beginning in 2016, AIB subjects are offered in basic banking education as well as advanced courses to suit both Associate and Bachelor's Degree programs. The curricula are customized for each type of Degree and yet allow for a high amount of diversity to ensure graduates are well grounded in ACLEDA's ethical banking principles and practices. Courses offer specialization in areas as diverse as accounting, credit analysis, financial reporting analysis, internal audit, good governance, skills of a marketing officer, ethics in banking, customer service and fair treatment of customers, and fintech applications that require special customer service and equal—not less—due diligence than traditional products.[13]

All of AIB's banking and finance courses are taught by skilled banking professionals, most of whom worked or currently work at ACLEDA Bank Plc., or one of its subsidiaries, such as ACLEDA Bank Lao, ACLEDA MFI Myanmar, and ACLEDA Securities Plc.

This innovation was sometimes challenged with scheduling headaches within the ACLEDA Group of Companies, but it was considered well worth the effort from the perspective of both bank staff, students, and prior training participants of the ACLEDA Training Center. Students appreciate the diversity of experience and expertise that is brought to the courses, and Bank staff values the challenge.

Transforming Bank staff into AIB professors and instructors revolutionized the business school curriculum at AIB in Cambodia. It also provided a positive disruptive energy for ACLEDA Bank staff, as they viewed teaching as a prestigious honor and, more often than not, a benefit of their employment at the Bank.

As Mrs. Kim Sotheavy, ACLEDA's Group Chief Internal Audit Officer notes, teaching helps develop clear communications skills and the ability to think through problems more thoroughly. It is one matter to know how to do your job with skill, but it's completely different to teach someone else (Kim 2018). And, as Mr. Thath Dynoth, Head of Internal Audit Development Division, emphasizes both mentorship in the office and encouragement in the classroom go hand in hand, as he notes Mrs. Kim Sotheavy's encouraging advice, "There is no problem, where a solution cannot be found."

Transforming Bank staff into AIB instructors represents another major innovation that distinguishes the AIB from the established community of higher education institutions in business and finance in Cambodia. AIB professors are practitioners, who understand what skills, aptitudes, and attitudes banking professionals need to succeed in the workplace. They are ethical bankers, and they understand and can convey both the theory and—most importantly—the practice of ethical banking which underpins the daily practices of customer service, accounting, business ethics, teamwork, and communications.

[13] For further information on some of the less obvious challenges of fintech applications, see, for example, a recent publication by Mr. Anup Singh, Principle Consultant, Banking and Financial Services at MicroSave, "An Open Letter to Central Bank of Kenya Governor, Patrick Njoroge," Singh (2018) MicroSave is an international financial inclusion consulting firm with 20 years of experience, 11 offices around the world, 175 staff, managing projects in around 50 developing countries.

10.2.1 *ACLEDA Institute of Business: Joining a "Flight to Quality"*

ACLEDA Bank Plc. transformations were inspired by and rooted in the context of Cambodia's financial services market as it developed over the past two decades. Through every transformation they aimed to initiate changes to serve the market better by building on progress and learning from it, as well as by applying rigorous measures of achievement often during uncertain times.[14]

ACLEDA staff and management were regularly challenged to navigate a "true heading" in murky waters. Knowledge about how the market changed—and the agility to respond quickly and sometimes dramatically—allowed ACLEDA Bank Plc. to remain relevant in the market and build a banking institution of lasting value.

Just as ACLEDA Bank Plc. was built to keep up with Cambodia's rapid pace of change in the banking sector while adhering to its fundamental values and international standards of excellence, AIB, too, has been built to embrace progress and remain true to its vision and values but in a vastly different context.

There has not yet been the "flight to quality" in the higher education sector that the banking sector experienced so dramatically by culling many moribund or ruthless banking institutions in 1999.[15] But it may be on the horizon. With the announcement of its Higher Education Vision 2030 in 2014, the Royal Government of Cambodia committed to postsecondary education as a national priority. The lofty aims are to build its higher education institutions to become competitive in the region.

To date, Cambodia's schooling system lacks quality assurance and credibility especially at the postsecondary level leading to low degree recognition within the labor market nationally and within the region. There is an immediate call for academic institutions to revamp their programs to better serve the labor market (IFC 2017).

MoEYS's Vision 2030 is promising, as is the energy and commitment of the Minister to make change happen. In many ways AIB aspires to contribute to a similar "flight to quality" in the higher education sub-sector as Cambodia experienced in the banking sector.

And, AIB will do its best to make it happen.

10.2.2 *AIB and Its Many Transitions*

The three major AIB transformations are plotted in the following flow diagram (Fig. 10.3).

[14] See Chaps. 5 and 6 for ACLEDA Bank Plc. prior transformations.

[15] For a discussion of "flight to quality" in the Cambodian banking sector and the difficult reforms it required, see the Prologue to Part 2, "Flight to Quality."

In 2000 when ACLEDA Bank was established as a full service bank, the Training Division within the Human Resources Department built the capacity of ACLEDA staff to contribute to the Bank's success over the exciting and difficult years of establishing a new bank. At the time, ACLEDA Bank was quite different from any other bank in Cambodia, with a national network within every province and focused on serving micro and small businesses. The Bank continued to focus on microfinance and small enterprise credit, just as it developed and expanded products to serve the people of Cambodia and their demand for new products and services.

At the time, and to this day, ACLEDA Bank continues staff training and opportunities for development and advancement of the enterprise and its staff as a normal part of business operations. Indeed, banks and MFIs in Cambodia have long enjoyed a synergetic relationship with ACLEDA Bank with the advent of the ACLEDA Training Center and its predecessor within the ACLEDA Training Division. The benefits of what would normally be considered "staff poaching" continue to this day. MFIs that recruit ACLEDA staff save costs on training, but are willing to pay much higher salaries—a major advantage for MFIs and small banks, as they generally do not have sufficient internal training capacity.

For ACLEDA training costs are high, but attention to training also guarantees staff quality. As a flat organization, there are many talented and experienced young staff, but few promotion opportunities emerge. As a result, the competition recruits senior staff from ACLEDA Bank. In fact, as Dr. In Channy is fond of saying, ACLEDA's former senior staff positively influences the operations of other banks and the banking industry as a whole.

For the ACLEDA Group of Companies, AIB is the guardian of quality of training for ACLEDA staff in Cambodia, the Lao PDR and Myanmar, and the financial sectors where they work. Since 2000, several major transitions have enabled AIB to evolve to the learning institution that it is today.

The transitions presented in Fig. 10.3 show a means of recognizing and following a more effective way of improving staff training and human resource development

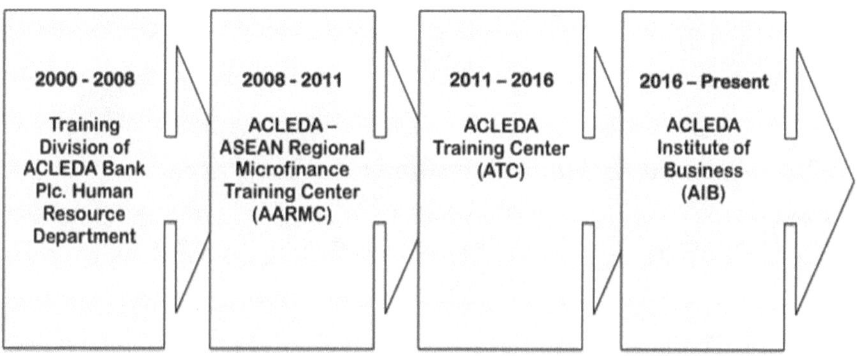

Fig. 10.3 AIB and its many transitions
Source: AIB Achievement Report Various Years through June 2019

over almost 20 years as the Cambodian economy grew and the ACLEDA Group of Companies expanded beyond borders to the Lao PDR and Myanmar.

10.2.2.1 The ACLEDA Training Division (2000–2008)

From 2000 to 2008 ACLEDA Bank's Training Division played the critical role of building the capacity of ACLEDA staff to make a successful transition to a full service commercial bank. The Bank's transition to a more complex level of operations, the array of products offered, and newly promulgated regulations were matched by the Training Division's acuity to perceive, understand, and deliver the human resources that built ACLEDA Bank Plc. during the critical early years.

The first transition from the Training Division in the Human Resources Department occurred in 2008 as ACLEDA Bank began to see the potential of expanding within the region.

10.2.2.2 ASEAN Regional Microfinance Training Center (AARMC) (2008–2011)

The new training center, the ACLEDA-ASEAN Regional Microfinance Training Center (AARMC) was established and co-financed by ACLEDA Bank Plc. and the Federal Republic of Germany through KfW. AARMC provided training locally and internationally and focused on MFIs in the ASEAN region and China.

At the time, AARMC also provided Training of Trainers to the AARMC staff. The AARMC staff and instructors continued to excel in this specialty over the years. With the advent of AARMC, ACLEDA cast its reach further afield in its expansion to Laos and other countries, primarily in Asia, and developed a consulting service as a companion to training.

As the Bank began to grow, the thinking of ACLEDA leadership at the time viewed separating the Human Resource management function from the training function as a positive development. Such a designation as a separate cost center would improve efficiency as the operation began to grow and additional staff members at all levels were required. This became important because the Human Resources Department had to focus on and keep pace with ACLEDA's new recruits and staffing newly established departments that were required for growth. A move toward increasing efficiency and preparing for growth for the Bank underpinned the rationale for transition.

The second reason was to prepare the training center to build the groundwork for the future dream of establishing a foundation for a university.

ACLEDA Bank was one of the first and also one of the many financial institutions in Cambodia—particularly microfinance institutions—to recognize the importance of ensuring management focused on professional growth and development of their staff. ACLEDA Bank required staff to attend professional training as part of their development. This was readily accepted by staff and mostly seen by them as an added benefit of their employment with ACLEDA Bank Plc. Later they were also tapped to serve as instructors.

10.2.2.3 The ACLEDA Training Center (2011–2016)

The second transition occurred in August 2011 as a strategic response to the growth and complexity of ACLEDA's training needs, which had been predicted by ACLEDA's management and leadership. ACLEDA Bank Plc. merged the internal Training Division and the ACLEDA-ASEAN Regional Microfinance Training Center to form the ACLEDA Training Center (ATC).

The ACLEDA Training Center trained ACLEDA staff and staff from local and international organizations, managed an International Visitors program, and offered courses to the public. The ATC established a curriculum consistent with international standards of teaching in banking with a focus on microfinance and small enterprise lending, teaching new fields of finance and banking management and governance, new bank organizational forms through NGO transformation, and ethical banking just as they were being developed in real time by ACLEDA Bank.

Since the founding of ATC, and prior to that, as an in-house staff training resource, business ethics were incorporated into the AIB curriculum. Mr. Chan Serey, a Buddhist scholar and head of the HR Department, taught a required curriculum that consisted almost entirely of business ethics, personal morality, and commitment to do the right thing.

During this time, ACLEDA Bank also began to train the competition in Cambodia as part of a deliberate strategy to increase the quality of the microfinance sector with the skills and the human resources they would need to contribute to improving Cambodia's banking sector.

Even though the idea of NGO transformation to a bank was still in the early stages in Cambodia, the example had already been set by ACLEDA Bank. The Kingdom's central bank—the National Bank of Cambodia—was supportive, and there was no reason to believe that such a transformation from an NGO lender to an organization that could provide deposit services couldn't happen again, and again, and again…

With the advent of ATC in 2011, ACLEDA cast its reach further afield in its expansion to Laos and other countries, primarily in Asia, and developed a consulting service as a companion to training services. ACLEDA's ATC quickly moved beyond its initial status as an in-house training center, focused only on Cambodia. ATC started producing graduates of training courses from many countries, who understood and began to apply a commercial and a financial system approach to microfinance. The ACLEDA approach was also strong on business ethics and how to serve the customer well and fairly.

The percentages of the 386 financial sector course participants from both Cambodian and international organizations as of April 2019 are shown in Figs. 10.4 and 10.5, respectively.

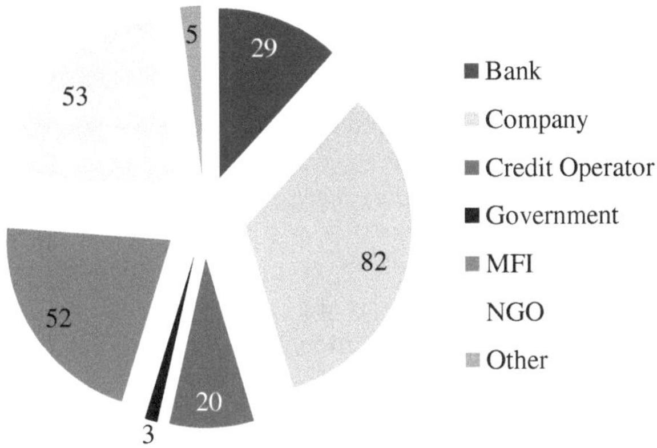

Fig. 10.4 Cambodian financial sector participants in AIB courses (%) (2008–2019)
Source: AIB Achievement Report Various Years through June 2019

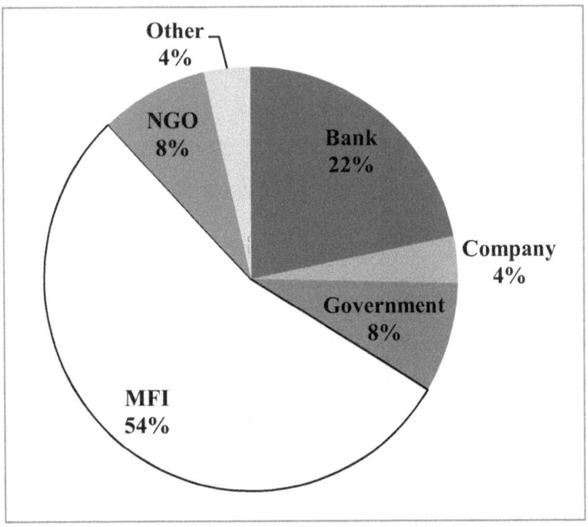

Fig. 10.5 International financial sector participants in AIB courses % (2000–2019)
Source: AIB Achievement Report Various Years through June 2019

ATC partnered with international schools, such as the Frankfurt School of Finance and Management to co-host a "Winter Academy" as a counterpart to the Frankfurt School's famous "Summer Academy." They also hosted seminars featuring regional and international specialists on specific topics, such as NGO transformation.

The International Visitors Program, initiated within the AARMC, thrived under the ATC. ATC focused Visitors Program efforts to support learning in best practices across countries. The program was designed to arrange study tours to Cambodia for visitors from the Central Banks, private banks, MFIs, and capacity builders from other countries. The program was tailor-made for small groups of people to visit and learn from and exchange experience with their counterparts in Cambodia.

It was a very popular and successful program, contributing to the understanding of the approach to microfinance as part of a country's broader financial system. One of the most popular visits was to the National Bank of Cambodia to understand their policies and regulations for advancing financial inclusion through formally regulated microfinance institutions.

In partnership with the HR Department, which had for 11 years been the center of ACLEDA's staff training, development, and advancement, the new ATC quickly proved the power of practical experience to ASEAN neighbors and microfinance practitioners and regulators from as far afield as Nepal, Ethiopia, and China.

The international experience helped to realize the dreams of Mr. Chan Serey and Mr. Chhan Ponloeu of becoming the most practical center of business training, dedicated to finance and banking to new heights in Cambodia. It also fostered and incubated a broader vision for ACLEDA Bank to expand beyond its national borders.

10.2.3 The Birth of the ACLEDA Institute of Business (2016–Present)

By 2014, ATC had created a strong foundation for ACLEDA to seriously consider becoming a licensed private higher education institution. The vision of the ACLEDA leadership, a group of teachers turned into bankers, was getting closer with every inspiration and every year.

ACLEDA Bank Plc. and ATC leadership and management were prepared to apply for a license from the Ministry of Education, as an institute of higher education. They planned to defend their position with a range of evidence that presented past experience and potential future contributions to the higher education sector, its students, and graduates.

Even though other universities had been established for sometime, since 1991, the ACLEDA Institute of Business aspired to teach students from a broad spectrum of society about finance and banking—not just prospective employees.

By 2016 AIB staff and management were committed to expand their reach from training 398,000 Cambodian staff intensely to serve customers directly and 4300 professional participants from many banking and finance organizations from as far away as Nigeria, Peru, and Eritrea and as close as the Lao PDR, Myanmar, and China.

ACLEDA Bank had its roots in providing financial services to small, medium, and microenterprises. The Bank continued to focus on their primary customers in both rural and urban areas, while expanding outreach to employees in the public and private sectors, and anyone who needed a bank account. The Bank's penchant for high-tech innovation to better serve all customers nationwide and in the region expanded with fintech innovations. The idea that they just might qualify as an institute of higher education surfaced and began to gain momentum.

Within the higher education sector, however, ACLEDA's competition expressed concerns about ACLEDA's intentions to become a licensed institution of higher learning able to establish a course of study and offer degrees worth the investment. Several private sector HEIs were concerned not only that ACLEDA would dominate the market but that standards would have to improve throughout the sector, including their own.

Competitive practices were suspect. As noted earlier in this chapter, many critics within the higher education sector believed that intense competition among private sector HEI's led to a worthless degree, and an admissions system where the capacity of a student to pay was more important than academic ability.

In addition, not all of the existing group of private HEIs were particularly happy with the ACLEDA Training Center's intended transformation to an institution of higher learning. Attracting students with quality instruction and proven employability for qualified undergraduates created a concern within AIB's competition. Their opposition to ACLEDA's application was precisely because they viewed AIB as a threat instead of an opportunity to move their own sector of the economy toward a "flight to quality."

The initial reluctance of the Cambodian Higher Education Association (CHEA), a membership organization of existing HEIs, to support the license of the newcomer, created an atmosphere of uncertainty within ATC, yet they redoubled their determination to continue their quest. The concerns of CHEA as well as AIB's would-be competitors were many.

AIB's presence in the market with its ability to attract students with experts in the field, quality courses that met international standards and demonstrated employability were valid concerns of AIB's competitors.

On January 25, 2016, the ATC obtained a license as a higher education institution—the ACLEDA Institute of Business (AIB).

The ACLEDA Institute of Business celebrated its Opening Ceremony for the new Academic Year 2016–2017 on November 21, 2016.[16] And the first AIB undergraduate class of Associate and Bachelor's Degree candidates enrolled in the first semester beginning in January 2017.

[16] AIB. Achievements as of August 31, 2018.

10.2.4 ACLEDA Institute of Business: The First Day of School

In June 2016, 396 students arrived in the spacious parking lot centered inside a group of temporary buildings that housed the ACLEDA Institute of Business at that time. They arrived on motorcycles, in shared taxis, by bus, and on bicycles. Some students were dropped off on the busy side street by their parents on their way to work.

The average age of this first batch of students was around 18 years old. One can only imagine a few brave souls eventually coming to class on skateboards ripping down Street 516 in Toul Kork, Phnom Penh and succeeding to arrive in one piece at the ACLEDA Institute of Business just in time for class.

Mr. Chhan Ponloeu, Ms. Sovanne Tourt, and Mrs. Hou Rasmey were all there to greet the newly accepted students, who would dedicate the next 2–4 years of their lives to the study of finance and banking. Smiling seriously, in their new roles as educators, organizers, and sergeants at arms, they corralled youthful enthusiasm into an organized and well-behaved crowd. Provided with directions to admissions, orientation to the campus, career guidance, course selection, and schedule, AIB's founding class of undergraduate students began their first day in pursuit of an undergraduate or associate degree in business administration.

For the students, this first day of school would set them on new and exciting career paths. For the founding members of ACLEDA, this first day of school was a long-cherished dream come true.

The new students received an orientation to the ACLEDA Institute of Business. They learned the directions to the classrooms and the Code of Conduct of the ACLEDA Institute of Business on campus—and off. Strategic career direction, course selection, and completion of classes that would support their academic decisions and intended career paths would soon follow.

But today was the first day of school, and it was an historic day in the development of 396 students in Cambodia's higher education system.

Each AIB staff member also had an eye-opening orientation that day. They were accustomed to orienting and teaching skilled adult professionals and newly recruited ACLEDA employees who were recent university graduates. The previous students were all at least 4 years older than the newly formed AIB class. The first experience with a class of recent high school graduates proved to be an unforgettable one.

"They are teenagers!" thought many AIB staff and faculty members. Teenage students were new for the AIB, but they were up to the challenge. They all took a deep breath. In short order, the first reaction quickly turned to the anticipation of accepting a new challenge.

AIB staff and faculty began to think about how they would manage such a group of very young students. And, they remembered their own experiences from the past and began to do what they were already very well prepared to do—adapt and find the best solution to a problem in a new situation.

And, true to ACLEDA Bank history, as the semester progressed, there was a lot more learning and appreciation going on, than only undergraduate students learning about banking and finance, and students appreciating their professors and AIB staff.

10.2.5 *ACLEDA Institute of Business: Performance*

ACLEDA Institute of Business celebrated its third anniversary on January 25, 2019.

In all phases of AIB's development over 20 years of experience from the beginnings of ATC and the International Visitors Program in 2011 to the official opening ceremony of AIB in 2018, the various incarnations for ACLEDA Bank's training services served more than 590,000 course participants and students inside and outside of Cambodia.

These 590,000 people—professionals in banks, MFIs, regulatory agencies, and students—sought out a reliable and innovative financial institution with a proven strategy of growth with equity. They achieved their objective to find professional training services, an international exchange of experience, an intensive banking staff training program, or skills development courses.

In 2016 AIB began its academic year with a Bachelor's Degree and an Associate's Degree in Banking and Finance. As of June 2019, there were 1,434 students, of whom 644 pursued a Bachelor's Degree and 102 students enrolled in the Associate's Degree Program. Another 688 signed up for the Bridging Course, which enables students to study further to enter a Bachelor or Associate Degree course of study.

A Decade of Growth

By 2019, participants from 30 countries representing almost 100 distinct institutions from around the globe attended training programs at AIB, from countries as diverse as China, Egypt, Nigeria, Tajikistan, Tunisia, Pakistan, and Peru.

Through its many transitions from an internal division of the ACLEDA Bank to a regional and national training center, AIB reports performance as follows in monthly reports (AIB June 2019):

- Local trainees increased from 305 as of December 31, 2009, to 7549 professionals from 251 institutions and members of the general public as of mid-2019.
- International trainees increased from 298 as of December 31, 2009, to 1886 from 163 institutions and 30 countries as of mid-2019.
- AIB commenced its first academic year offering Bachelor's Degree and Associate's Degree in the field of Banking and Finance in June 2016. By June 2019 AIB enrolled 1434 students of whom 644 are Bachelor's Degree students, 102 are Associate's Degree students, and 688 are enrolled in a Bridging Course.
- The number of internal training programs of ACLEDA Bank Plc.'s management and staff increased from 2664 courses with 37,379 employee participants as of December 31, 2009, to 53,605 courses attended by 583,288 employees as of early 2019.

- AIB staff grew from 34 staff as of December 31, 2009, to 127 staff as of the end of 2018. The training faculty consists of senior management and technical specialists from the Bank's branches and headquarters who complement the AIB faculty and specialists in course design, delivery, and training techniques.

10.2.6 ACLEDA Institute of Business: Discovering a New Business Model

It has been a long time since ACLEDA staff and management looked at an enterprise that was not making a profit nor designed to make a profit—or increase the profit within a short amount of time, generally within the life of the loan to improve the business. Rarely have ACLEDA staff and management looked at an enterprise that was designed to provide what is often thought of as a public good, but is still able to cover costs and make a profit, as proven in the Cambodian context.

The aim is not to produce wildly profitable performance, but to show a steady sustainable growth rate, and a redeemable contribution to society. The best theory of a higher educational institution that makes a profit is one that has established a reputation in the market and one that is considered to be an educational institution of choice in a sizeable market.

To this end, the indicators that AIB may choose to reveal progress may need to be adjusted and then subjected to continuous scrutiny, until the appropriate ones are found and agreed on by the AIB and ACLEDA Bank Plc. board. These indicators will benefit AIB, just as the ACLEDA Bank Cambodia, ACLEDA Bank Lao, and ACLEDA MFI Myanmar have benefited from rigorous monitoring of appropriate indicators against realistic benchmarks. Some decisions may be made and then adjusted as experience is gained in the following areas, among others:

- Profit making or providing a good return or subsidized and for how long.
- Finding the right quality measurements for serving the market well (not just profitability).
- Students who become employed by ACLEDA Bank and its subsidiaries, by other banks, or in the financial sector or in other businesses and agencies that use their expertise in finance and business.
- Students who complete their course of study and reasons for those who do not.
- Developing appropriate measures for building a strong ACLEDA Institute of Business Alumni Association.

On December 26, 2018, AIB finally occupied its own campus in Phnom Penh. The AIB campus sits on 7.57 hectares and consists of open spaces and buildings comprising a bookstore, a library, a football field, volleyball and basketball courts, a canteen, student dormitories, and other facilities. The institute, with state-of-the-art lecture halls, is capable of accommodating 627 employees in offices, lecture halls, and classrooms and 2866 students per academic term. (Hor 2018)

The phases and stages of AIB's development—from an in-house staff training program to a full-fledged and licensed higher education institution—show that it continues to focus on the field of banking and finance and its practice.

These areas are where ACLEDA Bank Plc. has always excelled and what it was originally founded in 2000 to achieve: provide the next generation with an extraordinary opportunity and an unparalleled education in banking, finance, and business ethics.

Along the way, they intend to contribute to the "flight to quality" that the Minster of Education hopes to foster and from which future generations will benefit.

References

ACLEDA Institute of Business (AIB) (2019) Achievement Report as of 30 June 2019. Available: http://www.acleda-aib.edu.kh/tc/eng/achievement Accessed August 9, 2019

Amaro, Yesenia (2018) "Higher Education must have Better Vision: Ministry" *The Phnom Penh Post*. Available: https://www.phnompenhpost.com/national/higher-education-must-have-better-vision-ministry. Accessed June 26, 2018.

Callejas-Albiñana et al. (2017) FE, Martínez-Rodríguez I, Callejas-Albiñana AI and de Vidales-Carrasco IM (2017) "Assessing the Growth of Ethical Banking: Some Evidence from Spanish Customers". Available: https://www.frontiersin.org/articles/10.3389/fpsyg.2017.00782/full. Accessed June 26, 2018.

Chea, Vannak (2018) "Budget to increase by11.4 pct." *Khmer Times*, Phnom Penh Available https://www.khmertimeskh.com/50551241/budget-to-increase-by-11-4-pct Accessed January 27, 2019.

Chealy C. (2006) Cambodia. In: UNESCO Higher Education in South-East Asia. Asia-Pacific Programme of Educational Innovation for Development, United Nations Educational, Scientific and Cultural Organization. Bangkok: UNESCO Bangkok, 2006. Available https://repository.ugm.ac.id/32578/1/UNESCO_Rihed_Higher_Education_nizam.pdf Accessed June 26, 2018.

Ford, David (2013) "Cambodian Higher Education–Subprime Degrees?" International Higher Education, Number 70, Winter 2013. Center for International Higher Education, Boston College, Chestnut Hill, MA, USA

Hang Chuon, Naron and Anne Lemaistre (2017) "Literacy Target of a Sustainable Development Goal" *The Phnom Penh Post*, Phnom Penh Available https://asiaviews.net/literacy-target-of-a-sustainable-development-goal-by-dr-hang-chuon-naron-and-anne-lemaistre Accessed January 26, 2019

Hor Kimsay (2018) ACLEDA inaugurates new business school campuses in PP's Sen Sok. December 27, 2018, *The Phnom Penh Post*, Phnom Penh Available https://www.phnompenhpost.com/business/acleda-inaugurates-new-business-school-campuses-pps-sen-sok. Accessed January 28, 2018.

International Finance Corporation (2017) "Cambodia's ACLEDA Institute of Business to Boost the Country's Academic Grade" Available https://www.ifc.org/wps/wcm/connect/news_ext_content/ifc_external_corporate_site/news+and+events/news/cambodias+acleda+institute+of+business+to+boost+the+countrys+academic+grade Accessed January 28, 2018.

Kim, Sotheavy (2018) Author Interview

Ministry of Education, Youth and Sport (2017) Public Education Statistics and Indicators 2016–2017. Phnom Penh. Available http://www.moeys.gov.kh/en/emis/2461.html Accessed February 16, 2018.

Ministry of Education, Youth and Sport (MoEYS website). Higher Education. https://www.moeys.gov.kh/index.php/en/higher-education.html. Accessed 20 April 2018, 2 January 2020

Ministry of Education Youth and Sport (2014) "Policy on Higher Education Vision 2030." Phnom Penh. Available http://www.moeys.gov.kh/en/policies-and-strategies/policy-on-higher-education-2030.html Accessed August 15, 2018.

National Institute of Statistics (2018) Cambodia Socio Economic Survey 2017 National Institute of Statistics. Ministry of Planning, Phnom Penh. Available https://www.nis.gov.kh/nis/CSES/Final%20Report%20CSES%202017.pdf. https://www.nis.gov.kh/index.php/en/about/general-information/14-cses/65-cses-report-2020 Accessed September 28, 2018.

Royal Government of Cambodia (2014) National Strategic Development Plan 2014–2018. Available https://www.ilo.org/asia/info/WCMS_364549/lang%2D%2Den/index.htm Accessed February 16, 2018.

Sem, Ren and Hem, Kosal (2016) Educational Reform in Cambodia: Progress and Challenges in Basic Education. Regional Research Paper. Parliamentary Institute of Cambodia. Phnom Penh. Available https://www.pic.org.kh/images/2017Research/20170523%20Education_Reform_Cambodia_Eng.pdf Accessed February 16, 2018.

Singh, Anup (2018) An Open Letter to Central Bank of Kenya Governor, Patrick Njoroge", http://startupmagazine.co.ke/2018/07/05/an-open-letter-to-central-bank-of-kenya-governor-patrick-njoroge/. Accessed July 28, 2018.

Smart Campaign website. http://www.smartcampaign.org/certification/all-about-certification Accessed October 25, 2018.

Tandon, Prateek; Fukao, Tsuyoshi. 2015. Educating the Next Generation: Improving Teacher Quality in Cambodia. Directions in Development--Human Development; Washington, DC: World Bank. © World Bank. Available https://openknowledge.worldbank.org/handle/10986/21002 Accessed July 28, 2018.

UNDP. 2016. Asia Pacific Human Development Report. Shaping the Future: How Changing Demographics Can Power Human Development. New York. Available http://hdr.undp.org/en/content/asia-pacific-human-development-report-2016 Accessed October 27–28, 2018.

UNDP (2018) Human Development Indicators and 2018 Statistical Update. United Nations Development Programme (UNDP), New York. Available http://hdr.undp.org/en/content/human-development-indices-indicators-2018-statistical-update

UNESCO. Sources: United Nations Educational, Scientific, and Cultural Organization (UNESCO) Institute for Statistics. Available http://uis.unesco.org/en/country/kh?theme=education-and-literacy Accessed October 27–28, 2018.

Williams, James, Yuto Kitamura, and Sopcheak Keng, (2014) Higher Education in Cambodia: Expansion and Quality Improvement. In: Kitamura Y., Edwards D.B., Sitha C., and Williams J.H. (eds.) The Political Economy of Schooling in Cambodia. International and Development Education. Palgrave Macmillan, New York. Available http://ir.lib.hiroshima-u.ac.jp/files/public/3/37025/20150423092237305377/HigherEducationForum_11_67.pdf Accessed July 25, 2018 and October 27–28, 2018.

World Bank. 2018. World Development Report 2018: Learning to Realize Education's Promise. Washington, DC: World Bank. Creative Commons Attribution CC BY 3.0 IGO. Available http://www.worldbank.org/en/publication/wdr2018 Accessed October 29, 2018.

World Economic Forum. 2017. The Global Competitiveness Report 2017–2018. Geneva. Available: http://reports.weforum.org/global-competitiveness-report-2017-2018 Accessed October 27–28, 2018.

World Economic Forum (2018) The Global Competitiveness Report 2018. Geneva. Available: http://reports.weforum.org/global-competitiveness-report-2018 Accessed October 27–28, 2018.

Epilogue

The Changing Landscape in the Financial Sector: Cambodia's Microfinance Segment, Ownership, and Governance

Today, in the new age of private social investing, poor and low-income borrowers, depositors, and remittance senders and receivers are seen as worthy participants in inclusive financial markets.

A decade ago, a new breed of socially responsible investment funds—microfinance investment vehicles (MIVs)—was eager to place their capital in Cambodia's robust microfinance institutions. Yet, the slow pace of change and the perceived trade-off between a social purpose enterprise and a commercial venture initially bested these new market players. In the mid-2000s, few MFIs had reached the levels of profitability with their social purpose intact, when they would merit such an investment (Clark 2006).

With this new category of MFI investors came an entirely new set of issues: globalization tempted philosophical debates on ownership of capital, repatriation of profit to foreign sources, good governance practices, and the slow pace of creating domestic private investors who could uphold the bargain of social mission within a commercial enterprise (Ibid.).

The prognosis in 2005 was that these very issues would continue to play out in the future, based on the failures and successes of the emerging phenomenon of banking for the people. In Cambodia, the market for MIV investments quickly developed from 2010 onward. Cambodian MFIs, particularly the microfinance deposit-taking institutions (MDIs), expanded in an increasingly robust market in both urban and rural areas and gradually reached profitability tied to a social purpose.

The NBC's prudent decision to increase the minimum capital from USD 2.5 million to USD 30 million (NBC 2016) for all microfinance deposit-taking institutions ushered in a new age for microfinance in Cambodia. As part of Basel III, the NBC

© Springer Nature Singapore Pte Ltd. 2020
H. A. Clark, *Beyond Borders, Beyond Banking*,
https://doi.org/10.1007/978-981-15-1687-0

required all bank and financial institutions to increase their minimum registered capital by March 22, 2018. See Chap. 4.

Unfortunately, the timing coincided with the maturation of the closed-end funds—the microfinance investment vehicles (MIVs)—from which many Cambodian MDIs accessed their primary or significant sources of equity capital. In fact, from 2010 to 2016, MIVs increasingly took the place of Development Finance Investors (DFIs) as the main equity investors in microfinance institutions in Cambodia.

By March 2018, as the deadline neared to raise the new minimum capital of USD 30 million, every microfinance deposit-taking institution in Cambodia was at least partially owned by a microfinance investment vehicle—some to a greater extent than others.

A Question of Governance in MFI Ownership Transitions

In 2005, most commercial microfinance advocates viewed the entrance of MIVs as a positive step to advance the integration of microfinance into the broader finance system. MIVs represented private social investors, and their market entrance would complement the work of DFIs that are temporary financiers of initiatives that are not yet primed for commercial investors. DFIs were designed to finance and develop investment worthy enterprises to become part of the private sector in any sector of the economy, including financial services.

There was good reason to make a better match to the more commercial approach advanced by Cambodian MFIs that most MIVs fulfilled. Yet, the practice may not have worked out as expected by the MFIs.

DFIs have played an important standard-setting role in MFI governance within many MFIs. This role may have been weakened or lost, when MIVs—and their more arm's length method of investing—took the place of DFIs, as MFIs experienced so dramatically in Cambodia. But it took almost a decade to notice how it affected governance.

As one prominent expert in the field noted, "Governance is perceived as a key risk in microfinance, as shown in the Microfinance Banana Skins surveys [1], with weaknesses prevailing in main governance areas such as clear ownership structure, disclosure and transparency, and the role and responsibilities of the board. Equity investors are not fully capitalizing on the opportunity to strengthen MFI governance. They must more actively engage in and beyond the boardroom and ensure adequate qualifications, commitment and continuity of their board nominees" (Maurer 2013).

[1] The Microfinance "Banana Skins" surveys are dedicated to exploring the risks of financial inclusion. The yearly surveys are undertaken by the Centre for the Study of Financial Innovation and supported by the Citi Foundation and the Center for Financial Inclusion at Accion. "Each year the Banana Skins series provides a barometer of the risks facing the banking, insurance and microfinance industries" (CSFI 2019).

Over the last decade, just when many of the "closed-end funds" investing in Cambodian microfinance deposit-taking institutions reached maturation, several challenges were raised by the investees—the MDIs—about the role such MIV funds play in governance. At the time, one particular concern was the MIV governance responsibility to ensure proper buyers for their equity stakes in the institution in a timely way.

As all Cambodian MDIs found, perhaps a bit too late, few MIV's are active participants in governance. And, even when they appoint independent directors, some act in the interest of their employers. As one CEO of a Cambodian MFI notes, "you have to realize that the MIV is working on behalf of their own investors. In our experience they do not have the interests of the microfinance institution at the forefront. They play an insignificant role in governance and their duty to care for the MFI."[2]

Ownership Transitions and Responsibilities

As advances are made with multiple investment transactions and ownership and governance options, the responsibilities of social investors—both buyer and seller—get more complex. Yet the bottom line remains quite clear, "...socially responsible investing means just that –investing in a manner that not only generates financial returns but also produces positive social value" (Rozas and Mendelson 2018).

Socially responsible sellers of equity stakes must undertake their due diligence to ensure the social mission of the buyer. Experts in the field of microfinance equity transactions note, "...The responsibility of finding the right buyer lies very much with those doing the selling. And if the sale means handing over control—a majority stake—this creates an even greater burden" (Mendelson and Rozas 2018).

> They note in conclusion, "*A buyer selection practice which gives primacy to the financial offer and considers social mission and strategic value to the investee – the investee's best interests – only to reject egregiously unsuitable buyers– fails to keep in mind that the best interests of the MFI and its clients are, for the investors who put funds into the MIV, arguably the primary reason for investing in the financial inclusionsector in the first place.*" (Ibid.)

In the wake of new minimum capital requirements and the staged exit of many MIVs from Cambodia, six of the seven remaining microfinance deposit-taking institutions turned to interested and financially stable foreign banking establishments, mostly located in the region. (See Chap. 4 for an account of the challenges and benefits of Cambodian MDI transitions to wholly owned and partially owned subsidiaries of foreign banks and financial institutions.)

"Buyer selection" choices among the original eight MDIs appear not to have compromised their original mission, with one exception. In this case, new ownership rebranded the financial services provider's operation and modified its product

[2] Author interview.

line and customer base. It moved toward consumer finance, drifting away from the original social mission and customer base.

As discussed in Chap. 4, only time will tell if all the new owners will invest in the continued strengthening of MFI governance and formulate strategies and policies to combat over-indebtedness, which, as of early 2020, appears to be approaching crisis proportions in microcredit lending.

The NBC Rules and Informs

Increasing Vigilance of Governance Practices

The National Bank of Cambodia Rules on Independent Directors Independent directors are important to quality governance to keep inappropriate shareholder influence at bay. However, due diligence to ensure appropriate qualifications, commitment, and continuity of independent directors is just as important to the investee as it is to the shareholder. The National Bank of Cambodia officially recognizes the importance of independent directors for commercial banks and microfinance institutions, noting that financial institutions must have a "Qualified, Active and Independent Board" (NBC 2008):

> For commercial banks, except foreign bank branches, the board shall include at least two independent members. Independent members are defined as being capable of exercising judgment independent of the views of management, political interests or inappropriate outside interests. (Ibid.)

> For specialized banks and Microfinance Institutions, the body acting as a board of directors shall at least be composed of three board members, among whom one should be independent under the definition provided above. Should such institutions have a board of directors composed of more than three members, they shall ensure that, a minimum, one third of its members are independent. (NBC 2008)

Independent Directors Play an Important Role for Banking Establishments

It is not only the NBC that recognizes the importance of strong, qualified, and active independent boards. Cambodia's MDIs recognize the importance, as well. ACLEDA Bank Plc. knew the importance of good governance even from the early days in the mid-1990s when the LEDAs were first forming themselves from informal provincial organizations into one national organization with non-governmental status.[3]

John Brinsden is a Seasoned Banker, who has served as a Director, Vice-Chair, and Chair of the Board of Directors of ACLEDA Bank Plc. He provides the strong

[3] See Chaps. 5 and 6.

rationales for ensuring qualified independent directors are active on the board of any banking institution:

> The more narrowly held a company is, the more important is the role of the independent director. Individual shareholders can exert great influence over the affairs of the bank through their board appointees, especially if they are officials of the shareholder concerned. No matter how impartial they may try to be, it is only natural that they will look at things through the prism of their employers. (Brinsden 2019)
>
> "An Independent Director can bring an 'outsiders' perspective, and a specialist's skills set that may not be available amongst the institutional board members. This is very important in certain Committees such as Audit, IT, and Compliance. They act as a neutral referee and/or emollient in factional Board disputes." (Ibid.) Independent directors also play an important role to strengthen the technical expertise of the Board, and to ensure that institutional directors keep the health of the institution at the forefront of their concerns, balancing the concerns of shareholders and management.
>
> And finally, an Independent Director can use the powers that the law provides to Independent Directors to intercede or report on serious matters affecting the conduct or honesty of the company. In most jurisdictions such an intervention would be mandatory for an Independent Director with heavy penalties for failure to act. (Brinsden 2019)

Solid Governance Within the ACLEDA Group Receives Attention

Striking a balance between institutional members of the Board of Directors, Independent Directors, Institutional Directors, and members of the board employed by shareholders was often a complex process to manage. Perspectives frequently differed, distance could interfere with the timeliness of decision-making, and the disparate views could easily upset an otherwise smooth process requiring mutual concessions and appreciation of all points of view.

Yet in ACLEDA Bank Plc., the bottom line was always preserved throughout the years and with different personalities and cultures involved. The central position where all directors agreed was the importance of the health of the institution—financially, operationally, and ethically—quite a difficult combination to get right all the time.

Another innovation, another unifying thought process, and a milestone in governance began in March 2005:

> The board commenced a program called, *Three Years On - Building A Governance Structure for The Future*, to meet the needs of the bank's long-term strategic goals. Attention was focused on the role of the Board and the experience and skill-sets needed to provide the organization with the leadership to achieve these goals. As a start, members of the board and the two most senior executives participated in the Company Director's Course provided by the Australian Institute of Company Directors ('AICD') in July 2006. Many went on to obtain the AICD's Graduate Certificate. (Brinsden 2019)

> At their meeting in March 2007, the Directors decided to implement a board evaluation exercise as a logical follow-up to the board development program and called for various ideas as to how these are best carried out. (Brinsden 2007) As a result, the BOD initiated a 4-year program of self-assessment, which was completed in 2011, with follow-up reviews every three years, a relatively uncommon practice in Asia. (Ibid.)

Fintech in Cambodia and in the Region

New advances are on the horizon in the ASEAN region and globally brought about by the speed and the ease of technological developments. With the increasing accessibility to financial services and rapid acceptance by rich and poor alike, anyone who owns a mobile smartphone can participate in the financial services market.

New issues have emerged in the banking industry in Cambodia and the region as well. Along with easy access to financial services through digital finance comes a different kind of risk, one that is likely to have fewer warning signs, comes more quickly, and can be more difficult for the consumer to detect in a timely manner. With these developments come new strategies to protect financial consumers. One cornerstone of financial consumer protection has always been financial consumer education.

Financial Education Is a Fairly New Priority: Is Financial Consumer Protection Far Behind?

The National Bank of Cambodia (NBC) has inherited a legacy of a population that has never had a solid education in finance, except through those microfinance institutions and ACLEDA Bank Plc. that served customers with financial services. Over the last two decades, financial services providers have kept customer deposits safe, transferred their money reliably and quickly, and lent them funds for enterprise development and other purposes, including housing, education, and consumer goods. In this respect, financial education has become the province of financial services providers by fiat, if not by design. And, many financial services providers emphasize financial consumer education as a central pillar of their business models and customer service support.

Financial education should be a high on the priority of the NBC and the Ministry of Education, Youth and Sport (MoEYS). Collaborative efforts between the MoEYS, the NBC, and donors dedicated to these efforts such as Good Return in Australia[4] to develop an easily accessible and quality financial education program are welcomed by every segment of society. In fact, such efforts at the national level are not just looking forward to a better future, but preventing a potential crisis.

Yet, financial consumer education has often been neglected because the effort to ensure widespread understanding of basic finance within the general population often seems insurmountable. A regulatory and educational environment that encourages advancement, sometimes through technological innovation, must be at the forefront of the financial services industry. It should also be one that ensures consumers are aware of how to accept their own responsibilities for their own

[4] Good Return is an Australian nonprofit, working to end extreme poverty by 2030. Objectives include to empower those living in poverty by providing responsible microloans, financial capability training, and business investment opportunities throughout the Asia-Pacific. For more information: https://www.goodreturn.org.au/

protection in the advancing financial technology and on whom they can rely to report and remedy transgressions in this regard for the mutual benefit of consumers and providers of financial services.

There is movement on both avenues as evidenced by the NBC's efforts to establish financial education within the general population through public education campaigns and a more direct initiative within the school system. In addition, all of the MDIs and ACLEDA Bank Plc. have been certified in client protection as advanced by the Smart Campaign. See Chap. 3 for an overview of financial education and consumer protection.

Are these initiatives in consumer protection and financial education enough and in time to serve and to protect against harm to the consumer and the system? That is the question for the next 5 years. To be sure, successful approaches and specific challenges will become much more apparent before that time.

ACLEDA Bank Plc. Transitions and Transformations: Past and Future

The vision of ACLEDA Bank Plc. was always supported by a plan to transform: whether it was a new organizational form—transforming from an NGO to a specialized bank and later to a commercial bank or pioneering new financial services companies in neighboring countries. Another transformation, rooted in ACLEDA's history of staff training for the industry, is going beyond banking to enter Cambodia's higher education sector.

This book's decade-long unpacking of the ACLEDA Group of Companies shows that changes continue, some are gradual, some are transformative, some are reminiscent of the ACLEDA Bank's beginnings, and some are truly groundbreaking for the institution, its staff, and directors.

ACLEDA's organizational values and its traditions have inspired each and every transition. ACLEDA's core values—no tolerance for corruption, honesty and personal integrity, customer service, staff ownership and governance, and professionalization—were formed from its origins in 1993 as the ILO project that was developed to train demobilized soldiers into Cambodia's future generation of entrepreneurs.

Values guided ACLEDA's decision to transform from a skills training program into a national NGO with a mission to serve micro and small enterprises. ACLEDA's governing board and staff built a skills training and credit program from this foundation and later reached beyond organizational boundaries to influence the financial sector in Cambodia. (See Chaps. 5, 6, and 7 for an account of how values informed transitions.)

As the organization developed, ACLEDA began to contribute to building Cambodia's financial sector. With their key values embracing innovation and professionalism, there was hardly any choice. ACLEDA Bank developed innovative products on the open market; systems and methods were shared with other organizations through ACLEDA's many industry-wide training programs and seminars, and ACLEDA staff also found leadership positions within other agencies. (See Chap. 7 for a summary of the growth of new products and performance in the sector.)

ACLEDA Bank and the ACLEDA Group of Companies continue to progress with their bedrock values in place. Their values will be tested by future growth and transformation, just as they were tested in 1993, throughout the 1990s and during the new millennium in Cambodia as well as in neighboring countries. In fact, one could argue that testing values overtime—and in different circumstances—contributed to the strength of those values throughout the organization and over time to this day.

The Drive to Learn, Adapt, and Innovate Increased with Time

ACLEDA's market share and financial performance improved throughout the years. The building blocks that enabled the bank to grow were shared organizational values among staff, management, and the governing board. Together they developed a guiding vision of the inclusive growth of Cambodia's financial sector. And, they were determined to broaden and deepen inclusive growth in the financial sector.

Solid financial performance over time rested on this organizational coherence. The drive to learn, adapt, and innovate distinguishes ACLEDA Bank Plc. as an outstanding pillar of the banking community in the ASEAN region. It is acknowledged by the NBC and its peers as the bank that brought and continues to bring lasting value to society. They have contributed both small and monumental innovations to the Cambodian banking sector, which are emulated by their colleagues and their competitors alike.

With over two decades of experience, ACLEDA Bank Plc. employs 12,183 staff in Cambodia as of January 2020. By 2016 ACLEDA Bank Plc. accounted for 44% of all employees in the commercial banking sub-sector, and 25% of employees in the formally regulated banking sector.[5] ACLEDA Bank Plc. serves more than 403,632 borrowers and manages 2,355,819 deposit accounts for customers in all provinces and towns throughout Cambodia (ACLEDA Bank Plc. January 2020).

By early 2020, ACLEDA Bank, Plc. supported a network of 262 branches, 627 ATMs, and over 3,800 points of sale in all provinces and towns, including rural posts. Domestic and international funds transfers continue to grow, which have averaged over 1.55 million transactions per year, since 2013. Internet banking through ACLEDA Unity and ToanChet, a mobile phone application, conveniently allows customers to make banking transactions and purchases from "anywhere at any time." As of January 2020, 1,346,344 people in Cambodia use the ACLEDA

[5] NBC statistics reported, as of 2016 annual report. The report includes commercial banks and formally regulated microfinance deposit-taking institutions with reliable statistics. It excludes MFI NGOs and registered microfinance organizations that are not regulated, as information may not be reliable or current. ACLEDA staff includes AIB staff. Source: ACLEDA Bank Plc.'s Achievement As of December 31, 2018

Unity ToanChet application to make purchases and banking transactions throughout the country. And, thanks to the National Bank Cambodia and the Bank of Thailand's recent efforts to advance QR code compatibility, customers can conveniently transact in Khmer Reil in Thailand via ACLEDA ToanChet.[6]

Sometime ago, ACLEDA's management found that if people are encouraged to develop new ideas for improving their jobs and their own performance, they often do. This management principle inspired robust growth for ACLEDA. It also provided a solid platform for staff-led innovation in the marketplace of ideas, new positions to support the organization, as well as the development of new products, and—just as important—the courage to let old ones go.

Peter Kooi, ACLEDA's First Finance Expert Advisor and now on the Board of Directors, once commented on In Channy's drive for innovation, "He is concerned about staff's need to innovate, otherwise, he thinks, they will get bored. ACLEDA tried to support a direction – not only because it was the right thing to do, but also because 'if we get the direction right, if we get the incentives right, the rest will come.'" (See Chap. 5.)

The People of ACLEDA Care About Their Customers and Their Bank

"The care extends from the boardroom to the sidewalk, from the rice field to the factory. It includes the Customer Service Assistant who helps a new customer securely navigate the ATM with grace and charm and his colleague who confidently stops traffic in front of the HQ for customers with large cars, small cars, tuk-tuks, motorcycles, bicycles, and the occasional flock of very brave pedestrians." Both the ACLEDA pioneers and their protégés care about their bank, their colleagues and their customers. As Mr. Nay Sok Samnang says, reflecting the attitude of many others, "I like this new staff. I used to be one of them." (See Chap. 6.)

When product development efforts succeeded, they found great acceptance in the market. It is true that some products fell off a fast truck as it made a sharp turn around the bend. With such experience ACLEDA learned how best to build for the future and how to structure and manage an organization that grew with the customer.

As an example, Mrs. Sok Sophea's initial experiment succeeded to identify a new position as marketing officer at the branch level who could provide a dedicated link for new product ideas from the customer to the branch staff and management. The innovation succeeded because she had the support of her team who listened to branch managers, account officers, and customers. They all had plenty of ideas on how to improve products and services.

ACLEDA Bank Plc. considered and followed reasonable advice of experts and ensured a governing board of both shareholders and independent directors who could guide the organization to navigate "sharp turns" as well as speed along an

[6] Statistics as of March 2019 (ACLEDA Bank Plc. 2019).

open super highway to new destinations. Their best efforts were applied to the structure and management of an organization that grew with the customers and grew with the staff. ACLEDA Bank Plc. eventually became the market leader for inclusive financial services in Cambodia. See Chap. 7.

They Are Builders

The notion of building did not end when ACLEDA Bank Plc. became the largest bank in Cambodia by all measures and the first Cambodian Bank to make "The Banker's ASEAN top 100 Banks." They are still building. They still have the *drive to learn, adapt, and innovate*. And, as the pioneers retire, their protégés will follow through to the next decade and beyond.

The ACLEDA Staff Association (ASA): The Pioneer of Staff Association Ownership in MFIs and Banks in Cambodia

ACLEDA Bank has always valued staff ownership as a principle and as a practice through the ACLEDA Staff Association (ASA). The creation of ASA was not just a mechanism used to promote staff unity or to maintain a percentage of local ownership. The creation of ASA represented a fundamental value with respect to staff ownership of the institution. The association was a complex one to manage in the early days. Through staff initiatives and the value placed in the association by staff, management, and the board of directors, the ASA has become an important strength of ACLEDA's development and success. See Chaps. 5 and 6 for more detail on the history of ASA and partnership with the ACLEDA Financial Trust (AFT).

The future presents both challenges and opportunities for the ACLEDA Staff Association as it continues to grow and bring new staff members into the organization, as the pioneers retire. They seek to serve the Bank with both management and governance expertise and live up to their responsibilities as owners of the organization. They aspire to continue to support inclusive growth and the expansion of Cambodia's growing financial sector.

ACLEDA Securities Plc.

Within the strategic directions and plan approved by the Board, ACLEDA management and staff respond, and they innovate to build for the future. ACLEDA Securities is another example of such innovation. Established in November 2010, ACLEDA Securities Plc. received its broker's license from the Securities and Exchange

Commission of Cambodia (SECC) and became one of the first securities brokerage companies in Cambodia.

From this beginning and under the astute direction of Mrs. Mar Amara, Mr. Prom Visoth, and Dr. Svay Hay, ACLEDA Securities positions itself for an expanded role within the Cambodian stock market by serving a growing number of customers who are interested in participating in the CSX as shareholders in all listed companies.

And, the CSX itself may play an even more important role in the future of Cambodia's banking sector, as its stakeholders—the NBC, Banks, MDIs, and qualified local investors—embrace the notion of strengthening capital markets in support of financial inclusion by ACLEDA Bank's creation of a "People's IPO". See Chap. 3 for a discussion of Cambodia's nascent capital markets and the newest bond products, advanced by Cambodia's MDIs, in addition to the growth in securities brokerage firms and the secondary market.

The Drive for Institutional Innovation

The reason ACLEDA continues to build may be found in management's drive for institutional innovation: to design products and services people need to make their banking and financial management more productive, useful, and profitable for their own enterprises and households. ACLEDA seeks to help customers ease transactions whether in cash or through the ACLEDA Unity and "ToanChet" and "ThanChai" digital finance application on their smartphones.

As ACLEDA Bank expands and advances, it becomes more productive and more relevant to continue building Cambodia's future financial sector and the expansion of quality inclusive banking services in the ASEAN region. Institutional innovation as a management principle inspired solid growth from ACLEDA's birth to the present; it also laid the foundation for ACLEDA's future in the region.

And, ACLEDA Bank Plc. just may be the first financial institution to list and/or issue a People's IPO on the Cambodian Stock Exchange (CSX) following the unanimous approval of the ACLEDA Bank Plc. shareholders during the Annual General Meeting in April 2019. The process has begun; how it continues is now in the hands of the National Bank of Cambodia, the Securities Exchange Commission of Cambodia (SECC), and ACLEDA Bank Plc.

How does ACLEDA Bank leadership see this next innovation and transition? They consider the listing of ACLEDA Bank Plc. on the Cambodian Securities Exchange or an IPO as an outcome of an organic process over time and a part of the ACLEDA Bank Plc. vision. Listing was not a specific strategic goal in itself, notes ACLEDA leadership and board members.

As Dr. In Channy says with customary clarity and wisdom, "ACLEDA always viewed its customers as builders of the bank...Listing allows the customers to become *owners* the bank."

Banking Beyond Borders

Microfinance in Myanmar: Full Circle

On September 6, 2013, the ACLEDA Group returned to its founding vision and the value of microfinance—the original heart and soul of the company—when it invested in establishing ACLEDA MFI Myanmar (AMM). In Cambodia, ACLEDA discovered a pathway to universal banking from a modest microfinance base to achieve its vision of an inclusive financial sector. ACLEDA MFI Myanmar, like its parent, started with a vision to discover its own pathway to universal banking.

Over the past seven years, AMM has grown considerably with plans to expand branches, customers, and products over the next five years and beyond regulations permitting. (See Chap. 9). AMM, like the ACLEDA Bank Cambodia (ABC), contributes to regulatory discussions in Myanmar along with its MFI colleagues. It is appreciated for its multi-country experience with various saving, lending, and funds transfer products that are important to microfinance customers, but not yet completely covered by microfinance regulation in Myanmar.

What is the future of the "shining star" in Myanmar as Dr. In Channy, the ACLEDA President and Group Managing Director, likes to call AMM? Growth of inclusive finance faces a number of challenges in Myanmar, but not for lack of demand for financial services in both urban and rural areas. Indeed the demand is high, and the supply is limited in many areas, except for informal sources of finance.

The consultative process between the regulator and the MFI community continues on issues such as financial intermediation focused on accepting deposits from customers who are not loan recipients; expansion to unserved and underserved populations and geographic areas, which could be made possible by lowering the regulatory barriers to branch expansion; supporting fintech and product development; and reconciling current bank licensing rules with the global experience in MFI transformation to fully licensed and prudentially regulated banking establishments.

However, the Central Bank of Myanmar is enthusiastic about changing regulations to advance financial inclusion. New loan products for MFIs are advancing—those loans that do not require collateral, but are issued at a higher interest rate—and the BOL recently approved higher percentages of foreign ownership in domestic banks to improve stronger capitalization within the sector.

Lao PDR: A Small Enterprise Bank in the Making?

ACLEDA Bank Lao Ltd. (ABL) management and directors of ACLEDA Bank Plc. learned the disappointment in their belief "just like us" during their pioneering efforts to take banking beyond their borders to a neighboring country. Their expectations of an enabling regulatory environment in the Lao PDR at the time of start-up in 2008 became more restrictive almost immediately, only to continue restrictions throughout 2018.

Foreign exchange set asides imposed without much warning, and restrictions on foreign currency transfers plagued the ABL and its parent company early on. Later, the requirements and costs of official land titles to serve as collateral for small enterprise loans made ABL's core operation of small and medium enterprise lending more difficult and expensive, given the pervasive lack of official land titles within the small enterprise sector.

Further, ACLEDA Bank Lao's core value of "no tolerance for corruption" was quickly tested by the conventional practice of loan officers to take commissions from their clients against ABL policy and code of conduct. When the Lao government canceled service contracts with SMEs across a full range of sectors, it placed a high degree of debt stress on SMEs and their lending partners, including ABL. (See Chap. 8 for a detailed discussion of ABLs tenacious progress under pressure.)

What is the future of inclusive finance in Lao PDR? Will ABL remain on the solid ground that took so long to evolve, or will it slip adrift with new regulatory conditions that make lending to small enterprises particularly vulnerable?

So far, there is high consumer acceptance of fintech applications in both Cambodia and the Lao PDR. However, the jury is still out on advancing the regulatory environment to become more enabling for financial inclusion in the Lao PDR.

Will the hopes of fintech applications, such as ToanChet in Cambodia and the innovative ThanChai in Lao PDR, fulfill the promise to make funds transfers work for people who need to move money throughout the country and beyond its borders? Perhaps the time has come. ACLEDA Bank was recently selected by the NBC to participate in an ASEAN fintech pilot to develop an efficient QR code based payment system between Thailand and Cambodia. The pilot was completed successfully, and ready for customer use by early 2020. The hopes for the near future are high as several years of experience, infrastructure, and customer acceptance are in place within the ACLEDA Group of Companies. (See Chap. 3 for more detail about the ASEAN fintech pilot.)

There are some signs that enabling regulation for microfinance and small enterprise finance can improve through the financial services providers' continuous advocacy and active involvement together with the regulators and supervisors in the Bank of the Lao PDR. For example, new models of community-based microfinance with strong accountability mechanisms in place are making headway. Action research and enabling regulations for fintech products are advancing. Using this experience in the process may further the development of small enterprise lending and a stronger banking sector overall. (See Chap. 8 for a history of ABL and a more detailed discussion of the issues.)

Beyond Boundaries: Banking to Higher Education

ACLEDA Institute of Business (AIB): The Beginnings

Unique among bankers, ACLEDA Bank Plc. staff and management looked for their chance to teach others about the business of financial inclusion and to bring lasting value to the next generation. Since 2008 they aimed to reach beyond borders to the Lao PDR and to Myanmar in 2013, where ACLEDA Bank rediscovered its roots as a microfinance institution.

With an entrepreneurial spirit and the intention to broaden financial inclusion within ASEAN, the ACLEDA pioneers and protégés discovered their roots beyond banking. They began a gradual transformation of the ACLEDA Bank Plc. Training Department established in 2000 into the ACLEDA Institute of Business that was licensed in 2016 as an Institute of Higher Education in Cambodia.

The question always asked is "why." Why did ACLEDA Bank Plc.—a privately held commercial bank—take on such a responsibility for creating, developing, and investing in the educational sector, particularly in an Institution of Higher Education and Learning?

It seems so unusual, so distant from their main business, and possibly a distraction.

> Can a bank build an Institution of Higher Education, or a University, and infuse it with the same corporate ethos, favoring innovation while managing risk?

Related questions include several asked at the beginning of this book.

> How will Cambodia and its local institutions begin to match the highest standards set in the ASEAN region, readying the country for the challenge of regional and global integration? Will the aim to ensure benefits for Cambodia's new generation secure future economic and social gain or—at the least—ensure that they are not left behind?

The answers to these questions are informed by the history of ACLEDA Bank Plc. and the history of higher education in Cambodia. Both factors merit consideration as discussed in Chaps. 5, 6, 7 and 10 and briefly noted here as part of ACLEDA Bank's legacy and future.

ACLEDA Institute of Business (AIB): The Rationale

ACLEDA staff valued education perhaps because there were few options in Cambodia for such a long time. Access to higher education may have faired well for some, but few educational services and opportunities, particularly higher specialization in a field of expertise, existed for the majority.

Another reason was the confluence of two practice areas of the ACLEDA founders' history and backgrounds. They were teachers before they were bankers. In addition, several of the original ACLEDA staff and leadership spent most of the 1980s in refugee camps where their teaching skills were enhanced by professional teachers and eager students. They were also exposed to international curricula.

A third factor that weighed heavily in their investment choices was a practical matter. Simply, at the time of greatest need for the young ACLEDA pioneers there was no easy access in Cambodia to schools of higher learning or practical learning about the entire array and depth of banking and finance subjects. That was in the early and mid-1990s and throughout the early 2000s. Only in 2005 and beyond did the first dedicated private and public business schools begin to emerge within Cambodia's institutions of higher education.

There were really no other options to acquire an experienced and educated staff other than to employ their own resources to teach newly recruited staff. And that is exactly what they did: they employed their experienced staff as teachers.

It was a gamble, but they took it—and it worked. ACLEDA Bank built the capacity of its own staff to contribute to the Bank's success over the years. In the process, they also developed a professional cadre of experienced business, banking, and finance teachers.

ACLEDA Institute of Business (AIB): Performance

The sheer size of ACLEDA's employment roster to support its national network of branches required a dedicated and skilled training facility. In 2017, ACLEDA Bank accounted for 40% of the employment in the commercial and specialized banking sub-sector.

In fact, ACLEDA Bank's percentage contribution to the commercial and specialized banking sector employment somewhat dropped over the years, even while the absolute numbers of ACLEDA staff have more than doubled, reaching 12,456 staff members since 2008 when 6,128 staff worked for the Bank. This is a positive sign of the health and resilience of the Cambodian banking sector, as employment in the overall sector increased from 21,000 in 2008 to 31,445 by the end of 2017.[7]

AIB and its predecessors held over 59,000 courses for over 655,000 staff of ACLEDA Bank Plc. in Cambodia, ACLEDA Bank Lao, and ACLEDA MFI Myanmar since its inception and through early 2020. Staff with few options for higher education in global banking standards and practices and financial inclusion have had the opportunity to learn new on-the-job techniques and skills.

These facts alone support ACLEDA's choice to create an independent training entity in 2011 by merging the training division of the bank with the ACLEDA ASEAN Regional Microfinance Center. These merged entities later became the ACLEDA Institute of Business in 2016.

Yet, the decision to create AIB has much deeper significance. Over the period from 2008 through January 2020, the ACLEDA Institute of Business, and its

[7]Commercial bank and specialized bank employment figures for 2017 from the NBC Annual Supervision Report 2017.

predecessors, held 590 courses for over 11,000 participants from other Cambodian financial institutions and financial sector organizations and the public. Participants came from 400 local and international organizations including banks, MFIs, NGOs, companies, and government agencies. The impact on Cambodia's financial sector has been significant.

In addition many previous ACLEDA staff members take their qualifications and use their ACLEDA training to work for other financial institutions in Cambodia, the Lao PDR, and Myanmar.

They follow the sage advice of Dr. In Channy, who advocates for capacity building in the financial sectors of all countries where ACLEDA Bank works. He is fond of saying:

> "It's a way that the industry will grow and become more like us. It's good for us. It's good for them. It's good for everyone; no one loses."

The original merger of ATC and the ACLEDA Bank training division continues to contribute to the success of all three of the ACLEDA financial services providers in the ASEAN region and the financial sectors where they work.[8]

The ACLEDA Bank Group of Companies has gained experience banking in the Lao PDR and Myanmar by training staff in an array of banking and finance areas of expertise, as well as developing the skills of a cadre of expert trainers and mentors in new countries. AIB still has a long way to go to reach its aims, yet the foundation is based on more than 10 years of experience of training staff for ACLEDA Bank, and staff who work in Cambodia's, Lao's, and Myanmar's financial sectors. The AIB begins to bring practical experience into the realm of academia. This contribution to higher education is something for Cambodia to celebrate!

ACLEDA Institute of Business (AIB): Lessons from the First Years

The ACLEDA Institute of Business (AIB) track record grows as an Institute of Higher Education. AIB intends to study the possibility of transforming to a full-fledged business school at some point in the future. A long-term goal is to become an ASEAN-qualified center of educational excellence in the fields of banking and finance and a multifaceted business school beyond banking.

In this context, AIB has in place a number of strategies to increase new student enrollments, a faculty with broader mix of subject matter specialties, and a range of academic and skills training courses designed to appeal to a broader range of business students—including entrepreneurs— while at the same time increasing finance and banking specialties.

[8] See Chap. 7 for more detail regarding ACLEDA's employment growth rates in the Cambodian financial sector and Chap. 10 for AIB and its predecessors' professional development and training statistics.

The performance of AIB continues to show strength in the crowded higher education market in Cambodia. As a newcomer in the highly competitive market, AIB's discovery and application of a specialized and targeted business model as the basis for expansion will take time and research. AIB's distinctive offer to newly minted high school graduates which combines both academic and practical experience will prepare them as market-ready employees for ACLEDA, other banking institutions, growth businesses, or entrepreneurs in their own right.

Just as the ACLEDA pioneers created a bank within the financial sector that does not discriminate between poor and rich borrowers and savers aspiring to serve all people well, the new generation of job seekers may be just as fortunate to have a worthy competitor in the higher education market.

In some small way, AIB may begin to leverage Cambodia's local experience to match the highest standards set in the ASEAN region, readying the country for the challenge of regional and global integration. The aim to ensure Cambodia's new-generation benefits from a secure future with economic and social gain through a quality education—or at the least to ensure that they are not left behind—seems within reach.

A Retrospective Journey: 2005–2020

The retrospective 14-year journey of ACLEDA's vision within and beyond its borders in financial and educational services has touched the lives of so many more people beyond its origins as a business training and credit program for demobilized solders. Banking services for millions of Cambodians—young and old, rich and poor—have been joined by tens of thousands of customers in Lao PDR and in Myanmar. ACLEDA's track record gives credence to their motto "The bank you can trust, the bank for the people."

As services grow regionally so do customers, staff, managers, and leadership that bring about opportunity for a new generation of "protégés" in Cambodia, Lao PDR, and Myanmar.

The ACLEDA Institute of Business provides specialized technical higher education in ethical banking practices, systems, and products from basic savings and credit to fintech applications that make banking easier, faster, and safer for customers and managers alike. The AIB's current role is to ensure the future generation of bankers and their customers are skilled and experienced in conventional banking as well as fintech.

A new generation of customers, staff, and managers in Cambodia, Lao PDR, and Myanmar count on ACLEDA's support. People continue using the services of ACLEDA Bank Plc., ACLEDA Bank Lao, and ACLEDA MFI Myanmar in greater numbers. Customers come because ACLEDA's suite of products helps them manage their businesses and their future. They come to ACLEDA because they value ACLEDA's reputation for transparency and customer service, the "no tolerance for corruption" policies and practices, and the opportunity to build a relationship over time.

This book began with a Foreword by HE Keat Chhon, Cambodia's Former Deputy Prime Minister and former Minister of Economy and Finance. He noted:

> "Innovators pushed the envelope, creating new institutions and operational models that appealed to customers, investors, policy makers and regulatory authorities alike in Cambodia, the Lao PDR and Myanmar. Later, these wider groups in different countries re-double their efforts to ensure they support the people to sustain and build their businesses now and in the future."
>
> ..."The ACLEDA Story is a story that is relevant to all of us now, and to future generations who will lead the financial sectors in their countries with a fundamental understanding of what it takes to begin, evolve and build an inclusive financial sector."

And, that is the good news story, a story that continues "beyond borders, and beyond banking."

References

ACLEDA Bank Plc. (2019) Performance Statistics. Available www.acledabank.com.kh; Accessed 8 January 2019, July 12 2019

Brinsden, John (2007) Vice-chairman's memo to Board of Directors, November 12 2007. On Independent Directors. Author interview.

Brinsden, John (2019) On the Role of the Board and Directors' Skill Set. Author interview

Centre for the Study of Financial Innovation (CSFI). (2019) Financial Inclusion Banana Skins. Available http://www.csfi.org/financial-inclusion-banana-skins. Accessed 8 January 2019

Clark, Heather A (2006) When There Was No Money. Springer, Berlin – Heidelberg

Maurer, Klaus (2013) The Role of DFIs in the Emerging 3.0 Responsible Funding Landscape – Responsible Corporate Governance and Beyond. In: Köhn D. (eds.) Microfinance 3.0. Reconciling Sustainability with Social Outreach and Responsible Delivery Springer, Berlin, Heidelberg D.KöhnMirofinance3.0: 155c©TheAuthor(s)2013 Available: https://core.ac.uk/download/pdf/81067857.pdf. Accessed 20 December 2018

Mendelson, Sam and Daniel Rozas (2018) Caveat Venditor: Towards a Conceptual Framework for Buyer Selection in Responsible Microfinance Exits. Available http://www.e-mfp.eu/resources/caveat-venditor-towards-conceptual-framework-buyer-selection-responsible-microfinance (Accessed 8 September 2018)

National Bank of Cambodia (NBC) (2008) Prakas on Governance in Banks and Financial Institutions, Article 6, dated 25 November 2008. Phnom Penh

National Bank of Cambodia (NBC) (2016) Regulation on Minimum Registered Capital of Banking and Financial Institutions dated 22 March 2016. Phnom Penh

Rozas, Daniel and Sam Mendelson (2018) Caveat Venditor: A New Model for Buyer Selection in Responsible Microfinance Equity Exits Available http://www.e-mfp.eu/blog/caveat-venditor-new-model-buyer-selection-responsible-microfinance-equity-exits Accessed 8 December 2018

Index

© Springer Nature Singapore Pte Ltd. 2020
H. A. Clark, *Beyond Borders, Beyond Banking*,
https://doi.org/10.1007/978-981-15-1687-0

FSC
www.fsc.org
MIX
Papier | Fördert
gute Waldnutzung
FSC® C083411

Kolibri 360 GmbH
Ferdinand-Jühlke-Straße 7
99095 Erfurt, Deutschland
produktsicherheit@kolibri360.de